Better Homes and Gardens

baking

Raspberry French Silk Pie Bars,
recipe page 96

Better Homes and Gardens®

baking

MORE THAN 350 RECIPES PLUS TIPS AND TECHNIQUES

Houghton Mifflin Harcourt
Boston New York 2013

Better Homes and Gardens® Baking

Editor: Jessica Saari Christensen

Recipe Testing: Better Homes and Gardens® Test Kitchen

Better Homes and Gardens® Test Kitchen Product Supervisor: Lori Wilson

Photographers: Blaine Moats, Jason Donnelly, Kritsada Panichgul

Food Stylist: Dianna Nolin

Contributing Editor: Mary Williams

Contributing Writer: Lois White

Contributing Copy Editors: Peg Smith, Gretchen Kauffman

Contributing Photographers: Andy Lyons, Karla Conrad

Contributing Stylists: Greg Luna, Sue Mitchell, Jennifer Peterson, Janet Pittman, Charles Worthington

Houghton Mifflin Harcourt

Publisher: Natalie Chapman

Editorial Director: Cindy Kitchel

Executive Editor: Linda Ingroia

Associate Editor: Heather Dabah

Managing Editor: Marina Padakis Lowry

Production Director: Tom Hyland

Design Director: Ken Carlson, Waterbury Publications, Inc.

Associate Design Director: Doug Samuelson, Waterbury Publications, Inc.

Production Assistants: Mindy Samuelson, Waterbury Publications, Inc.

Library of Congress Cataloging-in-Publication Data is available upon request.

ISBN 978-1-118-45326-1 (pbk); 978-0-544-17781-9 (ebk)

Book Design: Waterbury Publications, Inc., Des Moines, Iowa.
Cover Photograph: Jason Donnelly, Meredith Corporation

DOW 10 9 8 7 6 5 4 3 2 1
4500436582
Printed in the United States of America.

Our seal assures you that every recipe in *Better Homes and Gardens®* Baking has been tested in the Better Homes and Gardens® Test Kitchen. This means that each recipe is practical and reliable and meets our high standards of taste appeal. We guarantee your satisfaction with this book for as long as you own it.

Sticky Pecan Upside-Down
Baby Cakes, recipe page 448

Contents

introduction

Baking is about love. It's the warm feeling you get when a pan of homemade deliciousness is pulled hot from the oven. It's the comforting, soul-soothing aromas wafting through your kitchen. It's the first bite that makes you happy from head to toe. And all of these depend on baking recipes and techniques that work without fail.

So we set out to create a book that touches on every type of baking—from the easiest quick breads and cupcakes to the most wonderous cheesecakes and croquembouche—along with the hows, whys, and what-fors to go with each. This all-encompassing, handpicked baking collection is the first, last, and only baking book you'll ever need.

Croquembouche with Maple Cream, recipe page 471

Focaccia, recipe page 307

baking basics

WHETHER A NOVICE OR PRO, every baker can benefit from a refresher course on the basics of baking. From the role each ingredient plays in a recipe to the types of tools and pans you'll need, this guide lays out all the hows, whys, and what-nows that pop up when you don the apron and start mixing.

Flour

Flour is the foundation of most baked recipes because it provides structure. When combined with water and kneaded, flour's protein (gluten) begins to develop. This tough, elastic substance traps and holds air produced by yeast and other leaveners, enabling baked goods to rise. For tender cakes, pastries, and crusts, avoid overmixing flour mixtures once the liquid is added to prevent overdevelopment of gluten. For doughs that require kneading, gluten development is key to obtain texture.

All-purpose flour: All-purpose flour is made up of a blend of "soft" (low-protein) and "hard" (high-protein) wheats. All-purpose flour is used in a wide range of baked goods. It comes bleached—chemically made whiter—and unbleached. These two are often used interchangeably.

Bread flour: Bread flour is made of hard wheat and has a higher protein content than all-purpose flour, making it ideal for most yeast bread recipes.

Cake flour: Cake flour is made of more soft wheat and has a finer texture than other wheat flours. It is low in protein but high in starch. Many bakers use it for angel and chiffon cakes to create a tender, delicate crumb.

Whole wheat flour: Whole wheat flour is a coarse-textured flour that contains the nutritious wheat germ. Whole wheat flour makes heavier breads and baked goods and is rarely used exclusively in recipes. Blending it with all-purpose flour will lighten the texture of the finished product while providing nutritious benefits.

Measuring basics: Proper measuring of flour is critical. Start by stirring it with a fork in the bag or canister to aerate it. (Except for cake flour, sifting is not necessary.) Gently spoon flour into a dry measuring cup; fill it to overflowing. Level off the top with the edge of a knife. Never pack flour into a measuring cup, which will increase the amount of flour added to the recipe and cause dryness.

MEASURING FLOUR
Fill the measuring cup without packing or shaking. Using the back edge of a knife blade, level the overflow back into the flour bag.

Sweeteners

Sweeteners are essential to add flavor, tenderness, and moisture to baked goods. Sweeteners are also effective in feeding and activating yeast in breads, stabilizing whipped egg whites in meringues, and creating a caramelized golden brown color in finished baked goods.

Granulated sugar: Also referred to as white or table sugar, granulated sugar is the most common sugar used in baking. It is a refined product from sugar cane and sugar beets.

Superfine (ultrafine or castor) sugar: This white sugar is a finer granulation. Because superfine sugar dissolves so quickly, it works well in frostings and meringues.

Brown sugar: Brown sugar is a mixture of white sugar and molasses. The molasses gives it the trademark color and makes it more moist and richer with a caramel flavor. It's available in both light and dark varieties; dark brown sugar has more molasses and a stronger flavor.

Powdered sugar: Also known as confectioners' sugar, powdered sugar is a mixture of crushed (powderized) granulated sugar and cornstarch (which helps prevent clumping). Sifting is often recommended to remove lumps that may have developed (see photo, right).

Molasses: During the refining process, the juice that is removed from sugar beets and sugar cane is boiled down, then has the sugar crystals removed. The remaining syrup is called molasses. Purchase either light or dark molasses; dark syrup is less sweet and more robust.

Corn syrup: Corn syrup is the thick, sweet product created from processing cornstarch. Both dark and light corn syrups perform similarly in baked recipes and can usually be used interchangeably. Use light corn syrup when a delicately sweet flavor is desired. Dark corn syrup has a more robust flavor and color, which is ideal for some baked products.

Honey: This natural sweetener is made when bees extract the syrupy nectar from flowers. Its flavor and color—from off-white to dark brown—depend on the source of the nectar.

Measuring Sweeteners

LIQUID SWEETENER Coat a liquid measuring cup with nonstick cooking spray and look at eye level to fill just to the line.

BROWN SUGAR Pack brown sugar into the measuring cup with the back of a spoon or your fingers.

POWDERED SUGAR If the powdered sugar is lumpy, pass it through a sieve before you measure.

Eggs

An egg is a simple ingredient that is essential to the success of many baked goods. Not only are eggs the glue that holds ingredients together, they also help give rise (as a leavener) to the end product.

Eggs add structure, richness, moisture, and leavening to baked goods. Egg yolks are high in fat and flavor. Egg whites, a mixture of protein and water, add moisture and build structure in baked products. The recipes in this book were developed and tested using large eggs—they're your best bet for consistent results. Store eggs in the original carton in the coldest part of the refrigerator for up to 5 weeks after the packing date.

Have eggs at room temperature when you begin to put a recipe together. Room-temperature eggs give baked goods more volume; place eggs on the counter 30 minutes before using them. If a recipe calls for separating yolks and whites, do so as soon as you take the eggs out of the refrigerator. If you try to separate a room-temperature egg, you're likely to end up with egg yolk in the whites.

Brushing the tops of breads and pastries with an egg wash—a beaten mixture of egg and water or milk—before baking gives a glossy sheen. Egg washes that include only whites become very shiny, while those that include yolks give a brilliant golden hue.

Beating Eggs

EGG YOLKS Beat on high speed for about 5 minutes or until thick and lemon color.

SOFT PEAKS Beat egg whites on medium speed until a soft peak forms with a tip that curls when beaters are lifted. (Be sure to use very clean beaters and bowl.)

STIFF PEAKS With an electric mixer, beat egg whites on high speed until peaks form that stand straight when beaters are lifted. This often requires the addition of sugar to stabilize the egg whites.

Fats

Fats and oils—most prominently butter where baking is concerned—are essential to add rich taste and delicate texture to final baked goods. Here are the fat facts you need to know.

Butter: Nothing beats the flavor and richness that butter adds to baked goods. It's critical to use butter in baked desserts that rely strictly on butter for flavor, such as pound cake. Shortbread, too, needs to be made with butter to retain its characteristic butter flavor, richness, and dense crumb. Streusel toppings should also be made with butter for flavor and crispness.

Vegetable oil: Oil adds tenderness and moisture to baked goods and coats flour proteins better than shortening. This prevents the proteins from absorbing liquid and forming gluten, yielding moister cakes.

Shortening: Shortening is a solid fat made from vegetable oils. It's often used to create tender, flaky piecrusts and biscuit toppers. Plain and butter-flavor types are available; use whichever you prefer.

Measuring Basics: Measure solid shortening by pressing it firmly into a dry measuring cup with a spoon or a rubber scraper. Level off the excess with the straight edge of a knife. To measure oil, pour oil into a liquid measuring cup. Check at eye level to make sure it lines up exactly (see Liquid Sweetener photo, page 13).

Degrees of Softness

MELTED BUTTER Melt butter in the microwave or on the stove until it is liquid in form. Sometimes melted butter is used instead of cooking oil in a recipe.

SOFTENED BUTTER Let cold butter stand at room temperature for 30 minutes until it is soft and easy to spread and blend. To quickly soften butter, microwave on defrost for 15 seconds. Check and repeat.

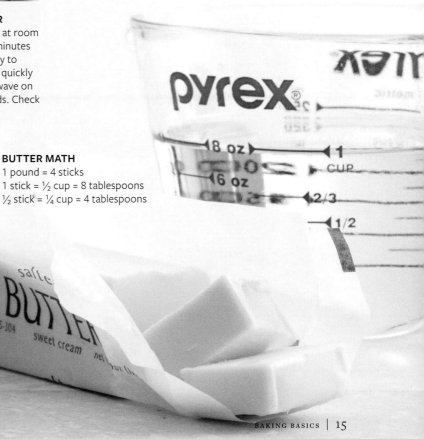

BUTTER MATH
1 pound = 4 sticks
1 stick = ½ cup = 8 tablespoons
½ stick = ¼ cup = 4 tablespoons

Dairy

Much of the liquid called for in baking originates at the dairy farm. Here's what you need to know about milk products for baking.

Whole, reduced-fat, low-fat, and skim milk: These milk types may be used interchangeably in recipes because they differ only in the amount of fat each contains, but keep in mind this will directly affect the richness and flavor in foods. Recipes in this cookbook were tested using reduced-fat (2 percent) milk.

Buttermilk: Buttermilk is low-fat or fat-free milk to which a bacterial culture has been added. It is thick and creamy with a mildly acidic taste. Do not substitute with regular milk. Instead make sour milk to replace it (see below).

Measuring Basics: Always measure milk and liquid ingredients (including oils) in a clear glass or plastic measuring cup. Place the cup on a flat work surface and pour the liquid in the cup until it reaches the desired measurement marking on the cup. Check at eye level to make sure it lines up exactly (see Liquid Sweetener photo, page 13). Baking is an exact science, and the success of recipes depends on accurate measurements.

Making Sweetened Whipped Cream

1. In a chilled mixing bowl combine 1 cup whipping cream, 2 tablespoons sugar, and ½ teaspoon vanilla. Beat with an electric mixer on medium speed until soft peaks form (tips curl). Serve at this stage if you wish to softly drape it over a dessert.

2. Or continue beating until stiff peaks form (tips stand straight). Do not overbeat or the cream will turn to butter.

TRY ADDING ONE OF THESE FLAVORFUL INGREDIENTS TO YOUR WHIPPED CREAM.

ADD WITH THE VANILLA: 2 tablespoons unsweetened cocoa powder plus 1 tablespoon sugar; 2 tablespoons amaretto, coffee, or hazelnut liqueur; or ¼ teaspoon ground cinnamon, nutmeg, or ginger

FOLD IN AT THE END: ½ teaspoon finely shredded lemon, lime, or orange peel

Making Sour Milk

In a liquid measuring cup, combine 1 tablespoon lemon juice or vinegar with enough milk to make 1 cup total liquid. Let stand for 5 minutes before using.

Flavorful Extras

When a recipe needs a flavorful boost, vanilla, nutmeg, and nuts are go-to ingredients. Here are the best ways to work with each.

Vanilla: This all-purpose flavor enhancer lends aroma, taste, and depth to all varieties of baked goods. Vanilla beans are the long, dark pods of a specific type of tropical orchid that have been dried and cured. Look for them in the spice aisle or at spice stores.

When a recipe calls for a whole vanilla bean, the pod is split lengthwise and the seeds scraped out (see photo, below). Vanilla bean paste is the next best thing to the whole bean and contains actual seeds from the bean. Pure vanilla extract is less expensive and is made by combining chopped vanilla beans with a mixture of alcohol and water. Cheap imitation vanilla should be avoided.

Nutmeg: Freshly grated whole nutmeg is a must in recipes where nutmeg is the featured flavor or is used as a garnish. The freshly grated variety is light, fluffy, and deliciously sweet and aromatic. In a pinch, you can use preground nutmeg in half the amount of freshly grated (½ teaspoon ground nutmeg replaces 1 teaspoon freshly grated nutmeg).

Nuts: Almonds, pecans, walnuts, and other nuts will add crunch, richness, and flavor to your baking. Use a large chef's knife to chop nuts to desired degree (see photos, below). Hazelnuts require a little extra work, but their flavor is well worth the effort (see tip, below). For tips on toasting nuts, see page 343.

VANILLA BEAN The seeds of the vanilla bean are delightful in baked goods. To prepare, use a paring knife to cut the vanilla beans in half lengthwise and scrape seeds out of the pod.

GRATING NUTMEG Freshly grated nutmeg is superior in all ways to the dense, ground variety. To grate whole spices, like nutmeg, run the seed back and forth across the serrated surface of a Microplane (rasp) grater.

HAZELNUT PREP Hazelnuts have a papery skin that is typically removed. Toast whole nuts in the oven in a single layer on a baking sheet at 350°F for 5 to 10 minutes or until golden brown. Stir or shake once or twice. To remove the skins, rub warm nuts in a dry dish towel until skins come loose.

CHOPPING AND GRINDING NUTS

Chopped nuts are called for in a variety of ways in recipes. The two photos (below left and center) show the two most commonly used.

For ground nuts, process in a food processor until ground but not oily. (Overdoing it can create nut butter.) To absorb some of the nut oil, add 1 tablespoon of the flour called for in the recipe to the nuts during grinding. Process with quick on/off turns, grind the nuts in small batches, and let them cool after toasting and before grinding.

CHOPPED NUTS

FINELY CHOPPED NUTS

GROUND NUTS

Chocolate

Chocolate is the ultimate indulgence, whether eaten out of hand or swirled into luscious desserts. Get the scoop on this ingredient favorite.

What Is Chocolate?

All chocolate starts from the beans of the cacao (kay-KAY-oh) tree. The beans are fermented, dried, roasted, and cracked. The extraction process produces cocoa butter and an intense brown paste called chocolate liquor. The percentage number noted on the chocolate package represents the amount of chocolate liquor contained in the bar. The rest is sugar. The greater the percentage of cacao content in proportion to sugar, the more pronounced and complex the chocolate flavor will be.

Types of Baking Chocolate

Milk chocolate: Dry milk gives this sweetened chocolate a creamy texture. Because of this addition, milk chocolate can't be substituted for other chocolates in recipes.

Sweet, semisweet, and bittersweet chocolate: These three chocolates, which contain varying amounts of chocolate liquor and sugar, can sometimes be used interchangeably in baking. Sweet and semisweet contain 15 to 35 percent chocolate liquor and have a higher sugar content than bittersweet. Bittersweet chocolate must contain 35 percent chocolate liquor or higher. These three varieties fall into the generic, hard-to-define category of dark chocolate.

Unsweetened chocolate: Also called baking chocolate, it is pure chocolate and cocoa butter with no added sugar. Recipes that call for it also require plenty of sugar.

White chocolate: This chocolate contains no chocolate liquor, so it's not technically a true chocolate. Instead, it's a mixture of cocoa butter (extracted from the cacao bean), milk solids, lecithin, and sugar. The recipes in this book call for white chocolate with cocoa butter. White baking pieces and candy coating do not contain cocoa butter and may diminish your baking success.

Cocoa powder: Unsweetened cocoa results from a final extraction of cocoa butter from chocolate liquor, resulting in a solid product that is ground to a powder.

Chocolate Garnishes

Try one of more of these ideas to create the ultimate garnish on your chocolate desserts.

Shards and cutouts: Line a baking sheet with foil; set aside. In a small saucepan stir chopped milk chocolate or semisweet chocolate over low heat until melted. Remove from heat. Spread chocolate ⅛ inch thick on prepared baking sheet. Let stand in a cool, dry place until firm (chill if necessary). For chocolate shards, carefully peel chocolate off foil. Break or cut chocolate into irregular pieces. For chocolate cutouts, use small cookie cutters to cut desired shapes from the sheet of chocolate. Cover and chill until needed.

Grated: Rub a solid piece of chocolate across a handheld grater using the fine or large section, depending on which size you want the pieces to be. Clean the grater as needed to prevent clogging.

Curls or shavings: For large curls, draw a vegetable peeler across the broad surface of a room-temperature bar of chocolate (milk chocolate works best). For small curls, use the narrow side of the chocolate piece. To make shavings, make short strokes with the peeler across the chocolate.

Chocolate designs: Line a baking sheet with parchment paper; set aside. Place tempered chocolate, melted white baking bar, candy coating, or a combination of these in a resealable plastic bag. Cut a small hole in one corner and pipe or drizzle small designs onto prepared baking sheet (see example, page 181). Let the garnishes stand in a cool, dry place until firm. Carefully peel designs from paper.

GRATED CHOCOLATE   **LARGE AND SMALL CHOCOLATE CURLS**

Quick-Tempering Chocolate

Tempering is the process of slowly melting and cooling chocolate to allow exactly the right type of cocoa butter crystals to form. When set, tempered chocolate has a shiny, glossy surface without streaks or evidence of bloom—the harmless but unattractive grayish patches that form on old or improperly stored chocolate. While this quick-temper process is not a true tempering method (the true method is a very time-consuming and tedious process), it allows the chocolate to melt slowly over controlled heat so it doesn't fall out of temper.

PREPARE BOWLS Place up to 1 pound finely chopped chocolate in a 1½-quart glass mixing bowl or 4-cup glass measure; set aside. Pour very warm water (100°F to 110°F) into a larger glass bowl or casserole to a depth of 1 inch.

COMBINE BOWLS Place the bowl containing chocolate inside the larger bowl of hot water. Water should cover the bottom half of the bowl containing the chocolate. Do not splash any water into the chocolate or it may seize (become thick and lumpy).

MELT AND STIR Stir chocolate with a spatula until completely melted and smooth. This should take 15 to 20 minutes (don't rush). Change the water as necessary to keep it at 100°F to 110°F. When chocolate is melted, it is ready to use.

Leaveners

Baked goods can be leavened by technique, added leavening agents, or both. Techniques such as creaming butter and whipping egg whites incorporate air into a batter. Two types of ingredients can be used for leavening, chemical (baking soda or baking powder) and biological (yeast).

Baking soda: Baking soda, or sodium bicarbonate, is primarily used in batters that contain acidic ingredients—such as buttermilk, yogurt, sour cream, molasses, honey, or fruit juices—because it requires an acid to help it break down at the correct rate for adequate carbon dioxide production.

Baking powder: Baking powder is a mixture that contains baking soda and just the right amount of a powdered acidic ingredient (such as cream of tartar) to react without additional acids being added to the batter. It also contains cornstarch to absorb moisture and keep these two ingredients perfectly dry. Most baking powders are "double-acting". They produce gases in two stages—once when liquids are added and again during baking. Be sure to thoroughly stir baking powder into a flour or dry ingredient mixture to prevent oversize gas bubbles from forming, which results in tunnels or large air pockets. Recipes often call for small amounts of baking powder and baking soda. Don't be tempted to leave either out of the recipe. The leaveners are necessary for proper rising.

Because the chemical properties of the two are different, one cannot be substituted for another. Some recipes call for both baking powder and baking soda, typically so the baking soda will neutralize an added acid (such as brown sugar).

Yeast: Active dry yeast is a dehydrated single-cell organism that is activated by warm liquid, which then converts its food (such as sugar) into carbon dioxide gas that makes dough rise.

Eggs: Beaten egg whites trap and hold quite a bit of air. When other ingredients are folded in (such as flour or beaten egg yolks), they act as a leavener in recipes such as Angel Food Cake (see recipe, page 125) and Hot Cocoa Soufflé (see recipe, page 297).

CHECK DATES Before you start baking, look at the expiration dates on all your packaged leaveners to ensure they are as fresh as possible. Toss any expired products to avoid problems during baking.

Pan Preparation

Keep cakes, bars, cookies, and other baked goodies from sticking to the pans with these simple preparation steps. Each recipe will specify how the pan is to be prepared before the batter or dough is added, so once you choose a recipe, you can refer back to this page to get started.

Greasing and flouring a pan

Cake recipes will call for a greased and floured pan, while many other recipes will simply call for greasing.

STEP-BY-STEP 1. With a pastry brush or paper towel, brush shortening evenly over the bottom and sides of the pan. **2.** Sprinkle a few spoonfuls of all-purpose flour into the bottom of the pan. **3.** Hold one edge and tap the other with your free hand to distribute flour around the pan. Be sure to tilt the pan to coat the sides. Tap any extra flour into the garbage.

Lining a pan with foil

Most of the bar cookie and brownie recipes in this book recommend lining the pan with foil for easy removal.

STEP-BY-STEP 1. Tear a piece of foil that is longer than the pan (allow for overhang on either end) and shape over the outside of the pan bottom, folding foil smoothly at the corners. **2.** Gently lift the shaped foil off the pan and turn the pan over. **3.** Fit the shaped foil into the inside of the pan, leaving the extra overhang to use as "handles" to lift the recipe out of the pan.

Lining a pan with waxed paper or parchment paper

This technique is commonly used for delicate cakes that are likely to stick, such as carrot cake and sponge cakes.

STEP-BY-STEP 1. Grease bottom and sides of pan as directed in recipe. Set pan on a large sheet of waxed paper or parchment paper; trace around the pan with a pencil. **2.** Cut around the traced line on waxed paper. **3.** Fit the waxed paper cutout to the bottom of the pan, pressing the corners and smoothing out wrinkles or bubbles. Grease the paper if directed in recipe.

Lowering Fat

Making your baked goods more healthful without sacrificing taste and texture takes a little substitution know-how.

Replace fats with pureed fruit.

Try replacing a portion of the fat in your recipe with an equal amount of pureed fruit (this works best in certain cakes, quick breads, and cakelike bars). Options include applesauce, pear butter, and pureed pumpkin. Begin by replacing only small amounts of the total fat and keep it under half the total fat being replaced. Some experimentation will be necessary to find the right balance.

Incorporate heart-healthy oils.

You can also experiment with substituting an equal portion of a heart-healthy oil, such as canola oil or olive oil, for some of the butter or shortening. Begin by replacing small amounts to see how you like the results.

Choose flour alternatives.

White whole wheat flour and regular whole wheat flour offer better nutrition and unique texture. Begin by replacing an equal amount of whole wheat flour for some of the all-purpose flour called for in the recipe. Because the texture of these flours is coarser, swapping 100 percent whole wheat flour into a recipe is not recommended.

Try a lower-fat milk.

Milk plays a big role in binding ingredients, while the fat in milk makes recipes tender and adds moisture. But replacing whole milk with lower-fat milk (even skim milk, in most cases) doesn't noticeably alter flavor or texture.

Make chocolate more healthful.

To replace 1 ounce of unsweetened baking chocolate, substitute 3 tablespoons antioxidant-rich unsweetened cocoa powder and 1 tablespoon heart-healthy canola oil.

PUREED FRUIT Lower fat by swapping in nutrient-rich fruit purees to replace some of the butter in your recipe.

HEART-HEALTHY OILS Use an equal amount to replace some of the butter or shortening in a recipe.

LOWER-FAT MILK If you typically use whole milk in recipes, try reduced-fat or low-fat milk instead.

CHOCOLATE SWAP
Boost the antioxidants and healthfulness with cocoa powder and canola oil.

FLOUR ALTERNATIVE
Substitute healthful whole wheat flour for a portion of the all-purpose flour.

MEASURING MATH
1 tablespoon = 3 teaspoons
¼ cup = 4 tablespoons
½ cup = 8 tablespoons
1 cup = 16 tablespoons

Substitutions

If you forgot to buy an ingredient, take a moment to look through your cupboards. If you have other ingredients on hand, these combinations make acceptable substitutions.

If you don't have:	Substitute:
Egg, 1 whole	¼ cup refrigerated or frozen egg product, thawed
Baking powder, 1 teaspoon	½ teaspoon cream of tartar plus ¼ teaspoon baking soda
Chocolate, semisweet or bittersweet, 1 ounce	3 tablespoons semisweet chocolate pieces, or 1 ounce unsweetened chocolate plus 1 tablespoon granulated sugar, or 1 tablespoon unsweetened cocoa powder plus 2 teaspoons sugar and 2 teaspoons shortening
Chocolate, sweet baking, 4 ounces	¼ cup unsweetened cocoa powder plus ⅓ cup granulated sugar and 3 tablespoons shortening
Chocolate, unsweetened, 1 ounce	3 tablespoons unsweetened cocoa powder plus 1 tablespoon cooking oil or shortening, melted
Butter, 1 cup	1 cup shortening plus ¼ teaspoon salt if desired
Buttermilk, 1 cup	1 tablespoon lemon juice or vinegar plus enough milk to equal 1 cup (let stand 5 minutes before using) or 1 cup plain yogurt
Cornstarch, 1 tablespoon (for thickening)	2 tablespoons all-purpose flour
Flour, cake, 1 cup	1 cup minus 2 tablespoons all-purpose flour
Flour, self-rising, 1 cup	1 cup all-purpose flour plus 1 teaspoon baking powder, ½ teaspoon salt, and ¼ teaspoon baking soda
Half-and-half or light cream, 1 cup	1 tablespoon melted butter or margarine plus enough whole milk to equal 1 cup
Sour cream, dairy, 1 cup	1 cup plain yogurt or 1 cup light sour cream
Sugar, brown, 1 cup packed	1 cup granulated sugar plus 2 tablespoons molasses
Sugar, granulated, 1 cup	1 cup packed brown sugar or 2 cups sifted powdered sugar
FLAVORINGS	
Vanilla bean, 1 whole	2 teaspoons vanilla extract
Apple pie spice, 1 teaspoon	½ teaspoon ground cinnamon plus ¼ teaspoon ground nutmeg, ⅛ teaspoon ground allspice, and dash ground cloves or ginger
Ginger, grated fresh, 1 teaspoon	¼ teaspoon ground ginger
Pumpkin pie spice, 1 teaspoon	½ teaspoon ground cinnamon plus ¼ teaspoon ground ginger, ¼ teaspoon ground allspice, and ⅛ teaspoon ground nutmeg
Herbs, snipped fresh, 1 tablespoon	½ to 1 teaspoon dried herb, crushed, or ½ teaspoon ground herb

Equivalents

Apple: 1 medium equals 1 cup sliced, ⅔ cup chopped
Banana: 1 medium equals ⅓ cup mashed, ¾ cup sliced
Blueberries: 1 pound equals 3 cups
Carrot: 1 medium equals ½ cup finely shredded
Cherries: 1 pound equals 3 cups whole, 2½ cups halved
Cranberries: 1 pound equals 4 cups
Cream, whipping: 1 cup equals 2 cups whipped
Gingersnaps: 15 cookies equals 1 cup crumbs
Graham crackers: 14 squares equals 1 cup crumbs

Lemon: 1 medium equals 2 teaspoons finely shredded peel, 3 tablespoons juice
Lime: 1 medium equals 1½ teaspoons finely shredded peel, 2 tablespoons juice
Orange: 1 medium equals 1 tablespoon finely shredded peel, ⅓ cup juice, ⅓ cup sections
Peach: 1 medium equals 1 cup sliced, ¾ cup chopped
Rhubarb: 1 pound equals 4 cups sliced
Zucchini: 1 medium equals 1⅓ cups shredded

Standard Mixing Methods

Doughs and batters are not all created equal. While most recipes call for a mixture of the same basic ingredients—flour, sugar, fat, milk, and eggs—the manner in which you combine them (as well as the ratio used) creates a variety of textures. With baking, you'll likely use one of these standard mixing methods to get the job done.

Butter-Style Cakes Method (Creaming)

Most butter-based cakes call for this method of beating first the butter, then slowly beating in sugar, and later eggs, one at a time, to work in as much air as possible. Later, flour and liquid are added alternately in batches to evenly incorporate each addition. First add some of the flour and limit the mixing after the first addition of liquid. Once liquid is combined with flour, gluten begins to develop and overmixing will cause toughness.

CREAMING Start by beating softened butter to incorporate air. Beat sugar into butter in small batches.

ADD EGGS Beat in eggs, one at a time to further incorporate air into the butter mixture.

ALTERNATELY ADD FLOUR Start by beating about one-third or one-fourth of the flour mixture into the butter mixture until combined.

ALTERNATELY ADD LIQUID After the first flour addition, add a portion of the liquid. Beat just until combined. Repeat alternating until all the flour and liquid are added.

Quick Bread Method

Most muffin and quick bread recipes use this simple method. Dry and wet ingredients are combined in two separate bowls. The wet ingredients are then added to the dry ingredients all at once and stirred just until combined. The stirring is so brief—again, to avoid toughness—that the batter will be lumpy.

MIX DRY INGREDIENTS Thoroughly whisk together all dry ingredients—such as flour, baking powder, salt, and/or spices—in a large bowl so they are well blended.

MIX WET INGREDIENTS In a separate bowl stir to combine wet ingredients—such as eggs, milk, oil, butter, zucchini, pumpkin, or banana.

ADD WET TO DRY. Press dry ingredients against the sides of bowl to create a well (indentation) in the center. Pour wet ingredients into the well.

MIX Stir the wet and dry ingredients together just until the two are combined; some flour lumps will remain. Overmixing may cause toughness from excess gluten.

Biscuit/Piecrust Method

Biscuits and piecrust rely on pockets of fat in the dough mixture to create tender flakiness. These pockets are made by cutting fat and flour together to create small pieces of flour-coated fat before the liquid is added.

CUT IN FAT Use a pastry blender to cut cold fat into flour until it is the size of peas.

SCRAPE AS NEEDED Use a butter knife to clean off the pastry blender as necessary.

WET INGREDIENTS Add the wet ingredients all at once to a well in the flour mixture.

MIX TOGETHER Stir the wet and dry ingredients just until all is moistened.

Folding Method

Folding calls for mixing light ingredients (such as beaten egg whites) with heavier mixtures without decreasing the volume of the egg whites. You will cut down vertically through the mixture with a spatula and sweep back along the side of the bowl.

BEAT EGG WHITES Start by beating egg whites until stiff peaks form.

LIGHTEN MIXTURE Fold in some of the egg whites by cutting down vertically and sweeping back up the side.

ADD MIXTURE Pour the lightened chocolate mixture into the remaining beaten egg whites.

FOLD Continue cutting down into mixture with spatula and sweeping back up and over the other side. Mixture will be light and airy.

Stir-Together Method

Instead of adding wet ingredients to dry all at once or beating the batter with an electric mixer, this simple method calls for stirring in ingredients, one at a time, with a wooden spoon.

COMBINE WET Begin by combining fat and liquid.

ADD FLOUR Other ingredients, such as flour or sugar, are stirred in all at once.

ADD EGGS Ingredients, such as eggs, are stirred in one at a time.

FINISH The combined mixture from this method is often thick and smooth.

Bakeware

While few bakers have every single pan on the market, there are some basics that you'll see often in the recipes in this book. If you're just starting out, buy a few pieces as you need them rather than getting everything at once. You may find your style of baking doesn't require certain pans.

A **Pie plate:** When the recipes in this book call for a pie plate, they refer to one that is 1¼ inches deep. It can be made of glass, ceramic, stoneware, or aluminum. Deep-dish pie plates are 1½ to 2 inches deep.

B **Ramekins and custard cups:** Use these small dishes for baking individual desserts and custards.

C **Fluted tube pan:** This ring-shape cake pan is perfect for making cakes and monkey bread.

D **2½-inch muffin pan:** Use this pan for muffins and cupcakes. Or look for miniature muffin pans in 1¾-inch size.

E **Springform pan:** A latch on this pan opens to release the sides from a baked dessert, such as cheesecake, for easy serving.

F **Cookie sheets:** Buy at least two cookie sheets so you can prep one batch of cookies while the other is in the oven. Here are some things to look for when purchasing new cookie sheets.
Light to medium color: Avoid dark-color pans.
Sturdy and heavy-duty: Avoid lightweight pans.
One or two raised sides: More than two raised sides prevents good air circulation.
Noninsulated: Insulation increases baking time and causes cookies to spread.
Nonperforated: Crumbs stick in the holes of perforated pans/mats.

G **Wire cooling rack:** Most recipes call for a rack to completely cool recipes after removing from oven.

H **Round cake pans:** Aim to buy two of these for baking standard layer cakes, although one will do. Pans come in an 8- or 9-inch diameter, which are interchangeable.

I **15×10×1-inch pan:** Also commonly called a jelly roll pan, this pan is used for a variety of recipes, including sponge cakes for jelly rolls and certain bar cookies and brownies.

J K L **Rectangular and square pans and dishes:** Stock up on rectangular (13×9×2-inch) and square (8×8×2-inch or 9×9×2-inch) baking pans for brownies, cakes, bars, and more. Loaf pans are used for yeast breads, quick breads, and pound cakes. They come in 8×4×2-inch and 9×5×3-inch—both of which are called for in this book.

Baking dishes: In this book, a baking dish means an oven-safe glass or ceramic vessel. A baking pan refers to a metal container.

M **Baking dishes (glass or ceramic):** Use when a 2- or 3-quart baking dish is called for—specifically when baking egg dishes or acidic foods, including citrus- and other fruit-based desserts. Ceramic dishes should be reserved for cobblers, crisps, and other crustless fruit desserts.

N **Baking pans (metal):** Aluminum—nonstick or not—is a great choice for baking pans. They are lightweight and conduct heat well for even baking and browning. Pale or shiny metal pans, such as heavy-gauge aluminum, deliver a tender, delicate crust, good for breads and cookies. Use dark metal pans, which conduct, retain, and distribute heat well, for fruit pies and other baked items that require more crispness and browning.

Baking Pan Capacities

Pan Shape	Pan Dimensions	Approximate Volume
Fluted tube pan	10 inches	12 cups
Jelly roll pan	15×10×1 inches	10 cups
Loaf pan	8×4×2½ inches	4 cups
Loaf pan	9×5×3 inches	8 cups
Muffin cup	2¾×1½ inches	½ cup
Muffin cup (mini)	1¾×¾ inches	2 tablespoons
Pie pan	9×1½ inches	6 cups
Pie pan (deep-dish)	9×2 inches	8 cups
Rectangular pan	11×7×2 inches	6 cups
Rectangular pan	13×9×2 inches	14 cups
Round pan	8×1½ inches	4 cups
Round pan	8×2 inches	6 cups
Round pan	9×1½ inches	6 cups
Round pan	9×2 inches	8 cups
Springform pan	8×3 inches	11 cups
Springform pan	9×3 inches	12 cups
Square pan	8×8×1½ inches	6 cups
Square pan	9×9×1½ inches	8 cups
Square pan	9×9×2 inches	10 cups
Tube pan	10 inches	16 cups

Baking Tools

Before you start baking, you'll need a few basic tools for the job. Here are the essentials—and a few extras you can stock up on over time.

A **Fine-mesh sieve:** Use a sieve to drain wet ingredients, sift together dry ingredients, and to dust a pan of brownies with powdered sugar. Sifting dry ingredients breaks up any lumps and aerates the ingredients so cakes and pastries turn out lighter and lump-free.

B **Pastry bag/tips/coupler:** Use pastry bags and tips to decorate cakes and cupcakes with frosting. Tips come in a variety of shapes and sizes, but the most common are star and round tips. The coupler fits into the bag so you can screw on different tips to use the same color frosting. Find these items in the cake decorating department of hobby and crafts stores (see Decorated Cakes chapter, page 150, for how to use these items).

C **Bench scraper:** A bench scraper can easily cut large masses of dough and pastry in half or into smaller pieces (such as dinner rolls). It can also be used to handle and move the dough and to clean and scrape sticky dough remnants from work surfaces.

D **Pastry blender:** When making piecrust and biscuits, the pastry blender is used for cutting fat into flour. You can use two butter knives—moved in a crisscross motion—but it's much easier and more efficient to use a pastry blender.

E **Microplane rasp grater/zester:** This is the ultimate gadget for finely grating citrus peel, ginger, and fresh nutmeg. You can also use it to grate chocolate over a frosted cake as a simple garnish.

F **Pastry brush:** This soft-bristle tool has many baking applications. Use it to grease a pan, brush melted butter on layers of phyllo, spread milk on top of a piecrust, and apply an egg wash to the top of bread and pastry dough.

G **Wooden spoon:** Sturdy wooden spoons are great for stirring heavy doughs and hot sauces or mixtures. They can take on odors, such as onions or garlic, so keep wooden spoons for baking and cooking separate.

H **Metal turner/spatula:** Off-set spatulas are a must for moving delicate cutout cookies from the pan to a cooling rack after baking. An especially thin metal blade is handy. It's flexible enough to easily slip under the item you're moving without squishing the dough or breaking the cookie or cake. To prevent scratching, avoid using metal spatulas on nonstick surfaces.

I **Scraper:** This all-purpose utensil is used for scraping batters from the sides of bowls and pans. Scrapers are also ideal for folding together wet and dry ingredients. Silicone scrapers stand up to high heat better than those made of rubber or other materials.

J **Flat or off-set spatula/spreader:** This spatula is ideal for frosting cakes. The off-set spatula allows you to spread batter or frost products in a baking pan without dragging your knuckles across the surface.

K **Serrated knife:** Most delicate baked goods require a good serrated knife for cutting and serving. The serrated edge is also used to level delicate cakes and slice into crusty bread. Use a gentle sawing motion to cut through your baked goods.

L **Whisk:** A wire whisk is a must for beating eggs, and it has plenty of other uses too. It's perfect for stirring homemade custards and terrific for thoroughly mixing and aerating dry ingredients.

M **Rolling pin:** There are two basic types of rolling pins. The one shown at right is the classic roller style. The other is the French-style rolling pin—an elongated rod with tapered ends. Rolling pins come in a variety of materials, including wood, ceramic, metal, silicone, and marble. Use them to roll out piecrust, cookie dough, and pastry.

N **Measuring spoons:** Shapes can vary for the bowls of measuring spoons, but they typically come in 1 tablespoon, 1 teaspoon, ½ teaspoon, and ¼ teaspoon measures. Use for measuring small amounts of ingredients, such as spices, baking powder, and baking soda.

O **Liquid measuring cups:** Any time you measure out liquids—such as milk, water, oil, honey, or even melted butter—you'll want to use these cups. A 1 cup and 2 cup are essential, but larger options can be helpful too.

P **Nesting glass mixing bowls:** Nesting glass mixing bowls typically have a variety of sizes, including 1½-, 3-, and 5-quart that you can nest and store easily.

Q **Dry measuring cups:** Use these when measuring dry goods like flour or sugar that require leveling off the top for an accurate measure. They're also good for loose ingredients, such as chocolate chips and oatmeal, or solid ingredients, such as shortening. Most sets come in 1 cup, ¾ cup, ½ cup, ⅓ cup, and ¼ cup sizes.

Storing & Freezing

Yeast breads, rolls, and quick breads
Short-term storage: Place cooled yeast breads and rolls in resealable plastic bags and store at room temperature for 2 to 3 days; avoid refrigerating.
Freezer: Wrap cooled bread tightly with plastic wrap; place in resealable plastic freezer bag. Freeze for up to 3 months. Thaw at room temperature. If desired, wrap bread in foil and reheat in a 350°F oven for 10 minutes.

Cakes
Short-term storage: Most cakes can be covered and stored at room temperature for up to 3 days. If you don't have a cake cover, turn a large bowl upside down over the cake. (Or stick a few toothpicks in the cake to protect the frosting and cover loosely with plastic wrap.) If the filling or frosting contains whipped cream, cream cheese, or eggs, store it, covered, in the refrigerator.
Freezer: Wrap unfrosted cakes in a layer each of plastic wrap and foil. If possible, place in a large resealable plastic freezer bag. Freeze for up to 3 months. Thaw at room temperature. Fill and frost as directed.

Cookie and bars
Short-term storage: Arrange cooled, unfrosted cookies in an airtight container in single layers separated by sheets of waxed paper or place in a reasealable plastic bag; store at room temperature for up to 3 days. (Do not mix soft and crisp cookies in the same container because the crisp cookies will soften.) Frost as directed. To store bars, place in a tightly covered container or store them in the baking pan, tightly covered with plastic wrap or foil. Any cookies or bars with cream cheese, yogurt, or egg-based frosting or filling must be stored in the refrigerator.
Freezer: Layer unfrosted cookies or bars in layers separated by sheets of waxed paper in a freezer container or in a large resealable plastic bag. Freeze for up to 3 months. Thaw at room temperature. To freeze cookie dough, place dough in a tightly sealed container or resealable freezer bag and freeze for up to 6 months. Thaw in the refrigerator, then shape and bake as directed. (Avoid freezing brownie batter and meringue mixtures.)

Cheesecakes
Short-term storage: Cover cheesecakes with plastic wrap and refrigerate for up to 3 days.
Freezer: Cover tightly in a layer each of plastic wrap and foil. Place in a large resealable plastic freezer bag. Freeze for up to 1 month. Thaw in the refrigerator.

Pies
Short-term storage: Baked fruit pies may stand at room temperature for 24 hours; cover and refrigerate for longer storage. Cover custard and cream pies loosely with plastic wrap and refrigerate for up to 2 days.
Freezer: Cover cooled, baked pies with a layer each of plastic wrap and foil; place pie in a large resealable freezer bag. Freeze for up to 4 months. To serve, thaw the pie, covered, at room temperature. If desired, reheat pie, covered, in a 325°F oven. Do not freeze custard, cream, and meringue-topped pies.

Troubleshooting Guide

Regardless of your level of baking expertise, recipes can go awry from time to time. Take a peek at the chart below to determine what may have happened and ways to prevent it in the future. From-scratch baking is all about learning from past experience.

Cakes

Problem	Possible causes/solutions
Coarse texture	• Excess baking soda • Too little liquid • Butter and sugar not thoroughly blended
Cake sticks to pan	• Insufficient greasing • Cake removed from pan too quickly • Cake cooled in pan too long
Cake is dry	• Excess flour or baking powder • Too little shortening, butter, or sugar • Oven too hot or cake baked too long
Cake is heavy/dense	• Too little baking powder • Too many eggs • Overmixing of batter
Cake sinks in the middle	• Use of small pans • Too much liquid • Opening oven or moving pans during baking • Oven temperature too low or cake not baked long enough

Cookies

Problem	Possible causes/solutions
Cookies are tough and hard	• Too much flour • Overmixing
Cookies bake unevenly	• Misshapen dough balls
Cookies too brown on the bottom	• Dark-color cookie sheets
Cookies spread too much	• Unnecessary greasing of cookie sheet • Dough placed on warm cookie sheets • Oven temperature too low • Too much sugar
Burned cookies	• Baked too long • Left on baking sheet too long

Yeast Bread

Problem	Possible causes/solutions
Loaf did not rise enough before baking	• Expired yeast • Liquid too hot • Not enough sugar • Environment too cool or drafty • Dough not kneaded enough
Loaf did not rise enough during baking	• Oven temperature too low • Dough raised too much before baking
Crust did not brown	• Oven temperature too low • Not enough sugar
Bread is dense on bottom	• Oven temperature too high
Bread collapsed in oven	• Dough raised too much before baking

Quick Bread

Problem	Possible causes/solutions
Bread is dense	• Not baked long enough • Not enough liquid
Bread is tough	• Too much liquid • Batter overmixed • Too much flour
Muffins have tunnels	• Batter overmixed • Not enough liquid • Too much flour • Muffins overbaked

Pie

Problem	Possible causes/solutions
Pastry is crumbly and hard to roll	• Not enough water • Rolled out with too much flour
Pastry is tough	• Too much water • Dough overworked • Fat not thoroughly worked into dough • Too little shortening
Crust shrinks	• Crust was stretched • Too much shortening
Bottom crust is soggy	• Used a shiny metal pan instead of dull metal or glass • Cracks in the dough before filling was added • Oven temperature too low
Crust sticks to rolling pin	• Too little flour on rolling pin and work surface
Edges of crust burn	• Cover edges with aluminum foil
Meringue sweats/beads	• Overcooked meringue
Meringue slides off filling	• Meringue was spread over cool filling • Spread meringue thoroughly over filling to edges to seal
Meringue is soggy	• Environment is too humid

Miscellaneous

Problem	Possible causes/solutions
Egg whites will not whip	• Dirty bowl • Eggs too cold
Overbeaten egg whites	• Add 1 unbeaten white and whip again until stiff peaks form. Remove ¼ cup of whipped egg white.
Overbeaten whipped cream	• Start over
Chocolate seized during melting	• Liquid got into chocolate

Thin-and-Crispy Chocolate Chip Cookies, recipe page 34

Soft-and-Cakelike Chocolate Chip Cookies, recipe page 34

Chocolate Chip Cookies, recipe page 34

cookies

CHEWY, GOOEY, CRISPY, OR CRUNCHY— cookies bring joy to every occasion and turn ordinary weekdays into something special. Choose from old-fashioned favorites like Classic Sugar Cookies or modern treats such as Double-Almond Macarons. Plus, learn how to tweak Chocolate Chip Cookies three ways—soft and cakey, thin and crispy, and the original.

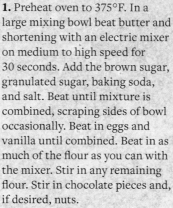

Chocolate Chip Cookies

Everyone has a favorite style of chocolate chip cookies—soft, crispy, or somewhere in between. Our best basic recipe provides two variations so you can please everyone!

PREP: 40 minutes
BAKE: 8 minutes per batch at 375°F
MAKES: 60 cookies

- ½ cup butter, softened
- ½ cup shortening
- 1 cup packed brown sugar
- ½ cup granulated sugar
- ½ teaspoon baking soda
- ½ teaspoon salt
- 2 eggs
- 1 teaspoon vanilla
- 2¾ cups all-purpose flour
- 1 12-ounce package semisweet chocolate pieces or miniature candy-coated semisweet chocolate pieces (2 cups)
- 1 cup chopped walnuts or pecans (optional)

1. Preheat oven to 375°F. In a large mixing bowl beat butter and shortening with an electric mixer on medium to high speed for 30 seconds. Add the brown sugar, granulated sugar, baking soda, and salt. Beat until mixture is combined, scraping sides of bowl occasionally. Beat in eggs and vanilla until combined. Beat in as much of the flour as you can with the mixer. Stir in any remaining flour. Stir in chocolate pieces and, if desired, nuts.

2. Drop dough by rounded teaspoons 2 inches apart onto ungreased cookie sheets. (Or use a ¼-cup measure or scoop to drop mounds of dough 4 inches apart onto ungreased cookie sheets. If desired, flatten dough mounds to circles about ¾ inch thick.)

3. Bake for 8 to 9 minutes or just until edges are light brown. Cool on cookie sheet for 2 minutes. Transfer to a wire rack; cool.

To Store: Layer cookies between sheets of waxed paper in an airtight container; cover. Store at room temperature for up to 3 days or freeze for up to 3 months.

PER COOKIE: *83 cal., 4 g fat (2 g sat. fat), 9 mg chol., 37 mg sodium, 11 g carb., 0 g fiber, 1 g pro.*

Thin-and-Crispy Chocolate Chip Cookies: Prepare as directed except increase butter to 1 cup and omit shortening; reduce brown sugar to ¾ cup and increase granulated sugar to ¾ cup; and reduce flour to 2 cups. Bake about 9 minutes or just until edges are light brown. Cool on cookie sheet for 1 minute. Transfer to a wire rack; cool completely.

PER COOKIE: *92 cal., 5 g fat (3 g sat. fat), 15 mg chol., 55 mg sodium, 12 g carb., 0 g fiber, 1 g pro.*

Soft-and-Cakelike Chocolate Chip Cookies: Omit butter and granulated sugar. Increase brown sugar to 1½ cups and baking soda to 1 teaspoon. Reduce flour to 2½ cups and semisweet chocolate pieces to 1½ cups. In a large mixing bowl beat shortening with an electric mixer on medium to medium-high speed for 30 seconds. Add brown sugar, baking soda, salt, and ½ teaspoon baking powder. Beat in eggs and vanilla until combined. Beat in one 8-ounce carton sour cream just until combined. Beat in as much flour as you can with the mixer. Stir in any remaining flour. Stir in chocolate pieces and, if desired, nuts. Drop dough onto cookie sheet as directed. Bake for 9 to 11 minutes or just until edges are light brown. Transfer to a wire rack; cool completely.

PER COOKIE: *85 cal., 4 g fat (2 g sat. fat), 9 mg chol., 51 mg sodium, 12 g carb., 0 g fiber, 1 g pro.*

Secrets to Success

This chocolate chip cookie recipe calls for an equal mixture of butter and shortening. Butter adds exceptional flavor and contributes to the texture, while shortening helps the cookies hold their shape during baking and prevents excessive spreading and crisping. Our Test Kitchen recommends always using butter instead of margarine for cookies because results will be different.

Beat the butter and sugars together well, but be careful not to overbeat the mixture, which will begin to deflate the air bubbles just achieved.

Always bake cookies on a cookie sheet—a pan that has, at most, one or two raised sides. If all sides are raised, (like a jelly roll pan), the cookies won't have good air circulation during baking. Select pans that are light color, sturdy, and noninsulated (insulated pans may increase baking time and can cause cookies to spread). Use an ungreased cookie sheet for this recipe because greasing will cause excessive spreading. Many cookie recipes call for ungreased cookie sheets because there is enough fat in cookies to prevent them from sticking to the pan.

Vary the flavor of this cookie by changing the chips. Have a little fun with milk chocolate pieces, butterscotch-flavor pieces, or candy-coated chocolate pieces.

CREAMING BUTTER AND SUGAR Beat butter and shortening with an electric mixture until smooth. Beat in the sugars, incorporating air into the dough.

BEAT IN THE EGGS Also beat in other liquid ingredients, such as vanilla, until uniformly combined. There should be no streaks of egg in the mixture.

WORK IN THE FLOUR After beating in as much flour as you can with the mixer, stir in any remaining flour with a wooden spoon or heavy-duty scraper.

ADD THE STIR-INS Stir the chocolate pieces and, if desired, nuts into the dough until all of the ingredients are incorporated.

DROP DOUGH BY SPOONS Using a flatware teaspoon (not a measuring teaspoon), push a scoop of dough onto cookie sheet with a second spoon.

LET COOKIES COOL Transfer baked cookies to a wire rack to cool completely. Let softer cookies stand on the cookie sheet for a minute before cooling.

Make-It-Mine Oatmeal Cookies

Who doesn't love options? Tweak the fat, sugar, spice, flavoring, flour, and stir-ins to make one-of-a-kind treats with each batch.

PREP: **30 minutes**
BAKE: **8 minutes per batch at 350°F**
MAKES: **48 cookies**

> *Fat* (choose option)
> *Sugar* (choose option)
> 1 teaspoon baking soda
> *Spice* (choose option)
> ½ teaspoon salt
> 2 eggs
> *Flavoring* (choose option)
> *Flour* (choose option)
> 3 cups regular or quick rolled oats
> *1 cup Stir-Ins* (choose option)

1. Preheat oven to 350°F. In a large mixing bowl beat *Fat* with an electric mixer on medium to high speed for 30 seconds. Add *Sugar*, baking soda, *Spice*, and salt. Beat until combined, scraping sides of bowl occasionally. Beat in eggs and *Flavoring*. Beat in as much of the *Flour* as you can with the mixer. Stir in any remaining Flour and the oats. If desired, add *Stir-Ins*.
2. Drop dough by rounded teaspoons or tablespoons or by a ¼-cup measure or cookie scoop 2 to 3 inches apart onto ungreased cookie sheets.
3. Bake for 8 to 10 minutes for rounded teaspoons or tablespoons or 12 to 14 minutes for ¼ cup or cookie scoop portions or until cookies are light brown and centers appear set. Cool on cookie sheets for 2 minutes. Transfer cookies to a wire rack; cool.

FAT (PICK ONE)
- 1 cup butter (note: cookies made with all butter are thin and crisp)
- ½ cup butter and ½ cup shortening
- ½ cup butter and ½ cup peanut butter

SUGAR (PICK ONE)
- 1 cup packed brown sugar and ½ cup granulated sugar
- 1½ cups packed brown sugar
- 1 cup granulated sugar and ½ cup molasses (add ¼ cup additional all-purpose flour)
- 1 cup granulated sugar and ½ cup honey

SPICE (PICK ONE)
- 1 teaspoon ground cinnamon
- 1 teaspoon pumpkin pie spice
- 1 teaspoon apple pie spice
- ½ teaspoon ground allspice

FLAVORING (PICK ONE)
- 1 teaspoon vanilla
- ½ teaspoon coconut flavoring
- ½ teaspoon maple flavoring

FLOUR (PICK ONE)
- 1½ cups all-purpose flour
- ¾ cup all-purpose flour and ¾ cup whole wheat flour
- 1 cup all-purpose flour and ½ cup oat bran
- 1¼ cups all-purpose flour and ¼ cup toasted wheat germ

STIR-INS (PICK ONE)
Raisins or mixed dried fruit bits
Snipped dried apricots or tart red cherries
Semisweet or milk chocolate pieces
White baking pieces
Butterscotch-flavor baking pieces
Peanut butter-flavor baking pieces
Flaked coconut
Chopped pecans, walnuts, or other nuts

Classic Sugar Cookies

PREP: **35 minutes**
BAKE: **12 minutes per batch
at 300°F**
MAKES: **48 cookies**

½ cup butter, softened
½ cup shortening
2 cups sugar
1 teaspoon baking soda
1 teaspoon cream of tartar
⅛ teaspoon salt
3 egg yolks
½ teaspoon vanilla
1¾ cups all-purpose flour

1. Preheat oven to 300°F. In a large mixing bowl beat butter and shortening with an electric mixer on medium to high speed for 30 seconds. Add sugar, baking soda, cream of tartar, and salt. Beat until combined, scraping sides of bowl occasionally. Beat in egg yolks and vanilla. Beat in as much of the flour as you can with the mixer. Using a wooden spoon, stir in any remaining flour.
2. Shape dough into 1-inch balls. Place balls 2 inches apart on ungreased cookie sheets.
3. Bake for 12 to 14 minutes or until edges are set; do not let edges brown. Cool cookies on cookie sheet for 2 minutes. Transfer cookies to wire racks; cool completely.

To Store: Layer cookies between sheets of waxed paper in an airtight container; cover. Store at room temperature for up to 2 days or freeze for up to 3 months.

PER COOKIE: *88 cal., 4 g fat (2 g sat. fat), 18 mg chol., 47 mg sodium, 12 g carb., 0 g fiber, 1 g pro.*

Tips for Cookie-Baking Success

• Leave enough room between pieces of dough for cookies to spread while baking. One to 2 inches is typical.
• When baking consecutive batches, do not place dough directly onto hot baking sheets. Wait for the baking sheets to cool to prevent spreading and uneven baking.
• Check cookies for even doneness as they bake. Switch cookie sheets from the bottom to the top rack and rotate them if necessary.

Soft Maple Sugar Cookies

PREP: 30 minutes
BAKE: 12 minutes per batch at 300°F
MAKES: 48 cookies

- ½ cup butter, softened
- ½ cup shortening
- 1½ cups granulated sugar
- ¼ cup packed brown sugar
- ¼ cup pure maple syrup
- 1 teaspoon baking soda
- 1 teaspoon cream of tartar
- ⅛ teaspoon salt
- 3 egg yolks
- ½ teaspoon vanilla
- 1¾ cups all-purpose flour
- 1 recipe Maple Icing

1. Preheat oven to 300°F. In a large mixing bowl combine butter and shortening. Beat with an electric mixer on medium to high speed for 30 seconds. Add granulated sugar, brown sugar, maple syrup, baking soda, cream of tartar, and salt. Beat until combined, scraping sides of bowl occasionally. Beat in egg yolks and vanilla until combined. Beat in as much of the flour as you can with the mixer. Using a wooden spoon, stir in any remaining flour.
2. Shape dough into 1-inch balls. Place 2 inches apart on an ungreased cookie sheet.
3. Bake for 12 to 14 minutes or until edges are light brown. Cool cookies on cookie sheet for 2 minutes. Transfer to a wire rack; cool. Centers will dip as cookies cool. Drizzle with Maple Icing.

Maple Icing: In a medium bowl stir together ¼ cup whipping cream or milk, ¼ cup melted butter, and 3 tablespoons pure maple syrup. Whisk in 3 to 4 cups powdered sugar to make icing drizzling consistency.

To Store: Layer cookies between sheets of waxed paper in an airtight container; cover. Store at room temperature for up to 2 days or freeze for up to 3 months.

PER COOKIE: *134 cal., 6 g fat (3 g sat. fat), 22 mg chol., 54 mg sodium, 20 g carb., 0 g fiber, 1 g pro.*

Giant Ginger Cookies

PREP: **40 minutes**
BAKE: **12 minutes per batch
at 350°F**
MAKES: **48 cookies**

4½ cups all-purpose flour
4 teaspoons ground ginger
2 teaspoons baking soda
1½ teaspoons ground cinnamon
1 teaspoon ground cloves
¼ teaspoon salt
1½ cups shortening
2 cups granulated sugar
2 eggs
½ cup molasses
¾ cup coarse sugar or
granulated sugar

1. Preheat oven to 350°F. In a medium bowl stir together flour, ginger, baking soda, cinnamon, cloves, and salt; set aside.
2. In a large mixing bowl beat shortening with an electric mixer on low speed for 30 seconds to soften. Gradually add the 2 cups granulated sugar. Beat until combined, scraping sides of bowl occasionally. Beat in eggs and molasses. Beat in as much of the flour mixture as you can with the mixer. Using a wooden spoon, stir in any remaining flour mixture.
3. Shape dough into 2-inch balls using ¼ cup dough. Roll balls in the ¾ cup coarse or granulated sugar. Place about 2½ inches apart on an ungreased cookie sheet.

4. Bake for 12 to 14 minutes or until cookies are light brown and puffed. (Do not overbake or cookies will not be chewy.) Cool on cookie sheet for 2 minutes. Transfer cookies to a wire rack; cool.

To Store: Layer cookies between sheets of waxed paper in an airtight container; cover. Store at room temperature for up to 3 days or in the freezer for up to 3 months.

PER COOKIE: *299 cal., 12 g fat (3 g sat. fat), 15 mg chol., 133 mg sodium, 45 g carb., 1 g fiber, 3 g pro.*

Make It Mini

Shape dough into ¾-inch balls. Increase coarse or granulated sugar for rolling to 1 to 1¼ cups; roll balls in the sugar. Place about 1 inch apart on an ungreased cookie sheet. Bake in a 350°F oven for 5 to 7 minutes or until cookies are light brown and puffed. (Do not overbake or cookies will not be chewy.) Cool on cookie sheet for 2 minutes. Transfer cookies to a wire rack to cool. Store in a tightly covered container at room temperature for up to 3 days or in the freezer for up to 3 months. Makes about 160 (1¾-inch) cookies.

Salted Chocolate-Caramel Rounds

PREP: **30 minutes**
BAKE: **8 minutes per batch**
at **375°F**
MAKES: **36 cookies**

2¾ cups all-purpose flour
¾ cup unsweetened cocoa
  powder
1 teaspoon baking soda
¼ teaspoon salt
1 cup butter, softened
1 cup granulated sugar
1 cup packed brown sugar
2 eggs
2 teaspoons vanilla
36 milk chocolate-covered
  round caramels
12 vanilla caramels,
  unwrapped
1 tablespoon whipping cream,
  half-and-half, or light cream
  Coarse salt

1. In a medium bowl stir together flour, cocoa powder, baking soda, and salt; set aside.

2. In a large mixing bowl beat butter with an electric mixer on medium to high speed for 30 seconds. Add granulated and brown sugars. Beat until combined, scraping sides of bowl occasionally. Beat in eggs and vanilla until combined. Beat in as much of the flour mixture as you can with the mixer. Stir in any remaining flour mixture. If necessary, cover and chill for 1 hour or until dough is easy to handle.

3. Preheat oven to 375°F. Shape dough into 1½-inch balls. Press a chocolate-covered caramel into each ball and shape dough around caramel to enclose. Place cookies 2 inches apart on an ungreased cookie sheet.

4. Bake for 8 to 10 minutes or until edges are firm. Transfer cookies to a wire rack; cool.

5. For caramel drizzle, in a small saucepan combine vanilla caramels and whipping cream. Heat over medium-low heat until caramels melt and mixture is smooth. Drizzle melted caramel mixture over cookies and then sprinkle with coarse salt.* Let stand until set.

To Store: Layer undecorated cookies between sheets of waxed paper in an airtight container; cover. Store at room temperature for up to 3 days or freeze for up to 3 months. To serve, thaw cookies if frozen. Drizzle cookies with caramel mixture and sprinkle with salt as directed in Step 5.

PER COOKIE: *177 cal., 8 g fat (5 g sat. fat), 27 mg chol., 140 mg sodium, 26 g carb., 1 g fiber, 2 g pro.*

*****Test Kitchen Tip:** A light sprinkling of coarse salt provides the ideal finishing touch to these chocolaty treats. The light, flaky texture of the salt brings out the rich complexity of the caramel topping, not just the sweetness. Flaky or coarse sea salts are ideal for topping baked goods because they have a light, crunchy texture and don't dissolve like other salts.

How to Place Candy in Dough Balls

1. Shape dough into balls and press a chocolate-covered caramel into each ball.

2. Use your hands to wrap the dough around the caramel to enclose. Roll ball gently to smooth.

Snickerdoodles

PREP: **35 minutes**
CHILL: **1 hour**
BAKE: **10 minutes per batch
at 375°F**
MAKES: **48 cookies**

   1 cup butter, softened
1½ cups sugar
   1 teaspoon baking soda
   1 teaspoon cream of tartar
   ¼ teaspoon salt
   2 eggs
   1 teaspoon vanilla
   3 cups all-purpose flour
   ¼ cup sugar
   2 teaspoons ground cinnamon

1. In a large mixing bowl beat butter with an electric mixer on medium to high speed for 30 seconds. Add the 1½ cups sugar, baking soda, cream of tartar, and salt. Beat until combined, scraping sides of bowl occasionally. Beat in eggs and vanilla until combined. Beat in as much of the flour as you can with the mixer. Using a wooden spoon, stir in any remaining flour. Cover and chill dough about 1 hour or until easy to handle.
2. Preheat oven to 375°F. In a small bowl combine the ¼ cup sugar and the cinnamon. Shape dough into 1¼-inch balls. Roll balls in sugar mixture to coat. Place 2 inches apart on ungreased cookie sheets.
3. Bake for 10 to 12 minutes or until bottoms are light brown. Transfer cookies to wire racks; cool.

To Store: Layer cookies between waxed paper in an airtight container; cover. Store at room temperature for up to 3 days or freeze for up to 3 months.

PER COOKIE: *94 cal., 4 g fat (3 g sat. fat), 19 mg chol., 69 mg sodium, 13 g carb., 0 g fiber, 1 g pro.*

Praline Snickerdoodles:
Prepare as directed, except stir 1 cup toffee pieces and ½ cup chopped pecans into the dough before chilling.

PER COOKIE: *126 cal., 6 g fat (3 g sat. fat), 22 mg chol., 89 mg sodium, 16 g carb., 0 g fiber, 1 g pro.*

Old-Fashioned Sugar Cookies:
Prepare as directed, except omit the cinnamon and roll balls in ¼ cup sugar.

PER COOKIE: *94 cal., 4 g fat (3 g sat. fat), 19 mg chol., 69 mg sodium, 13 g carb., 0 g fiber, 1 g pro.*

To Grease or Not to Grease

Grease a cookie sheet only when specified in the recipe. Snickerdoodles, for example, don't require a greased cookie sheet because they do not stick to an ungreased pan. In fact, if you put them on a greased baking sheet, they'll spread out too much during baking.

Mexican Chocolate Snickerdoodles

PREP: **25 minutes**
BAKE: **10 minutes per batch at 350°F**
MAKES: **30 cookies**

½ cup butter, softened
¾ cup granulated sugar
¾ cup packed brown sugar
1 teaspoon cream of tartar
½ teaspoon baking soda
½ teaspoon salt
¼ teaspoon cayenne pepper (optional)
2 eggs
2 teaspoons vanilla
½ cup unsweetened cocoa powder
2¼ cups all-purpose flour
¼ cup granulated sugar
2 teaspoons ground cinnamon

1. In a large mixing bowl beat butter with an electric mixer on medium to high speed for 30 seconds. Beat in the ¾ cup granulated sugar, the brown sugar, cream of tartar, baking soda, salt, and, if desired, cayenne pepper until combined, scraping sides of bowl occasionally. Beat in eggs and vanilla until combined. Beat in the cocoa powder and as much of the flour as you can with the mixer. Using a wooden spoon, stir in any remaining flour. If necessary, cover and chill dough about 1 hour or until easy to handle.

2. Preheat oven to 350°F. In a small bowl stir together the ¼ cup sugar and the cinnamon. Shape dough into 1¼-inch balls. Roll balls in sugar mixture to coat. Place balls 2 inches apart on ungreased cookie sheets.

3. Bake for 10 to 12 minutes or until edges are set and tops are cracked. Cool on cookie sheet for 1 minute. Transfer cookies to a wire rack; cool.

To Store: Layer cookies between sheets of waxed paper in an airtight container; cover. Store at room temperature for up to 3 days or freeze for up to 3 months.

Make-Ahead Directions: Dough may be shaped into balls, rolled in cinnamon-sugar mixture, and then frozen on parchment-lined cookie sheets. Transfer frozen balls to an airtight container; cover. Freeze for up to 3 months. When ready to bake, arrange frozen balls on cookie sheets; bake as directed for 13 to 15 minutes.

PER COOKIE: *118 cal., 4 g fat (2 g sat. fat), 21 mg chol., 94 mg sodium, 20 g carb., 1 g fiber, 2 g pro.*

Make It Mini

Prepare cookies as directed in Steps 1 and 2, except shape dough into ¾-inch balls and place 1½ inches apart on ungreased cookie sheets. Bake for 8 to 10 minutes or until edges are set and tops are cracked. Cool on cookie sheet for 1 minute. Transfer to a wire rack; cool.

Zesty Lemon Tea Sandwiches

PREP: **45 minutes**
BAKE: **10 minutes per batch
at 325°F**
MAKES: **60 sandwich cookies**

- ¾ cup butter, softened
- 1½ cups granulated sugar
- 1½ teaspoons baking soda
- 1½ teaspoons cream of tartar
- ¼ teaspoon salt
- ¾ cup vegetable oil
- 1 egg
- 1 teaspoon vanilla
- 1 teaspoon lemon extract
- 4 cups all-purpose flour
- 1½ teaspoons finely shredded lemon peel (see tip, page 102)
  Granulated sugar
- ⅔ cup purchased lemon curd
  Powdered sugar (optional)

1. Preheat oven to 325°F. In a large mixing bowl beat butter with an electric mixer on medium to high speed for 30 seconds. Add the 1½ cups granulated sugar, the baking soda, cream of tartar, and salt. Beat until well combined. Add oil, egg, vanilla, and lemon extract. Beat until combined. Beat in as much of the flour as you can with the mixer. Using a wooden spoon, stir in any remaining flour and the lemon peel.

2. Shape dough into ¾-inch balls. Place balls 2 inches apart on an ungreased cookie sheet. Dip the bottom of a glass in additional granulated sugar and slightly flatten each cookie.

3. Bake about 10 minutes or just until edges start to brown. Transfer to a wire rack; cool.

4. Spread about ½ teaspoon of the lemon curd on the bottoms of half of the cookies. Top with remaining cookies, flat sides down, pressing lightly together. If desired, sprinkle sandwich cookies with powdered sugar.

To Store: Layer unfilled cookies between waxed paper in an airtight container; cover. Store at room temperature for up to 3 days or freeze for up to 3 months. To serve, thaw cookies if frozen. Assemble as directed in Step 4.

PER SANDWICH COOKIE:
110 cal., 5 g fat (2 g sat. fat), 12 mg chol., 62 mg sodium, 15 g carb., 1 g fiber, 1 g pro.

Toffee Crackle Cookies

PREP: 25 minutes
BAKE: 20 minutes per batch at 300°F
MAKES: 48 cookies

- 1 cup butter, softened
- 1 cup packed brown sugar
- 1 teaspoon baking powder
- ¼ teaspoon salt
- 1 egg
- 1 teaspoon vanilla
- 2¼ cups all-purpose flour
- 1 cup chocolate-covered toffee pieces
- Granulated sugar

1. Preheat oven to 300°F. In a large mixing bowl beat butter with an electric mixer on medium to high speed for 30 seconds. Add brown sugar, baking powder, and salt. Beat until combined, scraping sides of bowl occasionally. Beat in egg and vanilla until combined. Beat in as much of the flour as you can with the mixer. Using a wooden spoon, stir in any remaining flour. Stir in toffee pieces.

2. Shape dough into 1¼-inch balls. Place 2 inches apart on an ungreased cookie sheet. Dip the bottom of a glass in granulated sugar and flatten each ball to about ¼-inch thickness.

3. Bake about 20 minutes or until edges are firm but not brown. Transfer cookies to a wire rack; cool completely.

To Store: Layer cookies between sheets of waxed paper in an airtight container; cover. Store at room temperature for up to 3 days or freeze for up to 3 months.

PER COOKIE: *109 cal., 5 g fat (3 g sat. fat), 16 mg chol., 76 mg sodium, 14 g carb., 0 g fiber, 1 g pro.*

Flattening Out

A glass is often called for to flatten cookies because it is the perfect size, has an even flat bottom, and is something everyone has on hand. To make sugar stick to the bottom of the glass the first time, press a bit of dough on the glass bottom, then remove it. Dip the glass bottom in sugar, then press into a dough ball to flatten. Dip glass in sugar after flattening each dough ball. The sugar prevents the glass from sticking to the dough while creating a pretty finish on the cookies.

Peanut Butter Blossoms

PREP: 25 minutes
BAKE: 10 minutes per batch
at 350°F
MAKES: 54 cookies

½ cup shortening
½ cup peanut butter
½ cup granulated sugar
½ cup packed brown sugar
1 teaspoon baking powder
⅛ teaspoon baking soda
1 egg
2 tablespoons milk
1 teaspoon vanilla
1¾ cups all-purpose flour
¼ cup granulated sugar
54 milk chocolate stars or milk chocolate kisses, unwrapped

1. Preheat oven to 350°F. In a large mixing bowl combine shortening and peanut butter. Beat with an electric mixer on medium to high speed for 30 seconds. Add the ½ cup granulated sugar, brown sugar, baking powder, and baking soda. Beat until combined, scraping sides of bowl occasionally. Beat in egg, milk, and vanilla until combined. Beat in as much of the flour as you can with the mixer. Using a wooden spoon, stir in any remaining flour.

2. Shape dough into 1-inch balls. Roll balls in the ¼ cup granulated sugar to coat. Place 2 inches apart on an ungreased cookie sheet.

3. Bake for 10 to 12 minutes or until edges are firm and bottoms are light brown. Immediately press a chocolate star into center of each cookie. Transfer cookies to a wire rack; cool.

To Store: Layer cookies between sheets of waxed paper in an airtight container; cover. Store at room temperature for up to 3 days or freeze for up to 3 months.

PER COOKIE: *96 cal., 5 g fat (2 g sat. fat), 5 mg chol., 27 mg sodium, 11 g carb., 0 g fiber, 2 g pro.*

Butter Pecan Blossoms: Prepare as directed, except substitute ½ cup softened butter for the ½ cup peanut butter. If desired, substitute 2 tablespoons melted butter pecan ice cream for the 2 tablespoons milk. Increase flour to 2¼ cups and add ½ teaspoon ground cinnamon. Omit the ¼ cup granulated sugar for rolling. In a food processor process ⅔ cup pecans until finely ground. Transfer pecans to a bowl; stir in 2 tablespoons packed brown sugar. In a small bowl lightly beat 2 egg whites. Roll balls in egg whites, then in pecan mixture to coat. Bake as directed. If desired, substitute chocolate kisses filled with caramel for chocolate stars.

PER COOKIE: *99 cal., 5 g fat (2 g sat. fat), 8 mg chol., 38 mg sodium, 12 g carb., 0 g fiber, 1 g pro.*

Spiced Jam Sandwiches

PREP: 40 minutes
CHILL: 1 hour
BAKE: 7 minutes per batch
at 375°F
MAKES: 20 sandwich cookies

⅓ cup butter, softened
⅓ cup shortening
¾ cup granulated sugar
1½ teaspoons baking powder
¼ teaspoon salt
¼ teaspoon ground cinnamon
⅛ teaspoon ground cloves
1 egg
1 tablespoon milk
½ teaspoon vanilla
½ teaspoon finely shredded
   lemon peel (see tip,
   page 102)
2 cups all-purpose flour
   Powdered sugar
⅓ to ½ cup raspberry,
   strawberry, or cherry
   preserves or jam

1. In a large mixing bowl beat butter and shortening with an electric mixer on medium to high speed for 30 seconds. Add granulated sugar, baking powder, salt, cinnamon, and cloves. Beat until combined, scraping sides of bowl occasionally. Beat in egg, milk, vanilla, and lemon peel until combined. Beat in as much of the flour as you can with the mixer. Using a wooden spoon, stir in any remaining flour. Divide dough in half. Cover and chill dough about 1 hour or until easy to handle.

2. Preheat oven to 375°F. On a lightly floured surface, roll half the dough at a time to ⅛- to ¼-inch thickness. Using 2½-inch cookie cutters, cut dough into desired shapes. Place cutouts 1 inch apart on an ungreased cookie sheet. Using ¾-inch cookie cutters, cut desired shapes from centers of half of the cookies. Reroll scraps as necessary.

3. Bake for 7 to 10 minutes or until edges are light brown. Transfer cookies to a wire rack; cool.

4. Sift powdered sugar onto the cookies with the cut-out centers. Spread a scant teaspoon of preserves over the bottoms of the cookies with no cut-out centers. Press the bottoms of the sugared cookies against the preserves. Serve within 2 hours.

To Store: Layer unfilled cookies between sheets of waxed paper in an airtight container; cover. Store at room temperature for up to 3 days or freeze for up to 3 months. Thaw cookies if frozen. Assemble as directed in Step 4.

PER SANDWICH COOKIE:
154 cal., 7 g fat (3 g sat. fat), 17 mg chol., 89 mg sodium, 22 g carb., 0 g fiber, 2 g pro.

Make It Mini

Prepare dough as directed in Step 1. Preheat oven to 375°F. On a lightly floured surface, roll half of the dough to ⅛- to ¼-inch thickness. (Place the remaining half of dough in an airtight container and freeze for up to 1 month.) Using 1¼-inch cookie cutters, cut dough into desired shapes. Place 1 inch apart on an ungreased cookie sheet. Use a straw or sharp knife to cut desired shapes from centers of half of the cookies. Reroll scraps as necessary. Bake for 6 to 8 minutes or until edges are light brown. Transfer cookies to a wire rack; cool. Assemble sandwich cookies as directed in Step 4, except reduce the amount of preserves to ¼ teaspoon per cookie. Makes about 48 sandwich cookies.

Pecan Sandies

PREP: 35 minutes
CHILL: 2 hours 30 minutes
BAKE: 12 minutes per
batch at 325°F
MAKES: 30 cookies

1 cup butter, softened
½ cup powdered sugar
1 tablespoon water
1 teaspoon vanilla
2 cups all-purpose flour
1½ cups finely chopped pecans,
    toasted
1 cup powdered sugar

1. In a large mixing bowl beat butter with an electric mixer on medium to high speed for 30 seconds. Add the ½ cup powdered sugar. Beat until combined, scraping sides of bowl occasionally. Beat in the water and the vanilla until combined. Beat in as much of the flour as you can with the mixer. Stir in any remaining flour and the pecans. Wrap dough and chill 30 to 60 minutes or until firm enough to shape.

2. Divide dough in half. Shape each portion into a 5½×2½-inch log. Wrap logs in plastic wrap and chill for 2 hours or until firm.

3. Preheat oven to 325°F. Cut logs into ¼-inch-thick slices. Place slices 1 inch apart on ungreased cookie sheets. Bake for 12 to 15 minutes or until bottoms are light brown. Transfer to wire racks and let cool.

4. Place the 1 cup powdered sugar on a large plate or pie plate. Add a few cooled cookies at a time, turning to coat with powdered sugar.

Chocolate-Covered Sandies: If desired, decrease the 1 cup powdered sugar to ¾ cup and stir in ¼ cup unsweetened cocoa powder. Turn cooled cookies in cocoa powder mixture.

PER COOKIE: *80 cal., 6 g total fat (2 g sat. fat), 9 mg chol., 24 mg sodium, 7 g carb., 0 g fiber, 1 g pro.*

Lime Zingers

PREP: 40 minutes
BAKE: 8 minutes per batch
at 350°F
MAKES: 42 cookies

1 cup butter, softened
½ cup granulated sugar
2 teaspoons finely shredded
  lime peel (see tip, page 102)
¼ cup lime juice
1 teaspoon vanilla
2¼ cups all-purpose flour
¾ cup finely chopped Brazil
  nuts or hazelnuts (filberts)
1 recipe Lime-Cream Cheese
  Frosting
  Finely shredded lime
  peel (optional) (see tip,
  page 102)

1. Preheat oven to 350°F. In a large mixing bowl beat butter with an electric mixer on medium to high speed for 30 seconds. Add the granulated sugar. Beat until combined, scraping sides of bowl occasionally. Beat in the 2 teaspoons lime peel, the lime juice, and vanilla until combined. Beat in as much of the flour as you can with the mixer. Using a wooden spoon, stir in any remaining flour and the nuts. Divide dough in half.

2. On a lightly floured surface, roll half of the dough at a time to ¼- inch thickness. To roll, start from the center and push dough out toward the edges until it is a uniform thickness. Using 1- to 2-inch cookie cutters, cut out dough. Place cutouts 1 inch apart on ungreased cookie sheets.

3. Bake for 8 to 10 minutes or until edges are light brown. Transfer to a wire rack; cool.

4. Drizzle cookies with Lime-Cream Cheese Frosting, If desired, immediately sprinkle cookies with finely shredded lime peel. Let stand until frosting sets.

Lime-Cream Cheese Frosting: In a medium mixing bowl combine half of an 8-ounce package cream cheese, softened; 1 cup powdered sugar; 1 tablespoon lime juice; and 1 teaspoon vanilla. Beat with an electric mixer on medium speed until smooth.

To Store: Layer frosted cookies between sheets of waxed paper in an airtight container; cover. Store at room temperature for up to 3 days. Or freeze unfrosted cookies for up to 3 months. Thaw cookies before frosting.

PER COOKIE: *62 cal., 4 g fat (2 g sat. fat), 9 mg chol., 31 mg sodium, 6 g carb., 0 g fiber, 1 g pro.*

Brown Sugar Icebox Cookies

PREP: 30 minutes
CHILL: 4 hours
BAKE: 10 minutes per batch
at 375°F
MAKES: 24 cookies

½ cup shortening
½ cup butter, softened
1¼ cups packed brown sugar
½ teaspoon baking soda
¼ teaspoon salt
1 egg
1 teaspoon vanilla
2½ cups all-purpose flour
¾ cup ground toasted
    hazelnuts (filberts) (see tip,
    page 17) or ground toasted
    pecans (see tip, page 343)
⅔ cup finely chopped
    toasted hazelnuts (filberts
    or ground toasted
    pecans(optional)
1 to 1½ cups semisweet
    or milk chocolate pieces
    (optional)
1 tablespoon shortening
    (optional)

1. In a large mixing bowl beat the ½ cup shortening and the butter with an electric mixer on medium to high speed for 30 seconds. Add the brown sugar, baking soda, and salt. Beat until combined, scraping sides of bowl occasionally. Beat in egg and vanilla until combined. Beat in as much of the flour as you can with the mixer. Using a wooden spoon, stir in any remaining flour and the ¾ cup ground nuts. Divide dough in half.

2. On waxed paper, shape each dough portion into a 10-inch-long log. Lift and smooth the waxed paper to shape the logs. If desired, roll logs in the ⅔ cup finely chopped nuts. Wrap each log in plastic wrap. Chill about 4 hours or until firm enough to slice.

3. Preheat oven to 375°F. Cut logs into ¼-inch slices. Place slices 1 inch apart on an ungreased cookie sheet.

4. Bake for 10 to 12 minutes or until edges are firm. Transfer cookies to a wire rack set over waxed paper and let cool.

5. If desired, in a small saucepan combine chocolate pieces and the 1 tablespoon shortening. Heat and stir over low heat until melted and smooth. Cool slightly. Transfer chocolate mixture to a small resealable plastic bag; seal bag. Snip off a tiny piece of one corner of the bag. Drizzle melted chocolate over cookies as desired. Let stand until set.

To Store: Allow chocolate to set. Layer cookies between sheets of waxed paper in an airtight container; cover. Store at room temperature for up to 3 days or freeze for up to 3 months.

PER COOKIE: *65 cal., 4 g fat (1 g sat. fat), 7 mg chol., 33 mg sodium, 7 g carb., 0 g fiber, 1 g pro.*

How to Make Icebox Cookies

These old-fashioned refrigerator cookies are made by forming dough into a log or rectangular block and chilling it thoroughly. You can also freeze the dough. When you crave something sweet, simply slice off and bake as many cookies as needed.

1. Place dough on waxed paper. Use the waxed paper to lift and shape dough into a log.

2. Spread nuts on waxed paper. Roll log in nuts to coat, gently pressing nuts into the dough roll.

3. Wrap rolls in plastic wrap and place in tall glasses. To help keep rolls round, place glasses on their sides in the refrigerator.

4. Using a sharp knife, cut the rolls into slices. Rotate rolls while cutting to prevent flattening one side.

5. Place warm chocolate mixture in a resealable bag; snip one corner and drizzle over cookies.

Lemon-Walnut Biscotti

PREP: **40 minutes**
CHILL: **15 minutes**
BAKE: **25 minutes at 325°F**
COOL: **45 minutes**
BAKE: **12 minutes per batch at 300°F**
MAKES: **50 cookies**

  3 cups all-purpose flour
  1 teaspoon baking powder
  ½ teaspoon salt
  ¼ teaspoon baking soda
  10 tablespoons butter, softened
  1⅓ cups granulated sugar
  4½ teaspoons finely shredded
     lemon peel (see tip,
     page 102)
  2 eggs
  3 tablespoons lemon juice
  2 cups chopped walnuts
  1 egg white, lightly beaten
  3 tablespoons turbinado sugar

1. Lightly grease two cookie sheets or line with parchment paper; set aside. In a medium bowl combine flour, baking powder, salt, and baking soda; set aside. In a large mixing bowl beat butter with an electric mixer on medium to high speed for 30 seconds. Add granulated sugar and lemon peel. Beat until combined, scraping sides of bowl occasionally. Beat in the 2 whole eggs, one at a time, until combined. Beat in lemon juice until combined. Beat in as much of the flour mixture as you can with the mixer. Using a wooden spoon, stir in any remaining flour mixture and walnuts.

2. Preheat oven to 325°F. Divide dough into three equal portions.

On a lightly floured surface, shape each portion into a 10-inch-long roll about 1½ inches wide. Place rolls about 3 inches apart on prepared cookie sheets; flatten slightly until about 2 inches wide. Brush dough with egg white. Sprinkle with turbinado sugar. Chill cookie sheets for 15 minutes.

3. Bake for 25 to 30 minutes or until firm and light brown. Cool on cookie sheets for 45 minutes. Reduce oven temperature to 300°F.

4. Using a serrated knife, cut each loaf diagonally into ½-inch slices. Put slices, cut sides down, on cookie sheets. Bake about 7 minutes or until light brown. Turn slices over; bake for 5 to 6 minutes more or until crisp and dry. Transfer to wire racks: let cool.

To Store: Layer cookies between sheets of waxed paper in an airtight container; cover. Store at room temperature for up to 3 days or freeze for up to 3 months.

PER SERVING: *100 cal., 6 g fat (2 g sat. fat), 14 mg chol., 61 mg sodium, 11 g carb., 1 g fiber, 2 g pro.*

Almond Biscotti: Preheat oven to 325°F. Lightly grease two cookie sheets; set aside. In a large bowl combine 2¾ cups all-purpose flour, 1½ cups sugar, 1½ teaspoons baking powder, and 1 teaspoon salt. Make a well in the center of the flour mixture. Place 2 whole eggs and 2 egg yolks in the well; stir into the flour mixture. Add 6 tablespoons melted butter and, if desired, 1½ teaspoons finely shredded orange peel or lemon peel; stir until dough starts to form a ball. Stir in 1 cup coarsely chopped sliced almonds. Divide dough into three equal portions. On a lightly floured surface, shape each portion into a 14-inch roll. Place rolls about 3 inches apart on prepared cookie sheets; flatten rolls slightly until about 1½ inches wide. Bake for 25 to 30 minutes or until firm and light brown. Cool on cookie sheets on wire racks for 15 minutes. Using a serrated knife, cut each roll diagonally into ½-inch slices. Place slices, cut sides down, on cookie sheets. Bake for 10 minutes. Turn slices over; bake for 10 to 15 minutes more or until crisp and dry. Transfer to wire racks; cool. Makes about 84 cookies.

PER COOKIE: *45 cal., 2 g fat (1 g sat. fat), 11 mg chol., 43 mg sodium, 7 g carb., 0 g fiber, 1 g pro.*

Hazelnut Biscotti: Prepare Almond Biscotti as directed, except use the option of orange peel and substitute 1 cup chopped hazelnuts (filberts) for the almonds.

PER COOKIE: *48 cal., 2 g fat (1 g sat. fat), 11 mg chol., 43 mg sodium, 7 g carb., 0 g fiber, 1 g pro.*

Pistachio Biscotti: Prepare Almond Biscotti as directed, except use the option of lemon peel and substitute 1 cup chopped pistachio nuts for the almonds.

PER COOKIE: *47 cal., 2 g fat (1 g sat. fat), 11 mg chol., 43 mg sodium, 7 g carb., 0 g fiber, 1 g pro.*

Triple-Chocolate Cookies

PREP: **40 minutes**
STAND: **20 minutes**
BAKE: **9 minutes per batch at 350°F**
MAKES: **60 cookies**

  7 ounces bittersweet chocolate, coarsely chopped
  5 ounces unsweetened chocolate, coarsely chopped
  ½ cup butter
  ⅓ cup all-purpose flour
  ¼ teaspoon baking powder
  ¼ teaspoon salt
  4 eggs
  1 cup granulated sugar
  ¾ cup packed brown sugar
  ¼ cup finely chopped pecans, toasted (see tip, page 343)
  1 cup semisweet chocolate pieces
  4 teaspoons shortening

1. In a medium saucepan heat and stir bittersweet chocolate, unsweetened chocolate, and butter over low heat until melted and smooth. Remove from heat; cool for 10 minutes.
2. Meanwhile, in a small bowl stir together flour, baking powder, and salt; set aside.
3. In a large mixing bowl beat eggs, granulated sugar, and brown sugar with an electric mixer on medium to high speed for 2 to 3 minutes or until lighter in color. Beat in chocolate mixture. Beat in flour mixture until combined. Stir in pecans. Cover surface of dough with plastic wrap. Let stand for 20 minutes (dough will thicken as it stands).

4. Preheat oven to 350°F. Line a cookie sheet with parchment paper or foil. Drop dough by rounded teaspoons 2 inches apart onto the prepared cookie sheet.
5. Bake about 9 minutes or just until tops are set. Cool on cookie sheet for 1 minute. Transfer cookies to a wire rack; cool.
6. In a small saucepan combine semisweet chocolate pieces and shortening. Heat and stir over low heat until smooth. Remove from heat. Place cooled cookies on a cookie sheet lined with parchment or waxed paper. Drizzle melted chocolate mixture over cookies. Place in freezer for 4 to 5 minutes or until chocolate is set.

To Store: Layer cookies between sheets of waxed paper in an airtight container; cover. Store at room temperature for up to 3 days or freeze for up to 3 months.

PER COOKIE: *92 cal., 6 g fat (3 g sat. fat), 18 mg chol., 19 mg sodium, 11 g carb., 1 g fiber, 1 g pro.*

Big Triple-Chocolate Cookies: Prepare as directed, except for each cookie, drop 3-tablespoon-size mounds of dough 3 inches apart onto the prepared cookie sheet. Bake for 13 minutes. Makes about 18 cookies.

PER COOKIE: *307 cal., 19 g fat (2 g sat. fat), 61 mg chol., 63 mg sodium, 37 g carb., 3 g fiber, 4 g pro.*

Parchment for Perfection

Parchment paper lines the cookie sheets for this recipe because the undersides of the cookies are soft and delicate. Oven-safe parchment makes for easy transfer, removal, and cleanup. Find parchment near the waxed paper in supermarkets.

1. Stir pecans into the beaten chocolate mixture. Toasting the nuts enhances the flavor.

2. Drop dough by rounded teaspoons 2 inches apart on parchment paper-lined cookie sheets.

3. Drizzle melted chocolate over cookies. Using parchment to catch the drips makes cleanup a breeze.

Coconut Macaroons

PREP: **30 minutes**
BAKE: **20 minutes per batch at 325°F**
MAKES: **60 cookies**

4	egg whites
1	teaspoon vanilla
¼	teaspoon cream of tartar
⅛	teaspoon salt
1⅓	cups sugar
1	14-ounce package flaked coconut (5⅓ cups)

1. Preheat oven to 325°F. Line cookie sheets with parchment paper; set aside.

2. In a very large mixing bowl beat egg whites, vanilla, cream of tartar, and salt with an electric mixer on high speed until soft peaks form (tips curl). Gradually add sugar, about 1 tablespoon at a time, beating until stiff peaks form (tips stand straight). Fold in coconut, half at a time. Drop coconut mixture from a teaspoon 1 inch apart into small mounds on prepared cookie sheets.*

3. Bake for 20 to 25 minutes or until bottoms are light brown. Transfer macaroons to wire racks; cool completely.

*****Test Kitchen Tip:** If you cannot bake all the coconut mixture at the same time, cover and chill while first batch of cookies bakes.

To Store: Layer cookies between sheets of waxed paper in an airtight container; cover. Store at room temperature for up to 3 days or freeze for up to 3 months.

PER COOKIE: *49 cal., 2 g fat (2 g sat. fat), 0 mg chol., 28 mg sodium, 7 g carb., 0 g fiber, 1 g pro.*

Add Some Fun

Dress up these little cookies by combining 1 teaspoon finely shredded lemon or orange peel (see tip, page 102) with the coconut before stirring into the egg mixture. Or, for chocolate lovers, drizzle the tops of the cooled baked cookies with melted semisweet or white chocolate.

Double-Almond Macarons

PREP: **35 minutes**
STAND: **30 minutes**
BAKE: **9 minutes per batch at 325°F**
MAKES: **30 sandwich cookies**

1½ cups finely ground almonds
1¼ cups powdered sugar
 3   egg whites
 ½   teaspoon vanilla
     Dash salt
 ¼   cup granulated sugar
 1   recipe Almond-Butter Frosting

1. Line three large cookie sheets with parchment paper; set aside. In a medium bowl stir together almonds and powdered sugar.
2. In a large mixing bowl combine egg whites, vanilla, and salt. Beat with an electric mixer on medium speed until frothy. Gradually add granulated sugar, 1 tablespoon at a time, beating on high speed just until soft peaks form (tips curl). Stir in almond mixture.
3. Spoon egg white mixture into a large decorating bag fitted with a large (about ½-inch opening) round tip.* Pipe 1½-inch circles 1 inch apart onto the prepared cookie sheets. Let stand for 30 minutes before baking.
4. Meanwhile, preheat oven to 325°F. Bake for 9 to 10 minutes or until set. Cool on cookie sheets on wire racks. Carefully peel cookies from parchment paper.

5. Spread Almond-Butter Frosting on bottoms of half of the cookies. Top with the remaining cookies, bottom sides down.

Almond-Butter Frosting: In a medium mixing bowl beat ¼ cup softened butter with an electric mixer on medium speed for 30 seconds. Gradually beat in 2 cups powdered sugar, ¼ teaspoon vanilla, ¼ teaspoon almond extract, and enough milk (3 to 5 teaspoons) to make frosting spreading consistency.

*Test Kitchen Tip: If you don't have a decorating bag, spoon the meringue mixture into a large resealable plastic bag and snip a ½-inch hole in a corner of the bag.

To Store: Layer filled cookies between sheets of waxed paper in an airtight container; cover. Store at room temperature for up to 3 days.

PER SANDWICH COOKIE: 96 cal., 3 g fat (1 g sat. fat), 3 mg chol., 19 mg sodium, 16 g carb., 1 g fiber, 1 g pro.

Making Perfect Macarons

Classic macarons are composed of a meringue mixture into which a ground almond-powdered sugar mixture has been folded. Macarons require a resting period of about 30 minutes before they are baked. This allows the meringue-nut mixture to dry out slightly, helping to develop the texture and the "feet" (the frilly, ruffled base of the cookies).

1. Beat egg whites, gradually adding sugar, until soft peaks form (tips curl).

2. Using a rubber spatula, gently fold in the almond mixture until incorporated.

3. Pipe mounds 1 inch apart on parchment paper-lined cookie sheets. Gently smooth out any pointy tops.

Fudgy Saucepan Brownies, recipe page 74

bars & brownies

THERE'S SOMETHING ABOUT SWEET "SQUARES" that keeps us coming back for more. Here you'll find the best recipes for the classics, such as rich blondies, fudgy brownies, and tangy lemon bars, as well as indulgently delicious new flavors (how about dulce de leche and marshmallow fluff on brownies?).

Fudgy Saucepan Brownies

With just ⅔ cup flour, this treasured recipe is as rich and gooey as a brownie can get without having to change the name to fudge. Learn how to make fudgy brownies step-by-step.

PREP: 20 minutes
COOL: 15 minutes
BAKE: 30 minutes at 350°F
MAKES: 16 brownies

- ½ cup butter
- 3 ounces unsweetened chocolate, coarsely chopped
- 1 cup sugar
- 2 eggs
- 1 teaspoon vanilla
- ⅔ cup all-purpose flour
- ¼ teaspoon baking soda
- ½ cup chopped nuts (optional)
- 1 recipe Chocolate-Cream Cheese Frosting (optional)

1. In a medium saucepan heat and stir butter and chocolate over low heat until melted and smooth; set aside to cool. Meanwhile preheat oven to 350°F. Line an 8×8×2-inch baking pan with foil, extending foil about 1 inch over edges of pan (see photos, page 21). Grease foil; set pan aside.

2. Stir the sugar into cooled chocolate mixture. Add eggs, one at a time, beating with a wooden spoon just until combined. Stir in vanilla. In a small bowl stir together the flour and baking soda. Add flour mixture to chocolate mixture, stirring just until combined. If desired, stir in nuts. Spread the batter evenly into the prepared pan.

3. Bake for 30 minutes. Cool in pan on a wire rack. If desired, spread Chocolate-Cream Cheese Frosting over cooled brownies. Using the edges of foil, lift uncut brownies out of pan. Place on cutting board; cut into squares.

Chocolate-Cream Cheese Frosting: In a small saucepan heat and stir 1 cup semisweet chocolate pieces over low heat until melted and smooth. In a medium bowl stir together two 3-ounce packages cream cheese, softened, and ½ cup powdered sugar. Stir in melted chocolate until smooth.

To Store: Place brownies in a single layer in an airtight container; cover. Store in the refrigerator for up to 3 days.

PER BROWNIE: *157 cal., 10 g fat (6 g sat. fat), 43 mg chol., 90 mg sodium, 18 g carb., 1 g fiber, 2 g pro.*

Secrets to Success

All brownies have similar ingredients. Varying the amounts of chocolate, butter, sugar, and flour gives brownies a more cakey or fudgy characteristic.

Fudgy brownies are dense, with a moist and intensely chocolate interior. Using less flour and more chocolate will provide this coveted texture, so don't be alarmed at the lower amount of flour in the recipe. The eggs, chocolate, and butter help with the structure, but just enough to make it fudgy and chewy. (The more flour you add, the cakier the brownie will be.) Notice that only one baking time (30 minutes) is given for Fudgy Brownies because there isn't a good doneness test (brownies are overbaked if a toothpick inserted in the center comes out clean). Instead, use an oven thermometer to ensure your oven is the right temperature and bake the recipe for exactly the recommended time. Your brownies will have a perfectly fudgy texture.

CHOPPING CHOCOLATE Using a chef's knife, coarsely chop chocolate bars on a cutting board.

STIR UNTIL SMOOTH Heat and stir the butter and chocolate over low heat until smooth and melted.

ADD THE SUGAR After the chocolate mixture has cooled, stir in the sugar until dissolved.

ADD THE EGGS Stir the eggs one by one into the chocolate mixture. Stir mixture vigorously after each addition until egg is well incorporated.

ADD THE DRY INGREDIENTS Combine the flour and baking soda in a bowl, then add the flour mixture all at once to the chocolate mixture.

STIR IT ALL TOGETHER Gently stir just until all of the flour mixture is moistened. If desired, stir in the nuts.

Make-It-Mine Blondies

Packed with rich butterscotch flavor, plain Blondies are amazingly delicious on their own. But when you stir in your choice of spices, nuts, toppers, and other scrumptious ingredients, you'll have a customized treat that's all your own.

PREP: **20 minutes**
BAKE: **25 minutes at 350°F**
MAKES: **36 bars**

2 cups packed brown sugar
⅔ cup butter
2 eggs
2 teaspoons vanilla
2 cups all-purpose flour
1 teaspoon baking powder
½ *teaspoon Spice* (*choose option*)
¼ teaspoon baking soda
1 *cup chopped Nuts, toasted* (*choose option*) (*see tip, page 343*)
½ *cup Stir-Ins* (*choose option*) *Topper* (*choose option*)

1. Preheat oven to 350°F. Line a 13×9×2-inch baking pan with foil, extending the foil about 1 inch over edges of pan (see photos, page 21). Grease foil; set pan aside. In a medium saucepan heat brown sugar and butter over medium heat until butter melts and mixture is smooth, stirring constantly. Cool slightly. Stir in eggs, one at a time; stir in vanilla. Stir in flour, baking powder, *Spice* (if desired), and baking soda. Stir in *Nuts* and, if desired, *Stir-Ins*. Spread batter into prepared pan.
2. Bake for 25 to 30 minutes or until a wooden toothpick inserted near center comes out clean. Cool in pan on a wire rack. If desired, add *Topper*. Cut into bars while warm.

SPICE (PICK ONE)
Cinnamon
Ginger
Allspice
Pumpkin pie spice
Apple pie spice
Five-spice powder
Ground cardamom

NUTS (PICK ONE)
Pecans
Almonds
Peanuts
Honey-roasted peanuts
Cashews
Walnuts
Macadamia nuts

STIR-INS (PICK ONE)
Chocolate: Semisweet or milk chocolate pieces
Dried fruit: Dried cranberries, chopped dried tart red cherries, chopped dried apricots, chopped dates, or chopped dried pineapple
Fresh fruit: Chopped fresh apple or pears

TOPPERS (PICK ONE)
Cocoa powder: Sift 1 tablespoon unsweetened cocoa powder over the top.
Chocolate drizzle: Melt 2 ounces semisweet chocolate and drizzle over the top.
White chocolate drizzle: Melt 2 ounces white baking chocolate (with cocoa butter) and drizzle over the top.
Frosting: Spread with 1 cup homemade (see recipes, pages 148 to 149) or canned chocolate or vanilla frosting.
Icing: Drizzle Powdered Sugar Icing over bars (page 105).

Dulce de Leche Fluff Brownies

PREP: **30 minutes**
BAKE: **20 minutes at 350°F**
MAKES: **32 brownies**

- 1 cup butter
- 6 ounces unsweetened chocolate, coarsely chopped
- 2 cups sugar
- 4 eggs
- 2 teaspoons vanilla
- 1⅓ cups all-purpose flour
- ½ teaspoon baking soda
- 1 cup miniature semisweet chocolate pieces
- 1 13.4-ounce can dulce de leche
- 1 7-ounce jar marshmallow creme
- ½ cup chopped pecans, toasted

1. In a medium saucepan heat and stir butter and unsweetened chocolate over low heat until melted and smooth. Set aside to cool.
2. Meanwhile, preheat oven to 350°F. Line a 13×9×2-inch baking pan with foil, extending the foil about 1 inch over edges of pan (see photos, page 21). Grease foil; set pan aside.
3. Stir sugar into the cooled chocolate mixture in saucepan. Add the eggs, one at a time, beating with a wooden spoon after each addition just until combined. Stir in the vanilla. In a small bowl stir together flour and baking soda. Add flour mixture to chocolate mixture; stir just until combined. Stir in semisweet chocolate pieces. Spread batter evenly into prepared baking pan.
4. Bake for 20 to 25 minutes or until edges are set and center is almost set.
5. Meanwhile, transfer dulce de leche to a small microwave-safe bowl. Microwave on 100 percent power (high) about 1 minute or until softened, stirring once. Transfer baking pan from oven to a wire rack. Immediately spoon the marshmallow creme in mounds on top of hot brownies. Drop spoonfuls of the dulce de leche between mounds of marshmallow creme. Let stand a few minutes to soften. Use a knife or thin metal spatula to swirl marshmallow creme and dulce de leche together. Sprinkle with chopped pecans. Cool in pan on the wire rack.
6. Using the edges of the foil, lift uncut brownies out of pan. Cut into bars, wiping knife as needed between cuts.

To Store: Place brownies in a single layer in an airtight container; cover. Store in the refrigerator for up to 3 days.

PER BROWNIE: *264 cal., 13 g fat (8 g sat. fat), 45 mg chol., 91 mg sodium, 35 g carb., 1 g fiber, 4 g pro.*

Top It Off

Make sure your brownies are still piping hot when you add spoonfuls of the marshmallow creme and dulce de leche. The heat will soften the toppings so they are easy to swirl together.

1. Spoon marshmallow creme in mounds on top of the hot brownies.

2. Drop spoonfuls of dulce de leche between mounds of marshmallow creme.

3. Use a thin spatula or table knife to gently swirl the marshmallow creme and dulce de leche together for a marbled effect.

Four-Layer Caramel Crunch Nougat Brownies

PREP: **50 minutes**
BAKE: **15 minutes at 350°F**
CHILL: **2 hours**
MAKES: **64 brownies**

½ cup butter
3 ounces unsweetened chocolate, coarsely chopped
2¼ cups sugar
2 eggs
1 teaspoon vanilla
⅔ cup all-purpose flour
¼ teaspoon baking soda
1½ 14-ounce packages vanilla caramels (about 68 caramels total), unwrapped
⅔ cup evaporated milk
1 tablespoon water
1½ cups crisp rice cereal
⅓ cup butter
1 7-ounce jar marshmallow creme
¼ cup creamy peanut butter
1 12-ounce package semisweet chocolate pieces
¼ cup butter
¼ cup whipping cream

1. In a medium saucepan heat and stir ½ cup butter and unsweetened chocolate over low heat until melted and smooth. Remove from heat. Set aside to cool.

2. Meanwhile, preheat oven to 350°F. Line a 13×9×2-inch baking pan with foil, extending the foil about 1 inch over edges of pan (see photos, page 21). Grease foil; set pan aside.

3. For the brownie layer, stir 1 cup of the sugar into chocolate mixture. Add eggs, one at a time, beating with a wooden spoon after each addition just until combined. Stir in vanilla. In a small bowl stir together flour and baking soda. Add flour mixture to chocolate mixture; stir just until combined. Pour batter into the prepared baking pan, spreading evenly. Bake for 15 to 17 minutes or until edges start to pull away from sides of pan. Cool in pan on a wire rack.

4. For caramel layer, in a large microwave-safe bowl combine caramels, 2 tablespoons of the evaporated milk, and the water. Microwave on 100 percent power (high) about 3 minutes or until caramels are melted, stirring every 30 seconds. Stir in rice cereal. Spread caramel mixture evenly over brownie layer in pan, spreading to edges. Place pan in freezer while preparing nougat layer.

5. For nougat layer, in a medium saucepan combine remaining 1¼ cups sugar, remaining evaporated milk, and the ⅓ cup butter. Bring to boiling over medium-high heat, stirring constantly. Reduce heat to medium. Boil at a moderate, steady rate, without stirring, for 10 minutes. Meanwhile, place marshmallow creme and peanut butter in a large heatproof bowl. Gradually whisk hot sugar mixture into marshmallow mixture; pour nougat over caramel layer, spreading to edges. Place pan in freezer while preparing chocolate layer.

6. For chocolate layer, in a small saucepan heat and stir semisweet chocolate pieces, the ¼ cup butter, and the whipping cream over low heat until melted and smooth. Pour chocolate mixture over nougat layer, spreading to edges. Cover loosely and chill for 2 hours. Using the edges of the foil, lift uncut brownies out of pan. Cut into bars.

To Store: Place brownies in a single layer in an airtight container; cover. Store in the refrigerator for up to 3 days.

PER BROWNIE: *157 cal., 8 g fat (5 g sat. fat), 16 mg chol., 69 mg sodium, 22 g carb., 1 g fiber, 2 g pro.*

Triple-Chocolate and Espresso Brownies

PREP: **30 minutes**
BAKE: **30 minutes at 350°F**
MAKES: **20 brownies**

½ cup butter
4 ounces bittersweet chocolate, coarsely chopped
3 ounces unsweetened chocolate, coarsely chopped
1 cup sugar
2 eggs
1 tablespoon espresso powder
1 teaspoon vanilla
⅔ cup all-purpose flour
¼ teaspoon baking soda
⅛ teaspoon salt
1 cup miniature semisweet chocolate pieces
½ recipe Cocoa-Cream Cheese Frosting (see page 149)
Chocolate-covered espresso beans, chopped (optional)

1. In a medium saucepan heat and stir butter, bittersweet chocolate, and unsweetened chocolate over low heat until melted and smooth. Remove saucepan from heat. Set aside to cool.
2. Meanwhile, preheat oven to 350°F. Line an 8×8×2-inch baking pan with foil, extending foil about 1 inch over the pan edges (see photos, page 21). Grease foil; set pan aside.
3. Stir sugar into the cooled chocolate mixture. Add the eggs, one at a time, beating with a wooden spoon just until combined. Stir in espresso powder and vanilla. In a small bowl stir together the flour, baking soda, and salt. Add flour mixture to chocolate mixture, stirring just until combined. Stir in chocolate pieces. Spread the batter evenly into the prepared pan.

4. Bake for 30 minutes. Cool in pan on a wire rack. Spread Cocoa-Cream Cheese Frosting over cooled brownies. Using the edges of the foil, lift the uncut brownies out of the pan. Cut into bars. If desired, sprinkle with chocolate-covered espresso beans.

To Store: Place bars in a single layer in an airtight container; cover. Store in refrigerator for up to 3 days or freeze for up to 3 months. To serve, thaw bars if frozen. Let refrigerated bars stand at room temperature for 15 minutes before serving.

PER BROWNIE: *250 cal., 15 g fat (9 g sat. fat), 36 mg chol., 93 mg sodium, 29 g carb., 0 g fiber, 3 g pro.*

Make It Mini

Prepare batter and bake as directed above. Cool, frost, and remove brownies from pan. Cut into 1-inch squares. If desired, top each with a whole chocolate-covered espresso bean. Makes 64 brownie bites.

Fudge Ripple Pecan Brownies

PREP: **30 minutes**
BAKE: **30 minutes at 350°F**
STAND: **2 hours**
MAKES: **18 brownies**

½ cup butter
3 ounces unsweetened chocolate, coarsely chopped
1 cup sugar
2 eggs
1 teaspoon vanilla
⅔ cup all-purpose flour
¼ teaspoon baking soda
1 cup chopped pecans, toasted (see tip, page 343)
¾ cup semisweet chocolate pieces
20 vanilla caramels, unwrapped
1 tablespoon milk

1. In a medium saucepan heat and stir butter and unsweetened chocolate over low heat until melted and smooth. Remove from heat. Set aside to cool.

2. Meanwhile, preheat oven to 350°F. Line an 8×8×2-inch baking pan with foil, extending the foil about 1 inch over the edges of pan (see photos, page 21). Grease foil; set pan aside.

3. Stir sugar into the cooled chocolate mixture in saucepan. Add the eggs, one at a time, beating with a wooden spoon after each addition just until combined. Stir in vanilla. In a small bowl stir together the flour and baking soda. Add flour mixture to chocolate mixture, stirring just until combined. Stir in ½ cup of the pecans and ½ cup of the chocolate pieces. Spread batter evenly into the prepared pan.

4. Bake for 30 minutes. Cool in pan on a wire rack.

5. Meanwhile, in a small saucepan heat and stir unwrapped caramels and milk over medium-low heat until melted and smooth. Spread mixture over cooled brownies. Sprinkle with the remaining ½ cup pecans.

6. In a small saucepan heat and stir the remaining ¼ cup chocolate pieces over low heat until melted and smooth. Drizzle chocolate over the top of brownies. Let stand for 2 hours before serving.

7. Using the edges of the foil, lift the uncut brownies out of the pan; cut into triangles (see photos, right).

To Store: Cover pan of brownies; place pan in the refrigerator for up to 3 days. Before serving, let brownies stand about 1 hour or until room temperature.

To Make Ahead: Prepare brownies as directed through Step 5. Cover pan of brownies; freeze for up to 3 months. Before serving, top thawed uncut brownies as directed in Steps 6 and 7.

PER BROWNIE: *258 cal., 16 g fat (8 g sat. fat), 37 mg chol., 91 mg sodium, 29 g carb., 2 g fiber, 4 g pro.*

Creative Cuts

With just a few easy cuts, bar cookies can be whatever shape you like. Try cutting bars into long, thin sticks or cut on the diagonal to create diamond shapes. Or try the technique below to turn standard bars into triangles. (To get clean, even edges, cut straight down with a long chef's knife instead of sawing back and forth.)

1. Cut square into thirds by making two even cuts vertically across brownies.

2. Repeat, making two even cuts horizontally across brownies, to create 9 squares.

3. Cut each square in half diagonally to create two triangles.

Best-Ever Bourbon Brownies

PREP: **35 minutes**
BAKE: **25 minutes at 350°F**
MAKES: **16 brownies**

½ cup sugar
⅓ cup butter
2 tablespoons water
1 cup semisweet chocolate
pieces
2 eggs
1 teaspoon vanilla
¾ cup all-purpose flour
¼ teaspoon baking soda
¼ teaspoon salt
½ cup chopped pecans,
toasted (see tip, page 343)
2 to 3 tablespoons bourbon
1 recipe Bourbon Frosting
2 ounces semisweet
chocolate, melted
Pecan halves, toasted
(optional)

1. Preheat oven to 350°F. Line an 8×8×2-inch baking pan with foil, extending the foil about 1 inch over the edges of pan (see photos, page 21). Grease foil; set pan aside. In a medium saucepan combine sugar, butter, and the water. Cook and stir over medium heat just until boiling. Remove from heat.
2. Stir in 1 cup chocolate pieces until melted. Add eggs and vanilla, beating with a wooden spoon just until combined. Stir in flour, baking soda, and salt. Stir in chopped pecans. Pour batter into the prepared pan, spreading evenly.
3. Bake about 25 minutes or until a wooden toothpick inserted near center comes out clean and edges start to pull away from sides of pan.
4. Place pan on a wire rack. Brush top of hot brownies with bourbon. Cool in pan on rack.

5. Spread brownies with Bourbon Frosting. Cut into bars. Top each with some of the melted chocolate and, if desired, a pecan half.

Bourbon Frosting: In a medium mixing bowl beat 3 tablespoons softened butter with an electric mixer on medium to high speed for 30 seconds. Gradually add 1½ cups powdered sugar, beating well. Beat in 1 tablespoon bourbon or milk and ¼ teaspoon vanilla. If necessary, beat in additional bourbon or milk, 1 teaspoon at a time, to make frosting spreading consistency.

To Store: Place brownies in a single layer in an airtight container; cover. Store at room temperature for up to 3 days.

PER BROWNIE: *244 cal., 13 g fat (7 g sat. fat), 39 mg chol., 119 mg sodium, 29 g carb., 2 g fiber, 2 g pro.*

Orange-Kissed Chocolate Brownies

PREP: **55 minutes**
CHILL: **1 hour**
BAKE: **25 minutes at 350°F**
MAKES: **32 brownies**

- 4 eggs
- 2 cups sugar
- 1¼ cups all-purpose flour
- 1 cup unsweetened Dutch-process cocoa powder
- 1 cup butter, melted
- ¼ cup butter, softened
- 1 teaspoon finely shredded orange peel (see tip, page 102)
- 3½ cups powdered sugar
- 2 to 3 tablespoons orange juice
- 4 ounces semisweet chocolate
- ½ cup butter
- 2 tablespoons light-color corn syrup

1. Preheat oven to 350°F. Line a 13×9×2-inch baking pan with foil, extending foil about 1 inch over the edges of the pan (see photos, page 21). Grease foil. Set aside. In a large mixing bowl combine eggs and sugar. Beat with an electric mixer on medium speed for 3 to 5 minutes or until mixture is pale yellow and thickened. In a small bowl whisk together flour and cocoa powder. Add flour mixture to egg mixture, beating just until smooth. Using a wooden spoon, stir in the 1 cup melted butter until combined. Spread batter evenly into prepared pan.

2. Bake for 25 to 30 minutes or until a wooden toothpick inserted near center comes out clean. Cool in pan on a wire rack.

3. Meanwhile, for frosting, in a large mixing bowl combine the ¼ cup softened butter and the orange peel. Beat on medium speed until smooth. Add 1 cup of the powdered sugar and 1 tablespoon of the orange juice, beating until combined. Beat in the remaining 2½ cups powdered sugar and enough of the remaining 1 to 2 tablespoons orange juice to make frosting spreading consistency. Spread frosting evenly over cooled brownies. Cover and chill for 30 minutes.

4. Meanwhile, for glaze, in a medium saucepan combine semisweet chocolate and the ½ cup butter. Heat and stir over low heat until melted and smooth. Remove from heat; stir in corn syrup. Cool for 15 minutes.

5. Slowly pour glaze over the frosted brownies. Tilt pan gently to spread glaze evenly over top. Chill about 30 minutes or until set. Using the edges of the foil, lift the uncut brownies out of the pan. Cut into bars.

PER BROWNIE: *244 cal., 12 g fat (7 g sat. fat), 53 mg chol., 82 mg sodium, 34 g carb., 1 g fiber, 2 g pro.*

Make It Mini

Preheat oven to 350°F. Grease sixty 1¾-inch muffin cups; set aside. Prepare batter as directed. Spoon a scant tablespoon batter into each prepared muffin cup. Bake for 12 minutes (may not appear set). Cool in pans on wire racks for 5 minutes. Carefully remove brownies from pans and place on wire racks; let cool. Double frosting ingredients and prepare as directed. Fill a pastry bag fitted with a star tip with frosting. Pipe frosting in swirls onto each mini brownie. Prepare chocolate glaze as directed. Dip frosting tops into the glaze. Chill about 15 minutes or until set. Makes about 5 dozen.

Raspberry and White Chocolate Brownies

PREP: **30 minutes**
BAKE: **30 minutes at 350°F**
MAKES: **20 brownies**

½ cup butter
2 ounces white baking chocolate with cocoa butter, cut up
2 eggs
⅔ cup sugar
1 teaspoon vanilla
1 cup all-purpose flour
½ teaspoon baking powder
  Dash salt
½ cup chopped almonds, toasted (see tip, page 343)
1 cup fresh raspberries
2 ounces white baking chocolate with cocoa butter, melted

1. Preheat oven to 350°F. Line an 8×8×2-inch baking pan with foil, extending the foil about 1 inch over edges of pan (see photos, page 21). Grease foil; set aside.
2. In a medium saucepan heat and stir butter and the 2 ounces chopped white chocolate over low heat until melted and smooth. Remove from heat. Add eggs, sugar, and vanilla. Beat lightly with a wooden spoon just until combined. In a small bowl stir together flour, baking powder, and salt. Add flour mixture to white chocolate mixture, stirring just until combined. Stir in almonds. Spread batter evenly into the prepared pan. Sprinkle with raspberries.
3. Bake for 30 to 35 minutes or until golden. Cool in pan on a wire rack. Using the edges of the foil, lift uncut brownies out of pan. Cut with a 2-inch round cutter or cut into bars. Drizzle brownies with the 2 ounces melted white chocolate.

To Store: Place brownies in a single layer in an airtight container; cover. Store in the refrigerator for up to 2 days.

PER BROWNIE: *146 cal., 8 g fat (4 g sat. fat), 34 mg chol., 62 mg sodium, 16 g carb., 1 g fiber, 2 g pro.*

Save the Scraps

If you cut your brownies into circles using a round cutter, pack the leftover scraps into a resealable freezer bag. For a tasty treat, thaw the pieces and sprinkle them on ice cream. Or make mini trifles with layers of pudding or whipped cream, the brownie scraps, and fresh raspberries.

Chewy Butterscotch Brownies

PREP: 30 minutes
BAKE: 25 minutes at 350°F
BAKE: 3 minutes at 450°F
MAKES: 20 brownies

⅓ cup butter
1⅓ cups flaked or shredded coconut
¾ cup chopped pecans
⅔ cup packed brown sugar
½ cup butter, softened
1 cup packed brown sugar
½ teaspoon baking soda
¼ teaspoon salt
3 eggs
½ teaspoon vanilla
1½ cups all-purpose flour
1½ cup tiny marshmallows
½ cup chopped pecans
Caramel-flavor ice cream topping (optional)

1. Preheat oven to 350°F. Grease a 13×9×2-inch baking pan (if desired, line pan with foil before greasing; [see photos, page 21]); set aside. In a small saucepan heat the ⅓ cup butter over medium heat until melted. Stir in coconut, the ¾ cup pecans, and the ⅔ cup brown sugar. Press mixture evenly onto bottom of prepared pan; set aside.

2. In a large mixing bowl beat the ½ cup softened butter with an electric mixer on medium to high speed for 30 seconds. Add the 1 cup brown sugar, the baking soda, and salt. Beat until combined, scraping sides of bowl occasionally. Add eggs and vanilla; beat until combined. Beat in flour until combined. Stir in ½ cup of the marshmallows and the ½ cup pecans. Carefully spread mixture over coconut layer.

3. Bake about 25 minutes or until top is evenly browned (center may jiggle slightly when gently shaken). Increase oven temperature to 450°F. Sprinkle with the remaining 1 cup marshmallows. Bake about 3 minutes or until marshmallows are lightly browned. Cool in pan on a wire rack. Cut into bars. If desired, drizzle with caramel topping.

To Store: Place bars in a single layer in an airtight container. Cover and store at room temperature for up to 3 days.

PER BROWNIE: *211 cal., 13 g fat (6 g sat. fat), 43 mg chol., 113 mg sodium, 23 g carb., 1 g fiber, 2 g pro.*

An Irresistible Topper

Marshmallows and caramel sauce make a wonderfully soft and gooey topper for brownies. Sprinkle the miniature marshmallows on the brownies about 5 minutes before they are done, then pop them back into the oven until the marshmallows become soft and golden. Cool the brownies completely before cutting them into squares. For neat squares, wipe the blade of the knife clean between each slice.

Cream Cheese Marbled Brownies

PREP: 30 minutes
BAKE: 40 minutes at 325°F
MAKES: 40 brownies

- 1 3-ounce package cream cheese, softened
- 2 tablespoons butter, softened
- ¼ cup sugar
- 1 egg
- 1 tablespoon all-purpose flour
- 6 ounces unsweetened chocolate, coarsely chopped
- ¾ cup butter
- 2¼ cups sugar
- 4 eggs
- ¼ cup milk
- 1 tablespoon vanilla
- 1 teaspoon almond extract
- 1¼ cups all-purpose flour
- ¾ teaspoon baking powder
- ½ teaspoon salt
- 1 cup chopped pecans (optional)

1. Preheat oven to 325°F. Line a 13×9×2-inch baking pan with foil, extending foil about 1 inch over edges of pan (see photos, page 21). Grease foil; set pan aside.
2. In a small mixing bowl beat cream cheese and the 2 tablespoons butter with an electric mixer on medium to high speed until creamy. Gradually add ¼ cup sugar, beating until light and fluffy. Beat in 1 egg and 1 tablespoon flour until combined. Set aside.
3. In a medium saucepan heat and stir chocolate and the ¾ cup butter over low heat until melted and smooth. Transfer to a large mixing bowl. Gradually add the 2¼ cups sugar, beating on low speed until combined. Add 4 eggs, one at a time, beating on low speed after each addition just until combined. Beat in milk, vanilla, and almond extract. In a small bowl stir together the 1¼ cups flour, the baking powder, and salt. Gradually beat in flour mixture just until combined.

4. Pour chocolate batter into the prepared baking pan, spreading evenly. Spoon cream cheese mixture in mounds on top of chocolate batter. Using a table knife or narrow metal spatula, gently swirl cream cheese mixture into chocolate batter to marble. If desired, sprinkle with pecans.
5. Bake for 40 to 45 minutes or until a wooden toothpick inserted in the center comes out with moist crumbs attached. Cool in pan on a wire rack. Using the edges of the foil, lift uncut brownies out of pan. Cut into bars.

To Store: Place brownies in a single layer in an airtight container; cover. Store in the refrigerator for up to 3 days.

PER BROWNIE: *139 cal., 8 g fat (5 g sat. fat), 36 mg chol., 91 mg sodium, 17 g carb., 1 g fiber, 2 g pro.*

Make It Marbled

Creating a beautiful two-tone swirl in brownies is simple. Use two large spoons to drop mounds of filling at even intervals over the top of the brownie batter. Then drag the tip of a table knife back and forth through the layers to create the effect of marbling (see photos, page 485).

Raspberry French Silk Pie Bars

PREP: **40 minutes**
BAKE: **10 minutes at 375°F**
CHILL: **2 to 4 hours**
MAKES: **32 bars**

1 recipe Chocolate Crumb Crust
1 cup whipping cream
3 ounces semisweet chocolate, chopped
3 ounces bittersweet chocolate, chopped
⅓ cup sugar
⅓ cup butter
2 egg yolks, lightly beaten
3 tablespoons crème de cacao or whipping cream
½ cup raspberry preserves or seedless raspberry jam
1 recipe Raspberry Ganache
Fresh raspberries (optional)

1. Preheat oven to 375°F. Line a 13×9×2-inch baking pan with foil, extending the foil about 1 inch over the edges of the pan (see photos, page 21). Press Chocolate Crumb Crust onto the bottom and slightly up the sides of prepared pan. Bake about 10 minutes or until crust is set. Cool completely in pan on a wire rack.

2. Meanwhile, for filling, in a heavy medium saucepan combine whipping cream, semisweet chocolate, bittersweet chocolate, sugar, and butter. Heat and stir over low heat about 10 minutes or until chocolate is melted and smooth. Remove from heat. Gradually stir half of the hot mixture into the beaten egg yolks. Add egg yolk mixture to chocolate mixture in saucepan. Cook and stir over medium-low heat about 5 minutes or until mixture is slightly thickened and bubbly. Remove from heat. (Mixture may appear slightly curdled.) Stir in the crème de cacao. Place the saucepan in a bowl of ice water for 20 minutes or until filling thickens and becomes hard to stir, stirring occasionally. Transfer the filling to a medium bowl.

3. Spread raspberry preserves over bottom of cooled Chocolate Crumb Crust. Beat filling with an electric mixer on medium to high speed for 2 to 3 minutes or until light and fluffy. Spread filling over preserves. Cover and chill for 1 to 2 hours or until firm.

4. Meanwhile prepare Raspberry Ganache. Remove bars from refrigerator. Spoon Raspberry Ganache over bars, gently spreading evenly. Cover and chill for 1 to 2 hours more or until firm. Using the edges of the foil, lift the uncut bars out of the pan. Cut into bars. If desired, garnish with fresh raspberries.

Chocolate Crumb Crust: In a medium bowl stir together 2 cups finely crushed chocolate wafer cookies, chocolate graham crackers, or other crisp chocolate cookies; ¼ cup all-purpose flour; and 2 tablespoons granulated sugar. Stir in ½ cup melted butter until combined.

Raspberry Ganache: In a large glass measuring cup combine 1 cup chopped semisweet chocolate or chocolate pieces, ⅓ cup whipping cream, and 1 tablespoon seedless raspberry jam. Microwave on 100 percent power (high) about 1 minute or until melted, stirring every 30 seconds. Let stand about 1 hour or until slightly thickened.

To Store: Place bars in a single layer in an airtight container; cover. Store in the refrigerator for up to 3 days.

PER BAR: *201 cal., 13 g fat (8 g sat. fat), 39 mg chol., 104 mg sodium, 21 g carb., 1 g fiber, 2 g pro.*

Maple-Nut Pie Bars

PREP: 25 minutes
BAKE: 40 minutes at 350°F
MAKES: 24 bars

Nonstick cooking spray
1¼ cups all-purpose flour
½ cup powdered sugar
¼ teaspoon salt
½ cup butter, cut up
2 eggs, lightly beaten
1 cup chopped mixed nuts
   or pecans
½ cup packed brown sugar
½ cup pure maple syrup
2 tablespoons butter, melted
½ teaspoon maple flavoring
   or 1 teaspoon vanilla
½ cup white baking pieces
   (optional)
1 teaspoon shortening
   (optional)
24 pecan halves (optional)

1. Preheat oven to 350°F. Line an 11×7×1½-inch baking pan with foil, extending foil over the edges of the pan (see photos, page 21). Lightly coat foil with cooking spray; set aside.
2. For crust, in a medium bowl stir together flour, powdered sugar, and salt. Using a pastry blender, cut in the ½ cup butter until mixture resembles coarse crumbs. Press mixture evenly onto the bottom of the prepared pan. Bake about 20 minutes or until light brown.
3. Meanwhile, for filling, in a medium bowl combine eggs, mixed nuts, brown sugar, maple syrup, the 2 tablespoons melted butter, and the maple flavoring. Spread filling evenly over hot crust.

4. Bake about 20 minutes or until filling is set. Cool in pan on a wire rack. Using the edges of the foil, lift the uncut bars out of the pan. Cut into bars.
5. For garnish, if desired, in a large glass measuring cup combine white baking pieces and shortening. Microwave on 100 percent power (high) about 1 minute or until mixture is melted, stirring after 30 seconds. Spoon or drizzle white chocolate mixture over each bar and top with a pecan half.

To Store: Place bars in a single layer in an airtight container; cover. Store in the refrigerator for up to 2 days.

PER BAR: *153 cal., 9 g fat (4 g sat. fat), 30 mg chol., 91 mg sodium, 18 g carb., 1 g fiber, 2 g pro.*

Salted Peanut Bars

PREP: **25 minutes**
BAKE: **12 minutes at 350°F**
MAKES: **48 bars**

½ cup butter, softened
⅔ cup packed brown sugar
2 egg yolks
2 teaspoons vanilla
1 cup all-purpose flour
½ cup crushed pretzels
½ teaspoon baking powder
¼ teaspoon baking soda
1 7-ounce jar marshmallow creme
½ cup creamy peanut butter
¼ cup powdered sugar
1 cup salted cocktail peanuts
1 14-ounce package vanilla caramels, unwrapped
3 tablespoons milk

1. Preheat oven to 350°F. Line a 13×9×2-inch baking pan with foil, extending foil about 1 inch over the edges of the pan (see photos, page 21); set pan aside. In a large mixing bowl beat butter with an electric mixer on medium to high speed for 30 seconds. Add brown sugar, egg yolks, and vanilla. Beat until combined, scraping sides of bowl occasionally. In a small bowl combine flour, pretzels, baking powder, and baking soda. Beat in as much of the flour mixture as you can with the mixer. Using a wooden spoon, stir in any remaining flour mixture. Press mixture into the bottom of the prepared pan.
2. Bake for 12 to 14 minutes or until light brown. Meanwhile, in a medium microwave-safe bowl combine marshmallow creme and peanut butter. Microwave on 100 percent power (high) about 1 minute or until softened and slightly melted, stopping to stir after 30 seconds. Stir in powdered sugar. Spread mixture over crust. Sprinkle with salted peanuts.
3. In a large heavy saucepan combine unwrapped caramels and milk. Heat and stir over medium-low heat until melted and smooth. Pour caramel mixture evenly over peanut layer. Cool in pan on wire rack. Using the foil, lift the uncut bars out of the pan. Cut into bars.

To Store: Place bars in a single layer in an airtight container; cover. Store in the refrigerator for up to 1 week.

PER BAR: *127 cal., 6 g fat (3 g sat. fat), 13 mg chol., 97 mg sodium, 17 g carb., 1 g fiber, 2 g pro.*

Make It Mini

Prepare and cool bars as directed. Lift bars from pan. Cut into 60 bars (approximately 1×1¾ inches). Makes 60 bars.

Lemon Bars Deluxe

PREP: 20 minutes
BAKE: 45 minutes at 350°F
MAKES: 24 bars

2 cups all-purpose flour
½ cup powdered sugar
1 cup butter, softened
4 eggs, lightly beaten
1½ cups granulated sugar
1 tablespoon finely shredded lemon peel (set aside)
⅓ cup lemon juice
¼ cup all-purpose flour
   Powdered sugar
   Crushed lemon drops
   (optional)

1. Preheat oven to 350°F. For crust, in a large mixing bowl stir together 2 cups flour and ½ cup powdered sugar; add butter. Beat with an electric mixer on low to medium speed just until mixture begins to cling together. Press evenly into the bottom of an ungreased 13×9×2-inch baking pan (if desired, line pan with foil before pressing in crust; see photos, page 21). Bake about 25 minutes or until light brown.
2. Meanwhile, in a medium bowl combine eggs, granulated sugar, and lemon juice. Whisk in ¼ cup flour and lemon peel. Pour evenly over crust.

3. Bake about 20 minutes more or until edges begin to brown and center is set. Cool in pan on a wire rack. Cut into bars. Sprinkle with additional powdered sugar and, if desired, crushed lemon drops.

To Store: Place bars in a single layer in an airtight container; cover. Store in the refrigerator for up to 2 days.

PER BAR: *184 cal., 9 g fat (5 g sat. fat), 55 mg chol., 66 mg sodium, 25 g carb., 0 g fiber, 3 g pro.*

How to Finely Shred Citrus Peel

While you can use a box grater for shredding citrus peel, it is much more efficient to use a Microplane (rasp) grater. Look for this utensil at cooking supply stores. To use the Microplane grater, gently but firmly rub the fruit over the grater, turning the fruit frequently so you only remove the peel and not the white pith beneath.

Cherry Kuchen Bars

PREP: **25 minutes**
BAKE: **42 minutes at 350°F**
COOL: **10 minutes**
MAKES: **32 bars**

½ cup butter, softened
½ cup shortening
1¾ cups sugar
1½ teaspoons baking powder
½ teaspoon salt
3 eggs
1 teaspoon vanilla
3 cups all-purpose flour
1 21-ounce can cherry pie
   filling
1 recipe Powdered Sugar Icing

1. Preheat oven to 350°F. In a large mixing bowl beat butter and shortening with an electric mixer on medium speed for 30 seconds. Add sugar, baking powder, and salt. Beat until well combined, scraping sides of bowl occasionally. Beat in eggs and vanilla. Beat in as much of the flour as you can with the mixer. Using a wooden spoon, stir in any remaining flour. Set aside 1½ cups of the dough for topping. Spread remaining dough into the bottom of an ungreased 15×10×1-inch baking pan.

2. Bake for 12 minutes. Spread pie filling over crust in pan. Spoon reserved dough into small mounds on top of pie filling.

3. Bake about 30 minutes more or until top is light brown. Cool in pan on a wire rack for 10 minutes. Drizzle with Powdered Sugar Icing. Cool in pan on a wire rack. Cut into bars to serve.

Powdered Sugar Icing: In a small bowl combine 1½ cups powdered sugar, ¼ teaspoon vanilla or almond extract, and enough milk (3 to 4 teaspoons) to make a drizzling consistency.

To Store: Place bars in a single layer in an airtight container; cover. Store in the refrigerator for up to 2 days.

PER BAR: *189 cal., 6 g fat (3 g sat. fat), 27 mg chol., 84 mg sodium, 31 g carb., 0 g fiber, 2 g pro.*

All About Kuchen

Kuchen means "cake" in German and refers to a variety of hearty, fruit-filled breakfast or dessert-style cakes—many of which are made with yeast as the leavening agent. This luscious treat calls for baking powder as the leavener, but the texture is a cross between cake and bars. Customize these squares by swapping in a can of your favorite fruit filling—apple, peach, or blueberry.

Five-Spice Pear Pie Bars

PREP: 40 minutes
BAKE: 45 minutes at 350°F
MAKES: 32 bars

- 3 cups all-purpose flour
- 2 tablespoons sugar
- ½ teaspoon salt
- ½ cup shortening
- ½ cup cold butter
- 2 egg yolks, lightly beaten
- ⅓ cup milk
- Water
- 6 cups peeled, cored, and thinly sliced ripe pears (about 2¼ pounds)
- 1 cup sugar
- 1 cup crushed cornflakes
- 1 teaspoon five-spice powder
- 1 egg white, lightly beaten
- 1 recipe Orange Icing

1. For pastry, in a large bowl combine flour, the 2 tablespoons sugar, and the salt. Using a pastry blender, cut in shortening and butter until pieces are pea size. In a small bowl whisk together egg yolks and milk. Gradually stir egg yolk mixture into flour mixture, tossing with a fork to moisten. Sprinkle 1 to 2 tablespoons water over the mixture, gently tossing until all of the mixture is moistened. Gather mixture into a ball, kneading gently until it holds together. Divide pastry into two portions, making one portion slightly larger than the other. Wrap and chill until needed.
2. For filling, in an extra-large bowl combine pears, the 1 cup sugar, the cornflakes, and five-spice powder. Set aside.

3. Preheat oven to 350°F. Use your hands to pat the larger portion of pastry onto the bottom of a 15×10×1-inch baking pan. Spoon filling evenly into pastry-lined pan.
4. Roll the remaining pastry portion between two sheets of waxed paper to a 15×10-inch rectangle. Carefully peel off top sheet of waxed paper. Invert rectangle, pastry side down, over the filling. Carefully peel off waxed paper. Using damp fingers, press edges of the two pastry rectangles together. Cut a few slits in the top pastry; brush lightly with egg white.
5. Bake for 45 to 50 minutes or until pastry is golden, fruit is tender, and filling is bubbly. Cool completely in pan on a wire rack.
6. Drizzle cooled bars with Orange Icing. Let stand until icing is set. Cut into bars.

Orange Icing: In a medium bowl stir together 1½ cups powdered sugar, 1 teaspoon finely shredded orange peel (see tip, page 102), and ¼ teaspoon vanilla. Stir in enough pear nectar (1 to 2 tablespoons) to make icing drizzling consistency.

To Store: Place bars in a single layer in an airtight container; cover. Store in the refrigerator for up to 2 days.

PER BAR: *179 cal., 6 g fat (3 g sat. fat), 21 mg chol., 81 mg sodium, 29 g carb., 1 g fiber, 2 g pro.*

How to Handle Tender Pastry

Rolling this tender pastry between two sheets of waxed paper helps it hold together better and prevents excessive cracking. The waxed paper also serves as support for the large rectangle of pastry when it is inverted over the filling.

1. Press half of the pastry onto the bottom of the baking pan in an even layer.

2. Roll the remaining pastry between sheets of waxed paper, rolling from the center out to the edges for uniform thickness.

3. Peel off the top sheet of waxed paper. Use your hands to support the pastry as you invert it over the pear filling.

4. Position the top pastry over the pear filling, moving it as necessary to fit over top.

5. Carefully peel off the second sheet of waxed paper. Press edges of top and bottom pastries together.

Pumpkin Bars

PREP: **25 minutes**
BAKE: **25 minutes at 350°F**
COOL: **2 hours**
MAKES: **36 bars**

2 cups all-purpose flour
1½ cups sugar
2 teaspoons baking powder
2 teaspoons ground cinnamon
1 teaspoon baking soda
½ teaspoon salt
¼ teaspoon ground cloves
4 eggs, lightly beaten
1 15-ounce can pumpkin
1 cup vegetable oil
1 recipe Browned Butter Frosting

1. Preheat oven to 350°F. In a large bowl stir together flour, sugar, baking powder, cinnamon, baking soda, salt, and cloves. Add eggs, pumpkin, and oil; stir until combined. Spread batter evenly into an ungreased 15×10×1-inch baking pan.

2. Bake for 25 to 30 minutes or until a wooden toothpick inserted near the center comes out clean. Cool in pan on a wire rack for 2 hours.

3. Spread with Browned Butter Frosting. Cut into bars.

Browned Butter Frosting: In a small saucepan heat ⅓ cup butter over low heat until melted. Continue heating until butter turns a light golden brown.

Remove from heat. In a large mixing bowl combine 3 cups powdered sugar, 2 tablespoons milk, and 1 teaspoon vanilla. Add browned butter. Beat with an electric mixer on medium speed until spreading consistency, adding additional milk if necessary. Makes about 1½ cups.

To Store: To store, place bars in a single layer in an airtight container; cover. Store in the refrigerator for up to 3 days.

PER BAR: 178 cal., 8 g fat (2 g sat. fat), 28 mg chol., 109 mg sodium, 25 g carb., 1 g fiber, 2 g pro.

Nutty-Caramel Pumpkin Bars: Prepare as directed in Step 1. In a small bowl stir together 1½ cups chopped pecans, toasted (see tip, page 343), and ⅓ cup caramel-flavor ice cream topping. Spoon nut mixture over batter in pan. Continue as directed in Step 2. Use only half of the Browned Butter Frosting (chill or freeze the remaining frosting and use it to frost cupcakes). Stir enough milk into the frosting to make it a drizzling consistency. Drizzle over cooled bars.

PER BAR: 190 cal., 11 g fat (1 g sat. fat), 26 mg chol., 113 mg sodium, 23 g carb., 1 g fiber, 2 g pro.

Applesauce-Cranberry Bars: Prepare as directed, except substitute one 15-ounce jar (1¾ cups) applesauce for the pumpkin, replace ½ cup of the sugar with honey, and stir 1 cup dried cranberries and/or dried tart cherries into the batter. Lightly sprinkle top of frosted bars with ground cinnamon.

PER BAR: 193 cal., 8 g fat (2 g sat. fat), 28 mg chol., 108 mg sodium, 29 g carb., 1 g fiber, 2 g pro.

Cream Cheese Swirl Pumpkin Bars: Prepare as directed in Step 1. In a medium mixing bowl combine half of an 8-ounce package cream cheese, softened, and ¼ cup sugar. Beat with an electric mixer on medium speed until combined. Beat in 1 egg and 1 tablespoon milk. Drizzle the cream cheese mixture over pumpkin batter in pan. Use a knife to gently marble the mixtures together. Sprinkle ½ cup miniature semisweet chocolate pieces over batter before baking. Continue as directed in Step 2. Omit Browned Butter Frosting.

PER BAR: 160 cal., 9 g fat (2 g sat. fat), 33 mg cholesterol, 108 mg sodium, 19 g carb., 1 g fiber, 2 g pro.

Oatmeal Jam Bars

PREP: 15 minutes
BAKE: 35 minutes at 350°F
MAKES: 16 bars

1⅓ cups all-purpose flour
¼ teaspoon baking soda
¼ teaspoon salt
¾ cup quick-cooking rolled oats
⅓ cup packed brown sugar
1 teaspoon finely shredded lemon peel (see tip, page 102)
2 3-ounce packages cream cheese, softened
¼ cup butter, softened
¾ cup seedless blackberry or red or black raspberry jam
1 teaspoon lemon juice

1. Preheat oven to 350°F. Grease a 9×9×2-inch baking pan (if desired, line pan with foil before greasing; see photos, page 21); set aside. In a medium bowl stir together flour, baking soda, and salt. Stir in oats, brown sugar, and lemon peel; set flour mixture aside.

2. In a large mixing bowl combine cream cheese and butter. Beat with an electric mixer on medium to high speed for 30 seconds. Add flour mixture; beat on low speed until mixture is crumbly. Remove 1 cup of the crumb mixture for topping; set aside.

3. Press the remaining crumb mixture into the bottom of the prepared baking pan. Bake for 20 minutes.

4. Meanwhile, in a small bowl combine jam and lemon juice. Carefully spread jam mixture over hot crust. Sprinkle with the reserved 1 cup crumb mixture. Bake about 15 minutes more or until top is golden. Cool in pan on a wire rack. Cut into bars.

To Store: Layer bars between sheets of waxed paper in an airtight container; cover. Store in the refrigerator for up to 3 days or freeze up to 1 month.

PER BAR: *173 cal., 7 g fat (5 g sat. fat), 20 mg chol., 121 mg sodium, 25 g carb., 0 g fiber, 2 g pro.*

Sweet Success

Jam bars are among the easiest bar cookies to prepare because the filling comes straight from a jar. If you're not a fan of berry jam, switch it up with your favorite spread, such as apricot preserves or orange marmalade.

1. Spoon the crumb mixture over the bottom of the pan, then use your hands to press into an even layer.

2. After prebaking the crust, top with the jam mixture.

3. Use the back of the spoon to spread the jam mixture in an even layer over the crust.

4. Sprinkle the reserved crumb mixture evenly over the jam layer.

White Cake, recipe page 114

cakes & cupcakes

A CAKE SAYS "CELEBRATION!" in a way no other dessert can. Whether it's a one-, two-, or three-layer confection, these cakes make any occasion—even weeknight desserts—special. Choose from scrumptious recipes for cake classics such as white, yellow, and chocolate, as well as enticing new recipes.

White Cake

White cake calls for egg whites instead of whole eggs to keep the color pure white. You can use shortening to further clarify the color, but butter gives superior flavor without altering the color of the cake significantly.

PREP: **55 minutes**
BAKE: **20 minutes at 350°F**
COOL: **1 hour**
MAKES: **12 servings**

  4 egg whites
  ½ cup butter or shortening
  2 cups all-purpose flour
  1 teaspoon baking powder
  ½ teaspoon baking soda
  ½ teaspoon salt
  1¾ cups sugar
  1 teaspoon vanilla
  1⅓ cups buttermilk or sour milk
      (see tip, page 16)
  1 recipe Whipped Sour Cream
      Frosting (see page 149) or
      other desired frosting

1. Allow egg whites and butter (if using) to stand at room temperature for 30 minutes. Grease and lightly flour two 9×1½-inch or 8×1½-inch round cake pans or grease one 13×9×2-inch baking pan; set pan(s) aside. In a medium bowl stir together flour, baking powder, baking soda, and salt; set aside.
2. Preheat oven to 350°F. In a large mixing bowl beat butter with an electric mixer on medium to high speed for 30 seconds. Add sugar and vanilla; beat until well combined. Add egg whites, one at a time, beating well after each addition. Alternately add flour mixture and buttermilk to butter mixture, beating on low speed after each addition just until combined. Spread batter into prepared pan(s).
3. Bake for 20 to 25 minutes for 9-inch pans, 30 to 35 minutes for 8-inch pans or 13×9×2-inch pan, or until a wooden toothpick inserted near center(s) comes out clean. Cool cake layers in pans

on wire racks for 10 minutes. Remove cake layers from pans. Cool thoroughly on wire racks. Or place the 13×9×2-inch cake in pan on a wire rack; cool thoroughly. Frost with Whipped Sour Cream Frosting or other desired frosting.

To Store: Place frosted layer cake in an airtight container; cover. For 13×9-inch cake, cover pan with foil. Store for up to 3 days. Cakes frosted with Butter Frosting or Creamy White Frosting may be stored at room temperature. Cakes with frostings containing cream cheese, sour cream, or egg whites should be refrigerated.

PER SLICE WITHOUT FROSTING: *275 cal., 8 g fat (5 g sat. fat), 21 mg chol., 271 mg sodium, 47 g carb., 1 g fiber, 4 g pro.*

Coconut White Cake: Prepare as directed, except stir ¾ cup toasted flaked coconut into batter.

PER SLICE WITHOUT FROSTING: *310 cal., 11 g fat (7 g sat. fat), 21 mg chol., 291 mg sodium, 50 g carb., 1 g fiber, 5 g pro.*

Secrets to Success

Traditional butter-style cakes call for creaming, or beating, the butter—first alone and then with the sugar—to add the all-important air bubbles to the batter. Later the egg or egg whites are beaten in, which act as an emulsifier (binding agent) and allow more air bubbles to be incorporated. After this, the flour mixture and liquid are added alternately to the butter mixture.

There are a few things to keep in mind during this entire mixing process to ensure a perfect cake. First, to get good volume and plenty of air bubbles, start with room-temperature butter and eggs. As noted before, it is very important to beat the butter and sugar adequately to work in enough air bubbles (baking powder and baking soda will work by expanding the air bubbles during baking). Also, stir the leavening agents into the flour well to avoid the formation of large holes from clumps of leavener. Finally, when alternating liquid and flour mixture, begin and end with the flour mixture. Once the first addition of liquid is added, the gluten in the flour will begin to develop, so beat only until incorporated. Overbeating will further develop the gluten and cause undesirable toughness.

CREAMING STEP Beat room-temperature butter for 30 seconds to incorporate air bubbles. Beat in the sugar until the mixture is light and fluffy.

ADD EGG WHITES Add the egg whites, one at a time, beating well after each is added. The egg acts as an emulsifier and helps the batter hold even more air.

ADD SOME OF THE FLOUR Begin by beating in a portion of the flour mixture.

ADD SOME OF THE LIQUID Beat in a portion of the liquid just until incorporated. Continue adding the flour and liquid in small batches alternately.

POUR INTO PAN After beating in each addition of flour and liquid just until mixed in (but not overbeating), pour the batter into prepared pans.

Make-It-Mine Snack Cake

Dress up an easy one-bowl cake just the way you like it with your choice of flour, sweetener, liquid, and flavoring, plus fun toppers!

PREP: 15 minutes
BAKE: 35 minutes at 350°F
MAKES: 12 servings

Flour (choose option)
Sweetener (choose option)
1 teaspoon baking soda
½ teaspoon baking powder
½ teaspoon salt
Liquid (choose option)
⅔ cup vegetable oil
Flavoring (choose option)
2 eggs
Sprinkle (choose option)
Topper (choose option)

1. Preheat oven to 350°F. Grease a 13×9×2-inch baking pan; set aside. In a very large mixing bowl stir together *Flour*, dry *Sweetener* (such as sugar or brown sugar), baking soda, baking powder, and salt. Add the *Liquid*, vegetable oil, liquid *Sweetener* (such as honey or molasses), and *Flavoring*. Beat with an electric mixer on low to medium speed until combined. Beat in eggs. Scrape sides of bowl; continue beating on medium speed for 2 minutes more. Spread batter into prepared pan.
2. Bake for 20 minutes. Top evenly with *Sprinkle*. Bake about 15 minutes more or until top springs back when lightly touched and a wooden toothpick inserted near center comes out clean. Cool thoroughly in pan on a wire rack. Add *Topper*.

FLOUR (PICK ONE)

2 cups all-purpose flour and 1 cup unsweetened cocoa powder
3 cups all-purpose flour
3 cups cake flour
2 cups all-purpose flour and 1 cup whole wheat flour

SWEETENER (PICK ONE)

2 cups granulated sugar
1 cup granulated sugar and 1 cup packed brown sugar
1½ cups granulated sugar and ½ cup honey
1½ cups granulated sugar and ½ cup molasses

LIQUID (PICK ONE)

1 cup buttermilk and ½ cup water
1 6-ounce carton plain yogurt and ½ cup water
1½ cups milk
1 cup milk and ½ cup orange juice

FLAVORING (PICK ONE)

1 teaspoon vanilla
½ teaspoon almond extract
2 teaspoons instant espresso powder or coffee crystals
½ teaspoon peppermint extract
1 teaspoon finely shredded citrus peel (orange, tangerine, lemon, or lime) (see tip, page 102)

SPRINKLE (PICK ONE)

½ cup semisweet chocolate pieces, miniature semisweet chocolate pieces, milk chocolate pieces, or dark chocolate pieces
½ cup peanut butter pieces
½ cup chopped toasted nuts (pecans, walnuts, hazelnuts, almonds, or macadamia nuts)
½ cup flaked coconut
½ cup dried fruit (tart red cherries; raisins; apricots, snipped; cranberries)

TOPPER (PICK ONE)

Powdered Sugar: Sift 2 teaspoons powdered sugar over cake.
Cocoa Powder-Powdered Sugar: Combine 1 teaspoon cocoa powder with 1 teaspoon powdered sugar; sift over cake.
Chocolate Drizzle: Drizzle 2 ounces melted semisweet, milk, dark, or white chocolate over cake.
Icing: Combine ½ cup powdered sugar with 1 to 2 teaspoons milk; drizzle over cake.
Dulce de Leche: Drizzle about ½ cup warmed canned dulce de leche over cake.

Yellow Cake

PREP: 50 minutes
BAKE: 20 minutes at 375°F
COOL: 1 hour
MAKES: 12 servings

¾	cup butter
3	eggs
2½	cups all-purpose flour
2½	teaspoons baking powder
½	teaspoon salt
1¾	cups sugar
1½	teaspoons vanilla
1¼	cups milk
1	recipe Chocolate Butter Frosting (page 148) or other desired frosting

1. Allow butter and eggs to stand at room temperature for 30 minutes. Meanwhile, grease and lightly flour two 9×1½-inch or 8×1½-inch round cake pans or grease one 13×9×2-inch baking pan; set pan(s) aside. In a medium bowl stir together flour, baking powder, and salt; set aside.

2. Preheat oven to 375°F. In a large mixing bowl beat butter with an electric mixer on medium to high speed for 30 seconds. Gradually add sugar, about ¼ cup at a time, beating on medium speed until well combined. Scrape sides of bowl; beat for 2 minutes more. Add eggs, one at a time, beating well after each addition. Beat in vanilla. Alternately add flour mixture and milk to butter mixture, beating on low speed after each addition just until combined. Spread batter into the prepared pan(s).

3. Bake for 20 to 25 minutes for 9-inch pans, 30 to 35 minutes for 8-inch pans, 25 to 30 minutes for 13×9×2-inch pan, or until a wooden toothpick inserted near center(s) comes out clean. Cool cake layers in pans on wire racks for 10 minutes. Remove cake layers from pans; cool thoroughly on wire racks. Or place the 13×9×2-inch cake in pan on a wire rack; cool thoroughly. Frost with Chocolate Butter Frosting.

Citrus Yellow Cake: Prepare as directed, except stir 2 teaspoons finely shredded orange peel or lemon peel (see tip, page 102) into the batter.

To Store: Place frosted layer cake in an airtight container; cover. For 13×9-inch cake, cover pan with foil. Store for up to 3 days. Cakes frosted with Butter Frosting or Creamy White Frosting may be stored at room temperature. Cakes with frostings containing cream cheese, sour cream, or egg whites should be refrigerated.

PER SLICE PLAIN OR CITRUS VARIATION WITHOUT FROSTING: *342 cal., 14 g fat (8 g sat. fat), 885 mg chol., 257 mg sodium, 51 g carb., 1 g fiber, 5 g pro.*

How to Frost a Cake

There's no right or wrong way to frost a cake, but there are some techniques to make the task easier. Try these tips for frosting a two-layer cake.

1. Place strips of parchment or waxed paper under edges of bottom cake layer to keep the serving plate clean. Frost the top of the cake layer.

2. Top with the second cake layer. Use a thin metal spatula to spread frosting on cake sides first, then the cake top.

3. Gently slide the parchment paper out from under the edges of the cake.

4. The cake will have a clean, frosting-free serving plate.

Chocolate Cake

PREP: 1 hour
BAKE: 35 minutes at 350°F
COOL: 1 hour
MAKES: 12 servings

¾ cup butter
3 eggs
2 cups all-purpose flour
¾ cup unsweetened cocoa powder
1 teaspoon baking soda
¾ teaspoon baking powder
½ teaspoon salt
2 cups sugar
2 teaspoons vanilla
1½ cups milk
1 recipe Cocoa-Cream Cheese Frosting (page 149) or other desired frosting

1. Allow butter and eggs to stand at room temperature for 30 minutes. Meanwhile, lightly grease bottoms of two 8×8×2-inch square or 9×1½-inch round cake pans. Line bottoms of pans with waxed paper; grease and lightly flour pans (see photos, page 21). Or grease one 13×9×2-inch baking pan. Set pan(s) aside. In a medium bowl stir together flour, cocoa powder, baking soda, baking powder, and salt; set aside.
2. Preheat oven to 350°F. In a large mixing bowl beat butter with an electric mixer on medium to high speed for 30 seconds. Gradually add sugar, about ¼ cup at a time, beating on medium speed until well combined. Scrape sides of bowl; beat for 2 minutes more. Add eggs, one at a time, beating after each addition. Beat in vanilla. Alternately add flour mixture and milk to butter mixture, beating on low speed after each addition just until combined. Beat on medium to high speed for 20 seconds more. Spread batter into prepared pan(s).
3. Bake for 35 to 40 minutes for 8-inch pans and 13×9×2-inch pan, 30 to 35 minutes for 9-inch pans, or until a wooden toothpick inserted near center(s) comes out clean. Cool cake layers in pans on wire racks for 10 minutes. Remove cake layers from pans. Peel off waxed paper. Cool thoroughly on wire racks. Or place 13×9×2-inch cake in pan on a wire rack; cool thoroughly. Frost with Cocoa-Cream Cheese Frosting or other desired frosting.

To Store: Place cake in a covered container. Store in the refrigerator for up to 3 days.

PER SLICE WITHOUT FROSTING: *354 cal., 14 g fat (9 g sat. fat), 86 mg chol., 330 mg sodium, 54 g carb., 2 g fiber, 6 g pro.*

Make It Mini

Preheat oven to 350°F. Allow butter and eggs to stand at room temperature for 30 minutes. Meanwhile, line twenty-four to thirty 2½-inch muffin cups with paper bake cups. Prepare batter as directed. Spoon batter into prepared muffin cups, filling each one-half to two-thirds full. Use the back of spoon to smooth out batter in cups. Bake for 18 to 22 minutes or until a wooden toothpick inserted in centers comes out clean. Cool cupcakes in muffin cups on wire racks for 5 minutes. Remove cupcakes from muffin cups. Cool completely on wire racks. Frost with Cocoa-Cream Cheese Frosting (page 149). Makes 24 to 30 (2½-inch) cupcakes.

Red Velvet Cake

PREP: **50 minutes**
BAKE: **20 minutes at 350°F**
COOL: **1 hour**
MAKES: **16 servings**

¾ cup butter
3 eggs
3 cups all-purpose flour
1 tablespoon unsweetened cocoa powder
¾ teaspoon salt
2¼ cups sugar
1 1-ounce bottle red food coloring (2 tablespoons)
1½ teaspoons vanilla
1½ cups buttermilk or sour milk (see tip, page 16)
1½ teaspoons baking soda
1½ teaspoons vinegar
1 recipe Buttercream Frosting

1. Allow butter and eggs to stand at room temperature for 30 minutes. Meanwhile, grease and lightly flour three 9×2-inch round, 8×2-inch round, or 8×8×2-inch square cake pans. Or grease one 13×9×2-inch baking pan. Set pan(s) aside. In a medium bowl stir together flour, cocoa powder, and salt; set aside.

2. Preheat oven to 350°F. In a very large mixing bowl beat butter with an electric mixer on medium to high speed for 30 seconds. Gradually add sugar, about ¼ cup at time, beating on medium speed until well combined. Scrape sides of bowl; beat on medium speed for 2 minutes more. Add eggs, one at a time, beating well after each addition. Beat in red food coloring and vanilla. Alternately add flour mixture and buttermilk, beating on low speed after each addition just until combined. In a small bowl combine baking soda and vinegar; fold into batter. Spread batter into the prepared pan(s).

3. Bake for 25 to 30 minutes for 8-inch pans, 20 to 25 minutes for 9-inch pans, 30 to 35 minutes for 13×9×2-inch pan, or until a wooden toothpick inserted near the center(s) comes out clean. Cool cake layers in pans on wire racks for 10 minutes. Remove cake layers from pans. Cool thoroughly on wire racks. Or place 13×9×2-inch cake in pan on wire rack; cool thoroughly.

4. Prepare Buttercream Frosting (cut recipe in half if making 13×9×2-inch cake). Place one cake layer, bottom side up, on serving platter. Spread with one-third of the Buttercream Frosting. Top with second cake layer, bottom side up. Spread top with half of the remaining frosting. Top with third layer, rounded (top) side up. Spread top with remaining frosting. If using 13×9×2-inch pan, spread frosting over cake in pan.

Buttercream Frosting: In a medium saucepan whisk together 1½ cups sugar, 1½ cups milk, ⅓ cup all-purpose flour, and a dash salt. Cook and stir over medium heat until thickened and bubbly. Reduce heat; cook and stir for 1 minute more. Remove from heat; stir in 2 teaspoons vanilla. Cover and cool completely at room temperature.* Transfer to a large mixing bowl. Using an electric mixer on medium speed, gradually beat in 1½ cups softened butter, a few tablespoons at a time, until mixture is combined and smooth, scraping sides of bowl occasionally. (Frosting might look curdled until all the butter is incorporated.)

*Test Kitchen Tip: Be sure the milk mixture is completely cooled to room temperature before you beat in the butter. If the mixture is too warm, the butter will melt and cause the frosting to break (separate).

PER SERVING: *546 cal., 28 g fat (17 g sat. fat), 112 mg chol., 467 mg sodium, 70 g carb., 1 g fiber, 6 g pro.*

Angel Food Cake

PREP: 50 minutes
BAKE: 40 minutes at 350°F
COOL: 2 hours
MAKES: 12 servings

1½ cups egg whites (10 to
      12 large)
1½ cups sifted powdered sugar
  1 cup sifted cake flour or
      sifted all-purpose flour
1½ teaspoons cream of tartar
  1 teaspoon vanilla
  1 cup granulated sugar
  1 recipe Meringue Frosting
      (see page 149) or desired
      frosting or icing
      Sliced, peeled kiwifruit
      (optional)

1. In a very large mixing bowl allow the egg whites to stand at room temperature for 30 minutes. Meanwhile, sift powdered sugar and flour together three times (see photo, page 13); set aside.
2. Adjust baking rack to the lowest position in oven. Preheat oven to 350°F. Add cream of tartar and vanilla to egg whites. Beat with an electric mixer on medium speed until soft peaks form (tips curl). Gradually add granulated sugar, about 2 tablespoons at a time, beating until stiff peaks form (tips stand straight).
3. Sift about one-fourth of the flour mixture over beaten egg whites; fold in gently. (If bowl is too full, transfer to a larger bowl.) Repeat, folding in remaining flour mixture by fourths. Pour into an ungreased 10-inch tube pan. Gently cut through batter to remove any large air pockets.

4. Bake on the lowest rack for 40 to 45 minutes or until top springs back when lightly touched. Immediately invert cake; cool thoroughly in the inverted pan.
5. To remove cake from pan, loosen the cooled cake from the sides of the pan by sliding a metal spatula between the cake and pan. Constantly pressing the spatula against the pan, draw it around the pan in a continuous, not sawing, motion without cutting into the cake. Frost with Meringue Frosting and, if desired, garnish with sliced kiwifruit.

To Store: Cover cake and store at room temperature for up to 2 days.

Chocolate Angel Food Cake: Prepare as directed, except sift ¼ cup unsweetened cocoa powder with the flour mixture.

Honey Angel Food Cake: Prepare as directed, except in Step 2 after beating egg white mixture to soft peaks, gradually pour ¼ cup honey in a thin stream over the egg white mixture and reduce granulated sugar to ½ cup.

PER SLICE PLAIN, CHOCOLATE, OR HONEY VARIATIONS WITHOUT FROSTING: *172 cal., 0 g fat, 0 mg chol., 51 mg sodium, 39 g carb., 0 g fiber, 4 g pro.*

How to Make an Angel Food Cake

Homemade angel food cake starts with about a dozen egg whites, which are beaten to a fluffy meringuelike mixture before the flour and powdered sugar are folded in. Because the powdered sugar mixture is folded into the egg whites rather than beaten in, lumps of the powdered sugar would remain in the batter if not sifted first. Using a sieve to sift the flour and powdered sugar together blends the two and removes lumps.

1. Using a very clean bowl, beat egg whites, cream of tartar, and vanilla until soft peaks form (tips of the mixture will bend over slightly).

2. Add the granulated sugar a bit at a time, beating until stiff peaks form.

3. Sift about one-fourth of the flour mixture over the egg white mixture. Fold in gently. Repeat with remaining flour mixture.

4. Use a metal spatula to cut through the batter to remove large air bubbles.

Dark Cocoa Buttermilk Cake with Cocoa Mascarpone Frosting

PREP: **35 minutes**
BAKE: **30 minutes at 350°F**
COOL: **1 hour**
MAKES: **12 servings**

- ¾ cup butter
- 3 eggs
- 2⅓ cups all-purpose flour
- ¾ cup unsweetened dark Dutch-process cocoa powder or unsweetened cocoa powder
- 1 teaspoon baking soda
- ¾ teaspoon baking powder
- ½ teaspoon salt
- 1 cup granulated sugar
- 1 cup packed brown sugar
- 2 teaspoons vanilla
- 1½ cups buttermilk or sour milk (see tip, page 16)
- 1 recipe Cocoa-Mascarpone Frosting

1. Allow butter and eggs to stand at room temperature for 30 minutes. Meanwhile, lightly grease the bottoms of three 8×1½-inch round cake pans.* Line bottoms of pans with waxed paper or parchment paper. Grease and lightly flour paper and sides of pans; set pans aside. In a medium bowl stir together flour, ¾ cup cocoa powder, baking soda, baking powder, and salt; set aside.

2. Preheat oven to 350°F. In a large mixing bowl beat butter with an electric mixer on medium to high speed for 30 seconds. In a small bowl stir together granulated and brown sugars. Gradually add sugar mixture to butter, beating on medium speed until combined. Scrape sides of bowl; beat for 2 minutes more. Add eggs, one at a time, beating well after each addition. Beat in vanilla.

3. Alternately add flour mixture and buttermilk to beaten mixture, beating on low speed after each addition just until combined. Beat on medium to high speed for 20 seconds more. Pour batter into the prepared cake pans, spreading evenly.

4. Bake for 30 to 35 minutes or until a wooden toothpick inserted in the centers comes out clean. Cool cake layers in pans on wire racks for 10 minutes. Remove layers from pans; peel off waxed paper. Cool thoroughly on wire racks.

5. To assemble, place a cake layer on a cake plate. Spread with ½ cup of the Cocoa Mascarpone Frosting. Top with second cake layer; spread with another ½ cup of the frosting. Top with the remaining cake layer. Frost top and sides of cake with the remaining frosting.

Cocoa Mascarpone Frosting: Allow half of an 8-ounce tub mascarpone cheese or half of an 8-ounce package cream cheese and ½ cup butter to stand at room temperature for 30 minutes. In a large mixing bowl beat the mascarpone cheese, the butter, ⅓ cup unsweetened dark Dutch-process cocoa powder or unsweetened cocoa powder, 2 tablespoons milk, and 2 teaspoons vanilla with an electric mixer on medium to high speed until creamy. Gradually add 1 pound powdered sugar, beating until smooth. Beat in additional milk, 1 teaspoon at a time, to reach spreading consistency.

***Test Kitchen Tip:** To make the cake as shown in the photo, prepare cake as directed, except use a greased 13×9×2-inch baking pan and bake for 45 to 50 minutes. Cool thoroughly in pan on a wire rack. Spread with only half of the frosting.

To Store: Cover cake and store in the refrigerator for up to 3 days.

PER SERVING: *633 cal., 26 g fat (16 g sat. fat), 117 mg chol., 419 mg sodium, 98 g carb., 3 g fiber, 9 g pro.*

Classic Carrot Cake

PREP: **30 minutes**
BAKE: **35 minutes at 350°F**
COOL: **2 hours**
MAKES: **12 servings**

  4   eggs
  2   cups all-purpose flour
  2   cups sugar
  2   teaspoons baking powder
  1   teaspoon ground cinnamon
      (optional)
  ½   teaspoon salt
  ½   teaspoon baking soda
  3   cups finely shredded carrots
      (lightly packed) (see tip,
      page 506)
  ¾   cup vegetable oil
  1   recipe Cream Cheese
      Frosting (see page 149)
  ½   cup finely chopped pecans,
      toasted (see tip, page 343)
      (optional)

1. Allow butter and eggs to stand at room temperature for 30 minutes. Meanwhile, grease and lightly flour two 8×1½-inch round cake pans (for cupcakes, see right); line pans with waxed paper and grease the paper.

2. Preheat the oven to 350°F. In a large bowl stir together flour, sugar, baking powder, cinnamon (if desired), salt, and baking soda.

3. In another bowl combine eggs, carrots, and oil. Add egg mixture to flour mixture. Stir until combined. Pour batter into the prepared pans.

4. Bake for 35 to 40 minutes or until a wooden toothpick inserted near centers comes out clean. Cool cake layers in pans on wire racks for 10 minutes. Remove cake layers from pans; cool thoroughly.

5. Frost with Cream Cheese Frosting.* If desired, sprinkle chopped pecans over frosting. Cover and store cake in the refrigerator for up to 3 days.

*****Test Kitchen Tip:** To decorate carrot cake or carrot cake cupcakes with frosting carrots, reserve a portion of Cream Cheese Frosting. Tint part of the reserved portion orange; tint remaining portion green. Place frostings in separate heavy-duty resealable plastic bags; snip a small hole in one corner of each bag. Pipe orange frosting in zigzags to create carrot shapes. Pipe green frosting at top of each carrot for "leaves."

PER SERVING: *711 cal., 30 g fat (10 g sat. fat), 112 mg chol., 350 mg sodium, 108 g carb., 1 g fiber, 6 g pro.*

Cupcake Conversion

It's easy to turn favorite cake recipes into cupcakes. Choose a cake recipe that starts with butter and sugar that are beaten or an oil-based cake like Classic Carrot Cake. A two-layer cake makes 24 to 30 cupcakes. Line muffin cups with paper bake cups or grease and flour cups. Prepare cake batter as directed; fill muffin cups half to two-thirds full with batter. Bake at the same temperature called for in the cake recipe, but reduce the baking time by one-third to one-half. (Most cupcakes will bake between 15 and 22 minutes.) Check doneness of cupcakes by inserting a toothpick in centers of the cupcakes in the middle of the pan. Cool cupcakes in pans for 5 to 10 minutes; remove cupcakes from pan and cool completely on a wire rack. Frost and decorate as desired.

Bourbon-Chocolate Tipsy Cake

PREP: **35 minutes**
BAKE: **1 hour at 325°F**
COOL: **2 hours**
MAKES: **12 servings**

1 cup unsalted butter
3 eggs
1 tablespoon unsweetened cocoa powder
2 cups all-purpose flour
1 teaspoon baking soda
½ teaspoon salt
3 ounces unsweetened chocolate, coarsely chopped
2 ounces sweet baking chocolate, coarsely chopped
¼ cup instant coffee crystals or instant espresso coffee powder
2 tablespoons boiling water
½ cup bourbon
2 cups sugar
1½ teaspoons vanilla
2 tablespoons bourbon
¾ cup caramel-flavor ice cream topping
2 tablespoons bourbon

1. Allow butter and eggs to stand at room temperature for 30 minutes. Meanwhile, butter a 10-inch fluted tube pan. Add cocoa powder. Shake and tilt pan to coat bottom, sides, and tube; shake out any excess cocoa powder. Set pan aside. In a medium bowl stir together flour, baking soda, and salt; set aside.

2. Preheat oven to 325°F. In a small microwave-safe bowl combine unsweetened chocolate and sweet chocolate. Microwave, uncovered, on 100 percent power (high) for 1 minute; stir. Microwave, uncovered, for 30 seconds more; stir until smooth. Cool slightly.

3. In a 2-cup glass measuring cup combine coffee crystals and boiling water, stirring to dissolve coffee crystals. Add enough cold water to coffee to measure 1½ cups. Stir in the ½ cup bourbon.

4. In a large mixing bowl beat butter with an electric mixer on medium to high speed for 30 seconds. Add sugar. Beat until combined, scraping sides of bowl occasionally. Add eggs, one at a time, beating well after each addition. Beat in melted chocolate and vanilla. Alternately add flour mixture and coffee mixture to chocolate mixture, beating on low speed after each addition just until combined. Pour batter into the prepared pan, spreading evenly.

5. Bake about 1 hour or until a wooden toothpick inserted near the center of cake comes out clean. Cool in pan on a wire rack for 15 minutes. Remove cake from pan; cool thoroughly on a wire rack. Brush top and sides of cake with 2 tablespoons bourbon.

6. For sauce, in a small saucepan combine caramel topping and 2 tablespoons bourbon. Cook and stir over medium heat until warm. Spoon sauce over cake.

To Store: Prepare as directed through Step 5. Wrap cake in plastic wrap and store at room temperature for up to 2 days. To serve, prepare sauce as directed and spoon over cake.

PER SERVING: *519 cal., 22 g fat (12 g sat. fat), 87 mg chol., 281 mg sodium, 70 g carb., 2 g fiber, 5 g pro.*

Island Bananas Foster Cupcakes

PREP: 35 minutes
BAKE: 20 minutes at 350°F
COOL: 45 minutes
MAKES: 24 cupcakes

- 1 cup butter
- 3 eggs
- 2 cups all-purpose flour
- 2 teaspoons baking powder
- ½ teaspoon salt
- 1½ cups sugar
- ½ teaspoon vanilla
- ¾ cup unsweetened coconut milk
- ¾ cup shredded coconut, lightly toasted
- ¼ cup rum or unsweetened coconut milk
- 1 recipe Bananas Foster Topping
  Sweetened whipped cream (see tip, page 16) (optional)
  Shredded coconut, lightly toasted (optional)

1. Allow butter and eggs to stand at room temperature for 30 minutes. Meanwhile, line twenty-four 2½-inch muffin cups with paper bake cups. In a medium bowl stir together flour, baking powder, and salt. Set aside.

2. Preheat oven to 350°F. In a large mixing bowl beat butter with an electric mixer on medium to high speed for 30 seconds. Add sugar, about ¼ cup at a time, beating until combined. Add eggs, one at a time, beating well after each addition. Beat in vanilla. Alternately add flour mixture and coconut milk to butter mixture, beating on low speed after each addition just until combined. Fold in the ¾ cup coconut and the rum.

3. Spoon batter into the prepared muffin cups, filling each about three-fourths full. Use the back of a spoon to smooth out batter in cups.

4. Bake about 20 minutes or until a wooden toothpick inserted in centers comes out clean. Cool cupcakes in muffin cups on wire racks for 5 minutes. Remove cupcakes from muffin cups. Cool thoroughly on wire racks.

5. Spoon Bananas Foster Topping onto cupcakes. If desired, pipe whipped cream onto cupcakes and sprinkle with additional coconut.

Bananas Foster Topping: In a large skillet melt ⅓ cup butter over medium heat. Stir in ½ cup packed brown sugar, ¼ teaspoon ground cinnamon, and, if desired, ⅛ teaspoon freshly grated nutmeg (see photo, page 17). Slice 3 bananas and add to mixture in skillet; toss gently to coat. Cook and stir for 1 to 2 minutes or until bananas are heated through. Meanwhile, in a small saucepan heat ¼ cup rum over low heat just until rum almost simmers; remove from heat. If desired, use a long match to carefully ignite rum. Once the flame dies down, pour rum into banana mixture. Gently stir in ½ teaspoon vanilla.

To Store: Place cooled cupcakes in an airtight container; cover. Store at room temperature for up to 3 days or freeze for up to 1 month. Thaw frozen cupcakes at room temperature. Prepare topping just before serving.

PER CUPCAKE: *263 cal., 14 g fat (9 g sat. fat), 54 mg chol., 173 mg sodium, 31 g carb., 1 g fiber, 3 g pro.*

Pineapple Upside-Down Cake

PREP: 25 minutes
BAKE: 35 minutes at 350°F
COOL: 25 minutes
MAKES: 12 servings

½ cup butter
1 cup packed brown sugar
12 canned pineapple rings in juice*
2 cups all-purpose flour
2 teaspoons baking powder
½ teaspoon salt
¼ teaspoon ground nutmeg
½ cup butter, softened
½ cup granulated sugar
½ cup packed brown sugar
2 eggs
½ cup milk
1 teaspoon vanilla
1 cup vanilla Greek yogurt or sweetened whipped cream (see tip, page 16) (optional)
1 tablespoon packed brown sugar (optional)
12 maraschino cherries (optional)

1. Preheat oven to 350°F. Grease the bottom and sides of a 13×9×2-inch baking pan. Line bottom of pan with parchment paper; set pan aside.
2. For topping, in a medium saucepan melt ½ cup butter over low heat. Stir in the 1 cup brown sugar. Bring mixture to boiling over medium heat, stirring frequently. Pour into prepared pan. Drain pineapple rings, reserving ½ cup juice. Fit rings tightly into bottom of pan.
3. For cake, in a medium bowl whisk together flour, baking powder, salt, and nutmeg; set aside. In a large mixing bowl beat ½ cup softened butter, the granulated sugar, and the ½ cup brown sugar with an electric mixer on medium speed for 2 minutes, scraping sides of bowl occasionally. Beat in eggs until combined. Beat in half of the flour mixture on low speed. Beat in the reserved pineapple juice, the milk, and vanilla until combined. Beat in the remaining flour mixture. Spread batter carefully over pineapple slices in pan.
4. Bake for 35 to 40 minutes or until a toothpick inserted in center comes out clean. Cool in pan on a wire rack for 10 minutes. Loosen sides of cake; invert onto a serving plate. If any pineapple sticks to pan, gently replace on cake. Let cool at least 15 minutes; serve warm or cooled. If desired, in a small bowl combine yogurt and the 1 tablespoon brown sugar. Rinse cherries; pat dry with paper towels. If desired, serve cake with yogurt mixture and cherries.

*Test Kitchen Tip: You will need one 20-ounce can and one 8-ounce can pineapple slices for the 12 slices. There will be a few slices of pineapple leftover.

To Store: Loosely cover cake or mini cakes. Store at room temperature for up to 24 hours.

PER SERVING: *396 cal., 17 g fat (10 g sat. fat), 77 mg chol., 290 mg sodium, 60 g carb., 1 g fiber, 4 g pro.*

Make It Mini

Preheat oven to 350°F. Grease the bottoms and sides of twelve 10-ounce ramekins. Line bottoms of ramekins with parchment paper; set ramekins aside. Prepare topping as directed, except divide among prepared ramekins. Fit a pineapple ring into each ramekin. Prepare batter as directed; divide among ramekins. Use the back of a spoon to smooth out batter in ramekins. Bake about 30 minutes or until tops spring back when lightly touched. Cool in ramekins on wire racks for 5 minutes. Using a metal spatula, loosen cakes from ramekins. Invert cakes onto serving plates. Let cool at least 15 minutes before serving. If desired, serve as directed in Step 4. Makes 12 mini cakes.

White Chocolate and Almond Pound Cake

PREP: **50 minutes**
BAKE: **55 minutes at 350°F**
COOL: **2 hours**
MAKES: **16 to 20 servings**

 1 cup butter
 6 eggs
 4 ounces white baking
   chocolate with cocoa butter,
   chopped
 3 cups all-purpose flour
 ¼ cup blanched almonds,
   finely ground
 1 teaspoon baking powder
 ½ teaspoon baking soda
 ½ teaspoon salt
 2 cups sugar
 1 tablespoon vanilla
 1½ teaspoons almond extract
 1 8-ounce carton sour cream
 4 ounces white baking
   chocolate with cocoa butter,
   chopped
 1 teaspoon shortening
 ¼ cup sliced almonds, toasted
   (see tip, page 343) and
   chopped

1. Allow butter and eggs to stand at room temperature for 30 minutes. Grease and flour a 10-inch fluted tube pan; set aside.
2. In a small heavy saucepan heat and stir 4 ounces white chocolate over low heat until melted; set aside. In a medium bowl stir together flour, the finely ground almonds, the baking powder, baking soda, and salt; set aside.
3. Preheat oven to 350°F. In a very large mixing bowl beat butter with an electric mixer on medium to high speed for 30 seconds. Gradually add sugar, beating about 10 minutes or until mixture is fluffy and lighter in color. Add eggs, one at a time, beating about 1 minute after each addition and scraping sides of bowl frequently. Add vanilla, almond extract, and the melted white chocolate; beat just until combined.
4. Alternately add flour mixture and the sour cream to butter mixture, beating on low to medium speed after each addition just until combined. Do not overmix. Pour batter into the prepared pan, spreading evenly.

5. Bake for 55 to 60 minutes or until a wooden toothpick inserted near the center comes out clean. Cool in pan on a wire rack for 15 minutes. Remove cake from pan; cool thoroughly on wire rack.
6. For glaze, in a small heavy saucepan heat and stir 4 ounces white chocolate and the shortening over low heat until melted. Spoon glaze over pound cake; sprinkle with the chopped almonds. Let stand until chocolate is set.

To Store: Place cake in an airtight container; cover. Store at room temperature for up to 3 days.

To Make Ahead: Bake and cool cake as directed through Step 5. Wrap cooled cake in plastic wrap; overwrap tightly with foil. Freeze for up to 1 month. Thaw overnight in the refrigerator before serving. Serve as directed in Step 6.

PER SERVING: *447 cal., 23 g fat (13 g sat. fat), 120 mg chol., 270 mg sodium, 53 g carb., 1 g fiber, 7 g pro.*

Mocha-Filled Banana Cupcakes

PREP: 40 minutes
BAKE: 18 minutes at 350°F
COOL: 45 minutes
MAKES: 24 cupcakes

1   8-ounce package cream cheese
3   eggs
2¼ cups all-purpose flour
1½ cups sugar
1½ teaspoons baking powder
1   teaspoon baking soda
½   teaspoon salt
¼   cup sugar
1½ teaspoons instant espresso powder
    Dash salt
2   ounces semisweet chocolate, melted and cooled
1   cup mashed ripe bananas (2 to 3 bananas)
¾   cup buttermilk or sour milk (see tip, page 16)
½   cup shortening
1   teaspoon vanilla
1   recipe Banana Frosting
    Dried banana chips (optional)

1. Allow cream cheese and eggs to stand at room temperature for 30 minutes. Grease and flour twenty-four 2½-inch muffin cups. In a large mixing bowl combine flour, the 1½ cups sugar, the baking powder, baking soda, and the ½ teaspoon salt. Set aside.
2. Preheat oven to 350°F. For mocha filling, in a medium mixing bowl beat cream cheese and the ¼ cup sugar with an electric mixer on medium to high speed until combined. Beat in one of the eggs, the espresso powder, and the dash salt. Stir in melted chocolate.
3. Add bananas, buttermilk, shortening, and vanilla to flour mixture; beat on low speed until combined. Beat in the remaining 2 eggs on medium speed.
4. Spoon a rounded tablespoon of batter into each prepared muffin cup. Drop a rounded teaspoon of mocha filling into each cup. Spoon the remaining batter over mocha filling in muffin cups, filling each two-thirds to three-fourths full.
5. Bake for 18 to 20 minutes or until a wooden toothpick inserted in centers of cupcakes comes out clean. Cool cupcakes in muffin cups on wire racks for 5 minutes. Remove cupcakes from muffin cups. Cool thoroughly on wire racks.
6. Spread cupcakes with Banana Frosting. If desired, top each cupcake with a dried banana chip.

Banana Frosting: In a medium mixing bowl beat ½ cup softened butter with an electric mixer on medium speed until smooth. Beat in ½ cup mashed ripe banana. Gradually add 3 cups powdered sugar, beating well. Beat in 1 tablespoon milk and 2 teaspoons vanilla. Gradually beat in 3½ to 4 cups additional powdered sugar until frosting reaches piping consistency.

PER CUPCAKE: *364 cal., 13 g fat (6 g sat. fat), 47 mg chol., 205 mg sodium, 61 g carb., 1 g fiber, 3 g pro.*

Make It Mini

Lightly coat seventy-two 1¾-inch muffin cups with nonstick cooking spray. Prepare batter as directed. Spoon a rounded teaspoon of the batter into each prepared muffin cup. Drop 1 level teaspoon of mocha filling into each muffin cup. Scoop a spoonful of the remaining batter over mocha filling in each muffin cup (mocha filling will not be completely covered). Bake for 12 to 14 minutes or until a toothpick inserted near centers comes out clean. Cool cupcakes in muffin cups on wire racks for 5 minutes. Remove from muffin cups. Cool completely on wire racks. Frost as directed. Makes 72 (1¾-inch) cupcakes.

Triple-Citrus Pound Cake

PREP: **20 minutes**
BAKE: **40 minutes at 350°F**
COOL: **2 hours**
MAKES: **16 servings**

1¼ cups butter
3 eggs
2¼ cups all-purpose flour
¾ teaspoon baking powder
½ teaspoon baking soda
¼ teaspoon salt
½ cup milk
2 teaspoons finely shredded grapefruit peel (see tip, page 102)
2 teaspoons finely shredded lime peel
2 teaspoons finely shredded orange peel
1 tablespoon grapefruit juice
1½ cups sugar
1 teaspoon vanilla
2 tablespoons butter, melted
1 to 2 tablespoons orange juice
¾ cup powdered sugar
Finely shredded grapefruit peel, lime peel, and/or orange peel (optional)
1 recipe Sugared Orange Slices (optional)

1. Allow 1¼ cups butter and the eggs to stand at room temperature for 30 minutes. Meanwhile, grease and flour a 10-inch fluted tube pan; set aside. In a medium bowl combine flour, baking powder, baking soda, and salt; set aside. In a small bowl stir together milk, the 2 teaspoons grapefruit peel, the 2 teaspoons lime peel, the 2 teaspoons orange peel, and the grapefruit juice; set aside.
2. Preheat oven to 350°F. In a large mixing bowl beat butter with an electric mixer on medium to high speed for 30 seconds. Gradually add granulated sugar, beating until mixture is fluffy and lighter in color. Add eggs, one at a time, beating well after each addition. Beat in vanilla. Alternately add flour mixture and milk mixture to butter mixture, beating on low speed after each addition just until combined. Pour batter into the prepared pan, spreading evenly.
3. Bake for 40 to 45 minutes or until a wooden toothpick inserted near the center comes out clean. Cool in pan on a wire rack for 10 minutes. Remove cake from pan; cool thoroughly on wire rack.
4. To serve, in a small bowl combine the 2 tablespoons melted butter and 1 tablespoon of the orange juice. Add powdered sugar; beat until smooth. If necessary, add enough of the remaining 1 tablespoon orange juice to make drizzling consistency. Drizzle over cake. If desired, top cake with Sugared Orange Slices.

Sugared Orange Slices: Thinly slice one orange. In a saucepan combine 1 cup sugar and 1 cup water. Cook and stir over medium-high heat until mixture begins to simmer and is clear. Reduce heat to medium. Add orange slices; simmer for 15 to 20 minutes or until slices are softened, turning occasionally. Remove from heat; cool oranges in the saucepan. Place orange slices on a wire rack set over waxed paper to drain. Cover loosely with waxed paper; let stand overnight to dry. Dip orange slices in sugar to coat.

To Store: Place cake in an airtight container; cover. Store at room temperature for up to 3 days.

To Make Ahead: Bake and cool cake as directed through Step 3. Wrap cooled cake in plastic wrap; overwrap tightly with foil. Freeze for up to 1 month. Thaw overnight in the refrigerator before serving. Serve as directed in Step 4.

PER SERVING: *319 cal., 17 g fat (10 g sat. fat), 82 mg chol., 228 mg sodium, 39 g carb., 1 g fiber, 3 g pro.*

Vanilla Cake with Berries and Jam

PREP: **40 minutes**
BAKE: **22 minutes at 350°F**
COOL: **2 hours**
MAKES: **12 servings**

　4　egg whites
2½　cups all-purpose flour
　⅓　cup cornstarch
3½　teaspoons baking powder
　1　teaspoon salt
　¾　cup water
　⅔　cup vegetable oil
　½　cup milk
　1　tablespoon vanilla
　¼　teaspoon cream of tartar
1½　cups sugar
　1　recipe Vanilla-Butter
　　　Frosting
　1　cup strawberry jam
　3　cups cut-up fresh berries
　1　cup whole fresh berries

1. Allow egg whites to stand at room temperature for 30 minutes. Grease bottoms of two 8×1½-inch round cake pans. Line bottoms with parchment paper or waxed paper; grease and lightly flour pans. Set pans aside.
2. Preheat oven to 350°F. In a large bowl stir together flour, cornstarch, baking powder, and salt. Add the water, oil, milk, and vanilla. Beat with a wire whisk until smooth.
3. In a medium mixing bowl combine egg whites and cream of tartar. Beat with an electric mixer on medium speed until soft peaks form (tips curl). Gradually add sugar, beating on high speed until stiff peaks form (tips stand straight). Fold beaten egg whites

into batter. Pour batter into prepared pans, spreading evenly.
4. Bake for 22 to 25 minutes or until a toothpick inserted near centers comes out clean. Cool in pans on wire racks for 10 minutes. Remove from pans; cool thoroughly on wire racks.
5. To assemble, use a long serrated knife to cut cake layers in half horizontally (see photos, right). Place one cake layer, cut side down, on a serving plate. Spread with a generous ¾ cup of the Vanilla-Butter Frosting and ¼ cup of the jam. Top with 1 cup of the cut-up berries. Repeat with two more cake layers.
6. For top layer, add final cake layer, cut side down. Spread with ¾ cup frosting, ¼ cup jam, and top with the whole berries.

Vanilla-Butter Frosting: Allow ½ cup butter to stand at room temperature for 30 minutes. In a medium mixing bowl beat butter with electric mixer on medium to high speed for 30 seconds. Gradually beat in 3 cups powdered sugar. Beat in 3 tablespoons milk and 2 teaspoons vanilla bean paste or vanilla. Gradually beat in 3 cups additional powdered sugar. If necessary, beat in additional milk, 1 teaspoon at a time, to make spreading consistency.

To Store: Cover and store in the refrigerator for up to 2 days.

PER SERVING: *722 cal., 20 g fat (6 g sat. fat), 21 mg chol., 404 mg sodium, 132 g carb., 2 g fiber, 5 g pro.*

How to Cut and Layer the Cake

Four decadent layers of cake, frosting, jam, and berries make an impressive spring- or summertime dessert. It's much easier to create than you might think. Follow these steps for accurate measuring, cutting, frosting, and layering.

1. To get even layers, measure the height of each layer. Insert toothpicks halfway between the top and bottom at even intervals.

2. With a sharp serrated knife, cut each cake layer in half horizontally, using the toothpicks as guides.

3. Spread one-fourth of the frosting over the cut side of one half-cake layer.

4. Spread one-fourth of the jam over the frosting. Top with one-third of the cut-up berries.

5. Place another half cake layer over the berries, cut side down. Repeat layering with frosting, jam, berries, and cake.

Triple-Chocolate Cupcakes

PREP: 1 hour
BAKE: 15 minutes at 350°F
COOL: 45 minutes
MAKES: 12 cupcakes

- 3 eggs
- 6 ounces bittersweet chocolate, chopped
- ½ cup butter, cut into pieces
- 3 tablespoons crème de cacao
- ½ cup all-purpose flour
- ½ teaspoon baking powder
- ¼ teaspoon salt
- ½ cup sugar
- 1 teaspoon vanilla
- 1 recipe Dark Chocolate Butter Frosting
   Chopped bittersweet chocolate (optional)

1. Separate eggs. Allow yolks and whites to stand at room temperature for 30 minutes. In a medium saucepan combine the 6 ounces chocolate and the butter. Heat and stir over medium heat until melted and smooth. Remove saucepan from heat. Stir in crème de cacao; let cool.

2. Line twelve 2½-inch muffin cups with paper bake cups or parchment paper. In a small bowl stir together flour, baking powder, and salt. Set aside.

3. Preheat oven to 350°F. In a large mixing bowl beat egg yolks and sugar with an electric mixer on high speed about 3 minutes or until thick and lemon color. Beat in chocolate mixture and vanilla. Add flour mixture, beating just until combined; set aside.

4. Wash beaters. In a medium bowl beat egg whites on medium to high speed just until stiff peaks form (tips stand straight). Stir a small amount of beaten egg whites into chocolate mixture to lighten. Fold in the remaining egg whites.

5. Spoon batter into the prepared muffin cups, filling each about two-thirds full.

6. Bake for 15 to 18 minutes or until tops spring back when lightly touched. Cool cupcakes in muffin cups on wire racks for 5 minutes. Remove cupcakes from muffin cups. Cool thoroughly on wire racks.

7. Spoon Dark Chocolate Butter Frosting into a pastry bag fitted with a medium star tip. Pipe long stars of frosting onto tops of cupcakes. If desired, sprinkle with additional chopped chocolate.

Dark Chocolate Butter Frosting: Allow 6 tablespoons butter to stand at room temperature for 30 minutes. In a large mixing bowl beat butter with electric mixer on medium speed until smooth. Gradually add 1 cup powdered sugar, beating well. Beat in 2 ounces dark chocolate, melted and cooled; 2 tablespoons milk; and 1 tablespoon crème de cacao. Gradually beat in 3 cups additional powdered sugar. Beat in enough additional milk (1 to 2 tablespoons) until frosting reaches piping consistency.

To Store: Place cupcakes in an airtight container; cover. Store at room temperature for up to 3 days.

PER CUPCAKE: 473 cal., 23 g fat (14 g sat. fat), 90 mg chol., 180 mg sodium, 67 g carb., 2 g fiber, 5 g pro.

How to Pipe Stars

To pipe long stars of frosting, pull back slowly as you squeeze bag gently.

Hazelnut-Pear Torte with Dulce de Leche Filling

PREP: **45 minutes**
BAKE: **20 minutes at 350°F**
COOL: **2 hours**
CHILL: **1 hour**
MAKES: **12 servings**

2½ cups hazelnuts (filberts), toasted (see tip, page 17)
3   tablespoons all-purpose flour
4   teaspoons baking powder
1   teaspoon ground cinnamon
6   eggs
1   cup granulated sugar
1   3-ounce package cream cheese, softened
¼   cup butter, softened
½   cup canned dulce de leche
2   to 3 tablespoons milk
4½ cups powdered sugar
2   tablespoons butter
3   ripe pears, peeled, cored, and thinly sliced
    Chopped hazelnuts (filberts), toasted (optional)

1. Preheat oven to 350°F. Grease two 8×1½-inch round baking pans. Line pan bottoms with waxed paper or parchment paper; grease the paper. Lightly flour pans; set aside. Place half of the 2½ cups hazelnuts in a blender or food processor. Cover; blend or process until nuts are ground. Repeat with the remaining nuts. In a medium bowl combine ground hazelnuts, the 3 tablespoons flour, the baking powder, and cinnamon; set aside.

2. In a large mixing bowl combine eggs and granulated sugar. Beat with an electric mixer on medium to high speed until smooth. Add nut mixture. Beat until combined, scraping sides of bowl occasionally. Spread evenly into prepared pans.

3. Bake for 20 to 25 minutes or until light brown and tops spring back when lightly touched (centers may dip slightly). Cool in pans on wire racks for 10 minutes. Remove from pans; peel off waxed or parchment paper if necessary. Cool thoroughly on wire racks.

4. For dulce de leche filling, in a large mixing bowl combine cream cheese and the ¼ cup butter. Beat with an electric mixer on medium to high speed until combined. Add dulce de leche, beating until smooth. Beat in 2 tablespoons of the milk. Add 2 cups of the powdered sugar, beating until combined. Beat in the remaining 2½ cups powdered sugar and enough of the remaining 1 tablespoon milk to make a spreading consistency.

5. In a very large skillet melt the 2 tablespoons butter over medium heat. Add pears; cook for 8 to 10 minutes or until brown and tender, gently stirring occasionally. Set aside to cool.

6. To assemble, use a long serrated knife to cut cakes in half horizontally, making four cake layers (see photos, page 143). Place one cake layer, cut side up, on a serving platter. Spread ½ cup of the dulce de leche filling over cake layer. Top with one-fourth of the pears, arranging pears in a single layer. Repeat layers twice. Add the remaining cake layer, cut side down. Frost with the remaining dulce de leche filling; arrange the remaining pears on top. If desired, sprinkle with chopped toasted hazelnuts. Chill for up to 1 hour before serving.

PER SERVING: *601 cal., 29 g fat (8 g sat. fat), 132 mg chol., 238 mg sodium, 82 g carb., 4 g fiber, 9 g pro.*

Frostings

Whether you're looking for a thick, buttery frosting or a light and airy topping, these recipes have you covered. Pick one to turn your homemade cake into a sweet and decadent masterpiece.

Butter Frosting

START TO FINISH: 30 minutes
MAKES: about 4½ cups

- ¾ cup butter, softened
- 2 pounds powdered sugar (about 8 cups)
- ⅓ cup milk
- 2 teaspoons vanilla
  Milk
  Food coloring (optional)

1. In a very large mixing bowl beat butter with an electric mixer on medium speed until smooth. Gradually add 2 cups of the powdered sugar, beating well. Slowly beat in the ⅓ cup milk and the vanilla. Gradually beat in the remaining powdered sugar. Beat in additional milk until frosting reaches spreading consistency. If desired, tint with food coloring. This frosts the tops and sides of two 8- or 9-inch layers. (Halve the recipe to frost a 13×9×2-inch cake.)

Milk Chocolate Butter Frosting: Prepare as directed, except melt 1 cup milk chocolate pieces; cool. Beat into the butter before adding the powdered sugar.

Chocolate Butter Frosting: Prepare as directed, except substitute ½ cup unsweetened cocoa powder for ½ cup of the powdered sugar.

Strawberry Butter Frosting: Prepare as directed, except beat ⅓ cup strawberry jam into butter before adding the powdered sugar.

Irish Cream Butter Frosting: Prepare as directed, except substitute Irish cream liqueur for the milk.

Coffee Butter Frosting: Prepare as directed, except add 1 tablespoon instant espresso powder or coffee crystals to the butter or substitute strong brewed coffee for the milk.

PER ¹⁄₁₂ RECIPE (ALL VARIATIONS): *401 cal., 12 g fat (7 g sat. fat), 31 mg chol., 85 mg sodium, 76 g carb., 0 g fiber, 0 g pro.*

Sweetened Whipped Cream Frosting

START TO FINISH: 25 minutes
MAKES: about 4 cups

- 2 tablespoons cold water
- 1 teaspoon unflavored gelatin
- 2 cups whipping cream
- ¼ cup sugar

1. In a large saucepan bring about 1 inch water to boiling over high heat. Meanwhile, in a 1-cup heatproof glass measuring cup combine the cold water and the gelatin. Let stand for 2 minutes. Place measuring cup in the saucepan of boiling water. Cook and stir about 1 minute or until the gelatin is completely dissolved. Remove measuring cup from water; cool for 5 minutes.
2. In a chilled large mixing bowl beat whipping cream and sugar with the chilled beaters of an electric mixer on medium speed while gradually drizzling the gelatin mixture into the cream

mixture. Continue beating the cream mixture until stiff peaks form (tips stand straight).
PER ¹⁄₁₂ RECIPE: *29 cal., 3 g fat (2 g sat. fat), 10 mg chol., 3 mg sodium, 1 g carb., 0 g fiber, 0 g pro.*

Creamy White Frosting

START TO FINISH: 25 minutes
MAKES: about 3 cups

- 1 cup shortening
- 1½ teaspoons vanilla*
- ½ teaspoon almond extract
- 1 pound powdered sugar (about 4 cups)
- 3 to 4 tablespoons milk

1. In a large mixing bowl beat shortening, vanilla, and almond extract with an electric mixer on medium speed for 30 seconds. Slowly add about half of the powdered sugar, beating well. Add 2 tablespoons of the milk. Gradually beat in remaining powdered sugar and enough remaining milk to make frosting spreading consistency. This frosts the tops and sides of two 8- or 9-inch cake layers. (Halve recipe to frost a 13×9×2-inch cake. Or freeze half of the frosting in a freezer container for up to 3 months; thaw at room temperature before using.)

*Test Kitchen Tip: For a bright white frosting, use clear vanilla.
PER ¹⁄₁₂ RECIPE: *298 cal., 16 g fat (4 g sat. fat), 0 mg chol., 2 mg sodium, 38 g carb., 0 g fiber, 0 g pro.*

Butter
Frosting

Sweetened Whipped
Cream Frosting

Creamy White
Frosting

Cream Cheese
Frosting

Whipped Sour
Cream Frosting

Meringue Frosting

Cream Cheese Frosting

START TO FINISH: 20 minutes
MAKES: about 4 cups

- 1 8-ounce package cream cheese
- ½ cup butter
- 2 teaspoons vanilla
- 5½ to 6 cups powdered sugar

1. Allow cream cheese and butter to stand at room temperature for 30 minutes. In a large mixing bowl beat cream cheese, butter, and vanilla with an electric mixer on medium speed until light and fluffy. Gradually beat in powdered sugar until frosting reaches spreading consistency. This makes enough to frost the tops and sides of two 8- or 9-inch layers. (Halve the recipe to frost a 13×9×2-inch cake.) Cover and store the frosted cake in refrigerator.

Cocoa-Cream Cheese Frosting: Prepare as above, except beat ½ cup unsweetened cocoa powder into the cream cheese mixture and reduce powdered sugar to 5 to 5½ cups.
PER ¹/₁₂ RECIPE (PLAIN OR COCOA VARIATION): *348 cal., 14 g fat (9 g sat. fat), 41 mg chol., 116 mg sodium, 4 g carb., 0 g fiber, 1 g pro.*

Whipped Sour Cream Frosting

START TO FINISH: 15 minutes
MAKES: about 4 cups

- 2 cups whipping cream
- ⅓ cup sour cream
- ¼ cup sugar
- 1 teaspoon vanilla

1. In a chilled medium mixing bowl beat whipping cream, sour cream, sugar, and vanilla with an electric mixer on medium-high speed until medium-stiff peaks form. This frosts tops and sides of two 8- or 9-inch cake layers or one 10-inch tube cake. Store frosted cake in the refrigerator and serve the same day it is made.
PER ¹/₁₆ RECIPE: *124 cal., 12 g fat (7 g sat. fat), 43 mg chol., 15 mg sodium, 4 g carb., 0 g fiber, 1 g pro.*

Meringue Frosting

START TO FINISH: 25 minutes
MAKES: about 5 cups

- 1½ cups granulated sugar
- ⅓ cup cold water
- 2 egg whites
- ¼ teaspoon cream of tartar
- 1 teaspoon vanilla

1. In a 3-quart top of a double boiler combine sugar, water, egg whites, and cream of tartar. Beat with an electric mixer on low speed for 30 seconds.
2. Place the pan over boiling water (upper pan should not touch the water). Cook, beating constantly with the electric mixer on high speed, for 10 to 13 minutes or until an instant-read thermometer registers 160°F when inserted in the mixture, stopping beaters and quickly scraping bottom and sides of pan every 5 minutes to prevent sticking. Remove pan from the heat; add vanilla. Beat about 1 minute more or until frosting is fluffy and holds soft peaks. This frosts tops and sides of two 8- or 9-inch cake layers or one 10-inch tube cake. Store frosted cake in the refrigerator and serve the same day it is made.
PER ¹/₁₂ RECIPE: *101 cal., 0 g fat, 0 mg chol., 9 mg sodium, 25 g carb., 0 g fiber, 1 g pro.*

White Chocolate Birthday Cake,
recipe page 152

decorated cakes

BRIGHT, COLORFUL CAKES decked out with all the trimmings take parties to the next level. These inspiring ideas are fun and creative, yet easy enough for bakers of any skill level to successfully complete. And each calls for pans typically on hand! Add your own creative touches by customizing the colors and candy decorations for any of these designs.

White Chocolate Birthday Cake

With confetti sprinkles and frosting streamers, this classic design makes an excellent birthday cake for children and adults alike.

PREP: 1½ hours
BAKE: 30 minutes at 350°F
COOL: 1 hour
MAKES: 16 servings

10	tablespoons butter, softened
4	eggs
2¼	cups all-purpose flour
2¼	teaspoons baking powder
¼	teaspoon salt
8	ounces white baking chocolate with cocoa butter, chopped
1⅓	cups sugar
1½	teaspoons vanilla
1¼	cups milk
1	recipe White Chocolate Frosting
	Desired colors food coloring
	Multicolored edible confetti sprinkles and/or edible glitter

1. Allow butter and eggs to stand at room temperature for 30 minutes. Grease bottoms of two 9×1½-inch round cake pans. Line bottoms of pans with waxed paper; grease and lightly flour pans. Set pans aside. In a medium bowl stir together flour, baking powder, and salt; set aside.
2. In a medium saucepan heat and stir white chocolate over low heat until melted and smooth; cool.
3. Preheat oven to 350°F. In a large mixing bowl beat butter with an electric mixer on medium to high speed for 30 seconds. Gradually add sugar, about ⅓ cup at a time, beating on medium speed until well combined. Add eggs, one at a time, beating well after each addition. Beat in vanilla. Alternately add flour mixture and milk to butter mixture, beating on low speed after each addition just until combined. Beat in melted white chocolate just until combined. Divide batter between prepared pans, spreading evenly.
4. Bake about 30 minutes or until a wooden toothpick inserted in centers comes out clean. Cool cake layers in pans on wire racks for 10 minutes. Remove layers from pans; peel off waxed paper. Cool thoroughly on racks.
5. To assemble, use a long serrated knife to cut each cake layer in half horizontally (see photos, page 143). Place one layer, cut side up, on a serving plate. Spread with 1 cup White Chocolate Frosting. Top with the second layer; spread with another 1 cup frosting. Top with the third layer; spread with 1 cup frosting. Top with the fourth layer, cut side down. Spread top and sides of cake with frosting.
6. Place some of the remaining frosting in a pastry bag fitted with a large rose petal tip or other desired tip. Pipe a border around bottom edge of the cake. Divide remaining frosting among 3 or 4 small bowls; tint each with a different color of food coloring. Place each tinted frosting in a separate decorating bag fitted with a small round tip (or with just a tiny hole cut from the bottom of the bag). Pipe squiggly lines of each color on top edge of cake. Garnish cake with sprinkles.

White Chocolate Frosting: In a medium saucepan heat and stir 1 pound coarsely chopped white chocolate (with cocoa butter) over low heat until melted and smooth. Set aside. In a very large mixing bowl beat 1¾ cups softened butter with an electric mixer on medium-high speed until fluffy. Beat in melted white chocolate and 2 teaspoons vanilla until combined. Gradually beat in 7 cups powdered sugar until combined.

To Store: Loosely cover cake; refrigerate for up to 24 hours. Let cake stand at room temperature about 30 minutes before serving.

PER SERVING: *832 cal., 43 g fat (25 g sat. fat), 121 mg chol., 387 mg sodium, 107 g carb., 0 g fiber, 7 g pro.*

Secrets to Success

The frosting and decorations are what turn an ordinary cake into a special birthday cake. Creamed frosting, based on butter or shortening, works well for spreading and piping on cakes. If using a butter frosting, you might need to chill the frosting a bit because butter softens at room temperature. The frosting will soften further as you hold the pastry bag during piping. However, chilling too much may make it too firm to spread and pipe.

To color frosting, use either liquid, gel, or paste food coloring. Start with just a bit of each; it doesn't take much to color frosting (a few drops of the liquid or gel or a bit of paste on the end of a toothpick will do to start). Use either disposable or reusable pastry bags and tips (see tip, page 166). Or, in a pinch, you can use a heavy-duty resealable plastic bag and snip a small hole in one corner.

FROST THE CAKE To prevent crumbs in frosting, spread a crumb coat (a thin layer of frosting) on the cake. Follow that with a thicker layer of frosting.

PIPE ON THE BORDER Using a pastry bag fitted with a rose petal tip, pipe the border holding the tip flush to cake. The narrow end of the tip should be upright.

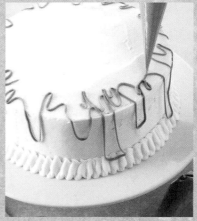

TINT FROSTING Divide remaining frosting among bowls and tint as desired. Place tinted frostings in separate pastry bags and use to pipe on streamers.

LAYER THE STREAMERS Continue to add different colors of frosting in layers for the streamers, letting them drape over the sides of the cake.

SPRINKLE WITH CONFETTI Add confetti or other desired sprinkles around the inside rim of the cake.

FINISH WITH GLITTER If desired, sprinkle edible glitter on top of confetti and insert candles into cake top.

Make-It-Mine Birthday Cake

Choose from white, yellow, chocolate, or red velvet cake baked in your choice of pan and decorated with a customized topping.

1 **recipe Cake** (choose option)
1 **recipe Frosting** (choose option)
Toppings or Decoration (choose option)

1. Preheat oven to 350°F. Grease and flour *Pan(s)*; set aside.
2. Prepare *Cake* recipe. Divide batter among pan(s). Bake *Cake* for recommended *Baking Time* or until a toothpick inserted near center of cake(s) comes out clean. Cool in pan(s) for 10 minutes. Remove from pan(s) and cool thoroughly on wire racks.
3. Prepare *Frosting*. If using round or square pans, spread about ½ cup Frosting over one cake layer. Top with remaining cake layer and spread frosting over top and sides of cake layers. If using 13×9-inch pan or tube pan, spread or drizzle Frosting over cake. Add *Toppings* or *Decoration* to cake.

PAN (PICK ONE)
Two 8×1½-inch or 9×1½-inch round cake pans
Two 8×8×2-inch square baking pans
One 13×9×2-inch baking pan,
One 10-inch fluted tube pan

CAKE (PICK ONE)
Chocolate Cake (see page 121)
Yellow Cake (see page 119)
White Cake (see page 114)
Red Velvet Cake (see page 123)

BAKING TIME
9-inch round or 8-inch square pans: 20 to 25 minutes*
8-inch round pans: 25 to 30 minutes*
13×9×2-inch pan: 30 to 35 minutes*
Fluted tube pan: 40 to 45 minutes*
***Note:** Chocolate Cake will take 5 to 10 minutes longer to bake in all pans.

FROSTING (PICK ONE)
Bittersweet Chocolate Ganache (see page 183)
Creamy White Frosting (see page 148)
Meringue Frosting (see page 149)
Whipped Sour Cream Frosting (see page 149)
Cream Cheese Frosting (see page 149)
Powdered Sugar Icing (see page 105)
Chocolate Butter Frosting (see page 148)
Buttercream Frosting (see Red Velvet Cake recipe, page 123)

TOPPINGS (PICK ONE)
Sprinkles: jimmies; nonpareils; candy-coated sunflower seeds; colored sugars; chopped, toasted nuts
Candies: candy-coated milk chocolate pieces, Jordan almonds, assorted colored candies

DECORATION (PICK ONE)
Almond flowers: Insert sliced almond "petals" around small round candies to look like flowers.
Frosting dots: Pipe different colors of Creamy White Frosting from pastry bags fitted with large and small round tips to form dots. If desired, practice technique on waxed paper first.
3-D white chocolate decoration: Melt white chocolate as directed for White Chocolate Bows (see page 174); place in resealable bag as directed. Pipe melted chocolate in a series of two to three loops. Chill as directed. Carefully press loop "pieces" into frosting to create designs.
Chocolate-covered cherries: Drain maraschino cherries with stems; pat dry with paper towels. Dip half of each cherry in melted chocolate, letting excess drip off. Let stand on waxed paper until set. Place on cake.

Tropical Fish Cake

START TO FINISH: 1½ hours
MAKES: 24 servings

- 1 recipe Yellow Cake (see page 119), Chocolate Cake (see page 121), or other 2-layer-size cake recipe
- 2 recipes Creamy White Frosting (see page 148) or three 16-ounce cans vanilla frosting (5 to 6 cups frosting total)
  Paste food coloring (red, orange and blue)
- 1 white candy coating disk (see tip, page 166) or other round white candy
- 1 miniature blue candy-coated milk chocolate piece
  Blue sanding sugar and/or edible glitter

1. Grease and flour a 13×9×2-inch baking pan. Line three 1¾-inch muffin cups with paper bake cups; set aside. Prepare batter for cake recipe as directed. Remove ¼ cup of the batter; divide among the paper-lined muffin cups. Spread the remaining batter into the prepared baking pan. Bake cupcakes for 10 to 12 minutes or until tops spring back when lightly touched. Bake cake as directed in recipe. Cool cupcakes in pan on a wire rack for 5 minutes. Remove cupcakes from pan; cool thoroughly on the rack. Cool cake in pan on a wire rack for 15 minutes. Remove from pan; cool cake thoroughly on rack.

2. Using a serrated knife, cut the corners off the 13×9-inch cake, creating a curved edge for an oval-shape piece. Place the oval cake on a large flat platter or tray. Position the corner pieces to create a top fin, bottom fin, and tail.
3. Remove 3¾ cups frosting and tint orange. Spread orange frosting over cake, leaving a space for the fin on the center of the cake. Remove 2 cups frosting and tint red-orange. Frost the fins, the space left on the body for the fin, and the tail. Use a metal spatula to swirl frosting to resemble scales. Make lips with red-orange frosting. For eye, position the candy coating disk upside down on the cake. Use a small amount of frosting to attach the blue candy-coated milk chocolate piece to the disk.
4. For bubble cupcakes, tint the remaining frosting light blue. Frost cupcakes with light blue frosting. Sprinkle with sanding sugar and edible glitter. Position the cupcakes to resemble bubbles.

To Store: Cover and store at room temperature for up to 3 days.

PER SERVING: *474 cal., 24 g fat (8 g sat. fat), 40 mg chol., 156 mg sodium, 63 g carb., 1 g fiber, 3 g pro.*

How to Shape a Tropical Fish Cake

Well-placed cuts turn a standard 13×9×2-inch cake into a creatively designed fish. To customize the fish cake, swap in any hues of paste food coloring for the tail, fins, and body. Trim the tail and fins as desired to make them smaller, more even, and rounder.

1. Cut four corners from the cake to create an oval shape.

2. Assemble the cake pieces with the corners placed on the top and bottom for fins and on the back for a tail.

3. Trim the top and bottom fin pieces as desired.

4. If you like, cut a notch in the center of the tail and/or round off the ends.

Cheeseburger-Ice Cream Cake

PREP: 1 hour
BAKE: 30 minutes at 350°F
FREEZE: 6 hours
MAKES: 12 servings

1   recipe Yellow Cake (see page 119)
⅓   cup white sprinkles
1   1.75-quart container chocolate ice cream
⅓   cup shredded coconut
    Green food coloring
    Purchased yellow rolled fondant icing
1   recipe Pound Cake Fries (optional)

1. Prepare cake recipe as directed for two 8-inch round layers. Very lightly brush one layer with water and top with white sprinkles. Place layers on a baking sheet and freeze until firm.
2. Line bottom of a 9-inch springform pan with waxed paper; set aside. Place ice cream in a bowl; stir until softened. Spread ice cream evenly in prepared pan. Cover ice cream with plastic wrap and freeze until firm.
3. For lettuce, place coconut in a resealable plastic bag. Add green food coloring, a few drops at a time, and mix in bag to tint; set aside. For cheese, roll yellow fondant to ¹⁄₁₆-inch thickness. Using a spatula, loosen the fondant periodically from the surface as you roll it. Cut into an 8- to 9-inch square. Set aside.
4. To assemble, place plain cake layer on a serving plate. Remove sides of springform pan and remove plastic wrap and waxed paper. Place ice cream on top of cake layer on plate. If necessary, trim ¼ to ½ inch from the edges of ice cream layer. If desired, drag a fork over surface of ice cream circle to add texture. Top with fondant cheese and coconut lettuce. Add remaining cake layer, sprinkle side up. Return to freezer and freeze for at least 1 hour or until firm. If desired, serve with Pound Cake Fries.

To Store: Place cake (or mini cakes) in an airtight container. Freeze for up to 3 days. Let stand at room temperature about 20 minutes before serving for cake or 5 to 10 minutes for mini cakes. Store Pound Cake Fries in an airtight container at room temperature for up to 3 days.

PER SERVING: *470 cal., 21 g fat (8 g sat. fat), 81 mg chol., 357 mg sodium, 69 g carb., 1 g fiber, 6 g pro.*

Pound Cake Fries: Thaw one 10.75-ounce loaf frozen pound cake. Preheat oven to 400°F. Line a large baking sheet with foil; lightly coat foil with nonstick cooking spray. Using a crinkle cutter or sharp knife, cut cake crosswise into ¼-inch slices. Cut each slice lengthwise into three sticks. Spread pound cake sticks on the prepared baking sheet. In a small bowl stir together 1 tablespoon sugar and ⅛ teaspoon ground cinnamon. Lightly coat pound cake sticks with nonstick cooking spray; sprinkle with cinnamon-sugar. Bake for 8 to 10 minutes or until light brown and crisp; cool.

Make It Mini

Use brick-style ice cream. Grease twenty-four 2½-inch muffin cups. Prepare cake batter as directed. Spoon batter into prepared muffin cups. Bake in 350°F oven for 18 to 22 minutes or until a toothpick inserted in centers comes out clean. Cool cupcakes in muffin cups on wire racks for 5 minutes. Remove from pans; cool on wire racks. (Set aside 4 cupcakes for another use.) Slice remaining cupcakes in half horizontally. Brush tops with water; top with sprinkles to resemble sesame seeds. Place bottom and top halves on a baking sheet. Freeze until firm. Slice ice cream ½ inch thick. Working in batches to prevent the circles from melting and using a 2½-inch round cookie cutter, cut 20 circles from ice cream. Place ice cream on a baking sheet; freeze. Tint coconut as directed. Roll fondant to a 10×8-inch rectangle. Cut fondant into twenty 2-inch squares. To assemble cupcakes, place ice cream rounds on bottom halves of cupcakes, trimming ice cream if necessary. Top with fondant cheese, coconut, and cupcake tops. Freeze 1 hour or until firm. If desired, serve with Pound Cake Fries.

Dragon Cake

START TO FINISH: **3 hours**
MAKES: **12 servings**

  1 recipe Yellow Cake (see page 119) or Chocolate Cake (see page 121)
  4 cups Creamy White Frosting (see page 148)
     Red or green paste food coloring
 13 large marshmallows
     Nonstick cooking spray
  1 tiny marshmallow
  2 miniature semisweet chocolate pieces
  2 semisweet chocolate pieces
  6 red or green fruit gel candy slices
  2 red or green rolled fruit leathers
  2 long skinny crisp breadsticks
     Black shoestring licorice

1. Preheat oven to 350°F. Grease and flour a 10-inch fluted tube pan. Prepare batter for cake recipe as directed. Spread batter evenly into prepared pan. Bake for 40 to 45 minutes (45 to 50 minutes for Chocolate Cake) or until a wooden toothpick inserted in center comes out clean. Cool in pan on a wire rack for 15 minutes. Remove cake from pan Cool thoroughly.
2. Slice a one-third crosswise section piece from the cake. Place remaining cake on a large platter. Connect the small piece to the large piece in an S shape. For the head, use a serrated knife to round off one end. Taper the remaining end to resemble a tail. Freeze until firm.

3. Tint the frosting red or green with food coloring. Pipe or spread icing on frozen cake to cover.
4. For each of the legs, stack 2 large marshmallows and press into the side of frosted cake. Cover the marshmallow legs with more red frosting.
5. For dragon teeth, use kitchen shears coated with cooking spray to cut a slice from top of a large marshmallow. Cut the slice almost in half. Spread the slice open and cut notches along the cut edges to make little triangle teeth that are in a row. Press teeth onto face of dragon. Repeat with remaining large marshmallows to make claws.
6. For eyes, cut the tiny marshmallow in half and place, cut sides out, on dragon face. Attach miniature chocolate pieces to tiny marshmallow halves. For nose, insert 2 chocolate pieces upside down on dragon's snout. Place citrus slice candies on the dragon's back for scales.
7. For each wing, unroll a fruit leather. Lay a breadstick on top diagonally, with one end extending beyond fruit leather. Fold square in half to make a triangle. Trim fruit leather to scallop. If desired, pleat the wing. Insert breadstick end into cake to attach the wing to dragon's back. Attach small pieces of shoestring licorice above the eyes for eyebrows.

To Store: Cover and store at room temperature for up to 3 days.

PER SERVING: *811 cal., 36 g fat (14 g sat. fat), 79 mg chol., 331 mg sodium, 117 g carb., 1 g fiber, 6 g pro.*

How to Shape the Dragon

Believe it or not, a few cuts with a serrated knife can turn a cake baked in a standard fluted tube pan into a twisty, snakey, fire-breathing dragon.

1. Use a serrated knife to cut the flat side of the cake even.

2. Cut off and remove one-third of cake.

3. Attach the one-third piece to create an S shape.

4. Use a serrated knife to round off the head and tail ends of the cake.

Pick-a-Sport Cupcakes

START TO FINISH: 2 hours
MAKES: 12 cupcakes

2¾ cups Creamy White Frosting
     (see page 148) or canned
     creamy white frosting
     Green food coloring
12   2½-inch cupcakes in paper
     bake cups (any flavor)
 1   cup white candy coating
     disks (see tip, page 166)
12   plain doughnut holes
     Red food coloring

1. In a medium bowl tint 2 cups of the Creamy White Frosting with green food coloring to make a grass color. Place frosting in a pastry bag fitted with a star tip or multiopening (grass) tip. Pipe frosting onto cupcakes to resemble grass.

2. For baseballs, in a small microwave-safe bowl microwave white candy coating disks on 100 percent power (high) for 1 minute. Stir; microwave for 30 to 60 seconds more or until melted, stirring once. Using a fork, dip the doughnut holes, one at a time, into melted candy coating, turning to coat completely. Place on waxed paper until set.

Baseball Cupcakes: Tint the remaining ¾ cup Creamy White Frosting red. Place frosting in a pastry bag fitted with a round tip. Pipe Xs onto doughnut holes to resemble the stitching on baseballs. Place a doughnut hole on each cupcake.

To Store: Place cupcakes in a covered container. Store at room temperature for up to 3 days.

PER CUPCAKE: *500 cal., 25 g fat (10 g sat. fat), 47 mg chol., 168 mg sodium, 66 g carb., 0 g fiber, 4 g pro.*

Soccer Ball Cupcakes: Soften a log-shape chocolate caramel candy in the microwave on 100 percent power (high) for 5 seconds. Use a rolling pin to flatten softened candy. Cut out small squares using aspic cutters. Arrange squares on coated doughnut holes, using white frosting to secure.

Basketball Cupcakes: Prepare as directed, except substitute orange candy coating disks for the white candy coating disks. Use a tube of chocolate icing to pipe lines onto coated doughnut holes to resemble basketballs.

PER SOCCER BALL OR BASKETBALL CUPCAKE: *495 cal., 24 g fat, (10 g sat. fat), 47 mg chol., 165 mg sodium, 66 g carb., 0 g fiber, 4 g pro.*

Zoo Animal Cupcakes

START TO FINISH: 2½ hours
MAKES: 12 cupcakes

- 2 cups Creamy White Frosting (see page 148) or one 16-ounce can creamy white frosting
  Black, yellow, and orange food colorings
- 1 cup Chocolate Butter Frosting (see page 148) or canned chocolate frosting
- 12 2½-inch cupcakes in paper bake cups (any flavor)
  Pink chewy fruit-flavor square candies, such as Starburst
- 12 miniature peanut butter sandwich cookies, such as Nutter Butter Bites
- 12 candy-coated milk chocolate pieces
- 8 miniature semisweet chocolate pieces
- 1 tube black icing
- 4 gummy worms
- 8 miniature pretzels
- 8 white candy-coated licorice candy, such as Good & Plenty
- 8 round oat cereal pieces, such as Cheerios
- 4 bite-size rich round crackers, such as Ritz Bits
- 8 miniature candy-coated chocolate pieces
- 4 miniature chocolate sandwich cookies with white filling
- 4 black jelly beans
- 8 black candy-coated sunflower kernels

1. Divide Creamy White Frosting into three portions. Use food colorings to tint one portion gray and one portion yellow; leave the remaining frosting white. Place some of the Chocolate Butter Frosting in a pastry bag fitted with a round tip. Place some of the white frosting in a separate pastry bag fitted with a round tip.

2. For monkey cupcakes, frost tops of three cupcakes with chocolate frosting. For ears, microwave a fruit-flavor square candy on 100 percent power (high) for 7 seconds; flatten candy. Cut out small candy rounds and attach to miniature peanut butter cookies with frosting. Press ears into frosting on opposite sides of each cupcake top. Place a cookie in center of each cupcake for mouth and nose. For eyes, place 2 candy-coated chocolate pieces on cupcake top; pipe a white frosting dot on each and top with miniature semisweet chocolate pieces. Pipe chocolate frosting for mouth and nose.

3. For elephant cupcakes, frost tops of 3 cupcakes with gray frosting. Pipe white frosting dots for eyes and top with a dot of black icing. In a microwave-safe bowl microwave some of the gray frosting on 100 percent power (high) for 10 seconds or until melted. Trim gummy worms to appropriate size for trunks (if they're too long, they may be heavy and fall off). Dip gummy worms in melted gray frosting, letting excess drip off. Place on waxed paper. For ears, dip pretzels in melted gray frosting, letting excess drip off; place on waxed paper. For pink on elephant

ears, microwave and flatten chewy fruit-flavor square candy as in Step 2. Using pretzel as a guide, cut outlines from candy. Press candy outlines into frosting on back side of each pretzel. Chill gummy worms and pretzels for about 5 minutes or until set. Arrange trunks on cupcakes. Stick white candy-coated licorice into frosting for tusks. Press ears into frosting on each cupcake top.

4. For lion cupcakes, frost tops of 3 cupcakes with yellow frosting. Tint half of the remaining yellow frosting orange. Spoon orange frosting along one side of a pastry bag fitted with a multiopening tip (see tip, page 166). Spoon yellow frosting along the other side of the pastry bag. Pipe frostings around edge of each cupcake for mane. Add oat cereal for ears. Pipe white frosting dots for eyes; top each dot with miniature candy-coated chocolate pieces. Place a rich round cracker in center of each cupcake; attach a candy-coated chocolate piece for nose. Pipe chocolate frosting for mouth.

5. For panda cupcakes, frost the tops of 3 cupcakes with white frosting. Split miniature chocolate sandwich cookies in half; press cookie halves into frosting for ears. Arrange jelly bean and sunflower kernels on cupcakes for nose and eyes. Pipe chocolate or black icing for mouth.

PER CUPCAKE: *490 cal., 22 g fat (9 g sat. fat), 50 mg chol., 164 mg sodium, 72 g carb., 1 g fiber, 3 g pro.*

Butterfly Cake

START TO FINISH: 1½ hours
MAKES: 12 servings

1 recipe Yellow Cake (see page 119), White Cake (see page 114), Chocolate Cake (see page 121), or other 2-layer-size cake recipe
1 10.75-ounce frozen pound cake, thawed, or 2 cream-filled sponge cakes*
1 recipe Creamy White Frosting (see page 148)
  Colored sugars
  Desired color paste food coloring
  Candy-coated licorice pieces, fruit-flavored jelly pieces, and/or pastel tiny marshmallows
2 pieces black shoestring licorice (see below)
2 candy eyes (see below) or miniature semisweet chocolate pieces (optional)

1. Prepare, bake, and cool cake as directed for two 8- or 9-inch round cake pans.
2. For butterfly body, use a serrated knife to cut pound cake into shape of a body. Frost with some of the Creamy White Frosting. Sprinkle with stripes of alternating colors of sugars. Place in center of platter.
3. Stack the two round cake layers together, spreading ½ cup frosting between layers. Cut the stacked cake in half crosswise.
4. For butterfly wings, arrange a cake half on each side of the frosted body, with the flat side facing out. Using a serrated knife, cut a small notch from the center of the straight side of each cake half. Tint the remaining frosting as desired with paste food coloring. Frost sides and tops of wing pieces. Decorate with symmetrically placed candies.

5. Cut two 2-inch pieces of shoestring licorice for antennae and insert into top end of butterfly body. If desired, add candy eyes.

*Test Kitchen Tip: If using cream-filled sponge cakes, sandwich cakes together with frosting, flat sides together. Spread with frosting and decorate as directed in Step 2.

To Store: Cover and store at room temperature for up to 3 days.

PER SERVING: *679 cal., 31 g fat (13 g sat. fat), 83 mg chol., 348 mg sodium, 96 g carb., 1 g fiber, 6 g pro.*

Stocking Up on Supplies

The best place to find cake decorating supplies is in the cake decorating department of hobby and crafts stores, such as Hobby Lobby and Michael's. There you can find pastry bags, tips, and couplers; a full color palette of paste food coloring; special sprinkles, sugars, and candies (such as the candy eyes and shoestring licorice for the butterfly); candy coating disks; frosting spatulas; rolled fondant; and much more. You can also visit *wilton*.com to purchase many of these items online.

Gumball Machine Cake

START TO FINISH: **2 hours**
MAKES: **24 servings**

- 2 recipes Yellow Cake (see page 119), Chocolate Cake (see page 121), or other desired 2-layer-size cake recipe
- 2 cups Creamy White Frosting (see page 148)
  Red food coloring
- 2 cups Chocolate Butter Frosting (see page 148) or purchased chocolate frosting
- ¾ cup large round candies or gumballs
- 1 thin chocolate square (Ghirardelli squares)
- 1 scoop-shape corn chip
  Decorating sugar (optional)

1. Prepare, bake, and cool one cake as directed for a 13×9-inch cake. Prepare, bake, and cool the remaining cake as directed, dividing batter between one 8×1½-inch round cake pan and one 8×8×2-inch square cake pan. Trim square cake into a 6-inch-wide rectangle. Trim one of the remaining ends into a curve shape that will fit against the round cake. Set aside.

2. Tint 1 cup Creamy White Frosting with red food coloring. Place the 13×9-inch cake upside down on serving platter and cover smoothly with the Chocolate Butter Frosting. Place round cake layer at one end of frosted 13×9-inch cake. Frost round cake with 1 cup white Creamy White Frosting. Place the cake rectangle under round cake and frost smoothly with red frosting.

3. Arrange round candies on the round cake, keeping them close together to look like gumballs in the machine. Add chocolate square to the gumball base to look like the gumball slot (if desired, carve "25 cents" on chocolate bar with a toothpick). Insert the large corn chip scoop above the chocolate square for the gumball dispenser. Place a round candy in the scoop (if necessary, use a small dab of frosting to secure the candy to the corn chip). If desired, sprinkle edge of round cake with decorating sugar.

To Store: Loosely cover cake and store at room temperature for up to 3 days.

PER SERVING: *498 cal., 22 g fat (11 g sat. fat), 86 mg chol., 330 mg sodium, 70 g carb., 1 g fiber, 6 g pro.*

How to Shape the Gumball Machine

To make this classic design, start with three cakes: a 13×9-inch, a round 8-inch, and a square 8-inch. Make a few simple cuts with a serrated knife and then assemble as shown below.

1. Trim the 8-inch square cake into a 6-inch-wide rectangle.

2. Cut a curve shape into one of the narrow ends to fit it against the 8-inch round cake.

3. Place the round cake and the trimmed square cake on the 13×9-inch cake.

Lollipop Cake

START TO FINISH: **3 hours**
MAKES: **12 servings**

- 1 recipe Yellow Cake (see page 119) or other 2-layer-size cake recipe or cake mix
- 1 recipe Creamy White Frosting (see page 148), Butter Frosting (see page 148), or 2½ cups purchased creamy white frosting
- 1 16-ounce box rolled fondant (see tip, page 166)
  Pink, blue, green, yellow, and purple paste food coloring
  Powdered Sugar
  Coarse sugar
- ¼ cup white candy coating disks (see tip, page 166)
- 1 pretzel rod
  Nonpareils

1. Prepare, bake, and cool cake as directed for two 8-inch round layers. Fill and frost layers with Creamy White Frosting.
2. For fondant lollipop, divide fondant into five portions. Wearing plastic or rubber gloves, knead one color paste food coloring into one portion of fondant.* Repeat with the remaining paste food colors and fondant portions.
3. Lightly dust work surface with powdered sugar. On the surface, roll fondant portions, one at a time, into 2-foot-long ropes. Brush ropes with a little water; press ropes together to make one rope. Roll the rope until sides are smooth. Twist the rope to twist colors together and continue rolling until rope is 6 feet long and about ¾ inch thick. (Or cut the rope in half and roll each half into a 3-foot-long rope.) On a baking sheet coil the rope (or ropes) to make an 8-inch circle. Slide the fondant circle from the baking sheet to the top of the cake, positioning the circle to cover the cake. Trim end of fondant rope so lollipop fits on top of cake. Sprinkle with coarse sugar.
4. Place candy coating in a small microwave-safe bowl. Microwave on 100 percent power (high) for 30 seconds. Stir; microwave for 20 to 30 seconds more or until melted. Hold the pretzel rod over a bowl and spoon melted candy coating over pretzel to cover, allowing excess to drip into bowl. While coating is still wet, decorate with nonpareils. Place on waxed paper until set. If desired, tie a ribbon on the coated pretzel. Insert pretzel into cake for lollipop stick. If desired, remove fondant lollipop before serving.

***Test Kitchen Tip:** If necessary, microwave fondant, one portion at a time, on 100 percent power (high) for 5 to 10 seconds or until fondant is pliable.

To Store: Cover cake with plastic wrap to keep fondant from drying out. Store at room temperature for up to 24 hours.

PER SERVING: *814 cal., 32 g fat (13 g sat. fat), 79 mg chol., 326 mg sodium, 128 g carb., 1 g fiber, 5 g pro.*

How to Shape Lollipop Swirls

While the process of making the lollipop swirl isn't difficult, it will take some time to complete (especially if you haven't worked with fondant before). Just take it slowly, one step at a time, and you'll be impressed with the results. Wear plastic gloves when kneading food coloring into the fondant pieces because it can stain your hands.

1. After kneading food coloring into pieces of fondant, roll each portion into a 2-foot-long rope.

2. Brush the ropes with a little bit of water, then stack and press ropes together.

3. Begin rolling the ropes together to create one long rope, rolling evenly from end to end to keep the rope a uniform thickness.

4. Continue rolling until rope is smooth and about 6 feet long. (Or, as the rope gets longer, cut it in half and roll halves separately.)

Chocolate-Berry Wreath Cake

PREP: **1 hour**
BAKE: **35 minutes at 350°F**
COOL: **1 hour**
MAKES: **12 servings**

1 tablespoon unsweetened cocoa powder
1½ cups all-purpose flour
1 cup sugar
½ cup unsweetened cocoa powder
1 tablespoon instant espresso coffee powder (optional)
1 teaspoon baking soda
½ teaspoon salt
2 eggs, lightly beaten
1 cup water
⅓ cup canola oil or vegetable oil
1 tablespoon cider vinegar or white vinegar
1 teaspoon vanilla
1 recipe Creamy Chocolate Frosting (see page 174)
1 to 2 cups assorted berries, such as blueberries, raspberries, blackberries, and/or small strawberries
2 tablespoons strawberry jelly
1 recipe White Chocolate Bow(s) (see page 174)

1. Preheat oven to 350°F. Grease a 9×2-inch round cake pan or a 9×9×2-inch baking pan. Sprinkle 1 tablespoon cocoa powder in pan. Shake and tilt pan to coat bottom and sides; shake out any excess cocoa powder. Set pan aside. In a large mixing bowl stir together flour, sugar, ½ cup cocoa powder, the espresso powder (if desired), baking soda, and salt; set aside.
2. In a medium bowl combine eggs, the water, oil, vinegar, and vanilla. Gradually add egg mixture to flour mixture, beating with an electric mixer on low speed just until combined. Beat on medium speed for 2 minutes, scraping sides of bowl occasionally.
3. Pour batter into the prepared pan, spreading evenly. Bake for 35 to 40 minutes or until a wooden toothpick inserted in the center comes out clean. Cool in pan on a wire rack for 10 minutes. Remove cake from pan; cool completely on wire rack.
4. Frost top and sides of cake with Creamy Chocolate Frosting. Arrange berries around edge of cake to resemble a wreath. Heat strawberry jelly until melted; brush evenly over berries. Place one or more White Chocolate Bow(s) on berry wreath.

Make It Mini

Preheat oven to 350°F. Line sixteen 2½-inch muffin cups with paper bake cups. Prepare cake batter as directed. Spoon batter into prepared muffin cups, filling each about two-thirds full. Use the back of a spoon to smooth out batter in cups. Bake for 15 to 18 minutes or until a wooden toothpick inserted in centers comes out clean. Cool cupcakes in muffin cups on wire racks for 5 minutes. Remove cupcakes from muffin cups. Cool completely on wire racks. Spread cupcakes with Creamy Chocolate Frosting. Arrange blueberries, raspberries, blackberries, or cut-up strawberries around edges of cupcakes to resemble wreaths. Heat strawberry jelly until melted; brush evenly over berries. Place a White Chocolate Bow on each cupcake wreath. Makes 16 cupcakes.

continued on page 174

continued from page 173

Creamy Chocolate Frosting: Heat ¼ cup milk chocolate pieces until melted; cool slightly. In a medium mixing bowl beat 3 tablespoons softened butter with an electric mixer on medium speed until smooth. Beat in melted chocolate. Gradually add 1 cup powdered sugar, beating well. Slowly beat in 2 tablespoons milk and 1 teaspoon vanilla. Gradually beat in 1½ cups additional powdered sugar. Beat in enough additional milk to reach spreading consistency.

White Chocolate Bow(s): Line a small baking sheet with waxed paper or parchment paper; set aside. In a small saucepan heat and stir 1 ounce chopped white baking chocolate with cocoa butter or vanilla-flavor candy coating (¼ cup) over low heat until melted and smooth. If desired, place melted white chocolate in a pastry bag fitted with a small round tip. Pipe white chocolate onto the prepared baking sheet to form one 3- to 4-inch bow or 16 small bows. Let stand until set (if necessary, chill in refrigerator until set). Carefully lift bow(s) off paper.

To Store: Loosely cover cake and store in the refrigerator for up to 1 day.

PER SERVING: *281 cal., 10 g fat (3 g sat. fat), 31 mg chol., 187 mg sodium, 49 g carb., 2 g fiber, 3 g pro.*

Easy Chocolate Chunk-Cherry Cake: Prepare as directed through Step 2, except stir ¾ cup maraschino cherries, drained, patted dry, and chopped, and ½ cup dark chocolate pieces into batter. Continue as directed.

PER SERVING: *457 cal., 17 g fat (7 g sat. fat), 41 mg chol., 254 mg sodium, 76 g carb., 3 g fiber, 5 g pro.*

How to Make a Chocolate Bow

Place the melted white chocolate in a pastry bag fitted with a small round tip. (Or fill a heavy-duty resealable plastic bag with the melted white chocolate; snip a small hole in one corner of the bag.) Pipe the melted white chocolate onto waxed paper in bow shapes. Allow bows to harden before gently lifting them from the waxed paper and placing on the cake or cupcakes.

Strawberry Santa Cake

START TO FINISH: 1½ hours
MAKES: 8 servings

- 1 recipe Yellow Cake (see page 119) or desired cake recipe
- 1 recipe Whipped Sour Cream Frosting (see page 149)
- 2 cups fresh whole strawberries, tops removed (one top reserved)
- 2 small blue candies

1. Prepare, bake, and cool Yellow Cake as directed for 8-inch round layers. Reserve 1 cup whipped Sour Cream Frosting for piping. Place a cake layer on a plate. Spread cake top with some of the remaining frosting. Add the second cake layer; frost cake top and sides.

2. Set aside 1 strawberry. For the hat, arrange remaining strawberries on the top one-third of the cake. Place reserved frosting in a pastry bag fitted with an extra-large star tip. Pipe an edge and pom-pom onto hat. Pipe eyebrows, mustache, and beard onto cake. Cut the tip and two slices from the remaining strawberry; place tip on cake for a nose. Place the slices on cake for cheeks. Cut pieces from the reserved green strawberry top; use for eyelashes. Before serving, add blue candies for eyes.

To Store: Loosely cover and store in the refrigerator for up to 2 days.

PER SERVING: *517 cal., 34 g fat (21 g sat. fat), 146 mg chol., 258 mg sodium, 49 g carb., 1 g fiber, 6 g pro.*

How to Pipe

The two must-have tools for this cake are a pastry bag and an extra-large star tip (see tip, page 166). These are used to create the pom-pom and edge for the hat, as well as the eyebrows, mustache, and beard. If you are a beginner at piping from a pastry bag, practice your technique on a piece of waxed paper. You can scrape the frosting from the waxed paper back into the bag when you're ready to try out your skills on the actual cake.

Spiderweb Cake

START TO FINISH: 2½ hours
BAKE: 20 minutes at 350°F
MAKES: 24 servings

1 recipe Yellow Cake (see page
   119), Chocolate Cake (see
   page 121), or other 2-layer-
   size cake recipe
2 recipes Creamy White
   Frosting* (see page 148)
   or Butter Frosting* (see
   page 148)
   Orange paste food coloring
   Black paste food coloring
2 2½-inch baked cupcakes
1 1¾-inch baked cupcake
3 tiny marshmallows
6 edible black pearl candies
   (see tip, page 166) or other
   tiny black candies
24 pieces black shoestring
   licorice (see tip, page 166)
   Desired paste food
   coloring(s)

1. Prepare, bake, and cool Yellow Cake as directed for 8-inch round layers.
2. Tint one recipe Creamy White Frosting with orange food coloring. Place one cake layer on a serving plate. Spread top of cake with orange frosting. Add second layer; spread top and sides with additional orange frosting. If desired, spoon some of the orange frosting into a decorating bag fitted with a small round tip; pipe a border around bottom of cake. Remove 1 cup of the remaining recipe of frosting and tint with black food coloring.** Spoon black frosting into a decorating bag fitted with a coupler and a small round tip. Pipe frosting in a spiderweb pattern over top and sides of cake.
3. For spiders, cut the rounded tops off two large cupcakes and one mini cupcake. Place one large cupcake top and the mini cupcake top on cake; place the remaining large cupcake top on plate. Change decorating tip on the bag of black frosting to a small star tip. Pipe stars of black frosting onto tops of cupcakes to cover completely. For eyes,

cut marshmallows in half crosswise; use a small amount of frosting to attach a black candy pearl to each marshmallow half. Place eyes on spider cakes. Attach 8 licorice pieces to each spider cake for legs. For spiders on cake, secure ends of legs in frosting. For spider on plate, use small dabs of black frosting to secure legs to plate.

*Test Kitchen Tip: You will have frosting left over. Cover and refrigerate for another use.

**Test Kitchen Tip: To reduce the amount of black paste food coloring needed, stir in some cocoa powder before tinting the frosting black.

To Store: Loosely cover cake and store at room temperature for up to 3 days.

PER SERVING: *649 cal., 31 g fat (12 g sat. fat), 79 mg chol., 308 mg sodium, 90 g carb., 1 g fiber, 5 g pro.*

Devil's Food Cake

PREP: **40 minutes**
BAKE: **30 minutes at 350°F**
COOL: **1 hour**
MAKES: **12 servings**

2¼ cups all-purpose flour
½ cup unsweetened cocoa powder
1½ teaspoons baking powder
1 teaspoon baking soda
½ teaspoon ground cinnamon (optional)
¼ teaspoon salt
½ cup shortening
1¾ cups sugar
1 teaspoon vanilla
3 eggs
1⅓ cups cold water
2 ounces semisweet chocolate pieces
¼ cup whipping cream
1 tablespoon butter
1 teaspoon light-color corn syrup
1 recipe Cocoa-Cream Cheese Frosting (see page 149)

1. Preheat oven to 350°F. Grease and lightly flour two 9×1½-inch round cake pans or one 13×9×2-inch baking pan; set pan(s) aside. In a medium bowl stir together flour, cocoa powder, baking powder, baking soda, cinnamon (if desired), and salt; set aside.
2. In a large mixing bowl beat the shortening with an electric mixer on medium to high speed for 30 seconds. Add sugar and vanilla; beat until well combined. Add eggs, one at a time, beating well after each. Add the flour mixture and water alternately to beaten mixture, beating on low speed after each addition just until combined. Spoon batter into prepared pan(s), spreading evenly.
3. Bake for 30 to 40 minutes or until a wooden toothpick inserted near the center(s) comes out clean. Cool layer cakes in pan on wire racks for 10 minutes. Remove from pans. Cool thoroughly on wire racks. Or place 13×9-inch cake in pan on a wire rack; cool thoroughly.
4. For glaze, in a heavy saucepan combine chocolate pieces, whipping cream, butter, and corn syrup. Heat and stir over low heat until chocolate begins to melt. Cook, uncovered, for 2 minutes more. Remove from heat. Cool to room temperature.
5. Frost tops and sides of layers or top of 13×9×2-inch cake with frosting, reserving 1 cup of frosting to make chocolate drops. Place glaze in a heavy resealable plastic bag. Snip off a very small piece from one corner of the bag. Pipe glaze in crisscross lines on top of cake. Spoon reserved frosting into a pastry bag fitted with a round tip. Pipe chocolate "drops" around base of cake.

To Store: Store in a covered container in the refrigerator for up to 3 days.

PER SERVING: *707 cal., 29 g fat (14 g sat. fat), 104 mg chol., 359 mg sodium, 107 g carb., 1 g fiber, 7 g pro.*

Make It Mini

Preheat oven to 350°F. Line twenty-four to thirty 2½-inch muffin cups with paper bake cups. Prepare batter as directed. Spoon batter into prepared muffin cups, filling each one-half to two-thirds full. Use the back of a spoon to smooth out batter in cups. Bake for 15 to 17 minutes or until a wooden toothpick inserted in centers comes out clean. Cool cupcakes in muffin cups on wire racks for 5 minutes. Remove cupcakes from muffin cups. Cool completely on wire racks. Prepare glaze and frosting as directed. To assemble, spread cupcakes with frosting, reserving 1 cup frosting to make chocolate drops. Drizzle frosted cupcakes with glaze. Fill a pastry bag fitted with small round tip with the reserved frosting. Pipe drops of frosting around the edges of the cupcakes. Cover and chill any remaining frosting for another use. Makes 24 to 30 cupcakes.

Ghost Cake

START TO FINISH: **2 hours**
MAKES: **12 servings**

 1 recipe White Cake (see
page 114), Yellow Cake (see
page 119), Chocolate Cake
(see page 121), or other
2-layer-size cake recipe
⅓ cup chocolate-flavor candy
coating disks
Chocolate jimmies
 1 recipe Meringue Frosting
(see page 149)
Black pearl sprinkles or tiny
black candies

1. Prepare, bake, and cool cake as directed for 8- or 9-inch layers.
2. For trees, line a large baking sheet with waxed paper. In a small microwave-safe bowl microwave candy coating on 100 percent power (high) for 30 seconds. Stir; microwave for 20 to 30 seconds more or until completely melted. Place in a heavy resealable plastic bag; seal. Snip off a small piece from one corner. On the prepared baking sheet, pipe 7 to 8 leafless trees, each 2 to 3 inches tall (make them thick so they won't break when hardened). Sprinkle trees with chocolate jimmies before candy coating sets. Chill until set.

3. Prepare Meringue Frosting. Fill and frost cake with some of the Meringue Frosting.
4. For ghosts, spoon remaining Meringue Frosting into a pastry bag fitted with a large round tip. Pipe frosting in mounds on top of cake. Arrange 2 candies on each ghost for eyes.
5. To serve, carefully peel trees from waxed paper. Press trees into frosting on sides of cake.

To Store: Loosely cover cake and store in the refrigerator for up to 24 hours.

PER SERVING: *410 cal., 10 g fat (6 g sat. fat), 21 mg chol., 310 mg sodium, 76 g carb., 1 g fiber, 5 g pro.*

How to Make Chocolate Trees

To pipe melted chocolate, a reseable plastic bag (with a corner snipped off) is recommended. Cleanup is a breeze—just throw away the bag. Or use a pastry bag fitted with a very small round tip.

1. Pipe melted candy coating onto waxed paper. If desired, sprinkle with chocolate jimmies.

2. Chill trees until set. Lift carefully from the waxed paper, being careful not to break the fragile trees.

Black and White Bows

START TO FINISH: **2 hours**
MAKES: **24 cupcakes**

- 4 ounces vanilla candy coating, coarsely chopped
- ¼ cup light-color corn syrup
- 4 ounces dark cocoa candy coating disks (see tip, page 166)
- 1 recipe Bittersweet Chocolate Ganache
- 12 2½-inch chocolate cupcakes in paper bake cups
- 1 recipe White Chocolate Ganache Frosting
- 12 2½-inch white cupcakes in paper bake cups
  Powdered sugar

1. For white clay, place vanilla candy coating in a microwave-safe dish. Microwave on 100 percent power (high) for 1 to 2 minutes or until melted, stirring once. Stir in 2 tablespoons of the corn syrup. Spoon onto plastic wrap. Cover and let stand for at least 1 hour or until cooled and firm. For chocolate clay, repeat with dark cocoa candy melts and the remaining 2 tablespoons corn syrup. When firm, unwrap and knead each mixture separately until smooth and pliable. Wrap each in plastic wrap; set aside.
2. Spoon Bittersweet Chocolate Ganache over chocolate cupcakes and White Chocolate Ganache Frosting over white cupcakes. Chill until firm.
3. Between separate sheets of waxed paper dusted with powdered sugar, roll out white clay and chocolate clay to ⅛-inch thickness. Using a pastry wheel, pizza cutter, or knife, cut clay into 1-inch-wide strips about 5 inches long. For each bow, bring ends of a strip together, making a double thickness. Turn upside down, with the seam underneath. Gently pinch in center. Trim scraps of clay into ribbon tails and center knots. Place two tails on top of each cupcake; top with a bow.

Bittersweet Chocolate Ganache: In a medium saucepan heat ½ cup whipping cream over medium heat just until boiling. Remove from heat. Add 6 ounces chopped bittersweet chocolate (do not stir). Let stand for 5 minutes. Whisk until smooth. Cool about 15 minutes or until thickened, stirring occasionally.

White Chocolate Ganache Frosting: In a small saucepan melt 2 ounces white baking chocolate with cocoa butter over low heat. Remove from heat. Stir in ¾ cup Creamy White Frosting (see page 148) or canned creamy white frosting. If necessary, stir in 1 tablespoon milk to make frosting smooth.

To Store: Place cupcakes in a covered container. Store in the refrigerator for up to 2 days.

PER CUPCAKE: 358 cal., 20 g fat (12 g sat. fat), 76 mg chol., 175 mg sodium, 44 g carb., 1 g fiber, 4 g pro.

How to Make a Chocolate Bow

These pretty bows are created from edible clay, each made from a different color of candy coating combined with corn syrup. Here's how to shape bows in four easy steps.

1. For each bow, bring the two ends of a strip of candy coating mixture together in the center.

2. Turn bow so the seam side is down. Pinch the two sides together in the center.

3. Cut a short, narrow piece from the scraps to use for the center knot. Wrap the piece over the top of the bow; trim as necessary.

4. Cut two tails for the bow. Assemble the pieces together on the tops of cupcakes.

Apple Pie, recipe page 186

pies & tarts

TAKE COMFORT IN WARM, HOMEBAKED PIES that feature seasonal fruits, sweet custards, tender crusts, billowy meringues, or buttery streusel toppings. With a handful of easy techniques and a little practice, you'll master the art of pie making in no time. Start with our classic recipe for an all-time American favorite—Apple Pie.

Apple Pie

For the most flavorful pie, use a mixture of sweet and tart apples. Choose baking varieties such as Granny Smith, Cortland, and Braeburn, that hold their shape and maintain texture.

PREP: 30 minutes
BAKE: 1 hour at 375°F
COOL: 2 hours
MAKES: 8 servings

- 1 recipe Pastry for Double-Crust Pie
- ¾ cup sugar
- 2 tablespoons all-purpose flour
- ½ teaspoon ground cinnamon
- ⅛ teaspoon ground nutmeg
- 6 cups thinly sliced, peeled cooking apples (about 2¼ pounds)
- 1 tablespoon lemon juice (optional)
- ⅓ cup dried cranberries (optional)
  Milk (optional)
  Sugar (optional)

1. Preheat oven to 375°F. Prepare Pastry for Double-Crust Pie. On a lightly floured surface, slightly flatten one portion of dough. Roll dough from center to edge into a circle about 12 inches in diameter. Wrap pastry circle around the rolling pin. Unroll into a 9-inch pie plate. Ease pastry into pie plate without stretching it. Set aside.
2. For filling, in a large bowl stir together the ¾ cup sugar, the flour, cinnamon, and nutmeg. If desired, sprinkle apples with lemon juice. Add apple slices and, if desired, cranberries to sugar mixture. Gently toss until coated. Transfer filling to pastry-lined pie plate. Trim pastry edge to edge of pie plate.
3. Roll the remaining dough portion into a 12-inch circle. Cut slits in pastry to allow steam to escape. Place pastry circle on filling; trim pastry to ½ inch beyond edge of pie plate. Fold top pastry edge under bottom pastry. Crimp edge as desired. If desired, brush top crust with milk and sprinkle with additional sugar. Cover edge of pie with foil to prevent overbrowning.

4. Bake for 40 minutes. Remove foil. Bake about 20 minutes more or until fruit is tender and filling is bubbly. Cool on a wire rack. To serve warm, let pie cool at least 2 hours.

Pastry for Double-Crust Pie: In a large bowl stir together 2½ cups all-purpose flour and 1 teaspoon salt. Using a pastry blender, cut in ½ cup shortening and ¼ cup cut-up butter until pieces are pea size. Sprinkle 1 tablespoon ice water over part of the flour mixture; toss gently with a fork. Push moistened dough to side of bowl. Repeat with additional ice water, 1 tablespoon at a time (½ to ⅔ cup total), until all of the flour mixture is moistened. Gather dough into a ball, kneading gently until it holds together. Divide dough in half. Shape each portion into a ball.

To Store: Cover pie and store at room temperature for up to 24 hours or in the refrigerator for up to 2 days.

PER SERVING: *395 cal., 18 g fat (7 g sat. fat), 15 mg chol., 219 mg sodium, 57 g carb., 3 g fiber, 4 g pro.*

Secrets to Success

Yes, there is an art to making pie pastry, but it is one that will become second nature with a little know-how and practice. Measure ingredients carefully. Cut the fat (usually butter and shortening) into the flour mixture until pieces of fat are the size of peas. These pockets of fat help separate the pastry into layers as it bakes, creating tender flakiness. To keep these pieces of fat intact during mixing, the water will have to be ice cold (add a couple of ice cubes to the water before measuring) to keep the fat from melting or softening and becoming too thoroughly incorporated. When tossing in the water and later rolling out the pastry, work the mixture as little as possible. Too much manipulation will develop the gluten in the flour, making the pastry tough rather than tender and flaky.

CUT IN THE FAT Use a pastry blender (or two knives) to cut the fat into the flour mixture until it is about the size of peas.

ADD WATER Sprinkle 1 tablespoon cold water over flour mixture; toss with a fork. Move moistened mixture to one side of bowl. Repeat moistening mixture.

GATHER IN BALL Once all the flour mixture is moistened and holds together (mixture should not be wet), use your hands to gather it into a ball.

ROLL AND TRANSFER Roll pastry out on a lightly floured surface. To transfer to the pie plate, roll pastry onto the rolling pin. Ease into plate without stretching.

FILL AND TRIM Evenly distribute filling in crust. Trim pastry even with the edge of the plate after adding the filling (so it doesn't pull pastry down).

ADD THE TOP CRUST Cut steam slits in top pastry while it is on work surface. Roll pastry around the rolling pin. Unroll over the filling without stretching pastry.

TRIM THE EDGE Use kitchen scissors to trim the edge of the top pastry ½ inch beyond the rim of the plate. Fold top pastry edge under bottom pastry edge.

SEAL THE EDGE For a rope edge, pinch the pastry edge by pushing forward on a slant with your bent index finger and pulling back with your thumb.

Make-It-Mine Streusel Pie

Choose your favorite fruits, spices, nuts, and toppings to create an amazing streusel pie that's all your own.

PREP: 35 minutes
BAKE: 55 minutes at 350°F
COOL: 2 hours
MAKES: 8 servings

- 1 cup granulated sugar
  Fruit Filling (choose option)
- 2 tablespoons water
  Crust (choose option)
- ½ cup regular or quick-cooking rolled oats
- ½ cup all-purpose flour
- ⅓ cup packed dark or light brown sugar
- ½ *teaspoon Spice* (choose option)
- ¼ teaspoon salt
- ⅓ cup butter
- ¼ *cup Crunch* (choose option)
  Topping (choose option) (optional)

1. Preheat oven to 350°F. In a 4-quart Dutch oven stir together the granulated sugar and *Fruit Filling*. Gently toss until coated.
2. Add the water to filling. Cook and stir over medium heat until thickened and bubbly. Cook and stir for 2 minutes more. Set aside.
3. If using refrigerated rolled pastry or Pastry for Single-Crust Pie, line a 9-inch pie plate with *Crust*. Trim overhang to an even 1 inch all the way around. Tuck the crust under and flute the edges. Do not prick pastry.

4. For crumb topping, in a medium bowl stir together the oats, flour, brown sugar, *Spice*, and salt. Using a pastry blender, cut in butter until mixture resembles coarse crumbs. If desired, add *Crunch;* toss to mix.
5. Transfer fruit mixture to the pastry-lined pie plate. Sprinkle crumb topping over fruit mixture. To prevent overbrowning, loosely cover pie with foil.
6. Place pie on middle rack in oven; place foil-lined baking sheet on the rack beneath pie. Bake for 20 minutes. Remove foil. Bake for 35 to 45 minutes more or until filling is bubbly and crumb topping is golden brown. Cool on a wire rack for at least 2 hours before serving.

To Store: Cover pie and store at room temperature for up to 24 hours or in the refrigerator for up to 3 days.

FRUIT FILLING (PICK ONE)

Cherry: 6 cups fresh or frozen pitted tart red cherries and 3 tablespoons cornstarch
Apple: 6 cups peeled, cored, and sliced apples and 2 tablespoons all-purpose flour
Blueberry: 5 cups fresh or frozen blueberries and 3 tablespoons cornstarch

Rhubarb: 6 cups sliced rhubarb and ¼ cup cornstarch

CRUST (PICK ONE)

Purchased Piecrust: Half of a 15-ounce package rolled refrigerated unbaked piecrust (1 piecrust)
Homemade Piecrust: Pastry for Single-Crust Pie (see page 195)
Frozen Piecrust: Purchased frozen 9-inch unbaked pie shell. (Remove ½ cup fruit mixture before adding to pie shell; place the ½ cup filling in a 6-ounce custard cup and sprinkle with some of the crumb topping. Bake beside the pie for 40 minutes total.)

SPICE (PICK ONE)

Ground cinnamon
Ground ginger
Pumpkin pie spice
Apple pie spice
Ground cardamom

CRUNCH

Chopped pecans or chopped, slivered almonds
Shredded or flaked coconut

TOPPING

Powdered Sugar Icing (see page 105)
Sweetened whipped cream (see tip, page 16)
Ice cream

Maple, Apple, and Cheddar Pie

PREP: **30 minutes**
BAKE: **1 hour at 375°F**
COOL: **1 hour**
MAKES: **8 servings**

- 1 recipe Pastry for Double-Crust Pie (see page 186)
- ½ cup sugar
- 2 tablespoons all-purpose flour
- ½ teaspoon ground cinnamon
- ¼ teaspoon salt
- 5 cups thinly sliced, peeled apples (such as Jonathan or McIntosh) (5 medium)
- 1½ cups shredded white cheddar cheese (6 ounces)
- ¼ cup maple syrup
- 1 tablespoon whipping cream
- 2 tablespoons maple syrup
- ¼ cup chopped pecans, toasted (see tip, page 343) (optional)

1. Preheat oven to 375°F. Prepare Pastry for Double-Crust Pie. On a lightly floured surface, slightly flatten one portion of dough. Roll dough from center to edge into a circle about 12 inches in diameter. Wrap pastry circle around the rolling pin; unroll into a 9-inch pie plate. Ease pastry into pie plate without stretching it. Set aside.

2. For filling, in a large bowl stir together sugar, flour, cinnamon, and salt. Add apples; toss gently to coat. Add cheese and the ¼ cup maple syrup; toss gently to combine. Transfer filling to pastry-lined pie plate. Drizzle with cream. Trim pastry even with edge of pie plate.

3. Roll the remaining dough portion into a 12-inch circle. Cut slits in pastry to allow steam to escape. Place pastry circle on filling; trim pastry to ½ inch beyond edge of pie plate. Fold top pastry edge under bottom pastry.

Crimp edge as desired. Cover edge of pie with foil to prevent overbrowning.

4. Bake for 40 minutes. Remove foil. Bake about 20 minutes more or until apples are tender and pastry is golden brown. Transfer pie to a wire rack. Brush the top crust with the 2 tablespoons maple syrup. If desired, sprinkle pie with pecans. Cool for 2 hours; serve pie slightly warm.

To Store: Cover pie and store in the refrigerator for up to 2 days.

PER SERVING: *524 cal., 26 g fat (12 g sat. fat), 40 mg chol., 540 mg sodium, 63 g carb., 2 g fiber, 29 g pro.*

How to Core an Apple

If you don't have an apple corer, you can core an apple by cutting the apple into four pieces from top to bottom. Cut away the core and the stem and blossom ends. When you want whole apples—for desserts such as apple dumplings—an apple corer makes quick work of removing the core without cutting the apple into wedges.

Sweet Glazed Cherry Pie

PREP: 20 minutes
STAND: 1 hour
BAKE: 1 hour 20 minutes
at 375°F
COOL: 1 hour
MAKES: 8 servings

½ cup granulated sugar
3 tablespoons cornstarch
1 16-ounce package frozen unsweetened pitted dark sweet cherries
½ teaspoon vanilla
1 recipe Pastry for Double-Crust Pie (see page 186)*
¾ cup sliced almonds, toasted (see tip, page 343)
1 21-ounce can cherry pie filling
¼ cup powdered sugar
1 to 1½ teaspoons milk

1. In a large bowl stir together granulated sugar and cornstarch. Add frozen cherries and vanilla; toss gently to coat. Let mixture stand about 1 hour or until a syrup forms, stirring occasionally.
2. Meanwhile, preheat oven to 375°F. Prepare Pastry for Double-Crust Pie. On a lightly floured surface, slightly flatten one portion of dough. Roll dough from center to edge into a circle about 12 inches in diameter. Wrap pastry circle around the rolling pin; unroll pastry into a 9-inch pie plate. Ease pastry into pie plate without stretching it. Sprinkle ½ cup of the almonds into pastry-lined pie plate. Stir sweet cherry mixture; spoon over almonds. Top with pie filling. Trim pastry even with edge of pie plate.
3. Roll the remaining dough into a 12-inch circle. Cut slits in pastry to allow steam to escape. Place pastry circle on filling; trim pastry to ½ inch beyond edge of pie plate. Fold top pastry edge under bottom pastry. Crimp edge as desired. Cover edge of pie loosely with foil to prevent overbrowning.

4. Place pie on middle oven rack. Line a baking sheet with foil; place on bottom rack to catch any drips. Bake for 50 minutes. Remove foil from pie. Bake about 30 minutes more or until pastry is golden and filling is bubbly. Cool on a wire rack for 1 to 1½ hours.
5. For glaze, in a small bowl stir together powdered sugar and enough of the milk to make glaze drizzling consistency. Drizzle glaze over pie. Sprinkle with the remaining ¼ cup almonds. Cool completely.

***Test Kitchen Tip:** If desired, substitute one 15-ounce package rolled refrigerated unbaked piecrust (2 crusts) for the Pastry for Double-Crust Pie. Allow piecrusts to stand at room temperature before using.

To Store: Cover pie and store at room temperature for up to 24 hours or in the refrigerator for up to 2 days.

PER SERVING: *463 cal., 16 g fat (5 g sat. fat), 5 mg chol., 290 mg sodium, 75 g carb., 3 g fiber, 4 g pro.*

Fresh Strawberry Pie

PREP: **35 minutes**
BAKE: **14 minutes at 450°F**
CHILL: **1 to 3 hours**
MAKES: **8 servings**

 1 recipe Pastry for Single-
     Crust Pie
 9 cups fresh strawberries,
     hulled and halved
 ½ cup water
 ⅔ cup sugar
 2 tablespoons cornstarch
     Several drops red food
     coloring (optional)
     Sweetened whipped cream
     (see tip, page 16) (optional)

1. Preheat oven to 450°F. Prepare Pastry for Single-Crust Pie. On a lightly floured surface, use your hands to slightly flatten pastry. Roll pastry from center to edges into a circle about 12 inches in diameter. Wrap pastry circle around the rolling pin. Unroll into a 9-inch pie plate. Ease pastry into pie plate without stretching it. Trim pastry to ½ inch beyond edge of pie plate. Fold under extra pastry even with the plate edge. Crimp edge as desired. Generously prick bottom and sides of pastry with a fork. Line pastry with a double thickness of foil. Bake for 8 minutes. Remove foil. Bake for 6 to 8 minutes more or until golden. Cool on a wire rack.

2. For strawberry glaze, in a food processor or blender combine 1½ cups of the strawberries and the water. Cover and process or blend until smooth. In a medium saucepan combine sugar and cornstarch; stir in pureed strawberry mixture. Cook and stir over medium heat until mixture is thickened and bubbly. Cook and stir for 2 minutes more. If desired, stir in red food coloring. Remove from heat; cool for 10 minutes without stirring.

3. In a large bowl combine the remaining strawberries and the strawberry glaze; toss gently to coat. Transfer strawberry mixture to the cooled pie shell.

4. Chill pie for 1 to 3 hours. (After 3 hours, bottom of crust will start to soften.) If desired, serve with sweetened whipped cream.

Pastry for Single-Crust Pie: In a medium bowl stir together 1½ cups all-purpose flour and ½ teaspoon salt. Using a pastry blender, cut in ¼ cup shortening and ¼ cup butter, cut up, or shortening until the pieces are pea size. Sprinkle 1 tablespoon ice water over part of the flour mixture; toss gently with a fork. Push the moistened flour mixture to side of bowl. Repeat moistening the flour mixture, using 1 tablespoon ice water at a time, until all of the flour mixture is moistened (¼ to ⅓ cup ice water total). Gather flour mixture into a ball, kneading gently until it holds together.

PER SERVING: *316 cal., 12 g fat (5 g sat. fat), 15 mg chol., 189 mg sodium, 49 g carb., 4 g fiber, 4 g pro.*

Make It Mini

Prepare as directed, except make 2 recipes Pastry for Single-Crust Pie. For each recipe, roll pastry from center to edges into a circle about 14 inches in diameter. Cut into 3½-inch rounds, cutting 12 rounds from each pastry circle. Line twenty-four 2½-inch muffin cups with pastry. Prick pastry. Bake in the 450°F oven about 6 minutes or until golden. Cool on wire racks. Prepare filling as directed in Steps 2 and 3, except halve amounts of all ingredients and slice the strawberries. Fill pastry-lined muffin cups with filling. Chill for 1 to 3 hours. Before serving, top with sweetened whipped cream. Makes 24 mini pies.

Shaker-Style Meyer Lemon Pie

PREP: 45 minutes
CHILL: overnight
BAKE: 1 hour at 350°F
COOL: 1 hour
MAKES: 8 servings

4 Meyer lemons or lemons
2¼ cups sugar
2 tablespoons all-purpose flour
¼ teaspoon salt
5 eggs
⅓ cup milk
¼ cup butter, melted
1 recipe Pastry for Single-Crust Pie (see page 195)
1 recipe Candied Lemon Slices (optional)

1. Finely shred enough of the peel from two of the lemons to measure 2 tablespoons (see tip, page 102). Juice one or two of the lemons to measure ¼ cup juice. Cover and chill juice and peel. Peel the remaining 2 lemons, cutting away any white pith. Very thinly slice lemons crosswise. Remove seeds. Pour ½ cup of the sugar into a medium bowl. Top with lemon slices; sprinkle with another ½ cup of the sugar to cover completely. If necessary, toss gently to coat. Cover and chill overnight.

2. Preheat oven to 350°F. For filling, in a large bowl combine the remaining 1¼ cups sugar, the flour, and salt. In a medium bowl whisk together the eggs, milk, butter, and the reserved lemon juice and lemon peel. Stir the egg mixture into the flour mixture until combined. Gently fold in the chilled lemon slice-sugar mixture. Set filling aside.

3. Prepare Pastry for Single-Crust Pie. On a lightly floured surface, use your hands to slightly flatten pastry. Roll pastry from center to edge into a circle about 12 inches in diameter. Wrap pastry circle around rolling pin. Unroll into a 9-inch pie plate. Ease pastry into pie plate without stretching it. Trim pastry to ½ inch beyond edge of pie plate. Fold under extra pastry even with pie plate edge. Crimp as desired. Pour filling into pastry-lined plate. To prevent overbrowning, cover edge of pie with foil.

4. Bake for 20 minutes. Remove foil. Bake about 40 minutes more or until evenly puffed and lightly browned (filling will still be jiggly). Cool completely on a wire rack. Cover and chill within 2 hours. If desired, top pie with Candied Lemon Slices.

Candied Lemon Slices: Thinly slice one lemon and remove seeds. In a saucepan combine 1 cup sugar and 1 cup water. Cook and stir over medium-high heat until mixture begins to simmer and is clear. Reduce heat to medium. Add lemon slices; simmer for 15 to 20 minutes or until slices are softened, turning occasionally. Remove from heat; cool lemons in the saucepan. Place lemon slices on a wire rack set over waxed paper to drain. Cover loosely with waxed paper; let stand overnight to dry. If desired, dip lemon slices in sugar to coat.

To Store: Cover pie and store in refrigerator for up to 24 hours. If desired, top with Candied Lemon Slices before serving.

PER SERVING: *478 cal., 16 g fat (9 g sat. fat), 164 mg chol., 350 mg sodium, 83 g carb., 3 g fiber, 8 g pro.*

Cream-Topped Pumpkin Pie

Spirited Pumpkin Pie

Cranberry-Pecan Pumpkin Pie

Classic Pumpkin Pie

Classic Pumpkin Pie

PREP: 30 minutes
BAKE: 1 hour at 400°F
COOL: 1 hour
MAKES: 8 servings

  1 recipe Pastry for Single-
     Crust Pie (see page 195)
  1 15-ounce can pumpkin
  ¾ cup packed brown sugar
 1¼ teaspoons ground cinnamon
  1 teaspoon ground ginger
  ½ teaspoon salt
  ¼ teaspoon ground cloves
  4 eggs, lightly beaten
 1½ cups half-and-half or light
     cream
     Sweetened whipped cream
     (see tip, page 16) (optional)

1. Preheat oven to 400°F. Prepare Pastry for Single-Crust Pie. On a lightly floured surface, use your hands to slightly flatten pastry. Roll pastry from center to edges into a circle about 12 inches in diameter. Wrap pastry circle around the rolling pin. Unroll into a 9-inch pie plate. Ease pastry into pie plate without stretching it. Trim pastry to ½ inch beyond edge of pie plate. Fold under extra pastry even with the plate edge. Crimp edge as desired.* Line pastry with a double thickness of foil. Bake for 15 minutes. Remove from oven; remove foil.
2. Meanwhile, for filling, in a large bowl combine pumpkin, brown sugar, cinnamon, ginger, salt, and cloves. Add eggs; beat lightly with a fork until combined. Gradually add half-and-half, stirring just until combined.
3. Place the partially baked pastry shell on the oven rack. Carefully pour filling into pastry shell. To prevent overbrowning, cover edge of pie with foil. Bake for 20 minutes. Remove foil. Bake about 25 minutes more or until a knife inserted near the center comes out clean. Cool on a wire rack. Cover and chill within 2 hours. If desired, serve with sweetened whipped cream.

*Test Kitchen Tip: For a decorative edge, prepare another recipe of Pastry for Single-Crust Pie. Roll pastry from center to edge into a 12-inch circle. With a small leaf- or star-shape cookie cutter, cut out pastry. Brush edge of pie with water. Overlap cutouts around edge of pie.

To Store: Cover pie and store in the refrigerator for up to 2 days,

PER SERVING: *333 cal., 14 g fat (8 g sat. fat), 138 mg chol., 394 mg sodium, 45 g carb., 2 g fiber, 8 g pro.*

Cream-Topped Pumpkin Pie: Prepare as directed through Step 2. Bake pie for 20 minutes as directed in Step 3. Remove foil. Meanwhile, combine one 16-ounce carton sour cream and ¼ cup packed brown sugar. After removing foil, bake for 15 minutes. Spoon sour cream mixture over pie, spreading evenly. Bake for 10 minutes more. Cool completely on a wire rack. If desired, sprinkle with white chocolate shavings instead of topping with whipped cream.

PER SERVING: *468 cal., 25 g fat (14 g sat. fat), 167 mg chol., 442 mg sodium, 54 g carb., 2 g fiber, 9 g pro.*

Cranberry-Pecan Pumpkin Pie: Prepare and bake pie as directed. For topping, in a medium bowl combine ⅓ cup dried cranberries and 3 tablespoons brandy or apple juice. Let stand for 15 minutes. Add 1½ cups toasted pecan halves (see tip, page 343) and ¼ cup caramel-flavor ice cream topping to the cranberry mixture. Toss to coat. Serve with pumpkin pie instead of the whipped cream.

PER SERVING: *529 cal., 29 g fat (9 g sat. fat), 138 mg chol., 430 mg sodium, 59 g carb., 5 g fiber, 10 g pro.*

Spirited Pumpkin Pie: Prepare as directed, except substitute ¼ cup liqueur (such as hazelnut, crème de cacao, or amaretto) for ¼ cup of the half-and-half.

PER SERVING: *348 cal., 13 g fat (7 g sat. fat), 135 mg chol., 391 mg sodium, 49 g carb., 2 g fiber, 10 g pro.*

Mallow-Praline Sweet Potato Pie

PREP: 45 minutes
BAKE: 14 minutes at 450°F
BAKE: 45 minutes at 375°F
COOL: 1 hour
MAKES: 8 servings

1 recipe Pastry for Single-Crust Pie (see page 195)
1⅔ cups cooked, mashed orange sweet potatoes* or one 17.2-ounce can whole sweet potatoes, drained and mashed
⅓ cup granulated sugar
¼ cup pure maple syrup
1 teaspoon finely chopped crystallized ginger or ½ teaspoon ground ginger
½ teaspoon ground cinnamon
½ teaspoon freshly grated nutmeg (see tip, page 17) or ¼ teaspoon ground nutmeg
¼ teaspoon ground allspice
⅛ teaspoon salt
3 eggs, lightly beaten
1 cup buttermilk or sour milk (see tip, page 16)
2 tablespoons butter
2 tablespoons packed brown sugar
2 tablespoons pure maple syrup
1 tablespoon milk
½ cup chopped pecans
1 cup tiny marshmallows

1. Preheat oven to 450°F. Prepare Pastry for Single-Crust Pie. On a lightly floured surface, use your hands to slightly flatten pastry. Roll pastry from center to edges into a circle about 12 inches in diameter. Wrap pastry circle around the rolling pin. Unroll into a 9-inch pie plate. Ease pastry into pie plate without stretching it. Trim pastry to ½ inch beyond edge of pie plate. Fold under extra pastry even with the plate edge. Crimp edge as desired.** Generously prick bottom and sides of pastry with a fork. Line pastry with a double thickness of foil. Bake for 8 minutes. Remove foil. Bake for 6 to 8 minutes more or until golden. Cool on a wire rack.

2. Reduce oven temperature to 375°F. For filling, in a large bowl stir together sweet potatoes, granulated sugar, the ¼ cup maple syrup, the ginger, cinnamon, nutmeg, allspice, and salt. Add eggs; beat lightly with a fork just until combined. Gradually stir in buttermilk until thoroughly combined.

3. Place the baked pastry shell on a foil-lined baking sheet on the oven rack. Carefully pour filling into pastry shell. Bake for 30 minutes.

4. Meanwhile, in a small saucepan melt the butter over medium heat. Gradually stir in brown sugar, the 2 tablespoons maple syrup, and the milk. Cook and stir until mixture comes to boiling. With pie on the oven rack, sprinkle partially baked pie with pecans and marshmallows. Carefully pour the hot brown sugar mixture over the top. Bake for 15 to 20 minutes more or until the center appears set when shaken. Cool on a wire rack for at least 1 hour. Cover and chill within 2 hours.

*Test Kitchen Tip: To prepare mashed sweet potatoes, in a covered medium saucepan cook about 18 ounces peeled, cubed sweet potatoes in enough boiling salted water to cover for 25 to 30 minutes or until tender. Drain potatoes. Mash potatoes with a potato masher or beat with an electric mixer on low speed until mashed.

**Test Kitchen Tip: For a decorative pie edge, prepare another recipe of Pastry for Single-Crust Pie. Roll pastry from center to edge into a 12-inch square. Using a pastry wheel, cut pastry into ½-inch-wide strips. Cut each strip into 1½-inch lengths. Brush edge of pie with water. Attach strips diagonally around edge of pie.

To Store: Loosely cover pie and store in the refrigerator for up to 2 days.

PER SERVING: *468 cal., 22 g fat (8 g sat. fat), 104 mg chol., 333 mg sodium, 61 g carb., 3 g fiber, 8 g pro.*

Classic Pecan Pie

PREP: **25 minutes**
BAKE: **45 minutes at 350°F**
COOL: **1 hour**
MAKES: **8 servings**

1 recipe Pastry for Single-Crust Pie (see page 195)
3 eggs, lightly beaten
1 cup corn syrup
⅔ cup sugar
⅓ cup butter, melted
1 teaspoon vanilla
1¼ cups pecan halves

1. Preheat oven to 350°F. Prepare Pastry for Single-Crust Pie. On a lightly floured surface, use your hands to slightly flatten pastry. Roll pastry from center to edges into a circle about 12 inches in diameter. Wrap pastry circle around the rolling pin. Unroll into a 9-inch pie plate. Ease pastry into pie plate without stretching it. Trim pastry to ½ inch beyond edge of pie plate. Fold under extra pastry even with pie plate edge. Crimp edge as desired. Do not prick pastry.
2. For filling, in a medium bowl combine eggs, corn syrup, sugar, butter, and vanilla. Stir in pecans.
3. Place the pastry-lined pie plate on the oven rack. Carefully pour the filling into the pastry shell. To prevent overbrowning, cover edge of pie with foil.
4. Bake for 25 minutes. Remove foil. Bake for 20 to 25 minutes more or until a knife inserted near the center comes out clean. Cool on a wire rack. Cover and chill within 2 hours.

To Store: Cover pie or mini pies and store in the refrigerator for up to 2 days.

PER SERVING: 532 cal., 34 g fat (12 g sat. fat), 115 mg chol., 281 mg sodium, 54 g carb., 2 g fiber, 6 g pro.

Make It Mini

Prepare Pastry for Double-Crust Pie (see page 186). Roll one portion of dough from center to edge into a circle about 12 inches in diameter. Using a 2½-inch round cookie cutter, cut 24 circles. Repeat with remaining dough for a total of 48 pastry rounds. Line forty-eight 1¾-inch muffin cups with the pastry rounds. Preheat oven to 350°F. Prepare filling as directed in Step 2, except chop the pecans. Fill each pastry-lined muffin cup with 1 tablespoon filling, stirring filling occasionally to keep the pecans evenly distributed. Bake for 20 to 25 minutes or until pastry is golden and filling is puffed. Carefully remove mini pies from muffin cups. Cool completely on a wire rack. Cover and chill within 2 hours. To store, place in a single layer in a covered container and chill for up to 48 hours. Makes 48 mini pies.

Spiced Sugar Cream Pie

PREP: 25 minutes
BAKE: 50 minutes at 350°F
COOL: 1 hour
MAKES: 8 servings

    1 recipe Nut Pastry
   ¾ cup packed brown sugar
   ⅓ cup all-purpose flour
   ¼ cup granulated sugar
   ½ teaspoon freshly grated
     nutmeg (see tip, page 17) or
     ¼ teaspoon ground nutmeg
   ½ teaspoon ground cinnamon
     Dash ground cloves
     (optional)
  2½ cups whipping cream
    1 vanilla bean, split
      lengthwise, or 1 teaspoon
      vanilla
    1 recipe Sugar Sprinkle
      (optional)

1. Preheat oven to 350°F. Prepare Nut Pastry. On a lightly floured surface, use your hands to slightly flatten pastry. Roll pastry from center to edge into a circle about 12 inches in diameter. Wrap pastry around the rolling pin; unroll into a 9-inch pie plate. Ease pastry into pie plate without stretching it. Trim pastry to ½ inch beyond edge of pie plate. Fold under extra pastry even with edge of plate. Crimp edge as desired. Do not prick pastry.
2. For filling, in a large bowl stir together brown sugar, flour, granulated sugar, nutmeg, cinnamon, and, if desired, cloves. Slowly whisk in whipping cream. If using, scrape seeds from vanilla bean (see photo, page 17). Whisk vanilla bean seeds or vanilla into the sugar mixture.
3. Pour filling into pie shell. Cover edge of pie with foil to prevent overbrowning.
4. Place pie on middle oven rack. Bake for 25 minutes; remove foil. Bake for 25 to 30 minutes more or until top is lightly browned and filling is bubbly across the surface (pie won't appear set but will firm up upon cooling). Cool completely on a wire rack. Cover and chill within 2 hours.
5. Just before serving, cut pie into wedges. If desired, sift Sugar Sprinkle over sliced pie.

Nut Pastry: In a medium bowl stir together 1¼ cups all-purpose flour; ¼ cup pecans, finely ground; and ½ teaspoon salt. Using a pastry blender, cut in ¼ cup shortening and ¼ butter, cut up, until pieces are pea size. Sprinkle 1 tablespoon ice water over part of the flour mixture; toss gently with a fork. Push moistened dough to side of bowl. Repeat with additional ice water, 1 tablespoon at a time (¼ to ⅓ cup total), until all of the flour mixture is moistened. Gather mixture into a ball, kneading gently until it holds together.

To Store: Cover pie and store in refrigerator for up to 24 hours.

PER SERVING: *584 cal., 42 g fat (23 g sat. fat), 118 mg chol., 221 mg sodium, 48 g carb., 1 g fiber, 5 g pro.*

Sugar Sprinkle: In a small bowl combine 1 tablespoon powdered sugar, ⅛ teaspoon freshly ground nutmeg (see page 17) or a dash ground nutmeg, and a dash of ground cinnamon.

Butterscotch Cream Pie

PREP: **50 minutes**
BAKE: **20 minutes at 425°F**
BAKE: **15 minutes at 350°F**
COOL: **1 hour**
CHILL: **3 to 6hours**
MAKES: **8 servings**

  1 recipe Flaky Pecan Pastry
  ¾ cup packed brown sugar
  ¼ cup cornstarch
  ¼ teaspoon salt
  1 12-ounce can evaporated
     milk, divided
  3 egg yolks
  1 cup milk
  3 tablespoons butter, cut into
     pieces
  1 teaspoon vanilla
  1 recipe Meringue for Pie

1. Preheat oven to 425°F. Prepare Flaky Pecan Pastry. On a floured surface, slightly flatten dough. Roll dough from center to edge into a 12-inch circle. Wrap pastry circle around rolling pin; unroll into a 9-inch pie plate. Ease pastry into pie plate. Trim pastry to ½ inch beyond edge of pie plate. Fold under extra pastry even with edge of plate. Crimp edge as desired. Do not prick pastry. Line pastry with a double thickness of foil. Bake for 12 minutes. Remove foil. Bake for 8 to 10 minutes more or until golden brown. Cool on a wire rack. Reduce oven temperature to 350°F.
2. For filling, in a medium saucepan combine brown sugar, cornstarch, and salt. Whisk in about ½ cup of the evaporated milk. Whisk in egg yolks until combined. Whisk in the remaining evaporated milk and the milk.

Cook and stir over medium heat until thickened and bubbly. Remove from heat. Stir in butter and vanilla. Cover and keep warm. Prepare Meringue for Pie.
3. Pour warm filling into pastry shell. Gently spread meringue over warm filling, sealing to edge of pie. Bake for 15 minutes. Cool on a wire rack for 1 hour. Chill for 3 to 6 hours before serving.

Flaky Pecan Pastry: In a large bowl stir together 1⅓ cups all-purpose flour and ¼ teaspoon salt. Using a pastry blender, cut in ¼ cup shortening and ¼ cup butter until pieces are pea size. Stir in ⅓ cup finely chopped pecans. Combine 2 tablespoons ice water and 2 teaspoons vinegar; sprinkle over part of the flour mixture; toss with a fork. Push moistened dough to side of bowl. Repeat with 2 tablespoons ice water until all of the flour mixture is moistened. Gather dough into a ball. Cover and chill about 1 hour.

Meringue for Pie: In a small bowl combine ¼ cup sugar and ¼ cup brown sugar. In a large mixing bowl combine 3 egg whites and ¼ teaspoon cream of tartar. Beat with an electric mixer on medium speed until soft peaks form (tips curl). Gradually add sugar mixture, 2 tablespoons at a time, beating on high speed until stiff peaks form (tips stand straight).

PER SERVING: 507 cal., 26 g fat (12 g sat. fat), 125 mg chol., 354 mg sodium, 60 g carb., 1 g fiber, 9 g pro.

How to Work with Meringue for Pie

Meringue pies are an old-fashioned favorite that are always in style. Here's how to prepare the meringue to top your pie.

1. Using a very clean bowl and beaters, whip egg whites until soft peaks form (the tips of the peaks will curl over).

2. Gradually beat in the sugar mixture, continuing to beat until stiff peaks form (the tips will stand straight).

3. Spread the meringue evenly over the filling and up to the edge of crust, sealing in the filling underneath.

Double Chocolate-Mascarpone Raspberry Pie

PREP: 30 minutes
BAKE: 14 minutes at 450°F
CHILL: 3 to 24 hours
MAKES: 10 servings

1 recipe Pastry for Single-Crust Pie (see page 195)
1 8-ounce carton mascarpone cheese
6 ounces bittersweet chocolate, chopped
½ cup powdered sugar
2 tablespoons raspberry liqueur
1 cup whipping cream
2 cups fresh raspberries
⅓ cup seedless raspberry jam, melted and cooled slightly
1 recipe White Chocolate Topping (optional) Semisweet chocolate, shavings (see tip, page 19) (optional)

1. Preheat oven to 450°F. Prepare Pastry for Single-Crust Pie. On a lightly floured surface, use your hands to slightly flatten pastry. Roll pastry from center to edges into a circle about 12 inches in diameter. Wrap pastry circle around the rolling pin. Unroll into a 9-inch pie plate. Ease pastry into pie plate without stretching it. Trim pastry to ½ inch beyond edge of pie plate. Fold under extra pastry even with the plate edge. Crimp edge as desired. Generously prick bottom and sides of pastry with a fork. Line pastry with a double thickness of foil. Bake for 8 minutes. Remove foil. Bake for 6 to 8 minutes more or until golden. Cool on a wire rack.

2. Meanwhile, in a medium saucepan combine mascarpone cheese, bittersweet chocolate, and powdered sugar. Cook and stir over medium-low heat until mixture is smooth. Remove from heat; stir in liqueur. Cool to room temperature.

3. In a chilled medium mixing bowl beat whipping cream with an electric mixer on medium speed until soft peaks form (tips curl). Stir about ½ cup of the whipped cream into chocolate mixture to lighten. Fold in the remaining whipped cream just until combined. Spoon chocolate mixture into pastry shell, spreading evenly. Cover and chill for 3 to 24 hours.

4. To serve, in a medium bowl gently stir together raspberries and melted jam; spoon over chocolate mixture. If desired, garnish with White Chocolate Topping and semisweet chocolate shavings.

To Store: Lightly cover pie and store in the refrigerator for up to 24 hours.

PER SERVING: *559 cal., 42 g fat (23 g sat. fat), 93 mg chol., 100 mg sodium, 44 g carb., 3 g fiber, 9 g pro.*

White Chocolate Topping: In a small heavy saucepan heat and stir 2 ounces coarsely chopped white baking chocolate and ¼ cup whipping cream over medium heat until chocolate is melted; cool. In a chilled small mixing bowl beat ⅔ cup whipping cream with an electric mixer on medium speed until mixture mounds but does not form peaks. Add white chocolate mixture. Beat on low speed just until stiff peaks form (tips stand straight).

Rustic Chocolate Tart

PREP: **30 minutes**
STAND: **30 minutes**
BAKE: **10 minutes at 400°F**
BAKE: **10 minutes at 350°F**
COOL: **45 minutes**
MAKES: **10 servings**

- 1 recipe Butter Pastry
- 6 ounces bittersweet chocolate (no more than 62% cacao), chopped
- 2 egg whites*
- ½ teaspoon vanilla
- ⅛ teaspoon cream of tartar
- ¼ cup sugar
- ⅛ teaspoon salt
- ¾ cup chopped pecans
- 3 tablespoons pine nuts, toasted (see tip, page 343)

1. Let Butter Pastry stand at room temperature about 30 minutes or until pliable enough to roll without cracking. Position rack in lower third of oven. Preheat oven to 400°F.
2. On a lightly floured surface, roll pastry into a 14×9-inch oval (about ⅛ inch thick), rotating and dusting with flour to prevent sticking. Brush excess flour from pastry; fold in half and transfer to a sheet of parchment paper slightly larger than pastry oval. Unfold pastry. Loosely fold and roll edges to form a rimmed crust, being careful not to press edges. Slide parchment paper with pastry onto a baking sheet. Bake for 10 to 12 minutes or until light golden brown (crust edges will be a little unbaked inside).
3. Place chocolate in a microwave-safe bowl. Microwave on 50 percent power (medium) about 2 minutes or until almost melted, stirring often. Stir until melted.
4. In a medium mixing bowl beat egg whites, vanilla, and cream of tartar with an electric mixer on medium to high speed until soft peaks form (tips curl). Gradually add sugar and salt, beating until egg whites are stiff but not dry. Add pecans and melted chocolate to beaten egg whites; fold together just until combined.
5. Reduce oven temperature to 350°F. Spread chocolate mixture over baked pastry. Bake about 10 minutes or until surface looks dry but filling is fudgy inside. Cool on baking sheet on a rack for 45 minutes. Sprinkle with pine nuts and, if desired, *chocolate curls* (see page 19). Cover; chill within 2 hours.

Butter Pastry: In a medium bowl stir together ¾ cup all-purpose flour and ¼ teaspoon salt. Using a pastry blender, cut in 5 tablespoons unsalted butter, cut up, until pieces are pea size. Sprinkle 1½ tablespoons cold water over flour mixture; toss gently with a fork just until moistened. If necessary, add 1½ teaspoons additional cold water to moisten all of the flour mixture. Gather flour mixture into a ball, kneading gently until it holds together. Cover with plastic wrap; chill for at least 30 minutes.

PER SERVING: *268 cal., 20 g fat (8 g sat. fat), 16 mg chol., 100 mg sodium, 23 g carb., 3 g fiber, 4 g pro.*

A No-Fuss Tart

A rustic (or country) tart is one of the easiest pastries to make because it doesn't require a pie plate or tart pan. First, roll out the dough as perfectly or imperfectly as you like. Either add filling to the center and fold over edges of the dough (as shown on page 212) or form a rimmed crust before adding the filling (as shown below).

1. Roll the pastry into a 14×9-inch oval (about ⅛ inch thick), rotating and dusting with flour to prevent sticking.

2. Fold pastry in half and transfer to a sheet of parchment paper.

3. Loosely fold and roll edges to form a rimmed crust, being careful not to press edges.

4. Fold pecans and chocolate into beaten egg whites just until combined.

5. Spread chocolate mixture evenly over partially baked pastry.

Country Peach Tart

PREP: **30 minutes**
BAKE: **50 minutes at 375°F**
COOL: **30 minutes**
MAKES: **8 servings**

- 1 recipe Pastry for Single-Crust Pie (see page 195)
- ¼ cup granulated sugar
- 4 teaspoons all-purpose flour
- ¼ teaspoon ground nutmeg, cinnamon, or ginger
- 3 cups sliced, peeled peaches or nectarines (about 1¼ pounds)
- 1 tablespoon lemon juice
- 1 tablespoon sliced almonds
  Milk
  Granulated or coarse sugar
  Sweetened whipped cream (see tip, page 16) (optional)

1. Preheat oven to 375°F. Prepare Pastry for Single-Crust Pie. On a large piece of lightly floured parchment paper, roll pastry into a 13-inch circle. Slide paper with pastry onto a baking sheet.

2. For filling, in a large bowl stir together the ¼ cup sugar, the flour, and nutmeg. Add peaches and lemon juice; toss until coated.

3. Mound filling in center of pastry, leaving a 2-inch border of dough around the edge. Fold uncovered pastry up over filling, pleating as necessary and using paper to lift pastry border. Sprinkle filling with sliced almonds. Lightly brush pastry top and sides with milk and sprinkle with additional granulated or coarse sugar.

4. Bake for 50 to 55 minutes or until filling is bubbly and crust is golden. If necessary to prevent overbrowning, cover edge of tart with foil the last 5 to 10 minutes of baking. Cool for at least 30 minutes on the baking sheet on a wire rack. If desired, serve with sweetened whipped cream.

To Store: Cover tart and store at room temperature for up to 24 hours or in the refrigerator for up to 2 days.

PER SERVING: *253 cal., 13 g fat (5 g sat. fat), 15 mg chol., 188 mg sodium, 32 g carb., 2 g fiber, 3 g pro.*

Country Pear Tart: Prepare as directed, except substitute 4 cups sliced, peeled pears (1½ pounds) for the peaches, substitute 1 tablespoon finely chopped crystallized ginger or ¼ teaspoon ground ginger and ¼ teaspoon ground cinnamon for the nutmeg, and increase sugar to ⅓ cup. Assemble tart as directed, except dot filling with 1 tablespoon butter. Bake as directed.

PER SERVING: *293 cal., 15 g fat (5 g sat. fat), 15 mg chol., 189 mg sodium, 43 g carb., 3 g fiber, 3 g pro.*

Rustic Pear Tart with Saffron Pastry

PREP: **40 minutes**
BAKE: **45 minutes at 375°F**
COOL: **30 minutes**
MAKES: **8 servings**

1 recipe Saffron Pasty
4 medium Anjou or Bartlett pears, peeled, cored, and sliced (about 4 cups)
¾ cup dried cherries
1 tablespoon lemon juice
2 tablespoons sugar
1 tablespoon all-purpose flour
¼ teaspoon ground cardamom or cinnamon
 Dash salt
¼ cup pear nectar or apple juice
3 tablespoons sugar
2 tablespoons finely chopped crystallized ginger
 Milk
 Sugar
1 pint ginger, cinnamon, or vanilla ice cream (optional)

1. Line a baking sheet with parchment paper; set aside. On a lightly floured surface, roll Saffron Pastry to a 13-inch circle. Transfer pastry to the prepared baking sheet; cover with plastic wrap and set aside.

2. Preheat oven to 375°F. For filling, in a large bowl gently toss together pears, dried cherries, and lemon juice. Add the 2 tablespoons sugar, the flour, cardamom, and the dash salt; gently toss to combine.

3. For pear syrup, in a small saucepan combine pear nectar, the 3 tablespoons sugar, and the crystallized ginger. Bring just to boiling over medium heat; reduce heat. Simmer, uncovered, for 5 minutes. Add to fruit mixture; gently toss to coat.

4. Spoon filling onto dough circle, leaving a 2-inch border of dough around the edge. Fold dough edge up and over filling, pleating as needed and leaving center uncovered. Spoon any liquid remaining in the bowl over filling. Brush dough edge with milk; sprinkle with additional sugar. Cover the filling in center of tart with foil.

5. Bake for 45 to 60 minutes or until dough is golden and filling is bubbly. Cool on baking sheet on a wire rack. If desired, serve with ice cream.

Saffron Pastry: In a small bowl pour 5 tablespoons boiling water over ¼ teaspoon saffron threads; let stand for 15 minutes. Add 4 ice cubes to chill the mixture; set aside. In a large bowl stir together 2 cups all-purpose flour, ¼ cup sugar, and ¾ teaspoon salt. Using a pastry blender, cut in ½ cup cold butter, cut into small pieces, until mixture resembles coarse cornmeal. In a small bowl combine 1 egg yolk and 3 tablespoons of the saffron-water mixture. Stir egg yolk mixture into flour mixture. Stir in enough of the remaining saffron-water mixture, 1 tablespoon at a time, to moisten the flour mixture. Gather dough into a ball, kneading gently until it holds together; flatten into a disk. Wrap in plastic wrap. Chill for at least 30 minutes or up to 3 days.

To Store: Cover tart and store at room temperature for up to 24 hours or in the refrigerator for up to 2 days.

To Make Ahead: Prepare Saffron Pastry up to 3 days before baking. Or place pastry in an airtight container and freeze for up to 1 month. Thaw overnight in the refrigerator before using.

PER SERVING: *394 cal., 13 g fat (8 g sat. fat), 57 mg chol., 326 mg sodium, 70 g carb., 4 g fiber, 5 g pro.*

Double-Coconut and Pineapple Cream Tart

PREP: **30 minutes**
BAKE: **30 minutes at 325°F**
COOL: **1 hour**
CHILL: **3 hours**
MAKES: **10 servings**

- 4 egg whites
- ⅓ cup sugar
- ¼ cup cornstarch
- ¼ teaspoon salt
- 1½ cups milk
- 1 15-ounce can cream of coconut (such as Coco Lopez)*
- 3 egg yolks, lightly beaten
- 2 tablespoons butter
- 1 8-ounce can crushed pineapple (juice pack), well drained
- ⅔ cup flaked coconut
- 1 tablespoon vanilla
- ½ teaspoon cream of tartar
- ½ cup sugar
- 1 recipe Macadamia Nut Tart Shell
- 2 tablespoons flaked coconut
- 2 tablespoons finely chopped macadamia nuts

1. Let egg whites stand at room temperature for 30 minutes. Meanwhile, for filling, in a medium saucepan combine the ⅓ cup sugar, the cornstarch, and salt; whisk in milk and cream of coconut until smooth. Cook and stir over medium heat until thickened and bubbly. Cook and stir for 2 minutes more. Remove from heat.

2. Gradually stir about 1 cup of the hot filling into egg yolks, stirring constantly. Pour yolk mixture into remaining hot filling in saucepan. Return to heat. Cook and stir for 2 minutes more. Remove from heat. Stir in butter until melted. Stir in pineapple, the ⅔ cup coconut, and 2 teaspoons of the vanilla. Cover; keep warm. Preheat oven to 325°F.

3. For meringue, in a large mixing bowl combine egg whites, the remaining 1 teaspoon vanilla, and the cream of tartar. Beat with an electric mixer on medium speed about 1 minute or until soft peaks form (tips curl). Gradually add the ½ cup sugar, 1 tablespoon at a time, beating on high speed about 4 minutes more or until stiff peaks form (tips stand straight) and sugar is dissolved.

4. Spoon warm filling into the Macadamia Nut Tart Shell, spreading evenly. Immediately spread meringue over warm filling, carefully sealing to edge to prevent shrinkage. Sprinkle with the 2 tablespoons coconut and the macadamia nuts. Bake for 30 minutes. Cool on wire rack for 1 hour. Chill for at least 3 hours before serving. For longer storage, cover with plastic wrap.

Macadamia Nut Tart Shell: In a medium bowl stir together 1½ cups all-purpose flour; ¼ cup macadamia nuts, finely ground; and ¼ cup sugar. Using a pastry blender, cut in ½ cup cold butter, cut up, until pieces are pea size. In a small bowl lightly beat 1 egg yolk. Stir in 1 tablespoon water. Gradually stir egg yolk mixture into flour mixture. Using your fingers, gently knead mixture until it holds together. Cover pastry with plastic wrap and chill for 1 hour or until easy to handle. Preheat oven to 450°F. On a lightly floured surface, use your hands to slightly flatten pastry. Roll pastry from center to edge into a 12-inch circle. Wrap pastry circle around a rolling pin. Unroll pastry into a 10-inch tart pan with a removable bottom. Ease pastry into pan without stretching it. Press pastry into fluted side of pan. Trim edges. Prick side and bottom with a fork. Line pastry with a double thickness of foil. Bake for 8 minutes. Remove foil. Bake for 5 to 6 minutes more or until golden. Cool on a wire rack.

*Test Kitchen Tip: Look for cream of coconut with the drink mixers in the liquor section of supermarkets or at a liquor store.

To Store: Insert several toothpicks into meringue to hold up plastic wrap. Cover pie loosely with plastic wrap. Store in the refrigerator for up to 2 days.

PER SERVING: *563 cal., 28 g fat (18 g sat. fat), 117 mg chol., 235 mg sodium, 72 g carb., 2 g fiber, 7 g pro.*

Key Lime Tart

PREP: 20 minutes
BAKE: 14 minutes at 450°F
BAKE: 15 minutes at 350°F
COOL: 1 hour
CHILL: 2 to 3 hours
MAKES: 8 servings

1 recipe Pastry for Single Crust Pie (see page 195)
4 egg yolks
1 14-ounce can (1¼ cups) sweetened condensed milk
1 teaspoon finely shredded lime peel (see tip, page 102)
½ cup fresh lime juice (14 to 16 Key limes or 4 to 6 Persian limes) or bottled Key lime juice
  Few drops green food coloring (optional)
  Sweetened whipped cream (see tip, page 16)

1. Preheat oven to 450°F. Prepare Pastry for Single-Crust Pie. On a lightly floured surface, use your hands to slightly flatten pastry. Roll pastry from center to edges into a circle 12 inches in diameter. Wrap pastry circle around a rolling pin. Unroll pastry into a 10-inch tart pan with removeable bottom. Ease pastry into pan without stretching it. Press pastry into fluted sides of tart pan. Trim edges even with tart pan. Prick pastry with a fork. Line pastry with a double thickness of foil. Bake for 8 minutes; remove foil. Bake for 6 to 8 minutes more or until golden. Cool on a wire rack.

2. Reduce oven temperature to 350°F. For filling, in a medium bowl beat egg yolks with a wire whisk or fork. Gradually whisk or stir in sweetened condensed milk; add lime peel, lime juice, and, if desired, food coloring. Mix well (mixture will thicken slightly).

3. Spoon filling into tart shell. Bake for 15 to 20 minutes or until set. Cool on a wire rack for 1 hour. Chill for 2 to 3 hours before serving; loosely cover for longer storage.

4. To serve, pipe sweetened whipped cream around the edge of the tart.

To Store: Lightly cover tart or mini tarts and store in the refrigerator for up to 2 days.

PER SERVING: *500 cal., 30 g fat (16 g sat. fat), 165 mg chol., 276 mg sodium, 51 g carb., 1 g fiber, 8 g pro.*

Make It Mini

Prepare as above, except cut pastry into eight 4½-inch rounds. Line eight 3¾-inch tart pans with removable bottoms with pastry. Prick pastry with a fork. Line tart shells with foil. Bake in the 450°F oven for 8 minutes. Remove foil; bake 4 minutes more. Reduce oven to 350°F. Spoon filling into tart shells. Bake for 12 to 15 minutes or until set. Cool, chill, and top as above. Makes 8 mini tarts.

Ganache-Glazed Peanut Butter Tart

PREP: 30 minutes
BAKE: 10 minutes at 350°F
CHILL: 4 to 27 hours
COOL: 10 minutes
STAND: 10 minutes
MAKES: 16 servings

1 cup crushed chocolate wafer cookies
3 tablespoons sugar
3 tablespoons butter, melted
1½ cups half-and-half or light cream
2 tablespoons all-purpose flour
¼ teaspoon salt
3 egg yolks
⅓ cup sugar
½ cup creamy peanut butter
1 teaspoon vanilla
4 ounces bittersweet chocolate, coarsely chopped
5 tablespoons butter, cut up
1 tablespoon light-color corn syrup

1. Preheat oven to 350°F. For crust, in a medium bowl combine crushed chocolate cookies and 3 tablespoons sugar. Drizzle with melted butter; toss to combine. Press crumb mixture onto the bottom and sides of an ungreased 9-inch tart pan that has a removable bottom. Bake about 10 minutes or until set. Cool on a wire rack.

2. For filling, in a medium saucepan combine half-and-half, flour, and salt. Cook over medium heat until simmering, stirring frequently. In a small bowl combine egg yolks and ⅓ cup sugar. Gradually stir about half of the hot mixture into egg yolk mixture. Return egg yolk mixture to saucepan. Cook and stir over medium heat until thickened and bubbly. Remove from heat. Whisk in peanut butter and vanilla until combined. Pour filling into crust-lined pan, spreading evenly. Cover and chill for 3 hours.

3. For ganache, in a small saucepan combine chocolate and 5 tablespoons butter. Heat and stir over low heat until melted. Remove from heat. Stir in corn syrup; cool for 10 minutes.

4. Pour ganache over filling; tilt pan to allow ganache to flow evenly over top of tart. Cover and chill for 1 to 24 hours.

5. Let stand at room temperature for 10 minutes before serving. Using a small sharp knife, gently loosen edges of tart from side of pan; remove side of pan. To cut, dip sharp knife into hot water; dry knife. Quickly score top of tart with warm knife. Cut tart along score marks.

To Store: Cover tart and store in refrigerator for up to 24 hours.

PER SERVING: *235 cal., 17 g fat (8 g sat. fat), 63 mg chol., 166 mg sodium, 19 g carb., 1 g fiber, 4 g pro.*

Salted Almond Praline Tart

PREP: **35 minutes**
BAKE: **35 minutes at 325°F**
COOL: **30 minutes**
CHILL: **2 to 24 hours**
MAKES: **12 servings**

    1   recipe Almond Crust
  12   ounces cream cheese,
         softened
  4½ ounces white baking
         chocolate with cocoa butter,
         chopped
    ⅓   cup sugar
    ½   cup light sour cream
    ¼   teaspoon almond extract
    1   egg
    1   egg yolk
    1   recipe Salted Almond
         Praline
         Sweetened whipped cream
         (see tip, page 16) (optional)
         Fresh raspberries (optional)

1. Prepare Almond Crust; set aside. Preheat oven to 325°F. In a medium saucepan combine 8 ounces of the cream cheese and the white chocolate. Heat and stir over low heat until melted. Remove from heat.
2. In a large mixing bowl beat the remaining 4 ounces cream cheese with an electric mixer on medium to high speed for 30 seconds. Beat in sugar until smooth. Beat in melted white chocolate mixture until combined. Beat in sour cream and almond extract just until combined. Beat in egg and egg yolk until combined. Pour into crust.
3. Bake about 35 minutes or until center is nearly set when gently shaken. Cool on a wire rack for 30 minutes. Loosen crust from sides of pan, but do not remove. Chill for 2 to 24 hours.
4. To serve, remove tart from pan. Top with Salted Almond Praline and, if desired, sweetened whipped cream and raspberries.

Almond Crust: In a food processor combine 2½ cups broken cinnamon graham crackers, 1 cup toasted sliced almonds (see page 343), and ⅓ cup sugar. Cover and process until finely ground. Add ⅓ cup softened butter. Process just until combined. Press into bottom and sides of a 10-inch fluted tart pan that has a removable bottom. Chill for 15 minutes. Preheat oven to 325°F. Place crust on foil-lined baking sheet. Bake about 20 minutes or until light brown; cool on a wire rack.

Salted Almond Praline: Preheat oven to 325°F. Line an 8×8×2-inch square baking pan with foil; grease foil. Set aside. In a small bowl combine 1 cup sliced almonds, ½ cup sugar, 2 tablespoons melted butter, 1 tablespoon water, 1 teaspoon ground cinnamon, and ½ teaspoon sea salt. Spread mixture evenly in the prepared pan. Bake about 20 minutes or until golden. Cool completely on a wire rack. Remove praline from pan and break into shards or bite-size pieces. Store praline in an airtight container for up to 3 days.

To Store: Cover tart and store in refrigerator for up to 24 hours.

PER SERVING: *562 cal., 30 g fat (14 g sat. fat), 91 mg chol., 237 mg sodium, 69 g carb., 22 g fiber, 10 g pro.*

Classic New York-Style Cheesecake,
recipe page 226

cheesecakes

CHEESECAKES HAVE INDULGENCE written all over them. Learn to achieve success the first time, every time with techniques for the perfect crumb crust, velvety filling, and a smooth surface. Polish your skills with Classic New York-Style Cheesecake and then expand to other amazing combinations using fruits, nuts, or chocolate.

Classic New York-Style Cheesecake

New York Cheesecake is a pure version of the dessert, consisting simply of eggs, cream cheese, and sugar in a graham cracker crust. We added a tangy sour cream topping to counter the classic creamy filling. Each slice is a study in dessert perfection.

PREP: 40 minutes
BAKE: 55 minutes at 350°F
STAND: 45 minutes
COOL: 45 minutes
CHILL: 4 hours
MAKES: 16 servings

- 4 8-ounce packages cream cheese
- 3 eggs, lightly beaten
- 2¼ cups finely crushed graham crackers
- 1 tablespoon sugar
- ⅔ cup butter, melted
- 1¼ cups sugar
- ¼ cup all-purpose flour
- 4 teaspoons vanilla
- 2 8-ounce cartons sour cream
- ¼ cup sugar

1. Allow cream cheese and eggs to stand at room temperature for 30 minutes. Meanwhile, for crust, in a large bowl combine crushed graham crackers and the 1 tablespoon sugar. Stir in melted butter. Press onto the bottom and 2 inches up the sides of a 10-inch springform pan.

2. Preheat oven to 350°F. In a large mixing bowl beat cream cheese and the 1¼ cups sugar with an electric mixer on medium to high speed until fluffy. Beat in flour on low speed until smooth. Stir in the eggs and 3 teaspoons of the vanilla. Gently stir in ½ cup of the sour cream. Pour batter into crust-lined pan. Place in a shallow baking pan in oven (if desired, see water bath tip, page 235).

3. Bake for 40 minutes or until a 2½-inch area around the outside edge appears set when gently shaken. Remove from oven. In a medium bowl stir together the remaining sour cream, the ¼ cup sugar, and the remaining 1 teaspoon vanilla. Using a spoon, spread mixture evenly over top of baked cheesecake. Return to oven and bake for 15 minutes more.

4. Cool in pan on a wire rack for 15 minutes. Using a small sharp knife, loosen crust from sides of pan. Cool for 30 minutes more. Remove sides of pan; cool completely on rack. Cover and chill for at least 4 hours or overnight before serving. Let stand at room temperature for 15 minutes before slicing.

To Store: Place cheesecake in an airtight container; cover. Store in the refrigerator for up to 5 days.

PER SERVING: *466 cal., 35 g fat (20 g sat. fat), 132 mg chol., 342 mg sodium, 34 g carb., 0 g fiber, 6 g pro.*

Secrets to Sucess

Cracks in cheesecakes are the bane of the baker's existence, but there are tricks to avoid this common problem. First, gently stir in the eggs after the cream cheese mixture is beaten. Overbeating the batter after adding the eggs will incorporate too much air and can cause the cheesecake to puff up during baking, then fall and crack.

Overbaking can also cause a cheesecake to crack. Baking it in a water bath can help (see Making a Water Bath, page 235) by providing protection from the oven's heat.

On that note, one of the hardest tasks in baking a cheesecake is determining when it is done but not overbaked. To check the cheesecake for doneness, shake it gently and look for a 2½-inch area around the outside edge of the cheesecake that appears set and doesn't jiggle (the very center will still jiggle slightly). It may go against everything in your nature to pull the cheesecake from the oven at this point, but success depends upon it. The satiny-smooth texture will develop during cooling and chilling. Unless instructed otherwise, cheesecakes should always be baked in springform pans with removable sides so clean slices can be cut and served.

PRESS CRUMBS INTO PAN Use your fingers to press the crumb mixture into the bottom and up the sides of the springform pan.

PRESS FIRMLY If you like, run a small measuring cup over the crumb crust to smooth out bumps and make it even.

BEAT UNTIL SMOOTH Beat softened cream cheese and sugar on medium to high speed until the mixture is smooth and fluffy. Stir in the eggs and vanilla.

FINISH BY STIRRING Gently stir the sour cream into the cream cheese mixture.

TRANSFER THE FILLING Pour the filling into the crust-lined pan, spreading evenly. Bake cheesecake as directed.

ADD THE TOPPING Gently spread the sour cream topping over the top of the baked filling. Finish baking as directed.

Make-It-Mine Cheesecake

Mix and match ingredients to create a new cheesecake favorite!

PREP: 30 minutes
BAKE: 40 minutes at 350°F
COOL: 2 hours
CHILL: 4 hours
MAKES: 12 servings

1¾ **cups Crumbs** (*choose option*)
¼ cup finely chopped pecans, almonds, or walnuts
1 tablespoon sugar
½ **teaspoon Spice** (*choose option*)
½ cup butter, melted
Dairy (*choose option*)
Sweetener (*choose option*)
2 tablespoons all-purpose flour
1 **teaspoon Flavoring** (*choose option*)
¼ cup milk
3 eggs, lightly beaten
Stir-In or Swirl-In (*choose option*)
Topping (optional)

1. Preheat oven to 350°F. In a medium bowl combine *Crumbs*, nuts, the 1 tablespoon sugar, and *Spice*. Stir in melted butter. Press onto bottom and 1½ inches up sides of a 9-inch springform pan.
2. In a large mixing bowl beat *Dairy, Sweetener,* flour, and *Flavoring* with electric mixer on medium to high speed until combined. Beat in milk. Stir in eggs and, if using, *Stir-In.* Pour into crust-lined pan. Dot with *Swirl-In* (if using); use a thin spatula to marble. Place pan in shallow baking pan.
3. Bake for 40 to 50 minutes or until a 2½-inch area around the outside edge appears set when gently shaken.
4. Cool in pan on a wire rack for 15 minutes. Loosen crust from sides of pan. Cool for 30 minutes more. Remove sides of pan; cool completely on rack. Cover and chill for at least 4 hours. If desired, serve with *Topping.*

CRUMBS (PICK ONE)
Crushed graham crackers
Crushed vanilla wafers
Crushed chocolate sandwich cookies (reduce melted butter to 3 tablespoons)
Crushed gingersnaps

SPICE (PICK ONE)
Ground cinnamon
Ground ginger
Ground allspice
Apple pie spice
Pumpkin pie spice

DAIRY (PICK ONE)
Cream cheese: Three 8-ounce packages cream cheese, softened
Sour cream: Two 8-ounce packages cream cheese, softened, and one 8-ounce carton sour cream (omit milk)
Yogurt: Two 8-ounce packages cream cheese, softened, and two 6-ounce cartons plain lowfat yogurt (omit milk)
Pumpkin: Two 8-ounce packages cream cheese, softened, and 1 cup canned pumpkin (omit milk)

SWEETENER (PICK ONE)
1 cup granulated sugar
½ cup granulated sugar and ½ cup packed brown sugar
⅔ cup packed brown sugar and ¼ cup maple syrup (omit Liquid)

FLAVORING (PICK ONE)
Vanilla
Almond extract
Finely shredded lemon or orange peel (see tip, page 102)

STIR-IN (PICK ONE)
1 cup semisweet, bittersweet, or milk chocolate pieces
3 ounces chopped white chocolate with cocoa butter
1 cup fresh or frozen blueberries or raspberries

SWIRL-IN (PICK ONE)
4 ounces semisweet chocolate melted with 2 tablespoons whipping cream
1 cup fresh or frozen blueberries or raspberries, pureed and sieved

TOPPING (PICK ONE)
Fruit pie filling, warmed
Sweetened whipped cream (see tip, page 16)
Caramel ice cream topping, warmed

White Chocolate Cheesecake

PREP: 30 minutes
BAKE: 45 minutes at 350°F
COOL: 2 hours
CHILL: 4 hours to overnight
MAKES: 8 servings

- 2 8-ounce packages cream cheese
- 3 eggs
- 1¼ cups finely crushed shortbread cookies
- 2 tablespoons butter, melted
- 6 ounces white baking chocolate with cocoa butter, melted and cooled
- ⅔ cup sugar
- ⅔ cup sour cream
- 1 teaspoon vanilla
  White Chocolate-Dipped Berries (optional)

1. Allow cream cheese and eggs to stand at room temperature for 30 minutes. Meanwhile, preheat oven to 350°F. For crust, in a small bowl toss together crushed cookies and melted butter until combined. Press crumb mixture onto the bottom of an 8-inch springform pan that has a removable bottom; set aside.
2. In a large mixing bowl beat cream cheese and the 6 ounces melted white chocolate with an electric mixer on medium to high speed until combined. Beat in sugar until fluffy. Using a fork, lightly beat eggs. Add eggs, sour cream, and vanilla to cream cheese mixture; beat on low speed just until combined. Pour filling over crust in pan, spreading evenly. Place in a shallow baking pan.
3. Bake about 45 minutes or until a 2½-inch area around outside edge appears set when gently shaken.
4. Cool in pan on a wire rack for 15 minutes. Using a small sharp knife, loosen cheesecake from sides of pan. Cool for 30 minutes more. Remove sides of pan; cool cheesecake completely on rack. Cover and chill for at least 4 hours or overnight before serving.

5. If desired, arrange White Chocolate-Dipped Berries on top of cheesecake.

White Chocolate-Dipped Berries: Rinse whole fresh berries such as raspberries, blackberries, and small strawberries under cool water; pat gently with paper towels to remove moisture. Let stand until completely dry. Dip berries in cooled, melted white chocolate (with cocoa butter), letting excess drip off. Let stand on waxed paper until chocolate is set.

Test Kitchen Tip: This cheesecake puffs during baking, then settles as it cools. The surface of the cheesecake may crack. To help prevent cracks from forming, try baking the cheesecake in a water bath (see tip, page 235). You can also use the berries to cover up cracks in the top.

To Store: Place cheesecake in an airtight container; cover. Store in the refrigerator for up to 5 days.

PER SERVING: *580 cal., 40 g fat (21 g sat. fat), 160 mg chol., 374 mg sodium, 47 g carb., 0 g fiber, 9 g pro.*

Chocolate Chip-Cookie Dough Cheesecake

PREP: 25 minutes
BAKE: 1 hour at 350°F
COOL: 2 hours
CHILL: 4 hours to overnight
MAKES: 12 servings

- 3   8-ounce packages cream cheese
- 3   eggs
- 1¾ cups finely crushed chocolate sandwich cookies with white filling or graham crackers
- 1   tablespoon granulated sugar
- 3   tablespoons butter,* melted
- ½   cup granulated sugar
- ½   cup packed brown sugar
- 2   tablespoons all-purpose flour
- 1   teaspoon vanilla
- ¼   cup milk
- 1   16.5- to 18-ounce roll refrigerated chocolate chip cookie dough
- ¼ to ½ cup semisweet chocolate pieces or miniature semisweet chocolate pieces

1. Allow cream cheese and eggs to stand at room temperature for 30 minutes. Meanwhile, preheat oven to 350°F. For crust, in a medium bowl stir together crushed cookies and 1 tablespoon granulated sugar. Stir in melted butter until combined. Press mixture onto the bottom and 1½ inches up the sides of a 9-inch springform pan; set aside.
2. In a large mixing bowl beat cream cheese, ½ cup granulated sugar, brown sugar, flour, and vanilla with an electric mixer on medium to high speed until combined. Beat in milk until smooth. Using a fork, lightly beat the eggs. Stir eggs into cream cheese mixture.
3. Pour half of the cream cheese mixture into crust-lined pan, spreading evenly. Gently drop half of the cookie dough by teaspoons onto cream cheese mixture in pan. Repeat with the remaining cream cheese mixture and the remaining cookie dough. Poke dough down just below surface. Sprinkle top with chocolate pieces. Place springform pan in a shallow baking pan.
4. Bake for 60 to 65 minutes or until a 2½-inch area around outside edge appears set when gently shaken.
5. Cool in pan on a wire rack for 15 minutes. Using a small sharp knife, loosen crust from sides of pan. Cool for 30 minutes more. Remove sides of pan; cool completely on rack. Cover and chill for at least 4 hours or overnight before serving.

*Test Kitchen Tip: If using finely crushed graham crackers, increase the butter to ½ cup.

To Store: Place cheesecake in an airtight container; cover. Store in the refrigerator for up to 5 days.

PER SERVING: 587 cal., 36 g fat (17 g sat. fat), 126 mg chol., 392 mg sodium, 61 g carb., 1 g fiber, 8 g pro.

Make It Mini

Prepare as directed, except omit the crust. Grease the springform pan. Pour filling directly into prepared pan. Bake and cool as directed. Line a baking sheet with waxed paper. Scoop cooled cheesecake filling into 1½-inch mounds onto prepared baking sheet. Roll mounds into balls, moistening your hands lightly with water if necessary. Freeze for 30 minutes. Microwave 12 ounces chopped chocolate-flavor candy coating and 12 ounces semisweet chocolate pieces on 50-percent power (medium) for 4 to 5 minutes or until melted, stirring twice. For each lollipop, dip one end of a lollipop stick into melted chocolate; insert that end into a cheesecake ball. Freeze about 1 hour or until firm. Working in small batches, dip pops into melted chocolate, spooning chocolate over balls and allowing excess to drip off. (Remelt mixture if necessary.) Sprinkle pops with chopped nuts. Place in a glass; let stand until set.

Snickerdoodle Cheesecake

PREP: 25 minutes
BAKE: 40 minutes at 350°F
COOL: 2 hours
CHILL: 4 hours to overnight
MAKES: 12 servings

2   8-ounce packages cream
    cheese
3   eggs
1   10-ounce package
    shortbread cookies, finely
    crushed
1   tablespoon sugar
¼   cup butter, melted
1   8-ounce carton sour cream
1   cup sugar
2   tablespoons all-purpose
    flour
2   teaspoons vanilla
1   teaspoon ground cinnamon
1   tablespoon sugar

1. Allow cream cheese and eggs to stand at room temperature for 30 minutes. Meanwhile, preheat oven to 350°F. For crust, in a medium bowl stir together crushed cookies and 1 tablespoon sugar. Stir in melted butter until combined. Press mixture onto the bottom and 1½ inches up the sides of a 9-inch springform pan; set aside.

2. In a large mixing bowl beat cream cheese, sour cream, the 1 cup sugar, the flour, vanilla, and ½ teaspoon of the cinnamon with an electric mixer on medium to high speed until smooth. Using a fork, lightly beat eggs. Stir eggs into the cream cheese mixture.

3. In a small bowl stir together the 1 tablespoon sugar and the remaining ½ teaspoon cinnamon. Pour cream cheese mixture into crust-lined pan, spreading evenly. Sprinkle with sugar-cinnamon mixture. Place springform pan in a shallow baking pan.

4. Bake for 40 to 50 minutes or until a 2½-inch area around outside edge appears set when gently shaken. Cool in springform pan on a wire rack for 15 minutes. Using a small sharp knife, loosen crust from sides of pan. Cool for 30 minutes more. Remove the sides of pan; cool cheesecake completely on wire rack. Cover and chill for at least 4 hours or overnight before serving.

To Store: Place cheesecake in an airtight container; cover. Store in the refrigerator for up to 5 days.

PER SERVING: 412 cal., 27 g fat (14 g sat. fat), 108 mg chol., 310 mg sodium, 39 g carb., 0 g fiber, 5 g pro.

Making a Water Bath

Although not necessary for most cheesecakes with added starch (such as flour), baking in a water bath can control the temperature to which the cheesecake is exposed, helping to prevent cracks and resulting in an extra-creamy texture. Place the crust-lined pan on a double layer of 18×12-inch heavy-duty foil. Mold the foil around pan, forming a water-tight seal. Prepare filling and pour into crust-lined pan. Place cheesecake in a roasting pan. Pour enough boiling water into roasting pan to reach halfway up the side of springform pan. Bake the cheesecake 10 to 20 minutes longer than directed in recipe. Turn off oven; allow cheesecake to stand in oven for 1 hour (cheesecake will continue to set up during this time). Carefully remove springform pan from water; remove foil from pan. Cool and chill as directed.

Place foil-wrapped cheesecake in pan; slowly add boiling water.

Blueberry-Topped Lemon Cheesecake

PREP: 1¼ hours
BAKE: 20 minutes at 350°F
BAKE: 1¼ hours at 325°F
COOL: 2 hours
CHILL: 6 hours to overnight
MAKES: 16 servings

⅓ cup butter
4 8-ounce packages cream cheese
1 8-ounce carton mascarpone cheese
2 eggs
¼ cup sugar
½ cup all-purpose flour
½ cup yellow cornmeal
⅛ teaspoon salt
1½ cups sugar
2 tablespoons finely shredded lemon peel (see tip, page 102)
3 tablespoons lemon juice
3 cups blueberries
½ cup sugar
3 tablespoons lemon juice
1 tablespoon water

1. Allow butter, cream cheese, mascarpone cheese, and eggs to stand at room temperature for 30 minutes. Meanwhile, preheat oven to 350°F. Wrap a double layer of foil around the bottom and sides of an ungreased 9-inch springform pan to form a watertight seal; set pan aside.

2. For crust, in a medium mixing bowl beat butter with an electric mixer on medium to high speed for 30 seconds. Add the ¼ cup sugar; beat until combined. Add flour, cornmeal, and salt; beat until crumbly. Press mixture onto the bottom of the foil-wrapped pan. Bake for 20 minutes. Reduce oven temperature to 325°F.

3. Meanwhile, in a very large mixing bowl combine cream cheese, mascarpone cheese, and the 1½ cups sugar. Beat on medium to high speed until smooth. Using a fork, lightly beat eggs. Add eggs, lemon peel, and 3 tablespoons lemon juice to cheese mixture, beating on low speed just until combined. Pour over crust, spreading evenly. Place the foil-wrapped springform pan in a roasting pan. Pour enough hot water into roasting pan to reach halfway up side of springform pan.

4. Bake for 1¼ to 1½ hours or until a 2-inch area around the outside edge appears set and the center appears nearly set when shaken.

5. Remove springform pan from water. Cool in pan on a wire rack for 15 minutes. Using a small sharp knife, loosen edges of cheesecake from sides of pan; cool completely on rack. Remove foil. Cover and chill for at least 6 hours or overnight before serving.

6. For blueberry topping, in a medium saucepan combine 2 cups of the blueberries, the ½ cup sugar, 3 tablespoons lemon juice, and the water. Cook and stir until mixture comes to boiling. Boil gently, uncovered, for 15 to 20 minutes or until slightly thickened. Stir in the remaining 1 cup blueberries; cook for 2 minutes more. Cool; cover and chill until ready to serve.

7. To serve, remove sides of springform pan. Slice cheesecake; spoon topping over each serving of cheesecake.

To Store: Place cheesecake in an airtight container; cover. Place blueberry topping in another airtight container; cover. Store in the refrigerator for up to 3 days.

PER SERVING: *456 cal., 31 g fat (17 g sat. fat), 114 mg chol., 252 mg sodium, 42 g carb., 1 g fiber, 6 g pro.*

Oatmeal-Butterscotch Cookie Cheesecake

PREP: **25 minutes**
BAKE: **45 minutes at 350°F**
COOL: **2 hours**
CHILL: **4 hours to overnight**
MAKES: **12 servings**

- 3 8-ounce packages cream cheese
- 3 eggs
- 2 cups rolled oats
- ½ cup broken pecans
- 2 tablespoons packed brown sugar
- ½ teaspoon ground cinnamon
- ½ cup butter, melted
- ½ cup granulated sugar
- ½ cup packed brown sugar
- 2 tablespoons all-purpose flour
- 1 teaspoon vanilla
- ½ teaspoon finely shredded orange peel (see tip, page 102) (optional)
- ¼ cup milk
- 1¼ cups butterscotch-flavor pieces

1. Allow cream cheese and eggs to stand at room temperature for 30 minutes. Meanwhile, preheat oven to 350°F. For crust, in a food processor combine oats, pecans, the 2 tablespoons brown sugar, and the cinnamon. Cover and process with on/off pulses until oats and nuts are finely chopped. Add melted butter; cover and process with on/off pulses just until combined. Remove ¼ cup of the oat mixture; set aside. Press the remaining oat mixture onto the bottom and about 1 inch up the sides of a 9-inch springform pan; set aside.

2. For filling, in a large mixing bowl beat cream cheese, granulated sugar, the ½ cup brown sugar, the flour, vanilla, and, if desired, orange peel with an electric mixer on medium to high speed until combined. Beat in milk until smooth. Using a fork, lightly beat eggs. Stir eggs and 1 cup of the butterscotch pieces into cream cheese mixture.

3. Pour filling into crust-lined pan, spreading evenly. Sprinkle the reserved oat mixture and the remaining ¼ cup butterscotch pieces around outside edge. Place springform pan in a shallow baking pan.

4. Bake for 45 to 50 minutes or until a 2½-inch area around outside edge appears set when gently shaken.

5. Cool in springform pan on a wire rack for 15 minutes. Using a small sharp knife, loosen crust from sides of pan. Cool for 30 minutes more. Remove sides of pan; cool cheesecake completely on wire rack. Cover and chill for at least 4 hours or overnight before serving.

To Store: Place cheesecake in an airtight container; cover. Store in the refrigerator for up to 5 days.

PER SERVING: *580 cal., 39 g fat (23 g sat. fat), 130 mg chol., 291 mg sodium, 50 g carb., 2 g fiber, 8 g pro.*

Chilling Out

Even though the temptation to dive in immediately is great, you'll want to cool and chill your cheesecake thoroughly before serving to allow the flavors and textures to intensify. Cool it completely on a wire rack, then refrigerate it for at least 4 hours before adding the topping or garnishes. Leftover cheesecake will hold better without sauces and other toppings. It's better to top each slice just before serving rather than adding topping to the entire cheesecake.

Chocolate-Peanut Butter Cheesecake

PREP: **35 minutes**
BAKE: **53 minutes at 350°F**
COOL: **2 hours**
CHILL: **4 hours to overnight**
MAKES: **12 servings**

  3 8-ounce packages cream cheese
  3 eggs
  2 cups finely crushed peanut butter-filled peanut sandwich cookies
  ¼ cup butter, melted
 12 ounces semisweet chocolate, chopped
  1 cup whipping cream
  ½ cup creamy peanut butter
 1¼ cups packed brown sugar
  2 teaspoons vanilla
 15 miniature chocolate-covered peanut butter cups, halved or coarsely chopped

1. Allow cream cheese and eggs to stand at room temperature for 30 minutes. Meanwhile, preheat oven to 350°F. For crust, in a medium bowl combine crushed cookies and melted butter. Press mixture onto the bottom and 1½ inches up the sides of a 9-inch springform pan. Bake for 8 minutes. Cool on a wire rack.
2. In a small saucepan combine chocolate and whipping cream. Cook over low heat until chocolate is melted and mixture is smooth, stirring frequently. Pour 1½ cups of the chocolate mixture into crust-lined pan, spreading evenly. Chill in the freezer for 10 minutes.
3. In a large mixing bowl beat cream cheese and peanut butter with an electric mixer on medium to high speed until smooth. Beat in brown sugar until combined. Using a fork, lightly beat eggs. Add eggs to cream cheese mixture, beating just until combined. Stir in vanilla. Carefully pour cream cheese mixture over chocolate layer in pan.

4. Bake about 45 minutes or until a 2½-inch area around outside edge appears set when gently shaken. Cool in pan on a wire rack for 15 minutes. Using a small sharp knife, loosen crust from sides of pan. Cool for 30 minutes more. Remove sides of pan. Cool cheesecake completely on wire rack. Spread the remaining chocolate mixture over top of cheesecake. Top with peanut butter cups. Cover and chill for at least 4 hours or overnight.

To Store: Place cheesecake in an airtight container; cover. Store in the refrigerator for up to 3 days.

PER SERVING: *746 cal., 53 g fat (27 g sat. fat), 146 mg chol., 397 mg sodium, 64 g carb., 3 g fiber, 12 g pro.*

Almond-Cherry Cheesecake Ribbon Pie

PREP: 45 minutes
BAKE: 23 minutes at 425°F
BAKE: 25 minutes at 350°F
COOL: 2 hours
CHILL: 5 hours to overnight
MAKES: 12 servings

2 15-ounce cans pitted tart red cherries (water pack)
1 cup sugar
¼ cup cornstarch
1 cup all-purpose flour
¼ cup finely ground almonds
1 teaspoon sugar
½ teaspoon salt
½ cup butter, cut up
3 to 4 tablespoons ice water
1 8-ounce package cream cheese
2 eggs
½ cup sugar
½ teaspoon vanilla
¼ teaspoon almond extract

1. Drain cherries, reserving 1 cup of the liquid. In a medium saucepan stir together the 1 cup sugar and the cornstarch. Add cherries and the reserved liquid. Bring to boiling, stirring to dissolve sugar; reduce heat. Boil gently, uncovered, for 1 minute; cool. Cover and chill until needed.

2. For pastry, in a medium bowl stir together flour, ground almonds, the 1 teaspoon sugar, and the salt. Using a pastry blender, cut in butter until pieces are pea size. Sprinkle 1 tablespoon of the water over part of the flour mixture; toss gently with a fork. Push moistened pastry to one side of bowl. Repeat moistening flour mixture, using 1 tablespoon of the water at a time, until all of the flour mixture is moistened. Gather flour mixture into a ball, kneading gently until it holds together. Cover and chill for 1 hour.

3. Meanwhile, allow cream cheese and eggs to stand at room temperature for 30 minutes. Preheat oven to 425°F. On a lightly floured surface, roll pastry into an 11-inch circle. Ease pastry circle into a 9-inch pie plate without stretching it. Trim pastry to ½ inch beyond edge of pie plate. Fold under extra pastry; crimp edge as desired. Bake for 8 minutes. Spoon half of the cherry mixture into pastry-lined pie plate. Bake for 15 minutes.

4. In a large mixing bowl beat cream cheese with an electric mixer on medium to high speed for 30 seconds. Add the ½ cup sugar, the vanilla, and almond extract; beat until combined. Using a fork, lightly beat eggs. Add eggs to cream cheese mixture; beat just until combined.

5. Reduce oven temperature to 350°F. Spread cream cheese mixture evenly over cherry layer in pie plate. Bake about 25 minutes more or until cream cheese layer is set. Cool on a wire rack.

6. Spread the remaining cherry mixture over pie. Cover and chill for at least 4 hours or overnight.

To Store: Loosely cover pie with foil or place in a covered container. Store in the refrigerator for up to 24 hours.

PER SERVING: *329 cal., 16 g fat (9 g sat. fat), 72 mg chol., 243 mg sodium, 44 g carb., 1 g fiber, 4 g pro.*

Milk Chocolate Cheesecake

PREP: 35 minutes
BAKE: 50 minutes at 350°F
COOL: 2 hours
CHILL: 4 hours to overnight
MAKES: 16 servings

3 8-ounce package cream
cheese
3 eggs
1¾ cups finely crushed
shortbread cookies
¼ cup finely chopped almonds
1 tablespoon sugar
¼ cup butter, melted
3 ounces milk chocolate,
grated
4 ounces milk chocolate,
chopped
¾ cup sugar
½ cup milk
2 teaspoons vanilla
2 tablespoons all-purpose
flour
4 ounces bittersweet
chocolate, chopped
2 tablespoons milk

1. Allow cream cheese and eggs to stand at room temperature for 30 minutes. Meanwhile, preheat oven to 350°F. For crust, in a medium bowl stir together crushed cookies, almonds, and the 1 tablespoon sugar. Stir in melted butter. Press crumb mixture onto the bottom and about 1½ inches up the sides of a 9-inch springform pan. Sprinkle crust with grated milk chocolate; set aside.

2. For filling, in a small heavy saucepan heat and stir chopped milk chocolate over low heat until melted and smooth; cool. In a large mixing bowl beat cream cheese, the ¾ cup sugar, ½ cup milk, and the vanilla with an electric mixer on medium to high speed until combined. Beat in flour. Beat in the cooled chocolate. Using a fork, lightly beat eggs. Add eggs to cream cheese mixture, beating on low speed just until combined. Set aside ½ cup of the filling. Pour the remaining filling into the crust-lined pan.

3. In a small heavy saucepan heat and stir chopped bittersweet chocolate over low heat until melted and smooth; cool slightly. Combine melted chocolate, the reserved ½ cup batter, and the 2 tablespoons milk. Dot bittersweet chocolate mixture over filling; use a thin metal spatula or table knife to swirl into filling. Place springform pan in a shallow baking pan.

4. Bake for 50 to 55 minutes or until a 2½-inch area around outside edge appears set with gently shaken.

5. Cool cheesecake in pan on a wire rack for 15 minutes. Using a small sharp knife, loosen the crust from sides of pan. Let cool for 30 minutes more. Remove the sides of the pan. Cool cheesecake completely on rack. Cover and chill at least 4 hours or overnight before serving.

To Store: Place cheesecake in an airtight container; cover. Store in the refrigerator for up to 5 days.

PER SERVING: *433 cal., 30 g fat (16 g sat. fat), 101 mg chol., 265 mg sodium, 36 g carb., 2 g fiber, 7 g pro.*

How to Create Marbled Swirls

1. Spoon the bittersweet chocolate mixture in small mounds on top of the cheesecake batter.

2. Use a table knife to gently swirl the two mixtures together to create the marble effect.

Maple-Mascarpone Cheesecake

PREP: 35 minutes
BAKE: 43 minutes at 350°F
COOL: 2 hours
CHILL: 8 hours to overnight
MAKES: 16 servings

- 2 8-ounce packages cream cheese
- 1 3-ounce package cream cheese
- 1 8-ounce carton mascarpone cheese
- 3 eggs
- 1½ cups walnut pieces
- ¼ cup granulated sugar
- ¼ cup butter, melted
- ⅓ cup granulated sugar
- ⅓ cup packed light brown sugar
- 1 teaspoon vanilla
- 1 teaspoon maple flavoring
- ¼ teaspoon salt
- 1 cup plain Greek yogurt
- ¼ cup pure maple syrup
- ½ teaspoon vanilla
- ⅛ teaspoon salt
  Candied walnuts (optional)

1. Allow cream cheese, mascarpone cheese, and eggs to stand at room temperature for 30 minutes. Meanwhile, preheat oven to 350°F. Grease a 10-inch springform pan; set aside. In a food processor or blender combine the 1½ cups walnut pieces and the ¼ cup granulated sugar; cover and process with several on/off pulses until fine crumbs form. Add the ¼ cup melted butter; pulse to mix. Press crumb mixture firmly into the bottom of the prepared springform pan. Bake for 8 to 10 minutes or until crust is firm and light brown on the edges. Cool in pan on a wire rack.

2. In a large mixing bowl combine cream cheese, mascarpone cheese, the ⅓ cup granulated sugar, and the brown sugar. Beat with an electric mixer on medium to high speed about 5 minutes or until very light and fluffy. Scrape down sides of bowl; beat for 1 minute more. Add eggs, one at a time, beating well after each addition. Stir in the 1 teaspoon vanilla, the maple flavoring, and the ¼ teaspoon salt; mix well.

3. Pour cheese mixture into cooled crust. Bake in the 350°F oven for 25 to 30 minutes or until cheesecake is puffy around the edges but jiggles slightly when gently shaken. Cool in pan on a wire rack for 20 minutes.

4. In a small bowl combine yogurt, maple syrup, the ½ teaspoon vanilla, and the ⅛ teaspoon salt. Spread yogurt mixture evenly over cheesecake, spreading to within ½ inch of edges. Bake in the 350°F oven for 10 minutes more. Remove cheesecake from oven; while hot, run a thin knife around the edges of cheesecake. Cool completely in pan on a wire rack. Cover and chill for at least 8 hours or overnight.

5. To serve, loosen cheesecake from sides of pan; remove sides of pan. If desired, garnish with candied walnuts.

To Store: Place cheesecake in an airtight container and store in refrigerator for up to 5 days.

PER SERVING: *359 cal., 29 g fat (13 g sat. fat), 103 mg chol., 212 mg sodium, 20 g carb., 1 g fiber, 9 g pro.*

Boston Cream Cheesecake

PREP: **30 minutes**
BAKE: **1¼ hours at 325°F**
COOL: **2 hours**
CHILL: **4 hours to overnight**
MAKES: **16 servings**

3 8-ounce package cream cheese
3 eggs
1 package 1-layer-size yellow cake mix (such as Jiffy)
2 tablespoons butter, melted
¾ cup sugar
1 teaspoon vanilla
1 8-ounce carton sour cream
¾ cup whipping cream
6 ounces semisweet chocolate, finely chopped
2 tablespoons butter, softened

1. Allow cream cheese and eggs to stand at room temperature for 30 minutes. Meanwhile, preheat oven to 325°F. Grease the bottom of a 9-inch springform pan; set aside. Prepare cake mix according to package directions, except add 2 tablespoons melted butter. Pour batter into the prepared pan, spreading evenly. Bake for 25 minutes.

2. Meanwhile, for cheesecake filling, in a large mixing bowl beat cream cheese, sugar, and vanilla with an electric mixer on medium to high speed until smooth. Using a fork, lightly the beat eggs. Add eggs all at once, beating on low speed just until combined. Stir in sour cream. Carefully pour filling over cake layer in pan.

3. Bake for 50 to 55 minutes or until a 2-inch area around the outside edge appears set when gently shaken. Cool in pan on a wire rack for 15 minutes. Using a small sharp knife, loosen edges of cheesecake from sides of pan. Cool completely on the rack. Remove sides of pan. Cover cheesecake and chill for at least 4 hours or overnight.

4. Before serving, in a small saucepan bring whipping cream to simmering. Remove from heat. Add chocolate; stir until chocolate is melted and mixture is smooth. Stir in the 2 tablespoons softened butter. Chill about 15 minutes or until slightly thickened, stirring once. Spoon chocolate mixture onto cheesecake, spreading to cover top.

To Store: Place cheesecake or mini cheesecakes in an airtight container; cover. Store in the refrigerator for up to 3 days.

PER SERVING: *347 cal., 24 g fat (12 g sat. fat), 102 mg chol., 272 mg sodium, 30 g carb., 1 g fiber, 5 g pro.*

Make It Mini

Grease twenty-four 2½-inch muffin cups. Prepare cake batter as directed, except divide batter among prepared muffin cups. Bake for 12 minutes. Prepare cheesecake filling as directed; pour over cake layers in the muffin cups. Bake for 20 to 22 minutes more or until centers appear set when gently shaken. Cool cheesecakes in muffin cups on a wire rack. Run a knife around edge of each cheesecake before gently removing from the cup. Cover and chill for at least 4 hours or overnight. Continue as directed in Step 4.

Café au Lait Cheesecake

PREP: 30 minutes
BAKE: 45 minutes at 350°F
COOL: 2 hours
CHILL: 4 hours to overnight
MAKES: 12 servings

  3 8-ounce packages cream
     cheese
  4 eggs
  1¾ cups finely crushed
     chocolate wafer cookies
  ⅓ cup butter, melted
  2 ounces semisweet
     chocolate, chopped
  2 tablespoons water
  1 tablespoon instant espresso
     coffee powder or regular
     instant coffee crystals
  2 tablespoons coffee liqueur
     or water
  1 cup sugar
  2 tablespoons all-purpose
     flour
  1 teaspoon vanilla
     Instant espresso coffee
     powder (optional)

1. Allow cream cheese and eggs to stand at room temperature for 30 minutes. Meanwhile, for crust, in a medium bowl combine the crushed cookies and butter. Press cookie mixture onto the bottom and about 2 inches up the sides of an 8-inch springform pan. Chill crust until needed.
2. In a small saucepan combine chocolate, the water, and the 1 tablespoon espresso coffee powder. Cook and stir over low heat until chocolate starts to melt. Remove from heat; stir until chocolate is melted and smooth. Stir in coffee liqueur; cool.
3. Preheat oven to 350°F. For filling, in a large mixing bowl beat cream cheese, sugar, flour, and vanilla with an electric mixer on medium to high speed until smooth. Using a fork, lightly beat eggs. Stir eggs into cream cheese mixture. Reserve 2 cups of the filling; cover and chill.
4. Stir cooled chocolate mixture into the remaining filling, stirring just until combined. Pour chocolate filling into crust-lined pan; place pan in a shallow baking pan.

5. Bake about 30 minutes or until edge is set (center will be soft-set). Remove reserved filling from the refrigerator 10 minutes before needed. Carefully pour reserved filling in a ring around the outside edge of the cheesecake filling (where the filling is set). Gently spread in an even layer over entire surface. Bake for 15 to 20 minutes more or until center appears nearly set when gently shaken.
6. Cool in pan on a wire rack for 10 minutes. Using a small sharp knife, loosen crust from sides of pan; cool for 30 minutes more. Remove sides of pan; cool cheesecake completely on rack. Cover and chill for at least 4 hours or overnight before serving. If desired, dust cheesecake with additional espresso coffee powder before serving.

To Store: Place cheesecake in an airtight container; cover. Store in the refrigerator for up to 5 days.

PER SERVING: *424 cal., 29 g fat (17 g sat. fat), 146 mg chol., 333 mg sodium, 35 g carb., 2 g fiber, 8 g pro.*

Vanilla-Scented Orange Cheesecake

PREP: 40 minutes
BAKE: 45 minutes at 375°F
COOL: 2 hours
CHILL: 4 hours to overnight
MAKES: 12 servings

2   8-ounce packages cream
     cheese
1   8-ounce carton sour cream
4   eggs
1½   cups finely crushed
     chocolate graham crackers
     or chocolate wafer cookies
¼   cup finely chopped pecans
1   tablespoon sugar
½   cup butter, melted
1   vanilla bean, split
     lengthwise, or 1 teaspoon
     vanilla bean paste
1   cup sugar
3   tablespoons all-purpose
     flour
½   teaspoon finely shredded
     orange peel (see tip,
     page 102)
     Few drops orange food
     coloring
½   cup orange marmalade

1. Allow cream cheese, sour cream, and eggs to stand at room temperature for 30 minutes. Meanwhile, for crust, in a medium bowl combine crushed graham crackers, pecans, and 1 tablespoon sugar. Stir in melted butter. Press mixture onto the bottom and about 2 inches up the sides of an 8- or 9-inch springform pan; set aside.
2. Preheat oven to 375°F. If using vanilla bean, use the tip of a small sharp knife to scrape out seeds (see tip, page 17); set aside. In a large mixing bowl beat cream cheese, sour cream, the 1 cup sugar, and the flour with an electric mixer on medium to high speed until combined. Using a fork, lightly beat eggs. Add eggs to cream cheese mixture, beating just until combined. Divide batter in half. Stir orange peel and food coloring into half of the batter. Stir vanilla seeds or vanilla bean paste into the remaining batter.
3. Pour orange batter into crust-lined pan, spreading evenly. Spoon vanilla batter over orange layer, gently spreading evenly. Place springform pan in a shallow baking pan.

4. Bake for 45 to 55 minutes for the 8-inch pan, 40 to 50 minutes for the 9-inch pan, or until a 2½-inch area around outside edge appears set when gently shaken.
5. Cool in pan on a wire rack for 15 minutes. Using a small sharp knife, loosen crust from sides of pan. Cool for 30 minutes more. Remove sides of pan; cool completely on wire rack.
6. Spoon marmalade over top of cheesecake; carefully spread to outside edge.* Cover and chill for at least 4 hours or overnight before serving.

*Test Kitchen Tip: If the marmalade is too thick to spread, microwave on 100 percent power (high) for 15 to 20 seconds to reach spreading consistency.

To Store: Place cheesecake in an airtight container; cover. Store in the refrigerator for up to 3 days.

PER SERVING: *431 cal., 28 g fat (15 g sat. fat), 134 mg chol., 293 mg sodium, 40 g carb., 1 g fiber, 6 g pro.*

Cranberry-Lemon Cheesecake

PREP: **40 minutes**
BAKE: **45 minutes at 350°F**
COOL: **2 hours**
CHILL: **4 hours to overnight**
MAKES: **12 servings**

- 3 8-ounce packages cream cheese
- 3 eggs
- 1¾ cups finely crushed gingersnap cookies (about 30 cookies)
- 1 tablespoon granulated sugar
- 1½ teaspoons finely shredded lemon peel (see tip, page 102)
- ⅓ cup butter, melted
- ½ cup granulated sugar
- ½ cup packed brown sugar
- 2 tablespoons all-purpose flour
- ¼ cup milk
- ⅓ cup snipped dried cranberries
- ½ cup fresh cranberries, coarsely chopped
  Sugared cranberries* (optional)
  Lemon peel curls (optional)

1. Allow cream cheese and eggs to stand at room temperature for 30 minutes. Meanwhile, preheat oven to 350°F. In a medium bowl combine crushed cookies, the 1 tablespoon granulated sugar, and 1 teaspoon of the lemon peel; stir in butter. Press mixture evenly onto the bottom and about 1½ inches up the side of a 9-inch springform pan; set aside.

2. In a large mixing bowl beat cream cheese with an electric mixer on medium to high speed for 30 seconds. Add ½ cup granulated sugar, the brown sugar, and flour. Beat until combined. Beat in milk until smooth. Using a fork, lightly beat eggs. Stir eggs and the remaining ½ teaspoon lemon peel into cream cheese mixture. Fold in dried cranberries. Pour cream cheese mixture into crust-lined pan. Sprinkle with fresh cranberries. Place springform pan in a shallow baking pan.

3. Bake for 45 to 50 minutes or until a 2½-inch area around the outside edge appears set when gently shaken.

4. Cool in pan on a wire rack for 15 minutes. Using a knife, loosen edges of cheesecake from sides of pan; cool for 30 minutes more. Remove sides of pan; cool completely on rack. Cover and chill for at least 4 hours or overnight before serving. If desired, garnish with Sugared Cranberries and lemon peel curls.

***Test Kitchen Tip:** To make sugared cranberries, roll frozen cranberries in sugar to coat. Place on waxed paper; let stand at room temperature until dry.

To Store: Place cheesecake or mini cheesecakes in an airtight container; cover. Store in the refrigerator for up to 3 days.

PER SERVING: *421 cal., 28 g fat (15 g sat. fat), 129 mg chol., 356 mg sodium, 39 g carb., 1 g fiber, 6 g pro.*

Make It Mini

Lightly grease sixty 1¾-inch muffin cups (or twenty 2½-inch muffin cups) or line with paper bake cups. Prepare gingersnap crumb crust mixture as directed. Place 1 teaspoon crust mixture in each cup (1 tablespoon for 2½-inch cups), pressing it down lightly. Spoon 1½ tablespoons cream cheese mixture (¼ cup for 2½-inch cups) into each cup. Increase fresh cranberries to 1 cup. Bake for 10 to 11 minutes (15 minutes for 2½-inch cheesecakes) or until centers appear set. Cool cheesecakes in muffin cups. Run a knife around edge of each cheesecake before gently removing from the cup.

Mocha-Chocolate Chip Cheesecake with Strawberries

PREP: 35 minutes
BAKE: 45 minutes at 350°F
COOL: 2 hours
CHILL: 4 hours to overnight
MAKES: 12 servings

- 3   8-ounce packages cream cheese
- 4   eggs
- 1¾ cups finely crushed chocolate wafer cookies (about 32 cookies)
- ⅓   cup butter, melted
- 5   ounces semisweet chocolate, chopped
- 1   ounce unsweetened chocolate or semisweet chocolate, chopped
- 1¼ cups sugar
- 2   tablespoons all-purpose flour
- 1   teaspoon vanilla
- 1   tablespoon instant coffee crystals
- ¼   cup milk
- ¾   cup miniature semisweet chocolate pieces
- 2   cups fresh strawberries, halved or quartered
- 2   tablespoons sugar
- ½   teaspoon shredded orange peel (see tip, page 102)
      Sweetened whipped cream (see tip, page 16) (optional)

1. Allow cream cheese and eggs to stand at room temperature for 30 minutes. Meanwhile, for crust, in a medium bowl combine crushed cookies and melted butter. Press mixture evenly onto bottom and 1¾ inches up the sides of an ungreased 9-inch springform pan. Chill until needed.

2. Preheat oven to 350°F. For filling, in a small heavy saucepan combine chopped semisweet chocolate and unsweetened chocolate. Cook over low heat until melted, stirring occasionally. Cool slightly.

3. In a large bowl combine cream cheese, 1¼ cups sugar, flour, and vanilla. Beat with an electric mixer on medium to high speed until smooth. With mixer running, slowly add melted chocolate, beating on low speed just until combined. Using a fork, lightly beat eggs. Add eggs all at once to cream cheese mixture, beating on low speed just until combined. Stir coffee crystals into milk until dissolved. Stir milk mixture and miniature chocolate pieces into cream cheese mixture. Pour filling into crust-lined pan. Place springform pan in a shallow baking pan.

4. Bake for 45 to 50 minutes or until the center appears nearly set when gently shaken.

5. Cool in springform pan on a wire rack for 15 minutes. Using a small sharp knife, loosen crust from sides of pan. Cool for 30 minutes more. Remove sides of pan; cool completely on rack. Cover and chill for at least 4 hours or overnight before serving.

6. Meanwhile, in a small bowl combine strawberries, 2 tablespoons sugar, and the orange peel. Cover and chill for up to 4 hours.

7. To serve, top cheesecake with strawberry mixture and, if desired, whipped cream.

To Store: Place cheesecake (without toppings) in an airtight container; cover. Store in the refrigerator for up to 5 days.

PER SERVING: *587 cal., 37 g fat (21 g sat. fat), 147 mg chol., 339 mg sodium, 59 g carb., 2 g fiber, 9 g pro.*

Chocolate-Almond Cheesecake: Prepare as directed, except omit chocolate cookies and melted butter. For almond crust, use 2 teaspoons butter to grease the bottom and sides of a 9-inch springform pan. Press 1 cup finely ground toasted almonds evenly on the bottom and 1¾ inches up the sides of the greased pan. Chill crust until needed. Continue as directed.

PER SERVING: *522 cal., 34 g fat, (18 g sat. fat), 135 mg chol., 214 mg sodium, 49 g carb., 3 g fiber, 9 g pro.*

Pumpkin Spice Cheesecake with Sugared Pepitas

PREP: 30 minutes
BAKE: 1 hour 33 minutes
at 350°F
COOL: 2 hours
CHILL: overnight
MAKES: 16 servings

¼ cup butter
4 8-ounce packages cream cheese
4 eggs
¼ cup sugar
½ cup all-purpose flour
½ cup crushed shortbread cookies
1½ cups sugar
1 15-ounce can pumpkin
2 teaspoons ground cinnamon
2 teaspoons vanilla
1½ teaspoons ground ginger
½ teaspoon ground nutmeg
¼ teaspoon ground allspice
¼ teaspoon ground cloves
1 recipe Sugared Pepitas

1. Allow butter, cream cheese, and eggs to stand at room temperature for 30 minutes. Meanwhile, preheat oven to 350°F. Wrap a double layer of foil around the bottom and sides of an ungreased 9-inch springform pan to form a watertight seal; set aside.
2. For crust, in a small mixing bowl combine the butter and the ¼ cup sugar. Beat with an electric mixer on medium to high speed until fluffy. Add flour and crushed cookies; beat until combined. Press mixture onto the bottom of the prepared pan. Bake for 18 to 20 minutes or until golden brown. Cool on a wire rack.
3. For filling, in a large mixing bowl combine cream cheese and the 1½ cups sugar. Beat on medium to high speed until fluffy. Using a fork, lightly beat eggs. Add eggs, pumpkin, cinnamon, vanilla, ginger, nutmeg, allspice, and cloves; beat on low speed just until combined. Pour into crust-lined pan, spreading evenly.
4. Place the foil-wrapped pan in a large roasting pan. Pour enough boiling water into roasting pan to reach halfway up sides of the springform pan.
5. Bake for 1¼ to 1½ hours or until a 2-inch area around the outside edge appears set and the center appears nearly set

when gently shaken. Carefully remove springform pan from water. Remove foil from pan. Cool cheesecake completely in pan on a wire rack. Cover cheesecake in pan and chill overnight.
6. Prepare Sugared Pepitas; set aside. Using a small sharp knife, loosen cheesecake from sides of pan. Remove sides of pan. Sprinkle pepitas over cheesecake.

Sugared Pepitas: Preheat oven to 325°F. Grease a 15×10×1-inch baking pan; set aside. In a small bowl combine 1 egg white, 2 tablespoons sugar, ¼ teaspoon ground cinnamon, and ⅛ teaspoon salt. Add ½ cup raw pepitas (pumpkin seeds); stir gently to coat. Spread pepitas in a single layer in the prepared baking pan. Bake for 15 to 20 minutes or until seeds start to brown, stirring occasionally. Cool completely (pepitas will crisp slightly while cooling).

To Store: Place cheesecake in an airtight container; cover. Store in the refrigerator for up to 5 days.

PER SERVING: *393 cal., 27 g fat (14 g sat. fat), 123 mg chol., 256 mg sodium, 34 g carb., 1 g fiber, 7 g pro.*

Saucy Apple Dumplings, recipe page 262

desserts

CAPTURE THE WARM AND COMFORTING FEELING that comes with homespun desserts such as creamy baked custards, rich bread puddings, sweet cobblers and crisps, shortcakes, and more. Begin your walk down memory lane with the sweetest, most tender apple dumplings you've ever tasted.

Saucy Apple Dumplings

This classic "grandmother" dessert has withstood the test of time, maintaining its popularity almost as well as apple pie. We'll show you how to make dumplings, from creating the most tender crust to filling and enclosing the apples.

PREP: 45 minutes
BAKE: 50 minutes at 350°F
MAKES: 6 servings

- 2 cups water
- 1¼ cups sugar
- ½ teaspoon ground cinnamon
- ¼ cup butter
- 3 cups all-purpose flour
- ½ teaspoon salt
- 1 cup shortening
- ½ to ⅔ cup half-and-half, light cream, or whole milk
- 2 tablespoons chopped golden raisins or raisins
- 2 tablespoons chopped walnuts
- 1 tablespoon honey
- 2 tablespoons sugar
- ½ teaspoon ground cinnamon
- 6 small Granny Smith, Rome Beauty, or other cooking apples (about 1½ pounds total)
- 1 tablespoon butter

1. For sauce, in a medium saucepan combine the water, the 1¼ cups sugar, and ½ teaspoon cinnamon. Bring to boiling; reduce heat. Simmer, uncovered, for 5 minutes. Stir in the ¼ cup butter. Set aside.

2. Meanwhile, for pastry, in a medium bowl combine flour and salt. Using a pastry blender, cut in shortening until pieces are the size of small peas. Sprinkle 1 tablespoon of the half-and-half over part of the mixture; gently toss with a fork. Push moistened dough to the side of the bowl. Repeat moistening dough, using 1 tablespoon of the half-and-half at a time, until all of the dough is moistened. Form dough into a ball. On a lightly floured surface, roll dough into a 21×14-inch rectangle.* Using a pastry wheel or sharp knife, cut pastry into six 7-inch squares.

3. In a small bowl combine raisins, walnuts, and honey; set aside. In another small bowl stir together the 2 tablespoons sugar and ½ teaspoon cinnamon; set aside.

4. Preheat oven to 350°F. Peel and core apples. Place an apple on each pastry square. Fill centers of apples with raisin mixture.

Sprinkle with sugar-cinnamon mixture; dot with the 1 tablespoon butter. Moisten edges of each pastry square with water; fold corners to center over apple. Pinch to seal. Place dumplings in an ungreased 13×9×2-inch baking pan or dish. Reheat sauce to boiling; pour hot sauce over dumplings.

5. Bake, uncovered, for 50 to 55 minutes or until apples are tender and pastry is golden brown. To serve, spoon sauce from pan or dish over dumplings.

*Test Kitchen Tip: If desired, roll pastry slightly larger so you'll have extra pastry to make pastry leaves for garnishing. Cut the 7-inch squares of pastry; then reroll scraps and cut into leaf shapes. Moisten undersides of leaf shapes with water; place on top of dumplings, pressing slightly to adhere.

To Store: Let dumplings cool completely. Transfer to a smaller baking dish. Cover and store in the refrigerator for up to 2 days. To reheat, loosely cover with foil and bake in a 350°F oven until warm.

PER SERVING: *910 cal., 48 g fat (16 g sat. fat), 33 mg chol., 294 mg sodium, 115 g carb., 5 g fiber, 8 g pro.*

Secrets to Success

A rich, flaky pastry is essential to the success of apple dumplings. To obtain the ideal flakiness, this recipe uses two methods: cutting the shortening into the flour mixture and using cream for the liquid. How does this work? Cutting the fat into the flour mixture will allow pockets of fat to be formed when rolled out. When baked, these pockets will create tender, flaky layers in the pastry. Using cream for the liquid in the pastry adds additional fat. The fat surrounds the protein in the flour, giving a rich texture and adding to the tenderness of the pastry. Choose an apple variety that is best for baking—such as Granny Smith or Rome Beauty—to prevent mealiness or mushiness once baked.

CUT PASTRY SQUARES Using a pastry wheel or sharp knife, cut pastry into six 7-inch squares.

CORE WHOLE APPLES Using an apple corer, twist and remove each apple core.

FILL THE APPLES Place the apples on the pastry squares and spoon the fruit and honey mixture into the center.

FORM DOUGH AROUND APPLES Top each apple with a small piece of butter and gather the corners of the dough squares at the apple tops.

SEAL DOUGH EDGES Pinch the edges of the dough to form a tight seal.

ADD THE SAUCE Heat sauce to boiling and pour over the dumplings.

Make-It-Mine Cobbler

Pick and choose from different flour, spice, fruit, and topping options to customize cobbler to your tastes.

PREP: 25 minutes
BAKE: 20 minutes at 400°F
COOL: 1 hour
MAKES: 6 servings

    Flour (choose option)
2 tablespoons sugar
1½ teaspoons baking powder
¼ teaspoon salt
¼ cup butter, cut up
    Fruit Filling (choose option)
    Spice (choose option)
1 egg
¼ cup milk
    Sprinkle (choose option)
    Sweetened whipped cream (see photos, page 16) or scoops of vanilla ice cream

1. Preheat oven to 400°F. For biscuit topper, in a medium bowl stir together *Flour*, 2 tablespoons sugar, the baking powder, and salt. Using a pastry blender, cut in butter until the pieces are pea size; set aside.
2. For filling, in a large saucepan combine the *Fruit Filling* and *Spice*. Cook over medium heat until thickened and bubbly. Keep filling hot.
3. In a small bowl stir together egg and milk. Add to *Flour* mixture, stirring just until moistened. Transfer hot filling to a 2-quart square baking dish. Using a spoon, immediately drop biscuit topper into six mounds on top of filling. Top with desired *Sprinkle*.

4. Bake for 20 to 25 minutes or until biscuits are golden. Cool in dish on a wire rack for 1 hour. If desired, serve warm cobbler with sweetened whipped cream or vanilla ice cream.

FLOUR (PICK ONE)

1 cup all-purpose flour
¾ cup all-purpose flour and ¼ cup whole wheat flour
¾ cup all-purpose flour and ¼ cup white whole wheat flour
¾ cup all-purpose flour and ¼ cup quick-cooking oats
¾ cup all-purpose flour and ¼ cup ground almonds

FRUIT FILLING (PICK ONE)

Cherry: 6 cups fresh or frozen unsweetened pitted tart red or sweet cherries and 1 cup sugar and 3 tablespoons cornstarch
Apple: 6 cups sliced, peeled apples and 1 cup sugar and 3 tablespoons cornstarch
Blueberry: 6 cups fresh or frozen blueberries and ¾ cup sugar and 2 tablespoons cornstarch
Rhubarb: 6 cups fresh or frozen sliced rhubarb and 1 cup sugar and 2 tablespoons cornstarch
Peach: 6 cups sliced, peeled fresh or frozen peaches and 1 cup sugar and 3 tablespoons cornstarch
Pear: 6 cups sliced, peeled pears and 1 cup sugar and 2 tablespoons cornstarch

Peach-Blueberry: 3 cups sliced, peeled fresh or frozen peaches and 3 cups fresh or frozen blueberries and 1 cup sugar and 3 tablespoons cornstarch
Cherry-Rhubarb: 3 cups fresh or frozen unsweetened pitted tart red or sweet cherries and 3 cups fresh or frozen sliced rhubarb and 1 cup sugar and 3 tablespoons cornstarch
Cherry-Berry: 3 cups fresh or frozen unsweetened pitted tart red or sweet cherries and 3 cups fresh or frozen blueberries and 1 cup sugar and 3 tablespoons cornstarch
Pear-Rhubarb: 3 cups sliced, peeled pears and 3 cups fresh or frozen sliced rhubarb and 1 cup sugar and 2 tablespoons cornstarch

---

SPICE (PICK ONE)

½ teaspoon ground cinnamon
¼ teaspoon ground allspice
½ teaspoon ground ginger
½ teaspoon apple pie spice
½ teaspoon pumpkin pie spice
¼ teaspoon ground nutmeg

SPRINKLE (PICK ONE)

1 tablespoon cinnamon-sugar
½ cup shredded white cheddar or cheddar cheese
¼ cup finely chopped pecans, almonds, or walnuts

Berry Cobbler with Brown Sugar-Pecan Biscuits

PREP: 30 minutes
BAKE: 35 minutes at 375°F
COOL: 20 minutes
MAKES: 8 servings

- ½ cup pecans, toasted (see tip, page 343)
- 1¾ cups all-purpose flour
- ½ cup packed brown sugar
- 2½ teaspoons baking powder
- ½ teaspoon baking soda
- ½ teaspoon salt
- ¼ cup butter, cut up
- ⅔ cup buttermilk or sour milk (see tip, page 16)
- 4 cups fresh blackberries
- 4 cups fresh blueberries
- ¾ cup granulated sugar
- ¼ teaspoon salt
- 2 teaspoons finely shredded lemon peel
- 1 teaspoon grated fresh ginger
- 3 tablespoons lemon juice
- 2 tablespoons cornstarch
- 1 tablespoon whipping cream
- 1 tablespoon coarse sugar
  Sweetened whipped cream (see tip, page 16)

1. Preheat oven to 375°F. For biscuits, place pecans in a food processor. Cover and process with several on/off pulses until coarsely chopped. Add flour, brown sugar, baking powder, baking soda, and the ½ teaspoon salt. Cover and process with several on/off pulses until combined. Add butter. Cover and process with several on/off pulses until the biggest butter pieces are no larger than small peas.

2. Transfer flour mixture to a large bowl. Add buttermilk all at once. Using a fork, stir just until moistened. Turn dough out onto a lightly floured surface. Knead dough by folding and gently pressing it just until dough holds together. Pat or lightly roll dough into a ½-inch-thick rectangle or circle. Cut dough into eight 2½-inch squares or rounds with a table knife or fluted round cutter, rerolling scraps as necessary. Set aside.

3. In a 3-quart rectangular baking dish combine blackberries and blueberries. In a small bowl combine the ¾ cup granulated sugar and the ¼ teaspoon salt. Using the back of a spoon, press lemon peel and ginger into sugar mixture until it becomes fragrant. Gently stir sugar mixture into berries. In another small bowl combine lemon juice and cornstarch; gently stir into berry mixture.

4. Brush tops of biscuits with whipping cream; sprinkle with coarse sugar. Arrange biscuits on top of berry mixture.

5. Bake for 25 minutes. Cover loosely with foil; bake for 10 to 20 minutes more or until filling is bubbly around edges. Remove foil. Cool on a wire rack for at least 20 minutes before serving.

6. To serve, divide berry mixture among serving bowls; place a biscuit on each serving. Top with sweetened whipped cream.

PER SERVING: *491 cal., 18 g fat (8 g sat. fat), 39 mg chol., 495 mg sodium, 6 g carb., 7 g fiber, 6 g pro.*

Make It Mini

Preheat oven to 375°F. Arrange eight 10-ounce ramekins or custard cups in a 15×10×1-inch baking pan; set aside. Prepare biscuit dough as directed in Steps 1 and 2, except cut dough into rounds slightly smaller than the diameter of the ramekins; set aside. Prepare berry filling as directed in Step 3. Divide filling among ramekins. Brush tops of biscuits with whipping cream; sprinkle with coarse sugar. Cut each round into 4 wedges. Assemble rounds on filling in ramekins. Bake cobblers in baking pan for 25 to 30 minutes or until filling is bubbly around edges. Cool on a wire rack for at least 20 minutes before serving. Serve in ramekins with sweetened whipped cream. Makes 8 mini cobblers.

Granny Smith Cobbler with White Cheddar Biscuits

PREP: 35 minutes
BAKE: 25 minutes at 400°F
COOL: 30 minutes
MAKES: 12 servings

3 pounds Granny Smith apples, peeled, cored, and sliced (about 9 cups)
1 cup packed dark brown sugar
1 tablespoon balsamic vinegar
1 teaspoon ground cinnamon
¼ cup cold water
3 tablespoons cornstarch
1½ cups all-purpose flour
½ cup finely ground pecans or almonds or ½ cup all-purpose flour
3 tablespoons granulated sugar
1 tablespoon baking powder
1 teaspoon salt
½ cup butter
2 eggs, lightly beaten
½ cup milk
½ cup shredded aged white cheddar cheese (2 ounces)
Vanilla ice cream (optional)

1. Preheat oven to 400°F. In a 4- to 6-quart Dutch oven combine apples, brown sugar, balsamic vinegar, and cinnamon. Bring to boiling, stirring occasionally once apples begin to release their juices. Reduce heat; simmer, covered, about 5 minutes or until apples are nearly tender, stirring occasionally. In a small bowl stir together the cold water and cornstarch; add to apple mixture. Cook and stir until thickened and bubbly. Keep hot over low heat.

2. In a large bowl combine flour, ground nuts, granulated sugar, baking powder, and salt. Using a pastry blender, cut in butter until pieces are pea size. In a medium bowl stir together eggs, milk, and cheese. Add egg mixture to flour mixture; stir just until combined. Spoon the hot apple mixture evenly into a 3-quart rectangular baking dish. Using a spoon, drop dough mixture into 12 mounds on top of fruit.

3. Bake for 25 to 30 minutes or until top is golden and filling is bubbly. Cool on a wire rack for 30 minutes. Serve warm. If desired, top with ice cream.

To Store: Transfer leftovers to a smaller ovenproof dish. Cover and store in the refrigerator for up to 2 days. To reheat, cover with foil and bake in a 350°F oven until warmed through.

PER SERVING: *326 cal., 14 g fat (7 g sat. fat), 61 mg chol., 390 mg sodium, 5 g carb., 2 g fiber, 5 g pro.*

Cherry Cobbler with White Chocolate-Almond Biscuits

PREP: 35 minutes
BAKE: 25 minutes at 375°F
COOL: 1 hour
MAKES: 12 servings

- 1¾ cups all-purpose flour
- ¼ cup granulated sugar
- 4 teaspoons baking powder
- ½ teaspoon salt
- ½ cup butter, cut up
- 12 cups frozen unsweetened pitted tart red cherries (3½ pounds)
- 2 cups granulated sugar
- 6 tablespoons cornstarch
- 2 eggs, lightly beaten
- ¾ cup milk
- 1 teaspoon almond extract
- ½ teaspoon vanilla
- 8 ounces white baking chocolate with cocoa butter, cut into ½-inch chunks
- 1 cup slivered almonds, toasted (see tip, page 343) and coarsely chopped
  Pearl or sanding sugar (optional)
- 1 recipe Mascarpone Dream (optional)

1. Preheat oven to 375°F. For biscuits, in a medium bowl stir together flour, the ¼ cup granulated sugar, the baking powder, and salt. Using a pastry blender, cut in butter until pieces are pea size. Make a well in the center of flour mixture. Cover and chill while preparing filling.

2. For filling, in a Dutch oven combine cherries, the 2 cups granulated sugar, and the cornstarch. Cook over medium heat until cherries release their juices, stirring occasionally. Increase heat to medium-high; cook and stir until thickened and bubbly. Keep filling hot.

3. In a small bowl combine eggs, milk, almond extract, and vanilla. Add egg mixture, white chocolate, and almonds all at once to flour mixture. Using a fork, stir just until mixture is moistened.

4. Transfer hot filling to a 3-quart rectangular baking dish. Immediately drop biscuit dough into 12 to 16 mounds onto filling. If desired, sprinkle biscuit mounds with pearl sugar.

5. Bake for 25 to 30 minutes or until biscuits are golden. Cool on a wire rack about 1 hour. Serve warm. If desired, serve with Mascarpone Dream.

Mascarpone Dream: Place one 8-ounce carton mascarpone cheese in a large mixing bowl. Let stand at room temperature for 30 minutes. Beat mascarpone cheese with an electric mixer on low speed for 30 seconds. Beat in 1 cup sugar. Gradually beat in 1 cup whipping cream and 1½ teaspoons almond extract until soft peaks form (tips curl). Use immediately or cover and chill for up to 6 hours.

To Store: Transfer leftovers to a smaller ovenproof dish. Cover and store in the refrigerator for up to 2 days. To reheat, cover with foil and bake in a 350°F oven until warmed through.

PER SERVING: *540 cal., 20 g fat (10 g sat. fat), 60 mg chol., 272 mg sodium, 86 g carb., 4 g fiber, 8 g pro.*

Perfect Peach Crisp

PREP: 25 minutes
BAKE: 35 minutes at 375°F
MAKES: 6 servings

- 6 cups sliced, peeled fresh ripe peaches or two 16-ounce packages frozen unsweetened peach slices
- ½ cup granulated sugar
- 2 tablespoons all-purpose flour
- ½ cup regular rolled oats
- ½ cup packed brown sugar
- ¼ cup all-purpose flour
- ¼ teaspoon ground cinnamon, ginger, or nutmeg
- ¼ cup butter
- ¼ cup chopped nuts or flaked coconut
- Vanilla ice cream (optional)

1. Preheat oven to 375°F. In a large bowl combine peaches, granulated sugar, and the 2 tablespoons flour. Transfer to a 1½- to 2-quart square baking dish; set aside.

2. For topping, in a medium bowl combine oats, brown sugar, flour, and cinnamon. Cut in butter until mixture resembles coarse crumbs. Stir in the nuts. Sprinkle topping over peach mixture.

3. Bake for 35 to 40 minutes or until peaches are tender and topping is golden. (If using frozen fruit, bake for 50 to 60 minutes or until filling is bubbly across entire surface.) If necessary, cover with foil the last 10 minutes to prevent overbrowning. If desired, serve warm with ice cream.

To Store: Transfer leftovers to a smaller ovenproof dish. Cover and store in the refrigerator for up to 2 days. To reheat, cover with foil and bake in a 350°F oven until warmed through.

PER SERVING: *358 cal., 12 g fat (5 g sat. fat), 20 mg chol., 60 mg sodium, 62 g carb., 3 g fiber, 4 g pro.*

Cherry Crisp: Prepare as directed, except substitute 6 cups fresh pitted tart red cherries (or two 16-ounce packages frozen unsweetened pitted tart red cherries) for the peaches.

PER SERVING: *377 cal., 12 g fat (5 g sat. fat), 20 mg chol., 65 mg sodium, 67 g carb., 4 g fiber, 5 g pro.*

Rhubarb Crisp: Prepare as directed, except substitute 6 cups sliced fresh rhubarb or two 16-ounce packages frozen unsweetened sliced rhubarb for the peaches. For the filling, increase granulated sugar to ¾ cup and add 3 tablespoons all-purpose flour.

PER SERVING: *358 cal., 12 g fat (5 g sat. fat), 20 mg chol., 65 mg sodium, 62 g carb., 4 g fiber, 4 g pro.*

Apple Crisp: Prepare as directed, except substitute 6 cups sliced, peeled cooking apples for the peaches. Reduce granulated sugar to 3 tablespoons and omit the 2 tablespoons all-purpose flour.

PER SERVING: *298 cal., 12 g fat (5 g sat. fat), 20 mg chol., 65 mg sodium, 67 g carb., 4 g fiber, 5 g pro.*

Strawberry-Raspberry-Rhubarb Crumble

PREP: **30 minutes**
BAKE: **1¼ hours at 375°F**
MAKES: **12 servings**

1⅔ cups all-purpose flour
½ cup packed brown sugar
½ cup slivered almonds (optional)
2 teaspoons baking powder
2 teaspoons finely shredded lemon peel (see tip, page 102)
½ cup butter, melted
6 cups fresh strawberries, hulled and quartered, or whole frozen unsweetened strawberries
3 cups fresh rhubarb, cut into ½-inch slices, or frozen unsweetened sliced rhubarb
2 cups fresh raspberries or frozen unsweetened raspberries
1 cup granulated sugar
⅓ cup cornstarch
¼ teaspoon salt
2 tablespoons Chambord or raspberry liqueur (optional)
Crème fraîche (optional)

1. Preheat oven to 375°F. Grease a 3-quart rectangular baking dish; set aside.

2. For topping, in a medium bowl stir together flour, brown sugar, almonds (if desired), baking powder, and lemon peel. Add melted butter; mix until clumps form. Cover and chill topping while preparing filling.

3. For filling, in a very large bowl combine strawberries, rhubarb, and raspberries. In a small bowl stir together granulated sugar, cornstarch, and salt. Add sugar mixture to fruit; toss well to combine. If desired, drizzle Chambord over fruit mixture; toss gently to combine. Transfer filling to the prepared baking dish. If using frozen fruit, allow filling to stand at room temperature for 45 minutes.

4. Cover filling with topping. Place baking dish in a 15×10×1-inch baking pan.

5. Bake about 1¼ hours (1½ hours if using frozen fruit) or until fruit is bubbly in the center and topping is golden. If necessary, cover with foil the last 30 minutes of baking to prevent topping from overbrowning. Serve warm or at room temperature. If desired, serve with crème fraîche.

To Store: Transfer leftovers to a smaller ovenproof dish. Cover and store in the refrigerator for up to 2 days. To reheat, cover with foil and bake in a 350°F oven until warmed through.

PER SERVING: *285 cal., 8 g fat (5 g sat. fat), 20 mg chol., 182 mg sodium, 52 g carb., 4 g fiber, 3 g pro.*

Make It Mini

Preheat oven to 375°F. Grease twelve 6-ounce or eight 10-ounce ramekins or custard cups. Place ramekins in two 15×10×1-inch baking pans; set aside. Prepare topping and filling as directed. Divide filling among ramekins. Cover filling with topping. Bake crumbles in baking pans for 40 to 45 minutes (50 to 60 minutes if using frozen fruit) or until filling is bubbly and topping is golden. If necessary, cover with foil the last 10 minutes of baking to prevent topping from overbrowning. Serve as directed. Makes 12 (6-ounce) or 8 (10-ounce) servings.

Apple-Cranberry Dessert

PREP: **30 minutes**
BAKE: **1 hour at 325°F**
MAKES: **15 servings**

- 2 12-ounce packages fresh or frozen cranberries or two 16-ounce packages frozen unsweetened pitted tart red cherries*
- 2 cups chopped, peeled cooking apples (3 medium)
- 2 tablespoons butter, cut up
- 1¼ cups sugar
- ¾ cup chopped walnuts or pecans
- 2 eggs, lightly beaten
- 1 cup sugar
- ¾ cup all-purpose flour
- ¾ cup butter, melted
  Vanilla ice cream (optional)

1. Preheat oven to 325°F. Grease the bottom of a 13×9×2-inch baking pan. Add cranberries and apples; toss gently to mix. Dot fruit with the 2 tablespoons butter. Sprinkle with the 1¼ cups sugar and the nuts.

2. In a medium bowl combine eggs, the 1 cup sugar, the flour, and ¾ cup melted butter. Pour evenly over cranberry mixture.

3. Bake, uncovered, for 1 to 1¼ hours or until the top is golden. Serve warm or at room temperature. If desired, top servings with ice cream.

*Test Kitchen Tip: If using frozen cranberries, do not thaw before tossing with apples. If using frozen cherries, let stand at room temperature for 30 minutes before tossing with apples.

PER SERVING: *312 cal., 16 g fat (6 g sat. fat), 58 mg chol., 91 mg sodium, 42 g carb., 3 g fiber, 3 g pro.*

Seasonal Crunch

Cranberries—commonly found fresh during the late fall and early winter months—complement apples in this mouthwatering dessert, adding a fresh pop of sweet-sour flavor and bright red color. While fruit bakes, the juices of the fruit bubble up and are absorbed by the sweet, rich crust on top. If you like, substitute cherries for the cranberries.

Maple Bread Pudding with Pecan Praline

PREP: 35 minutes
CHILL: 1 hour
BAKE: 40 minutes at 375°F
COOL: 30 minutes
MAKES: 12 servings

1 cup granulated sugar
¼ cup water
½ cup chopped pecans, toasted (see tip, page 343)
8 eggs
4 cups half-and-half or light cream
1 cup packed brown sugar
1 cup maple syrup
1 tablespoon vanilla
1 1-pound loaf egg bread, torn into bite-size pieces (about 14 cups)
Vanilla ice cream (optional)

1. For pecan praline, lightly grease a baking sheet; set aside. In a small saucepan combine granulated sugar and water. Cook over medium heat, stirring to dissolve sugar. Bring to boiling; reduce heat. Without stirring, boil gently, uncovered, about 7 minutes or until mixture turns a deep amber color. Remove from heat. Stir in pecans. Quickly pour onto the prepared baking sheet. Let cool. Break or chop praline into pieces; set aside.

2. In a very large bowl whisk together eggs, half-and-half, brown sugar, maple syrup, and vanilla. Add bread pieces; stir to moisten evenly. Cover and chill for 1 hour.

3. Preheat oven to 375°F. Lightly grease a 3-quart rectangular baking dish. Transfer bread mixture to the prepared baking dish. Bake, uncovered, about 40 minutes or until golden brown and a knife inserted in the center comes out clean. Cool on a wire rack for 30 minutes.

4. To serve, spoon warm bread pudding into bowls. If desired, top with scoops of ice cream. Sprinkle with pecan praline.

To Store: Let any leftover pudding cool completely on a wire rack. Transfer leftovers to a smaller ovenproof dish. Cover and store in the refrigerator for up to 2 days. To reheat, cover with foil and bake in a 350°F oven until warmed through.

PER SERVING: *647 cal., 26 g fat (13 g sat. fat), 222 mg chol., 331 mg sodium, 92 g carb., 2 g fiber, 13 g pro.*

Richness is Key

Egg bread, such as brioche or challah, produces a particularly rich texture and flavor in bread puddings. The bite-size pieces are perfect for soaking up all the custard, yet hold together well enough to give the baked dessert texture.

Chocolate-Walnut Bread Pudding with Coffee-Kahlúa Cream Sauce

PREP: **20 minutes**
BAKE: **50 minutes at 350°F**
MAKES: **12 servings**

6 cups dried French bread cubes (see below)
1¼ cups semisweet chocolate pieces
1 cup coarsely chopped walnuts
4 eggs, lightly beaten
3 cups milk
1 cup sugar
1 tablespoon vanilla
1 recipe Coffee-Kahlúa Cream Sauce

1. Preheat oven to 350°F. Generously grease a 3-quart rectangular baking dish. Spread bread cubes in the prepared baking dish. Sprinkle with chocolate pieces and walnuts.

2. In a large bowl combine eggs, milk, sugar, and vanilla. Pour egg mixture evenly over bread mixture. Using the back of a large spoon, gently press down on bread mixture to moisten.

3. Bake for 50 to 60 minutes or until a knife inserted near the center comes out clean. If necessary to prevent overbrowning, cover loosely with foil for the last 5 to 10 minutes of baking. Cool slightly. Serve warm with Coffee-Kahlúa Cream Sauce.

Coffee-Kahlúa Cream Sauce: In a medium saucepan stir together ½ cup sugar and 4 teaspoons cornstarch. Stir in 1 cup whipping cream; ½ cup strong freshly brewed coffee; and ½ cup Kahlúa, other coffee liqueur, or water. Cook and stir over medium heat until thickened and bubbly.

To Store: Let any leftover pudding cool completely on a wire rack. Transfer leftovers to a smaller ovenproof dish. Cover and store in the refrigerator for up to 2 days. Store Coffee-Kahlúa Cream Sauce in a covered container in the refrigerator for up to 2 days. To reheat, cover pudding with foil and bake in a 350°F oven until warmed through. Transfer sauce to a small saucepan and reheat over low heat just until warm.

PER SERVING: *455 cal., 22 g fat (9 g sat. fat), 103 mg chol., 175 mg sodium, 56 g carb., 2 g fiber, 9 g pro.*

Drying Out Bread Cubes

For dried bread cubes, preheat oven to 300°F. Cut bread into ½-inch cubes. Spread cubes in a shallow baking pan. Bake for 10 to 15 minutes or until dried, stirring twice; cool.

Browned Butter Bread Pudding

PREP: **40 minutes**
BAKE: **40 minutes at 350°F**
MAKES: **8 servings**

- 8 cups 1-inch cubes dry sweet egg bread* (such as challah or Hawaiian)
- 1 cup chopped pitted dates
- ¾ cup butter
- 6 eggs, lightly beaten
- 3 cups milk
- ⅓ cup sugar
- 1 tablespoon vanilla
- ¼ teaspoon ground nutmeg
- ¼ teaspoon ground cinnamon
- 2 tablespoons coarsely chopped hazelnuts, toasted (see tips, pages 17 and 343)
- 2 cups powdered sugar
- ¼ teaspoon vanilla
- 2 to 4 tablespoons milk

1. Preheat oven to 350°F. Grease a 2-quart rectangular baking dish; set aside. In a large bowl combine bread cubes and dates; set aside.
2. In a small skillet heat and stir butter until browned. Remove from heat. Place ¼ cup of the browned butter in another large bowl (set aside remaining butter for sauce). Beat in eggs, milk, sugar, the 1 tablespoon vanilla, the nutmeg, and cinnamon until combined. Pour egg mixture over bread mixture; toss to coat.

3. Turn bread mixture into the prepared baking dish. Place baking dish on baking sheet. Bake, uncovered, for 40 to 45 minutes or until a knife inserted near center comes out clean.
4. Remove baking dish from oven; cool slightly. Sprinkle with nuts.
5. For browned butter sauce, in a small bowl stir together the ½ cup reserved browned butter, the powdered sugar, and the ¼ teaspoon vanilla. Whisk in enough milk to make drizzling consistency. Serve sauce with warm bread pudding.

***Test Kitchen Tip:** To make dry bread cubes, spread the cubes on a large baking sheet. Let the bread cubes stand, uncovered, on a kitchen counter overnight, stirring them occasionally.

To Store: Completely cool leftover pudding or mini puddings on wire racks. Cover and store in the refrigerator for up to 3 days. To reheat, cover with lid or foil and bake in a 350°F oven until warmed through.

PER SERVING: *633 cal., 28 g fat (15 g sat. fat), 215 mg chol., 371 mg sodium, 84 g carb., 4 g fiber, 15 g pro.*

Make It Mini

Preheat oven to 350°F. Grease twenty-four 2½-inch muffin cups or line with foil bake cups; set aside. Prepare bread mixture as directed. Spoon bread mixture evenly into prepared muffin cups. Bake, uncovered, for 15 to 17 minutes or until puffed and a knife inserted near centers comes out clean. Cool in pans for 5 minutes. If using greased muffin cups, use a sharp knife to loosen puddings from sides of muffin cups. Transfer to a serving platter. Sprinkle puddings with nuts. Prepare sauce as directed; serve with warm puddings. Pass any additional sauce. Makes 24 desserts.

Campfire S'mores Bread Pudding

PREP: **25 minutes**
BAKE: **47 minutes at 325°F**
STAND: **5 minutes**
MAKES: **9 servings**

4 frankfurter buns, cut into 1-inch pieces
4 eggs, lightly beaten
1 14-ounce can sweetened condensed milk
¾ cup milk
1 teaspoon vanilla
¼ teaspoon ground nutmeg
1 cup tiny marshmallows
¾ cup semisweet chocolate pieces
½ cup coarsely crushed graham crackers (6 graham cracker squares)
2 tablespoons milk

1. Preheat oven to 325°F. Grease a 2-quart square baking dish; set aside. Place bun pieces on a baking sheet. Bake for 7 to 8 minutes or until dry and crisp; cool.

2. In a medium bowl combine eggs, sweetened condensed milk, the ¾ cup milk, the vanilla, and nutmeg; set aside.

3. Place bun pieces in the prepared baking dish. Sprinkle with ½ cup of the marshmallows and ½ cup of the chocolate pieces. Pour milk mixture evenly over layers in dish. Let stand for 5 minutes. Sprinkle with crushed graham crackers. Bake for 35 minutes. Sprinkle with ¼ cup of the marshmallows. Bake about 5 minutes more or until a knife inserted near the center comes out clean.

4. For drizzle, in a small saucepan cook and stir the remaining ¼ cup marshmallows, the remaining ¼ cup chocolate pieces, and the 2 tablespoons milk over low heat until melted and smooth. Drizzle over bread pudding. Serve warm.

To Store: Let any leftover pudding cool completely on a wire rack. Transfer leftovers to a smaller ovenproof dish. Cover and store in the refrigerator for up to 2 days. To reheat, cover with foil and bake in a 350°F oven until warmed through.

PER SERVING: *348 cal., 12 g fat (6 g sat. fat), 111 mg chol., 221 mg sodium, 52 g carb., 1 g fiber, 10 g pro.*

Toffee-Pear Sticky Pudding

PREP: 30 minutes
BAKE: 43 minutes at 350°F
COOL: 10 minutes
MAKES: 9 servings

1¼ cups water
1¼ cups pitted whole dates, preferably Medjool dates
 1 cup chopped, peeled fresh pears
 ½ teaspoon baking soda
 1 cup all-purpose flour
 1 teaspoon baking powder
 ½ teaspoon salt
 ¼ teaspoon ground nutmeg
 ¾ cup packed dark brown sugar
 ⅓ cup butter, softened
 2 eggs
 ½ teaspoon vanilla
 1 recipe Toffee-Pear Sauce

1. In a large saucepan combine the water, dates, and pears. Bring to boiling; reduce heat. Cook, covered, about 15 minutes or until fruit is tender and most of the liquid is absorbed. Mash with a potato masher, fork, or immersion blender until as smooth as possible. Stir in baking soda; set aside.

2. Preheat oven to 350°F. Grease an 8×8×2-inch baking pan; set aside. In a small bowl combine flour, baking powder, salt, and nutmeg; set aside. In a large mixing bowl combine brown sugar and butter. Beat with an electric mixer on medium speed about 1 minute or until combined. Beat in eggs, one at a time, and vanilla. Stir in date-pear mixture. Stir in flour mixture just until combined. Pour batter into prepared baking pan.

3. Bake for 40 to 45 minutes or until a wooden toothpick inserted near the center comes out clean. Place pan on a wire rack. Immediately use a long skewer to prick top of cake all over. Spoon the portion of Toffee-Pear Sauce without pears over cake. Bake for 3 minutes more. Cool on the wire rack for 10 minutes. Serve warm with the portion of Toffee-Pear Sauce with pears.

Toffee-Pear Sauce: Peel, core, and thinly slice 1 pear. In a medium skillet melt 1 tablespoon butter over medium heat. Add pear slices; cook for 2 to 3 minutes or until tender and light brown, turning pear slices occasionally and reducing heat to low if slices brown too quickly. Set aside. In a small saucepan heat ½ cup butter over medium heat until melted. Stir in ¾ cup packed brown sugar. Bring to boiling, stirring until sugar is dissolved. Reduce heat. Boil gently, uncovered, for 5 minutes, stirring occasionally. Carefully stir in ¾ cup whipping cream. Return to boiling. Remove from heat; stir in 1 teaspoon vanilla. Divide sauce in half. Stir pear slices into one portion.

To Store: Let any leftover pudding cool completely on a wire rack. Transfer to a smaller ovenproof dish. Cover and store in the refrigerator for up to 2 days. Store Toffee-Pear Sauce in a covered container in the refrigerator for up to 2 days. To reheat, cover pudding with foil and bake in a 350°F oven until warmed through. Reheat sauce in a small saucepan over low heat just until warm.

PER SERVING: *531 cal., 27 g fat (17 g sat. fat), 123 mg chol., 405 mg sodium, 72 g carb., 4 g fiber, 4 g pro.*

Blueberry Sugar Shortcake with Warm Peach Compote

PREP: **35 minutes**
BAKE: **35 minutes at 375°F**
MAKES: **8 servings**

2¼ cups all-purpose flour
 ⅓ cup granulated sugar
  1 tablespoon baking powder
  1 teaspoon salt
  1 cup fresh blueberries
1⅓ cups whipping cream
  2 tablespoons unsalted butter, melted
  2 tablespoons granulated sugar
  3 tablespoons butter
 ⅓ cup packed brown sugar
  8 cups sliced, peeled peaches (2 to 2½ pounds)
 ½ cup whipping cream
    Fresh thyme sprigs (optional)

1. Preheat oven to 375°F. Grease a large baking sheet; set aside. In a large bowl stir together flour, the ⅓ cup granulated sugar, the baking powder, and salt; gently stir in blueberries. Add the 1⅓ cups whipping cream, stirring with a fork just until moistened.
2. Turn dough out onto prepared baking sheet. Pat dough into a 6-inch circle. Brush top and sides with melted butter; sprinkle top with the 2 tablespoons granulated sugar. Bake for 35 to 40 minutes or until golden and a toothpick inserted in center comes out clean. Cool on baking sheet for 5 minutes. Transfer to a wire rack; cool completely.
3. For peach compote, in a large nonstick skillet melt the 3 tablespoons butter over medium-high heat. Stir in brown sugar; cook about 2 minutes or until brown sugar starts to melt.

Add the peaches; cook for 3 to 4 minutes or until peaches are heated through, stirring occasionally.
4. To serve, in a medium bowl whisk the whipping cream until soft peaks form (tips curl). To assemble, split shortcake horizontally in half. Place bottom of shortcake on a serving plate. Spoon peach compote onto bottom half and top with whipped cream. Replace top half of shortcake. If desired, garnish with fresh thyme sprigs.

PER SERVING: *410 cal., 19 g fat (12 g sat. fat), 60 mg chol., 410 mg sodium, 58 g carb., 2 g fiber, 4 g pro.*

How to Shape and Split a Shortcake

1. Use your hands to pat dough into a 6-inch circle.

2. Use a serrated knife to cut the shortcake in half horizontally.

Brownie Pudding Cake

PREP: 15 minutes
BAKE: 40 minutes at 350°F
COOL: 45 minutes
MAKES: 6 servings

1 cup all-purpose flour
¾ cup granulated sugar
2 tablespoons unsweetened cocoa powder
2 teaspoons baking powder
¼ teaspoon salt
½ cup milk
2 tablespoons vegetable oil
1 teaspoon vanilla
½ cup chopped walnuts
¾ cup packed brown sugar
¼ cup unsweetened cocoa powder
1½ cups boiling water
Vanilla ice cream (optional)

1. Preheat oven to 350°F. Grease an 8×8×2-inch baking pan; set aside. In a medium bowl stir together flour, granulated sugar, the 2 tablespoons cocoa powder, the baking powder, and salt. Stir in the milk, oil, and vanilla. Stir in the walnuts. Pour batter into prepared pan.

2. In a small bowl stir together the brown sugar and the ¼ cup cocoa powder. Stir in the boiling water. Slowly pour brown sugar mixture over batter.

3. Bake for 40 minutes. Cool on a wire rack for 45 to 60 minutes. To serve, spoon warm cake into dessert bowls; spoon pudding from the bottom of the pan over cake. If desired, add a scoop of vanilla ice cream.

To Store: Transfer leftovers to an ovenproof dish. Cover and store in the refrigerator for up to 2 days. To reheat, cover with foil and bake in a 350°F oven until warmed through.

PER SERVING: *406 cal., 12 g fat (2 g sat. fat), 2 mg chol., 237 mg sodium, 74 g carb., 3 g fiber, 5 g pro.*

Proof Is in the Pudding

This homey, old-fashioned pudding cake has two delicious layers, a moist chocolate cake and a thick chocolate pudding sauce. As it bakes, the cake miraculously rises to the top, leaving the pudding layer on the bottom. The cake is done when it starts to pull away from the sides of the pan. Its texture will be somewhere between cake and brownie. Complete each serving of the dessert with a scoop of vanilla ice cream.

White Chocolate Crème Brûlée

PREP: **20 minutes**
BAKE: **30 minutes at 325°F**
CHILL: **1 to 8 hours**
STAND: **20 minutes**
MAKES: **6 servings**

1¾ cups half-and-half or
   light cream
  4 ounces white baking
   chocolate with cocoa butter,
   chopped
  5 egg yolks, lightly beaten
⅓ cup sugar
  1 teaspoon vanilla
⅛ teaspoon salt
  2 tablespoons sugar

1. Preheat oven to 325°F. In a small heavy saucepan heat and stir ½ cup of the half-and-half and the white chocolate over low heat just until chocolate is melted. Gradually whisk in the remaining 1¼ cups half-and-half. Bring to simmering. Remove from heat.
2. In a medium bowl whisk together egg yolks, the ⅓ cup sugar, the vanilla, and salt just until combined. Slowly whisk hot chocolate mixture into egg mixture.
3. Place six 4-ounce ramekins or 6-ounce custard cups in a 3-quart rectangular baking dish. Divide egg mixture evenly among ramekins. Place baking dish on oven rack. Pour enough boiling water into baking dish to reach halfway up sides of ramekins.

4. Bake for 30 to 40 minutes or until a knife inserted near the centers comes out clean (centers will shake slightly). Remove ramekins from water; cool on a wire rack. Cover and chill for 1 to 8 hours.
5. Before serving, let custards stand at room temperature for 20 minutes. Meanwhile, for caramelized sugar, in an 8-inch heavy skillet heat the 2 tablespoons sugar over medium-high heat until sugar begins to melt, shaking skillet occasionally to heat sugar evenly. Do not stir. Once the sugar starts to melt, reduce heat to low and cook about 3 minutes or until all of the sugar is melted and golden, stirring as needed with a wooden spoon.
6. Quickly drizzle caramelized sugar over custards. (If sugar hardens in the skillet, return to heat; stir until melted.) Serve immediately.

PER SERVING: *307 cal., 18 g fat (10 g sat. fat), 180 mg chol., 98 mg sodium, 31 g carb., 0 g fiber, 6 g pro.*

How to Temper Eggs

For recipes with a custard base, such as a crème brûlée, you must "temper," or heat, the eggs gradually. First, whisk together the egg yolk and sugar mixture. Then slowly pour the simmered half-and-half or cream mixture into the yolk mixture, whisking constantly to heat the eggs slowly and prevent them from curdling (separating), which would ruin the mixture.

Slowly whisk half-and-half mixture into egg mixture.

Salted Caramel Pots de Crème

PREP: **35 minutes**
BAKE: **40 minutes at 325°F**
COOL: **30 minutes**
CHILL: **4 to 24 hours**
MAKES: **8 servings**

1¼ cups sugar
¼ cup water
¼ teaspoon salt
1½ cups whipping cream
½ cup whole milk
6 egg yolks
1 teaspoon fleur de sel or other flaked sea salt

1. Preheat oven to 325°F. Place eight 4-ounce pots de crème pots or ramekins or 6-ounce custard cups in a large roasting pan.
2. In a medium saucepan stir together sugar, the water, and the ¼ teaspoon salt. Heat and stir over low heat until sugar is dissolved. Using a soft pastry brush dipped in water, brush down any sugar crystals on the sides of the saucepan. Increase heat to medium-high; bring mixture to boiling. Boil, without stirring, for 8 to 10 minutes or until mixture turns an amber color. Remove from heat.
3. Whisking constantly, carefully add whipping cream and milk in a slow stream (mixture will steam and sugar will harden). Return to heat. Cook and whisk about 2 minutes more or until sugar has dissolved.
4. In a large bowl whisk egg yolks until light and foamy. Slowly whisk whipping cream mixture into beaten egg yolks.

Pour through a fine-mesh sieve into a glass 4-cup measure with a pouring spout. Divide mixture among pots de crème pots.
5. Add enough hot water to the roasting pan to come halfway up the sides of the dishes. Carefully place pan on the center rack of the oven. Bake about 40 minutes or until edges are set but centers jiggle slightly when shaken. Transfer dishes to wire racks; cool for 30 minutes. Cover with plastic wrap. Chill for 4 to 24 hours.
6. Before serving, sprinkle custards with fleur de sel.

To Store: Cover pots de crème with plastic wrap. Store in the refrigerator for up to 24 hours.

PER SERVING: *327 cal., 21 g fat (12 g sat. fat), 221 mg chol., 302 mg sodium, 34 g carb., 0 g fiber, 3 g pro.*

Bathing Beauties

You'll get extra-creamy results when you use a water bath to bake custards. A water bath provides a humid environment, and because the water in the pan never exceeds 212°F, the water bath insulates the custards for even baking. To make a water bath, see page 235.

Hot Cocoa Soufflé with Coffee Ice Cream

PREP: 25 minutes
STAND: 30 minutes
BAKE: 40 minutes at 350°F
MAKES: 6 servings

    4 egg yolks
    4 egg whites
    3 tablespoons sugar
    2 tablespoons unsweetened
       Dutch-process cocoa
       powder
  ¼   cup butter
  ½   cup sugar
  ½   cup unsweetened Dutch-
       process cocoa powder
  ¼   cup all-purpose flour
    1 cup milk
    2 tablespoons sugar
    1 quart coffee ice cream

1. Allow egg yolks and egg whites to stand at room temperature for 30 minutes.
2. Meanwhile, preheat oven to 350°F. Butter the sides of a 1½-quart ovenproof mixing bowl or soufflé dish. In a small bowl stir together 3 tablespoons sugar and 2 tablespoons cocoa powder. Sprinkle the inside of the prepared mixing bowl with enough of the sugar-cocoa mixture to coat bottom and sides; set bowl and the remaining sugar-cocoa mixture aside.
3. In a medium saucepan heat the butter over medium heat until melted. Stir in ½ cup sugar, ½ cup cocoa powder, and the flour. Add milk all at once. Cook and stir until thickened and bubbly. Remove from heat. In a medium bowl beat egg yolks with a fork until combined. Gradually stir milk mixture into beaten egg yolks. Set aside.
4. In a large mixing bowl beat egg whites with an electric mixer on medium to high speed until soft peaks form (tips curl). Gradually add 2 tablespoons sugar, beating until stiff peaks form (tips stand straight) and sugar is completely dissolved. Fold 1 cup of the beaten egg whites into egg yolk mixture. Fold egg yolk mixture into the remaining beaten egg whites. Transfer mixture to the prepared mixing bowl.
5. Bake for 40 to 45 minutes or until a knife inserted near the center comes out clean. Immediately sprinkle top of baked soufflé with the remaining sugar-cocoa mixture. Serve with scoops of ice cream or, if desired, place scoops of ice cream in center of soufflé and serve.

PER SERVING: 484 cal., 24 g fat (13 g sat. fat), 178 mg chol., 206 mg sodium, 59 g carb., 2 g fiber, 11 g pro.

What Makes a Soufflé Rise or Fall?

Room-temperature egg whites achieve greater volume when beaten than do cold egg whites. Beat the whites just until they hold stiff, upright, glossy peaks. Fold the whites gently into the chocolate mixture, being careful not to deflate the batter. With gentle handling, your soufflé will rise beautifully in the oven.

1. Heat the butter, then whisk in the sugar, cocoa powder, and flour and then add milk.

2. Gradually add the hot chocolate mixture to the beaten egg yolks.

3. Thoroughly whisk the chocolate and egg yolk mixture together.

4. With a rubber spatula, fold 1 cup beaten egg whites into the chocolate mixture.

5. Fold chocolate mixture into remaining beaten egg whites.

Classic White Bread, recipe page 300

yeast & artisan breads

THE HEADY AROMA OF YEAST BREAD baking in the oven is almost as tantalizing as the first bite from a warm, crusty loaf. It's an experience you just can't duplicate with a store-bought baguette. Introduce yourself to the homemade variety with Classic White Bread, then dive in to the rest of these fine artisan loaves and rolls.

White Bread

Before the invention of presliced bread, homemakers made loaves from scratch. Considering how much bread our society eats, it would be hard for the average baker to keep up. But one bite of this classic bread will encourage you to give it a try!

PREP: **30 minutes**
RISE: **1 hour 15 minutes**
BAKE: **35 minutes at 375°F**
MAKES: **2 loaves**
(12 slices per loaf)

5¾ to 6¼ cups all-purpose flour
1 package active dry yeast
2¼ cups milk or buttermilk
2 tablespoons sugar
1 tablespoon butter
1½ teaspoons salt

1. In a large mixing bowl combine 2½ cups of the flour and the yeast; set aside. In a medium saucepan heat and stir milk, sugar, butter, and salt just until warm(120°F to 130°F) and butter almost melts. Add milk mixture to flour mixture. Beat with an electric mixer on low to medium speed for 30 seconds, scraping sides of bowl constantly. Beat on high speed for 3 minutes, scraping sides of bowl occasionally. Using a wooden spoon, stir in as much of the remaining flour as you can.
2. Turn dough out onto a lightly floured surface. Knead in enough of the remaining flour to make a moderately stiff dough that is smooth and elastic (6 to 8 minutes total). Shape dough into a ball. Place in a lightly greased bowl, turning once. Cover; let rise in a warm place until double in size (45 to 60 minutes).
3. Punch dough down. Turn dough out onto a lightly floured surface; divide in half. Cover and let rest for 10 minutes. Meanwhile, lightly grease two 8×4×2-inch loaf pans.
4. Shape each dough half into a loaf by patting or rolling. To shape dough by patting, gently pat and pinch each half of dough into a loaf shape, tucking edges underneath. To shape dough by rolling, on a lightly floured surface, roll each half of dough into a 12×8-inch rectangle. Tightly roll up, starting from a short side, sealing seams with fingertips.

5. Place the loaves in the prepared pans, seam sides down. Cover and let rise in a warm place until nearly double in size (about 30 minutes).
6. Preheat oven to 375°F. Bake for 35 to 40 minutes or until bread sounds hollow when lightly tapped (if necessary, cover loosely with foil the last 5 to 10 minutes of baking to prevent overbrowning). Immediately remove bread from pans. Cool on wire racks.

Whole Wheat Bread: Prepare as directed, except decrease all-purpose flour to 3¾ to 4¼ cups and stir in 2 cups whole wheat flour after beating the mixture for 3 minutes in Step 1.

To Store: Place cooled loaves in an airtight container or wrap tightly in plastic wrap. Store at room temperature for up to 3 days. To freeze, place cooled loaves in an airtight container or resealable freezer bags; freeze for up to 2 months. Thaw wrapped bread at room temperature about 2 hours.

PER SLICE: *130 cal., 1 g fat (1 g sat. fat), 3 mg chol., 159 mg sodium, 25 g carb., 1 g fiber, 4 g pro.*

Secrets to Success

Choose bleached or unbleached all-purpose flour or bread flour when making yeast bread. These flours have the amount of protein needed for the best structure in bread. Bread flour has the most protein and works best for bread machine breads. For tender yeast breads, knead in just enough flour to make the dough smooth and not sticky. Kneading in too much flour will create a tough, dense bread. To ensure a light-textured loaf, make sure to use fresh yeast (check the date on the yeast package) and follow the temperatures given for the liquid used with the yeast. Yeast will not be active if the liquid is not warm enough or if it is too warm. Yeast creates air bubbles in the dough that contribute to the height and structure of the bread.

COMBINE INGREDIENTS Stir in the remaining flour until dough begins to pull away from the sides of the bowl and appears "ropey."

KNEAD DOUGH To knead dough, fold and push away with the heel of your hand. Turn dough and repeat until specified stiffness and smooth.

SLOW RISE Let dough rise in a lightly greased, covered bowl in a warm place until double in size.

READY OR NOT Dough is ready to shape when indentations stay after two fingers are pressed ½ inch apart in the top of the dough.

GIVE IT A PUNCH Use your fist to punch dough down to deflate it. Shape as directed.

Make-It-Mine Artisan Bread

In this recipe, we provide a rich no-knead dough base. You select ingredient options to create a bread to accompany any meal (or stand alone!).

PREP: 25 minutes
CHILL: 4 to 24 hours
STAND: 30 minutes
RISE: 1 hour
BAKE: 25 minutes at 400°F
MAKES: 12 servings

¾ cup warm water (105°F to 115°F)
1 package active dry yeast
Liquid (choose option)
2 tablespoons sugar
2 tablespoons butter or olive oil
Salt (choose option)
Stir-Ins (choose option)
Flour (choose option)
Olive oil or vegetable oil
Cornmeal
1 egg, lightly beaten
2 teaspoons water
Spread (choose option)

1. In a large bowl stir together the ¾ cup water and the yeast. Let stand for 5 minutes. Meanwhile, in a small saucepan heat and stir *Liquid*, sugar, butter, and *Salt* just until warm (120°F to 130°F) and butter almost melts. Stir *Liquid* mixture and *Stir-Ins* into yeast mixture until combined. Stir in *Flour* (dough will be sticky). Lightly brush a medium bowl with oil; transfer dough to bowl. Lightly brush a sheet of plastic wrap with olive oil; cover bowl with plastic wrap, oiled side down. Chill for 4 to 24 hours.

2. Using a dough scraper, carefully loosen dough from bowl and turn out onto a floured surface. Cover with oiled plastic wrap. Let stand for 30 minutes.

3. Grease a baking sheet; sprinkle lightly with cornmeal. Gently *Shape* dough as desired, lightly flouring the dough as needed. Transfer to the prepared baking sheet, using dough scraper or spatula if necessary. Cover and let rise in a warm place until nearly double in size (about 1 hour).

4. Preheat oven to 400°F. In a small bowl whisk together egg and the 2 teaspoons water; brush over loaf. Bake about 25 minutes or until an instant-read thermometer inserted in loaf registers at least 200°F. If necessary, cover with foil during the last 5 minutes of baking to prevent overbrowning. Remove bread from baking sheet or pan; cool on a wire rack. Serve with *Spread*.

LIQUID (PICK ONE)
½ cup milk
½ cup ale
½ cup coconut milk

SALT (PICK ONE)
1½ teaspoons salt
1½ teaspoons garlic salt

STIR-INS (PICK ONE)
Sweet Potato-Spice: ½ cup mashed, cooked sweet potato and ½ teaspoon pumpkin pie spice; reduce water in Step 1 to ½ cup
Almond-Smoked Gouda: ½ cup ground toasted almonds and ½ cup shredded smoked Gouda

continued on page 304

continued from page 302

cheese and ¼ cup stone-ground mustard and ¼ cup cooked and crumbled bacon and 2 teaspoons toasted caraway seeds

Rhubarb: 1 cup chopped fresh or frozen rhubarb and ½ cup golden raisins and 2 tablespoons finely chopped shallot and 2 teaspoons grated fresh ginger and ½ teaspoon ground coriander

Mediterranean: ½ cup crumbled feta cheese and ½ cup grated Asiago cheese and ¼ cup chopped pitted Kalamata olives and ¼ cup thawed and well-drained frozen chopped spinach and 4 cloves garlic, minced

Apricot-Swiss: ½ cup cooked, chopped onion and ½ cup finely snipped dried apricots and ½ cup shredded Swiss cheese and 1 tablespoon snipped fresh sage

FLOUR (PICK ONE)

2¾ cups all-purpose flour

2 cups all-purpose flour and ¾ cup whole wheat flour

SHAPE

Oblong loaf: Pat dough into an oblong loaf.

Square loaf: Omit baking sheet and pat dough into a greased 8×8×2-inch pan.

Round loaf: Pat dough into a 6-inch round loaf; if desired, cut an X into the top.

Squares rolls: Pat dough into 8-inch square; cut into sixteen 2-inch squares, flouring the dough and knife as necessary. Place about 1 inch apart on baking sheet (bake about 15 minutes).

Long loaf: Pat dough into an 11-inch long loaf.

Small round loaves: Divide dough into three portions. Pat each portion into a round loaf, about ½ inch thick.

SPREAD

Softened butter

Soft goat cheese

Garlic and herb semisoft cheese

Herbed Boule

PREP: 40 minutes
RISE: 1 hour 5 minutes
BAKE: 22 minutes at 450°F
MAKES: 2 loaves
(12 slices per loaf)

5½ to 6 cups all-purpose flour
2 packages active dry yeast
2 teaspoons salt
2 cups warm water (120°F to 130°F)
2 tablespoons snipped fresh thyme, snipped fresh sage, and/or snipped fresh rosemary
  Cornmeal
1 egg white, lightly beaten
1 tablespoon water
2 cups ice cubes

1. In a large mixing bowl stir together 2 cups of the flour, the yeast, and salt. Add the 2 cups warm water to the flour mixture. Beat with an electric mixer on low to medium speed for 30 seconds, scraping sides of bowl constantly. Beat on high speed for 3 minutes, scraping sides of bowl occasionally. Using a wooden spoon, stir in thyme and as much of the remaining flour as you can.
2. Turn dough out onto a lightly floured surface. Knead in enough of the remaining flour to make a stiff dough that is smooth and elastic (8 to 10 minutes total). Shape dough into a ball. Place in a lightly greased bowl, turning once to grease surface. Cover; let rise in a warm place until double in size (40 to 45 minutes).*
3. Punch dough down. Turn dough out onto a lightly floured surface. Divide dough in half. Cover; let rest for 10 minutes. Meanwhile, lightly grease a baking sheet; sprinkle with cornmeal.
4. Shape each dough portion into a 6-inch round loaf. Transfer the dough rounds to the prepared baking sheet. Cover; let rise in a warm place until nearly double in size (25 to 30 minutes).

5. Adjust one oven rack to lowest position and another oven rack to lower-middle position. Set a shallow baking pan on bottom rack. Preheat oven to 450°F. Using a sharp knife, make an X in the top of each loaf. Combine egg white and the 1 tablespoon water; brush loaves with egg white mixture. Place baking sheet with dough rounds on lower-middle rack. Place ice cubes in the shallow baking pan (as they melt, they will create steam to help dough take on a crisp crust).
6. Bake for 22 to 25 minutes or until loaves sound hollow when tapped. If necessary, cover baking loaves with foil after 15 minutes to prevent overbrowning.

*Test Kitchen Tip: Because this dough rises faster than many other yeast breads, watch the rising time carefully.

To Store: Place each cooled loaf in an airtight container or resealable plastic bag. Store at room temperature for up to 2 days or freeze for up to 2 months. If frozen, thaw at room temperature.

PER SLICE: 110 cal., 0 g fat, 0 mg chol., 198 mg sodium, 23 g carb., 1 g fiber, 3 g pro.

MAKE IT MINI

Focaccia

PREP: **30 minutes**
STAND: **2 to 8 hours**
RISE: **1 hour**
STAND: **40 minutes**
BAKE: **15 minutes at 400°F**
COOL: **15 minutes**
MAKES: **12 servings**

3¾ to 4 cups all-purpose flour
½ cup warm water (105°F to 115°F)
1 teaspoon active dry yeast
1 cup warm water (105°F to 115°F)
2 teaspoons coarse salt
1 tablespoon olive oil
Freshly ground coarse black pepper
Finely shredded Parmesan cheese (optional)
Coarse salt (optional)
Desired Topping Options* (optional)

1. For the sponge, in a large bowl combine ½ cup of the flour, the ½ cup warm water, and the yeast. Beat with a wooden spoon until smooth. Cover loosely with plastic wrap. Let sponge stand at room temperature for 2 to 8 hours.
2. Gradually stir in the 1 cup warm water, the 2 teaspoons salt, and just enough of the remaining flour to make a dough that pulls away from the sides of the bowl. Turn dough out onto a lightly floured surface. Knead in enough of the remaining flour to make a soft dough that is smooth and elastic (3 to 5 minutes total). Place dough in a lightly greased bowl, turning once to grease surface. Cover and let rise in a warm place until double in size (about 1 hour). Punch dough down. Let rest for 10 minutes.
3. Lightly grease a 12-inch pizza pan. Turn dough out into prepared pan. Using oiled hands, gently press dough to edges of pan. Brush dough with the oil. Using your fingers, make ½-inch deep indentations over the dough. Cover with plastic wrap; let stand in a warm place for 30 minutes.
4. Preheat oven to 400°F. If necessary, reindent top of dough round. Sprinkle dough round lightly with black pepper and, if desired, Parmesan cheese, additional coarse salt, and/or other desired Toppings.
5. Bake for 15 to 20 minutes or until golden, checking after 8 minutes and popping any large air bubbles with a sharp knife. (An instant-read thermometer should register at least 200°F when inserted in center of focaccia.) Use two large spatulas to transfer focaccia to a wire rack; cool for 15 minutes.

***Topping Options:** Fresh or dried rosemary or other herbs, thinly sliced onion or garlic, sliced roasted red sweet pepper, sliced Kalamata or ripe black olives, pine nuts, or shredded smoked Gouda cheese or other desired shredded cheese.

PER SERVING: *163 cal., 2 g fat (0 g sat. fat), 0 mg chol., 324 mg sodium, 32 g carb., 1 g fiber, 5 g pro.*

Make It Mini

To make 6 mini focaccia, lightly grease two large baking sheets; set aside. In Step 3, divide dough into six equal pieces, using oiled hands if necessary. Place three dough pieces on each baking sheet. Press each piece of dough into a 5-inch circle, leaving 2 to 3 inches of space between each dough circle. Continue as directed in Steps 4 and 5. Makes 6 mini focaccia (12 servings).

Mock Sourdough Bread

PREP: **45 minutes**
RISE: **1 hour 15 minutes**
BAKE: **30 minutes at 375°F**
MAKES: **2 loaves**
(12 slices per loaf)

6¾ to 7¼ cups all-purpose flour
1 package active dry yeast
1½ cups water
3 tablespoons sugar
3 tablespoons vegetable oil
2 teaspoons salt
1 6-ounce carton (⅔ cup) plain yogurt
2 tablespoons lemon juice
   Strawberry or other flavor jam (optional)

1. In a large mixing bowl combine 2½ cups of the flour and the yeast; set aside. In a medium saucepan heat and stir the water, sugar, oil, and salt just until warm (120°F to 130°F). Add water mixture, yogurt, and lemon juice to the flour mixture. Beat with an electric mixer on low to medium speed for 30 seconds, scraping sides of bowl constantly. Beat on high speed for 3 minutes, scraping sides of bowl occasionally. Using a wooden spoon, stir in as much of the remaining flour as you can.

2. Turn dough out onto a lightly floured surface. Knead in enough remaining flour to make a moderately stiff dough that is smooth and elastic (6 to 8 minutes total). Shape dough into a ball. Place in a greased bowl, turning once to grease surface. Cover; let rise in a warm place until double in size (45 to 60 minutes).

3. Punch dough down. Turn out onto a lightly floured surface. Divide in half. Cover and let rest for 10 minutes. Meanwhile, lightly grease two baking sheets.

4. Shape each dough half by gently pulling it into a ball, tucking edges under. Place dough rounds on prepared baking sheets. Flatten each round slightly to about 6 inches in diameter. Using a sharp knife, make 3 or 4 slashes in the top of each loaf. Cover and let rise in a warm place until nearly double in size (about 30 minutes).

5. Preheat oven to 375°F. Bake for 30 to 35 minutes or until bread sounds hollow when lightly tapped. (An instant-read thermometer should register at least 200°F when inserted into centers of loaves.) If necessary, cover loosely with foil the last 10 minutes of baking to prevent overbrowning. Immediately remove bread from baking sheets. Cool on wire racks. If desired, serve with jam.

To Store: Place cooled loaves in airtight containers or wrap tightly in plastic wrap. Store at room temperature for up to 3 days. To freeze, place cooled loaves in an airtight container or resealable freezer bags; freeze for up to 2 months. Thaw wrapped bread at room temperature about 2 hours.

PER SLICE: *155 cal., 2 g fat (0 g sat. fat), 0 mg chol., 200 mg sodium, 29 g carb., 1 g fiber, 4 g pro.*

No Starter Needed

Traditional sourdough bread requires a starter—composed of flour, sugar, water, and yeast—that ferments for hours until foamy. To cut down on time, this recipe gets its tanginess from a substitution of plain yogurt and lemon juice.

Almond and Fennel Wheat Bread

PREP: 35 minutes
RISE: 1 hour 30 minutes
BAKE: 30 minutes at 375°F
MAKES: 1 loaf (12 slices)

1⅓ cups warm water (105°F to 115°F)
1 package active dry yeast
1 teaspoon sugar
1 tablespoon olive oil
2 teaspoons fennel seeds, crushed
1½ teaspoons salt
1 cup whole wheat flour
½ cup chopped almonds or hazelnuts (filberts), toasted (see tip, page 343)
2¼ to 2¾ cups bread flour or all-purpose flour

1. In a large bowl stir together the warm water, yeast, and sugar; let mixture stand for 5 minutes. Add olive oil, fennel seeds, and salt.

2. Using a wooden spoon, stir in the whole wheat flour. Stir in nuts and as much of the bread flour as you can. Turn dough out onto a lightly floured surface. Knead in enough of the remaining bread flour to make a moderately stiff dough that is smooth and elastic (6 to 8 minutes total). Shape the dough into a ball. Place dough in a lightly greased large bowl, turning once to grease surface.

3. Cover and let rise in a warm place until double in size (about 1 hour).

4. Punch dough down. Turn dough out onto a lightly floured surface. Cover and let rest for 10 minutes. Meanwhile, lightly grease a baking sheet. Shape dough into an 8×4-inch oval loaf. Place on prepared baking sheet. Sprinkle lightly with additional bread flour. Cover and let rise in a warm place until nearly double in size (30 to 45 minutes).

5. Preheat oven to 375°F. Using a sharp knife, slash top of loaf several times, making each cut about ½ inch deep. For a crisp crust, spray or brush the loaf with cold water. Bake about 30 minutes or until bread sounds hollow when lightly tapped, brushing or spraying with cold water halfway through baking. Immediately remove bread from pan. Cool on a wire rack.

To Store: Place cooled bread in an airtight container or wrap tightly in plastic wrap. Store at room temperature for up to 3 days. To freeze, place cooled bread in an airtight container or resealable freezer bag; freeze for up to 2 months. Thaw wrapped bread at room temperature about 2 hours.

To Make Ahead: Prepared dough as directed through Step 2. Cover and chill dough for 2 to 24 hours. Let stand at room temperature for 30 minutes before continuing as directed in Step 4.

PER SLICE: *167 cal., 4 g fat (0 g sat. fat), 0 mg chol. 293 mg sodium, 28 g carb., 3 g fiber, 6 g pro.*

A Proofing Box for Bread

The draft-free, well-insulated environment of a microwave oven makes it the ideal place for proofing yeast bread dough (allowing it to rise). Make sure the bowl you plan to use for the dough fits inside the microwave oven. Bring a 2-cup measuring cup of water to boiling in the microwave; set the cup in the back corner and place the bowl of dough in the center. The heated water will maintain the proper temperature for rising.

Whole Grain Caramelized Onion and Kale Bread

PREP: 40 minutes
RISE: 1 hour 30 minutes
BAKE: 25 minutes at 350°F
MAKES: 1 loaf (16 slices)

3 ounces pancetta, chopped
1 tablespoon butter
1 cup chopped onion
½ cup chopped ripe pear
6 cloves garlic, minced
2 cups chopped fresh kale
3½ to 4 cups all-purpose flour
1 package active dry yeast
1 teaspoon sea salt
1½ cups warm water (105°F to 115°F)
1 cup shredded Gruyère cheese (4 ounces)
½ cup whole wheat flour
½ cup ground rolled oats*
½ cup flaxseed
1 egg
1 teaspoon honey
1 teaspoon water

1. In a large nonstick skillet cook pancetta over medium heat until crisp. Using a slotted spoon, transfer pancetta to a small bowl, reserving drippings in skillet. Add butter to drippings in skillet. Add onion, pear, and garlic; cook and stir about 5 minutes or until tender. Stir in kale and pancetta; cook until kale is tender. Remove from heat; cool.
2. In a large mixing bowl combine 1 cup of the all-purpose flour, the yeast, and salt. Add the 1½ cups warm water. Beat with an electric mixer on low to medium speed for 30 seconds, scraping sides of bowl constantly. Beat on high speed for 3 minutes, scraping sides of bowl occasionally. Stir in cooled kale mixture and cheese. Using a wooden spoon, stir in whole wheat flour, ground oats, and flaxseed. Gradually stir in as much of the remaining all-purpose flour as you can.
3. Turn dough out onto a lightly floured surface. Knead in enough of the remaining all-purpose flour to make a moderately stiff dough that is smooth and elastic (6 to 8 minutes total). Shape dough into a ball. Place in a lightly greased bowl, turning once to grease surface. Cover and let rise in a warm place until double in size (about 1 hour).
4. Punch dough down. Turn dough out onto a lightly floured surface. Cover and let rest for

10 minutes. Line a baking sheet with parchment paper; set aside. Shape dough by gently pulling it into a ball, tucking edges under. Place dough on prepared baking sheet. Flatten round slightly to about 9 inches in diameter.
5. Cover and let rise in a warm place until nearly double in size (30 to 40 minutes).
6. Preheat oven to 350°F. In a small bowl whisk together egg, honey, and the 1 teaspoon water; brush top of dough round with egg mixture. Bake for 25 to 30 minutes or until golden and bread sounds hollow when lightly tapped. Cool on a wire rack. Store in the refrigerator.

*Test Kitchen Tip: For ground oats, place ⅔ cup rolled oats in a food processor or blender. Cover and process or blend until ground.

To Store: Place bread in an airtight container or resealable plastic bag. Store in the refrigerator for up to 2 days or freeze for up to 2 months. Thaw bread in refrigerator.

To Make Ahead: Prepare dough through Step 4. Cover and chill for 2 to 24 hours. Let stand at room temperature for 30 minutes before baking as directed in Step 6.

PER SLICE: *229 cal., 7 g fat (3 g sat. fat), 27 mg chol., 237 mg sodium, 32 g carb., 3 g fiber, 9 g pro.*

Molasses Buckwheat Loaf

PREP: **35 minutes**
RISE: **2 hours**
BAKE: **40 minutes at 350°F**
MAKES: **12 servings**

½ cup warm water (105°F to 115°F)
¼ cup molasses
2 tablespoons canola oil
1 package active dry yeast
⅓ cup water
1¾ to 2¼ cups all-purpose flour
1 cup rye flour
½ cup buckwheat flour
1½ teaspoons salt
1 teaspoon butter, melted

1. In a large bowl whisk together the ½ cup warm water, the molasses, oil, and yeast. Cover and let stand about 5 minutes or until the mixture is cloudy and a little foamy.

2. Add the ⅓ cup water. Add 1½ cups of the all-purpose flour, the rye flour, buckwheat flour, and salt. Stir until nearly combined.

3. Turn dough out onto a lightly floured surface. Knead in enough of the remaining all-purpose flour to make a moderately soft dough that is smooth and elastic (5 to 7 minutes total).

4. Shape dough into a ball. Place in a lightly greased bowl, turning once to grease surface. Cover and let rise in a warm place until double in size (1½ hours).

5. Punch down dough. Turn dough out onto a lightly floured surface. Grease an 8×4×2-inch loaf pan. Shape dough by gently patting and pinching into a loaf shape, tucking edges under. Using a sharp knife, make a few diagonal slashes in the top of the loaf. Place in the prepared pan. Cover and let rise in a warm place until nearly double in size (about 30 minutes).

6. Preheat oven to 350°F. Brush dough with melted butter. Bake for 40 to 45 minutes or until mahogany in color and bread sounds hollow when lightly tapped. Remove from pan and cool on a wire rack.

To Store: Place cooled bread in an airtight container or wrap tightly in plastic wrap. Store at room temperature for up to 3 days. To freeze, place cooled bread in an airtight container or resealable freezer bag; freeze for up to 2 months. Thaw wrapped bread at room temperature about 2 hours.

PER SERVING: *163 cal., 4 g fat (1 g sat. fat), 3 mg chol., 302 mg sodium, 29 g carb., 3 g fiber, 4 g pro.*

Time to Knead

Kneading bread dough builds a protein structure called gluten, which gives body to the finished bread. To knead, fold the dough over and push down on it with the heels of your hands, curving your fingers over the dough. Give the dough a quarter turn and repeat the process of folding and pushing down until you have an elastic dough and the stiffness called for in a recipe. Here are familiar terms to know:
• Moderately soft dough—slightly sticky and is used for rich, sweet breads.
• Moderately stiff dough—not sticky and is slightly firm to the touch.
• Stiff dough—firm to the touch and will hold its shape. This description is used for breads with a chewy texture, such as French bread.

Spicy Apricot and Sausage Braid

PREP: 1 hour
RISE: 1 hour 40 minutes
BAKE: 20 minutes at 350°F
MAKES: 1 loaf (16 slices)

- 4 ounces andouille sausage, finely chopped
- ½ cup finely chopped dried apricots
- ½ to 1 teaspoon crushed red pepper
- ½ cup snipped fresh cilantro
- 2 tablespoons honey
- 3 to 3½ cups all-purpose flour
- 1 package active dry yeast
- 1 teaspoon kosher salt
- ⅔ cup warm water (105°F to 115°F)
- 2 eggs, lightly beaten
- ¼ cup olive oil
- 1 egg, lightly beaten
- 1 teaspoon water

1. In a large nonstick skillet cook sausage over medium-high heat until it starts to brown. Stir in apricots and crushed red pepper. Cook and stir for 1 minute. Stir in cilantro and honey. Remove from heat; cool.

2. Meanwhile, in a large mixing bowl combine 1 cup of the flour, the yeast, and salt. Add the ⅔ cup warm water, the 2 eggs, and the oil. Beat with an electric mixer on low to medium speed for 30 seconds, scraping sides of bowl constantly. Beat on high speed for 3 minutes, scraping sides of bowl occasionally. Stir in sausage mixture. Using a wooden spoon, stir in as much of the remaining flour as you can.

3. Turn dough out onto a lightly floured surface. Knead in enough of the remaining flour to make a soft dough that is smooth and elastic (3 to 5 minutes total). Shape dough into a ball. Place in a lightly greased bowl, turning once to grease surface. Cover and let rise in a warm place until double in size (about 1 hour).

4. Punch dough down. Turn dough out onto a lightly floured surface; divide dough into three portions. Cover and let rest for 10 minutes. Meanwhile, line a large baking sheet with parchment paper.

5. Gently roll each dough portion into a 16-inch-long rope. Place the ropes 1 inch apart on the prepared baking sheet; braid.

6. Cover and let rise in a warm place until nearly double in size (about 40 minutes).

7. Preheat oven to 350°F. In a small bowl combine the one egg and the 1 teaspoon water; brush over braid. Bake for 20 to 25 minutes or until loaf sounds hollow when lightly tapped. Cool on a wire rack.

To Store: Place cooled bread in an airtight container or wrap tightly in plastic wrap. Store in the refrigerator for up to 24 hours. To freeze, place cooled bread in an airtight container or resealable freezer bag; freeze for up to 2 months. Thaw wrapped bread in the refrigerator.

PER SLICE: *158 cal., 5 g fat (1 g sat. fat), 45 mg chol., 188 mg sodium, 3 g carb., 1 g fiber, 5 g pro.*

Bring It to Brunch

To prepare this bread fresh for a brunch, make the dough up to 24 hours ahead of time. Prepare and shape as directed through Step 5. Cover and chill for 2 to 24 hours. To prepare, let stand at room temperature for 30 minutes before baking. Continue as directed in Step 7. The cool environment slows but does not stop the rising; in fact, the slower rise creates a more delicate, even texture in the finished product.

Herbed Braidsticks

PREP: **35 minutes**
RISE: **1 hour 15 minutes**
BAKE: **15 minutes at 350°F**
MAKES: **16 breadsticks**

1 to 1¼ cups all-purpose flour
1 package active dry yeast
1 tablespoon snipped fresh rosemary, thyme, and/or oregano
¼ teaspoon coarsely ground black pepper
¾ cup milk
2 tablespoons butter
1 tablespoon sugar
½ teaspoon salt
1 cup semolina pasta flour*
1 egg white
1 tablespoon water

1. In a large mixing bowl stir together ¾ cup of the all-purpose flour, the yeast, rosemary, and pepper. In a small saucepan heat milk, butter, sugar, and salt just until warm (120°F to 130°F) and butter almost melts.

2. Add milk mixture to flour mixture. Beat with an electric mixer on low to medium speed for 30 seconds, scraping sides of bowl constantly. Beat on high speed for 3 minutes, scraping sides of bowl occasionally. Using a wooden spoon, stir in semolina flour. Let stand for 1 minute. Stir in as much of the remaining all-purpose flour as you can.

3. Turn dough out onto a lightly floured surface. Knead in enough of the remaining all-purpose flour to make a stiff dough that is smooth and elastic (8 to 10 minutes total). Shape into a ball. Place in a lightly greased large bowl, turning once to grease surface. Cover and let rise in a warm place until nearly double in size (45 to 60 minutes).

4. Punch down dough. Turn out onto a lightly floured surface. Divide dough in half. Cover and let rest for 10 minutes. Line a baking sheet with foil; grease foil. Roll one dough portion into a 10×9-inch rectangle. Cut lengthwise into 24 strips.

5. For each breadstick, pinch together ends of three strips; braid the dough strips. Pinch opposite ends together. Tuck under ends.** Place on the prepared baking sheet. Repeat with remaining dough portion. Cover; let rise in a warm place until nearly double in size (about 30 minutes).

6. Preheat oven to 350°F. In a small bowl beat together egg white and the water. Lightly brush egg white mixture on breadsticks. Bake for 15 to 20 minutes or until golden. Serve warm.

*Test Kitchen Tip: Instead of semolina flour, you can use ¾ cup all-purpose flour plus ¼ cup yellow cornmeal.

**Test Kitchen Tip: For faster shaping, cut rolled dough into 1-inch-wide strips. Hold each strip at both ends. Twist in opposite directions two or three times. Arrange on a greased baking sheet; press ends down. Let rise and bake as directed. Makes 20 breadsticks.

To Store: Place breadsticks in an airtight container or resealable plastic bag. Cover or seal and store at room temperature for up to 2 days or freeze for up to 3 months.

PER BREADSTICK: *58 cal., 1 g fat (0 g sat. fat), 0 mg chol., 60 mg sodium, 10 g carb., 0 g fiber, 2 g pro.*

No-Knead Bread

PREP: 25 minutes
STAND: 4 to 24 hours
RISE: 1 hour
BAKE: 40 minutes at 450°F
MAKES: 1 loaf (10 slices)

3 cups all-purpose flour
1¼ teaspoons salt
¼ teaspoon active dry yeast
1⅔ cups warm water (120°F to 130°F)
5 tablespoons all-purpose flour
1 tablespoon yellow cornmeal
Butter (optional)
Honey (optional)

1. In a large bowl combine the 3 cups flour, the salt, and yeast. Add the warm water. Stir until flour mixture is moistened (dough will be very sticky and soft). Cover and let stand at room temperature for 4 to 24 hours.
2. Generously sprinkle additional flour (3 to 4 tablespoons) on a large piece of parchment paper. Turn dough out onto floured parchment. Lightly sprinkle top of dough mixture lightly with additional flour (1 to 2 tablespoons); using a large spatula, gently fold dough over onto itself. Sprinkle lightly with additional flour (1 to 2 tablespoons). Cover and let rest for 15 minutes.
3. Grease a 5- to 6-quart Dutch oven or heavy pot that has a diameter of 8½ to 9½ inches; sprinkle cornmeal over bottom and about 2 inches up the sides. Gently turn dough into prepared Dutch oven, using a spatula to help scrape dough off the paper (some dough may remain on the paper). Cover and let rise at room temperature until dough has risen by about 1 inch in the pan (1 to 2 hours).
4. Preheat oven to 450°F. Cover Dutch oven with a lid or foil; bake for 30 minutes. Uncover; bake for 10 to 15 minutes more or until top is golden brown. Immediately remove bread from pan. Cool on wire rack. If desired, serve with butter and honey.

To Store: Place cooled bread in an airtight container or wrap tightly in plastic wrap. Store at room temperature for up to 3 days. To freeze, place cooled bread in an airtight container or resealable freezer bag; freeze for up to 2 months. Thaw wrapped bread at room temperature about 2 hours.

PER SLICE: *154 cal., 0 g fat, 0 mg chol., 293 mg sodium, 32 g carb., 1 g fiber, 4 g pro.*

A Little Rest

This easy bread uses very little yeast and just like the title claims requires no kneading. Time comes into play when the dough rests for several hours. A piping-hot Dutch oven provides the right amount of heat and humidity to produce a loaf that's deliciously moist and chewy inside yet still has the beautiful outer crust of rustic peasant loaves.

MAKE IT MINI

Chile-Cheddar Casserole Bread

PREP: 20 minutes
RISE: 1 hour
BAKE: 45 minutes at 350°F
COOL: 30 minutes
MAKES: 8 servings

¼ cup warm hot-style
   vegetable juice (105°F
   to 115°F)
1 package active dry yeast
1 cup sour cream
2 eggs
¼ cup finely chopped onion
2 tablespoons sugar
1 teaspoon salt
½ teaspoon ancho chile
   powder
2½ cups all-purpose flour
1⅓ cups finely shredded sharp
   cheddar cheese (about
   5 ounces)
1 4-ounce can fire-roasted
   diced green chiles,
   undrained
   Sliced green onions
   (optional)
   Ancho chile powder
   (optional)

1. In a large mixing bowl combine vegetable juice and yeast; let stand until mixture is foamy. Add sour cream, eggs, chopped onion, sugar, salt, the ½ teaspoon ancho chile powder, and 1 cup of the flour. Beat with an electric mixer on medium speed for 2 minutes. Using a wooden spoon, stir in the remaining 1½ cups flour, 1 cup of the cheese, and the green chiles until a soft, sticky dough forms.
2. Transfer dough to a greased 2-quart oval or rectangular baking dish. Cover and let rise in a warm place until double in size (1 to 1½ hours).
3. Preheat oven to 350°F. Bake for 40 minutes; remove from oven and sprinkle with remaining cheese. Return to oven; bake for 5 minutes more. Cool in dish on a wire rack for 10 minutes. Remove bread from dish. Let cool on wire rack for 20 minutes before serving. If desired, sprinkle with sliced green onions and additional ancho chile powder.

PER SERVING: *300 cal., 12 g fat (7 g sat. fat), 78 mg chol., 497 mg sodium, 36 g carb., 2 g fiber, 11 g pro.*

Make It Mini

Increase cheese to 1½ cups (6 ounces). Grease twenty-four 6-ounce ramekins or custard cups or 2½-inch muffin cups; set aside. Prepare dough as directed in Step 1. Using a cookie scoop or spoon, place about 2 tablespoons dough into each prepared ramekin. Cover and let rise in a warm place until double in size (about 1 hour). Preheat oven to 350°F. Bake for 15 minutes; remove from oven and sprinkle with the remaining cheese. Return to oven; bake for 5 minutes more. Remove bread from ramekins. Serve warm. If desired, sprinkle with additional ancho chile powder before serving. Makes 24.

Potato-Bacon Batter Bread with Caramelized Onions

PREP: 30 minutes
RISE: 40 minutes
BAKE: 45 minutes at 375°F
COOL: 10 minutes
MAKES: 8 servings

6 slices bacon, chopped
½ cup chopped onion
   (1 medium)
   Cornmeal
1 cup warm milk (105°F to
   115°F)
1 package active dry yeast
⅓ cup butter, melted
1 egg
1 teaspoon salt
3 cups all-purpose flour
1 cup mashed potatoes,* at
   room temperature

1. In a large skillet cook bacon over medium heat until crisp. Using a slotted spoon, transfer bacon to paper towels to drain.

2. Transfer 2 tablespoons of bacon drippings in skillet to a small bowl; set aside. Drain and discard all but 2 tablespoons of the remaining drippings from skillet. Cook onion in hot drippings in skillet over medium heat about 6 minutes or until dark brown. Remove from heat; set aside.

3. Brush the reserved bacon drippings over the bottom and sides of a 2-quart square baking dish. Sprinkle bottom and sides of dish generously with cornmeal. Set aside.

4. In a large mixing bowl combine warm milk and yeast; let stand until mixture is foamy. Add butter, egg, salt, and 1 cup of the flour. Beat with an electric mixer on medium speed for 2 minutes, scraping sides of bowl occasionally. Using a wooden spoon, stir in the remaining 2 cups flour, the mashed potatoes, bacon, and onion until a soft, sticky dough forms.

5. Transfer dough to the prepared baking dish. Cover; let rise in a warm place until double in size (about 40 minutes).

6. Preheat oven to 375°F. Bake for 45 to 50 minutes or until loaf is golden brown. Cool in dish on a wire rack for 10 minutes. Remove bread from dish. Serve warm or cool completely on wire rack.

*Test Kitchen Tip For 1 cup mashed potatoes, cook 2 small peeled and quartered red or russet potatoes (12 ounces total) in lightly salted boiling water for 15 to 20 minutes or until very tender. Drain well. Use an electric mixer or a masher to mash potato. Or use 1 cup leftover or refrigerated mashed potatoes.

To Store: Place cooled bread in an airtight container or wrap tightly in plastic wrap. Store in the refrigerator for up to 2 days. To freeze, place cooled bread in an airtight container or resealable freezer bag; freeze for up to 2 months. Thaw wrapped bread in the refrigerator.

PER SERVING: *391 cal., 19 g fat (9 g sat. fat), 62 mg chol., 596 mg sodium, 45 g carb., 2 g fiber, 10 g pro.*

Overnight Refrigerator Rolls

PREP: 35 minutes
CHILL: overnight
RISE: 45 minutes
BAKE: 12 minutes at 375°F
MAKES: 24 rolls

1¼ cups warm water (105°F to 115°F)
1 package active dry yeast
4 to 4¼ cups all-purpose flour
⅓ cup butter, melted, or vegetable oil
⅓ cup sugar
1 teaspoon salt
1 egg
Nonstick cooking spray
2 tablespoons butter, melted (optional)

1. In a large mixing bowl combine warm water and yeast. Stir to dissolve yeast. Add 1½ cups of the flour, the ⅓ cup melted butter, the sugar, salt, and egg. Beat with an electric mixer on low speed for 1 minute, scraping sides of bowl constantly.

2. Using a wooden spoon, stir in enough of the remaining flour to make a soft dough that just starts to pull away from sides of bowl (dough will be slightly sticky). Coat a 3-quart covered container with cooking spray. Place dough in container, turning once to coat surface. Cover and chill overnight.

3. Punch dough down. Turn dough out onto a lightly floured surface. Divide dough in half. Cover and let rest for 10 minutes. Lightly grease a 13×9×2-inch baking pan or baking sheets.

4. Shape dough into 24 balls or shape as desired (be careful not to overwork dough; it becomes more sticky the more you work with it) and place in prepared baking pan or 2 to 3 inches apart on baking sheets. Cover and let rise in a warm place until nearly double in size (about 45 minutes).

5. Preheat oven to 375°F. Bake for 12 to 15 minutes for individual rolls or about 20 minutes for pan rolls or until golden. Immediately remove rolls from pans. If desired, brush tops of rolls with melted butter. Serve warm.

continued on page 328

Shaping Know-How

Below, learn how to shape Parker House Rolls and Rosettes in just a few steps.

FOR PARKER HOUSE ROLLS

1. Use a 2½-inch round cutter to cut rolls. Brush centers with melted butter.

2. Make an off-center crease in each round.

3. Fold so large half overlaps slightly. The dough will crawl back during baking so the top half is shorter.

FOR ROSETTES

1. Roll each portion of dough into a pencil-like strand about 12 inches long.

2. Form rope into a loose knot, leaving two long ends.

3. Tuck top end under roll. Bring bottom end up and tuck into center of roll.

continued from page 327

To Store: Place leftover rolls in an airtight container or resealable plastic bags and store at room temperature for up to 2 days.

PER ROLL: 113 cal., 3 g fat (2 g sat. fat), 16 mg chol., 119 mg sodium, 1 g carb., 1 g fiber, 3 g pro.

Butterhorn Rolls: On a lightly floured surface, roll each dough half into a 10-inch circle. If desired, brush with melted butter. Cut each dough circle into 12 wedges. To shape rolls, begin at wide end of each wedge and loosely roll toward the point. Place, point sides down, 2 to 3 inches apart on prepared baking sheets. Make 24 rolls.

PER ROLL: 113 cal., 3 g fat (2 g sat. fat), 16 mg chol., 119 mg sodium, 1 g carb., 1 g fiber, 3 g pro.

Rosettes: Divide each dough half into 16 pieces. On a lightly floured surface, roll each piece into a 12-inch-long rope. Tie each rope in a loose knot, leaving two long ends. Tuck top end under knot and bottom end into the top center. Place 2 to 3 inches apart on prepared baking sheets. Makes 32 rolls.

PER ROLL: 85 cal., 2 g fat (1 g sat. fat), 12 mg chol., 89 mg sodium, 14 g carb., 0 g fiber, 2 g pro.

Parker House Rolls: On a lightly floured surface, roll each dough half until ¼ inch thick. Cut dough with a floured 2½-inch round cutter. Brush with melted butter. Using the dull edge of a table knife, make an off-center crease in each round. Fold each round along the crease. Press the folded edge firmly. Place, large half up, 2 to 3 inches apart on prepared baking sheets. Makes 24 rolls.

PER ROLL: 122 cal., 4 g fat (2 g sat. fat), 18 mg chol., 126 mg sodium, 19 g carb., 1 g fiber, 3 g pro.

Hamburger or Frankfurter Buns: Divide dough into 12 pieces. Cover and let rest for 10 minutes. For hamburger buns, shape each piece into a ball, tucking edges under. Place on a greased baking sheet. Using your fingers, slightly flatten balls to 4 inches in diameter. For frankfurter buns, shape each portion into a roll about 5½ inches long, tapering ends. Place 2 to 3 inches apart on prepared baking sheets. Makes 12 buns.

PER BUN: 226 cal., 6 g fat (3 g sat. fat), 31 mg chol., 238 mg sodium, 38 g carb., 1 g fiber, 5 g pro.

Keep It Dry

If you leave bread and rolls in the pans to cool, condensation forms between the pan and the bread, resulting in a soggy bottom. Placing bread and rolls on wire racks allows air to circulate around them, cooling them faster and preventing condensation. To reheat dinner rolls, wrap in foil and place in a 325°F oven about 10 minutes or until heated through. If they're frozen, wrap in foil and heat them about 30 minutes or until heated through.

Orange Bowknots

PREP: **45 minutes**
RISE: **1 hour 30 minutes**
BAKE: **12 minutes at 375°F**
MAKES: **24 rolls**

6 to 6½ cups all-purpose flour
1 package active dry yeast
1¼ cups milk
½ cup butter
⅓ cup sugar
½ teaspoon salt
2 eggs
2 tablespoons finely shredded orange peel (see tip, page 102)
¼ cup orange juice
1 recipe Orange Icing

1. In a large mixing bowl combine 2 cups of the flour and the yeast; set aside. In a medium saucepan heat and stir the milk, butter, sugar, and salt just until warm (120°F to 130°F) and butter almost melts. Add milk mixture and eggs to the flour mixture. Beat with an electric mixer on low to medium speed for 30 seconds, scraping sides of bowl constantly. Beat on high speed for 3 minutes, scraping sides of bowl occasionally. Using a wooden spoon, stir in orange peel, orange juice, and as much of the remaining flour as you can.

2. Turn dough out onto a lightly floured surface. Knead in enough remaining flour to make a moderately soft dough that is smooth and elastic (3 to 5 minutes total). Shape dough into a ball. Place in a lightly greased bowl, turning once to grease surface. Cover and let rise in a warm place until double in size (about 1 hour).

3. Punch dough down. Turn dough out onto a lightly floured surface. Divide in half. Cover and let rest for 10 minutes. Meanwhile, lightly grease two large baking sheets; set aside.

4. Roll each dough half into a 12×7-inch rectangle. Cut each rectangle into twelve 7-inch-long strips. Tie each strip loosely in a knot. Place knots 2 inches apart on prepared baking sheets. Cover and let rise in a warm place until nearly double in size (about 30 minutes).

5. Preheat oven to 375°F. Bake for 12 to 14 minutes or until golden. Immediately remove from baking sheets. Cool on wire racks. Drizzle with Orange Icing.

Orange Icing: In a medium bowl combine 1½ cups powdered sugar, 1½ teaspoons finely shredded orange peel (see tip, page 102), and enough orange juice (2 to 3 tablespoons) to make icing a drizzling consistency.

PER ROLL: *203 cal., 5 g fat (3 g sat. fat), 29 mg chol., 88 mg sodium, 35 g carb., 1 g fiber, 4 g pro.*

Homemade Checkerboard Rolls

PREP: 45 minutes
RISE: 1 hour 30 minutes
BAKE: 12 minutes at 400°F
MAKES: 16 rolls

- 1 cup milk
- ¼ cup sugar
- ¼ cup butter
- 1 teaspoon salt
- 1 package active dry yeast
- ¼ cup warm water (105°F to 115°F)
- 1 egg, lightly beaten
- 3½ to 4 cups all-purpose flour
- 2 tablespoons sesame seeds
- 2 tablespoons poppy seeds
- 2 teaspoons dried minced onion or dried minced garlic
- 2 tablespoons yellow cornmeal
- 2 tablespoons grated Romano or Parmesan cheese
- ¼ cup butter, melted

1. In a small saucepan combine milk, sugar, ¼ cup butter, and the salt; heat and stir over medium-low heat until warm (105°F to 115°F). Meanwhile, in a large bowl dissolve yeast in the warm water.
2. Add the milk mixture and egg to yeast mixture. Gradually stir in enough flour to make a soft dough.
3. Turn dough out onto a floured surface. Knead in enough of the remaining flour to make a moderately soft dough that is smooth and elastic (about 3 minutes). Shape dough into ball. Place in a greased bowl, turning once. Cover; let rise in warm place until double in size (about 1 hour).

4. Grease a 15×10×1-inch baking pan; set aside. Punch dough down; turn out onto a lightly floured surface. Let rest for 10 minutes. Divide dough into 24 pieces. Gently shape into balls.
5. In a shallow dish combine sesame seeds, poppy seeds, and dried minced onion. In another shallow dish combine cornmeal and cheese. Place ¼ cup melted butter in a third dish. Working quickly, roll dough pieces in butter and in one of the seasoning mixtures to lightly coat. Coat half of the rolls with one seasoning mixture and the remaining rolls with the other seasoning mixture (see "Rolls Perfected," top right). Alternate rolls in prepared pan. Cover rolls with greased plastic wrap and a towel. Let rise in a warm place for 30 minutes.
6. Preheat oven to 400°F. Bake for 12 to 15 minutes or until golden. Remove from pan. Serve warm or at room temperature.

To Make Ahead: Prepare as directed through Step 5. Chill for up to 24 hours. Let stand at room temperature for 30 minutes. Continue as directed in Step 6. Or prepare and bake rolls as directed. Wrap cooled rolls in plastic wrap; place in a resealable plastic freezer bag. Freeze for up to 2 months. To serve, heat rolls in a 375°F oven for 5 to 8 minutes.

PER ROLL: *129 cal., 5 g fat (3 g sat. fat), 20 mg chol., 137 mg sodium, 18 g carb., 1 g fiber, 3 g pro.*

Rolls Perfected

To keep the poppy seed topping out of the butter, coat all the Romano cheese rolls first. Place in alternating spots on the pan. Then coat the poppy seed rolls balls, filling in the remaining places on the pan.

1. Warmer temperatures hasten the first rise of the dough.

2. To make smooth tops, pull the edges of each dough ball under.

3. After coating the rolls with seasoning, arrange them checkerboard style in prepared pan.

Feather Rolls

PREP: **40 minutes**
CHILL: **2 hours**
RISE: **40 minutes**
BAKE: **20 minutes at 400°F**
MAKES: **15 rolls**

4¼ to 4¾ cups all-purpose flour
1 package active dry yeast
1½ cups warm water (120°F to 130°F)
½ cup mashed cooked potato*
⅓ cup butter, melted
¼ cup sugar
1¼ teaspoons salt
2 tablespoons butter, melted

1. In a large mixing bowl combine 2 cups of the flour and the yeast. In a medium bowl combine the warm water, mashed potato, the ⅓ cup melted butter, the sugar, and salt. Add potato mixture to flour mixture. Beat with an electric mixer on low speed for 30 seconds, scraping sides of bowl constantly. Beat on high speed for 3 minutes, scraping sides of bowl occasionally. Using a wooden spoon, stir in as much of the remaining flour as you can.
2. Turn dough out onto a lightly floured surface. Knead in enough of the remaining flour to make a moderately soft dough that is smooth and elastic (3 to 5 minutes total). Place dough in a greased bowl, turning once to grease the surface. Cover; chill for 2 hours.
3. Punch dough down. Turn out onto a lightly floured surface. Cover; let rest for 10 minutes. Grease a 13×9×2-inch baking pan. With lightly floured hands, divide dough into 15 pieces. Shape pieces into balls; arrange in prepared pan. Cover and let rise in a warm place until nearly double in size (about 40 minutes).

4. Preheat oven to 400°F. Bake for 20 to 25 minutes or until rolls are golden and sound hollow when lightly tapped. Brush tops with the 2 tablespoons melted butter. Immediately remove from pan. Serve warm.

*Test Kitchen Tip: For ½ cup mashed potato, cook 1 small peeled and quartered red or russet potato (6 ounces) in lightly salted boiling water for 15 to 20 minutes or until very tender. Drain well. Use an electric mixer or a masher to mash potato. Or use ½ cup leftover or refrigerated mashed potatoes.

To Store: Place leftover rolls in an airtight container or wrap tightly with plastic wrap. Store at room temperature for up to 2 days. Or place in a resealable plastic freezer bag. Seal, label, and freeze for up to 2 months. Thaw at room temperature.

PER ROLL: *198 cal., 6 g fat (4 g sat. fat), 15 mg chol., 245 mg sodium, 32 g carb., 1 g fiber, 4 g pro.*

Make It Mini

Prepare as directed, except divide dough into 32 pieces. Shape into balls and arrange in prepared pan. Cover and let rise in a warm place until nearly double in size (about 40 minutes). Bake in the 400°F oven for 18 to 20 minutes or until rolls are golden and sound hollow when lightly tapped. Continue as directed. Makes 32 mini rolls.

Curried Sweet Potato Rolls

PREP: 50 minutes
RISE: 1½ hours
BAKE: 25 minutes at 375°F
MAKES: 16 rolls

5¾ to 6¼ cups all-purpose flour
1 package active dry yeast
1 tablespoon packed brown sugar
1 tablespoon curry powder
2 teaspoons kosher salt
1 teaspoon ground coriander
1 teaspoon ground cinnamon
¼ to ½ teaspoon cayenne pepper
1 14-ounce can unsweetened coconut milk, warmed (120°F to 130°F)
2 tablespoons butter, melted
2 eggs, lightly beaten
1 recipe Roasted Sweet Potatoes and Garlic
1 teaspoon water
1 tablespoon black and/or white sesame seeds
1 recipe Mango Butter (optional)

1. In a large mixing bowl combine 2 cups of the flour, the yeast, brown sugar, curry powder, salt, coriander, cinnamon, and cayenne pepper. Add warmed coconut milk, melted butter, and one of the eggs. Beat with an electric mixer on low to medium speed for 30 seconds, scraping sides of bowl constantly. Beat on high speed for 3 minutes, scraping sides of bowl occasionally. Beat in Roasted Sweet Potatoes and Garlic. Using a wooden spoon, stir in as much of the remaining flour as you can.
2. Turn dough out onto a lightly floured surface. Knead in enough of the remaining flour to make a moderately stiff dough that is smooth and elastic (6 to 8 minutes total). Shape dough into a ball. Place in a lightly greased large bowl, turning once. Cover and let rise in a warm place until double in size (about 1 hour).
3. Punch dough down. Turn out onto a lightly floured surface. Divide dough in half. Cover let rest for 10 minutes. Meanwhile, grease a 13×9×2-inch baking pan.
4. Divide each portion of dough into eight pieces. Shape each portion into a round ball. Place in prepared pan.
5. Cover and let rolls rise in a warm place until nearly double in size (about 30 minutes.)
6. Preheat oven to 375°F. Bake rolls, uncovered, for 15 minutes. Meanwhile, in a small bowl whisk together the remaining egg and the water. Carefully brush rolls with egg mixture; sprinkle with sesame seeds. Bake for 10 to 15 minutes more or until rolls sound hollow when lightly tapped. Immediately remove rolls from pan. Cool on a wire rack. Serve warm or at room temperature. If desired, serve with Mango Butter.

Roasted Sweet Potatoes and Garlic: Preheat oven to 400°F. Lightly grease a 15×10×1-inch baking pan; set aside. Peel 1 pound sweet potatoes; cut into 1½-inch chunks. In a medium bowl combine sweet potatoes; 2 tablespoons olive oil; 6 cloves garlic, minced; 1 teaspoon kosher salt; and ½ teaspoon cayenne pepper. Toss to coat. Spread in the prepared baking pan. Roast about 25 minutes or until golden. Cool slightly. Mash with a potato masher or an electric mixer.

To Store: Place rolls in an airtight container or a resealable plastic bag. Store in the refrigerator for up to 2 days.

PER ROLL: *274 cal., 9 g fat (6 g sat. fat), 30 mg chol., 401 mg sodium, 43 g carb., 2 g fiber, 7 g pro.*

Mango Butter: Seed, peel, and chop 1 mango. In a food processor combine mango and ¾ cup softened butter. Cover and process with several on-off pulses until mango is finely chopped.

Banana Bread, recipe page 338

quick breads

FROM MUFFINS TO SCONES AND LOAVES TO BISCUITS,

FROM MUFFINS TO SCONES AND LOAVES TO BISCUITS, quick breads are the simplest of pleasures in the world of from-scratch baking. Learn the hows and whys of the classic banana, zucchini, and pumpkin bread—as well as inspiring new creations such as pear-ginger scones and extra chocolaty muffins.

Banana Bread

Soft, moist, and almost cakelike in texture, Banana Bread is the quintessential quick bread. The ease of making it comes from a basic stir-and-pour method—no kneading or rising.

PREP: **25 minutes**
BAKE: **55 minutes at 350°F**
STAND: **overnight**
MAKES: **1 or 2 loaves (16 slices)**

2	cups all-purpose flour
1½	teaspoons baking powder
½	teaspoon baking soda
½	teaspoon ground cinnamon
¼	teaspoon salt
¼	teaspoon ground nutmeg
⅛	teaspoon ground ginger
2	eggs, lightly beaten
1½	cups mashed bananas (4 to 5 medium)
1	cup sugar
½	cup vegetable oil or melted butter
¼	cup chopped walnuts

1. Preheat oven to 350°F. Grease bottom(s) and ½ inch up the sides of one 9×5×3-inch or two 7½×3½×2-inch loaf pan(s); set aside. In a large bowl combine flour, baking powder, baking soda, cinnamon, salt, nutmeg, and ginger. Make a well in the center of the flour mixture; set aside.
2. In a medium bowl combine eggs, bananas, sugar, and oil. Add egg mixture all at once to flour mixture. Stir just until moistened (batter should be lumpy). Fold in walnuts. Spoon batter into prepared pan(s), spreading evenly.
3. Bake for 55 to 60 minutes for 9×5×3-inch pan or 40 to 45 minutes for 7½×3½×2-inch pans or until a wooden toothpick inserted near center(s) comes out clean. If necessary to prevent overbrowning, cover loosely with foil for the last 15 minutes of baking.
4. Cool in pan(s) on a wire rack for 10 minutes. Remove from pan(s). Cool completely on rack. Wrap and store overnight before slicing.

To Store: Wrap cooled loaf or loaves in foil or plastic wrap. Store in the refrigerator for up to 1 week. Or place loaves in freezer bags or containers (do not frost Peanut Butter-Banana Bread) and freeze for up to 3 months. Thaw frozen loaves overnight in the refrigerator. Frost thawed Peanut Butter-Banana Bread.

PER SLICE: *200 cal., 9 g fat (1 g sat. fat), 23 mg chol., 119 mg sodium, 28 g carb., 1 g fiber, 3 g pro.*

Banana-Jam Swirl Bread: Prepare as directed through Step 2, except spoon ½ cup strawberry jam on top of the batter in pan(s) before baking. Use a knife or thin metal spatula to swirl jam into batter. Continue as directed in Steps 3 and 4.

PER SLICE: *227 cal., 9 g fat (1 g sat. fat), 23 mg chol., 122 mg sodium, 35 g carb., 1 g fiber, 3 g pro.*

Peanut Butter-Banana Bread: Prepare as directed, except omit walnuts and stir ½ cup chopped peanuts into batter. After cooling and storing bread overnight, spread with peanut butter frosting. For peanut butter frosting, in a medium mixing bowl combine ¼ cup peanut butter, 3 tablespoons softened butter, 1 tablespoon milk, and ½ teaspoon vanilla. Beat with an electric mixer on medium speed until smooth. Gradually add 1½ cups powdered sugar, beating until combined. If necessary, beat in 1 to 2 tablespoons additional milk to make desired consistency.

PER SLICE: *302 cal., 14 g fat (3 g sat. fat), 29 mg chol., 158 mg sodium, 41 g carb., 1 g fiber, 5 g pro.*

Secrets to Success

Banana bread is perhaps the most popular way to use overripe bananas, which are softer and easier to mash than just-ripened bananas. Choose bananas that have more brown on the skins than yellow. You can also freeze overripe unpeeled bananas in a resealable freezer bag until you're ready to use them. Simply thaw and mash as directed. Grease the bottom, corners, and ½ to 1 inch up the sides of the pan (see photo 1, below). Do not grease all the way up the pan sides. The batter needs to cling to the ungreased sides so the center of the loaf rises higher to create a rounded dome. Expect the top of the loaf to exhibit some cracks after baking because the loaf rises so quickly while baking. However, large tunnels in the bread may indicate overmixing. For best flavor and texture, wrap the loaf in plastic wrap and let stand overnight.

GREASE THE PAN Use a pastry brush or a paper towel to spread shortening in the bottom, corners, and ½ to 1 inch up the sides of the pan.

MASH THE BANANAS For this step, use soft, ripe (or slightly overripe) bananas that mash easily. Instead of a fork, you can also use a potato masher.

COMBINE WET AND DRY After stirring the wet ingredients into the mashed bananas, add the banana mixture to the dry ingredients.

MIX TO MOISTEN Stir the wet and dry ingredients together just until combined—overmixing will cause large tunnels in the loaf.

Make-It-Mine Muffins

Muffins brighten breakfasts and brunches. Now you can customize them with your choice of flours, liquids, stir-ins, and toppings.

PREP: **20 minutes**
BAKE: **15 minutes at 400°F**
COOL: **5 minutes**
MAKES: **12 muffins**

Flour (*choose option*)
¼ cup granulated sugar or packed brown sugar
1½ teaspoons baking powder
½ teaspoon baking soda
¼ teaspoon salt
2 eggs, lightly beaten
Liquid (*choose option*)
¾ cup buttermilk, sour milk (see page 16), or milk
2 tablespoons butter, melted, or vegetable oil
Stir-In (*choose option*)
Topping (*choose option*)
½ recipe Powdered Sugar Icing (see page 105)

1. Preheat oven to 400°F. Grease twelve 2½-inch muffin cups; set aside. In a medium bowl combine *Flour*, sugar, baking powder, baking soda, and salt. Make a well in center of flour mixture; set aside.
2. In a small bowl combine eggs, *Liquid*, buttermilk, and melted butter. Add egg mixture all at once to flour mixture. Stir just until moistened (batter should be lumpy). Fold in *Stir-In*.

3. Spoon batter into prepared muffin cups, filling each half to two-thirds full. If desired, sprinkle with *Topping*.
4. Bake for 15 to 18 minutes or until golden. Cool in muffin cups on a wire rack for 5 minutes. Remove from muffin cups. If desired, drizzle with Powdered Sugar Icing.

FLOUR (PICK ONE)
2 cups all-purpose flour
1⅓ cups all-purpose flour and ¾ cup buckwheat flour
1½ cups all-purpose flour and ¾ cup quick-cooking oats
1 cup all-purpose flour and 1 cup yellow cornmeal
1 cup all-purpose flour and 1 cup rye flour
½ cup all-purpose flour and 1½ cups whole wheat flour

LIQUID (PICK ONE)
¾ cup ricotta cheese
¾ cup sour cream
¾ cup plain yogurt
¾ cup finely shredded unpeeled zucchini
¾ cup canned pumpkin
¾ cup applesauce
¾ cup lemon curd

STIR IN (PICK ONE)
Green onion: 2 to 4 tablespoons thinly sliced green onions
Sweet pepper: 2 to 4 tablespoons finely chopped sweet pepper
Bacon: 2 to 4 tablespoons crumbled crisp-cooked bacon
Parmesan: 2 tablespoons grated Parmesan cheese
Blueberry: ¾ cup fresh or frozen blueberries
Dried Fruit: ⅓ cup dried fruit (blueberries; raisins; chopped cranberries or cherries; snipped dates, apricots, or figs)

TOPPING
(PICK ONE IF DESIRED)
Crunchy: ⅓ cup crushed potato chips, tortilla chips, or cereal flakes, or granola
Streusel: In a small bowl stir together 3 tablespoons all-purpose flour, 3 tablespoons packed brown sugar, and ¼ teaspoon ground cinnamon or ginger. Cut in 2 tablespoons butter until mixture resembles coarse crumbs. If desired, stir in 2 tablespoons chopped, shredded, or flaked coconut.

Apple Pie Bread

PREP: 35 minutes
BAKE: 1 hour at 350°F
STAND: overnight
MAKES: 1 loaf (14 slices)

½ cup butter, softened
1 cup sugar
¼ cup buttermilk or sour milk (see page 16)
2 teaspoons baking powder
2 eggs
1 teaspoon vanilla
2 cups all-purpose flour
½ teaspoon salt
2 cups shredded, peeled apples (about 4 medium)
1 cup chopped walnuts or pecans, lightly toasted (if desired) (see "Toasting Nuts," right)
½ cup raisins
1 recipe Streusel-Nut Topping

1. Preheat oven to 350°F. Grease the bottom and ½ inch up the sides of an 9×5×3-inch loaf pan; set pan aside.
2. In a large mixing bowl beat butter with an electric mixer on medium to high speed for 30 seconds. Beat in sugar until combined. Add buttermilk and baking powder; beat until combined. Add eggs and vanilla; beat until combined. Add flour and salt; beat until combined. Stir in apples, nuts, and raisins. Spoon batter into the prepared pan, spreading evenly. Sprinkle Streusel-Nut Topping over batter.
3. Bake for 60 to 65 minutes or until a wooden toothpick inserted near the center comes out clean. Cool in pan on a wire rack for 10 minutes. Remove bread from pan. Cool completely on wire rack. Wrap and store overnight before slicing.

Streusel-Nut Topping: In a small bowl stir together ¼ cup packed brown sugar and 3 tablespoons all-purpose flour. Cut in 3 tablespoons butter until mixture resembles coarse crumbs. Stir in ⅓ cup chopped walnuts or pecans.

To Store: Wrap cooled loaf in foil or plastic wrap. Store in the refrigerator for up to 1 week. Or place loaf in freezer bag or container and freeze for up to 3 months. Thaw frozen loaf overnight in the refrigerator.

PER SLICE: 326 cal., 17 g fat (6 g sat. fat), 52 mg chol., 193 mg sodium, 42 g carb., 2 g fiber, 5 g pro.

Toasting Nuts

Enhance the flavor of baked products by toasting the nuts, which makes them more fragrant and flavorful than raw nuts. Here are three ways to toast nuts.

Oven: To toast whole nuts, spread them in a shallow baking pan. Bake them in a 350°F oven for 5 to 10 minutes, shaking the pan once or twice. Check nuts often to avoid overbrowning.

Stove top: Toast finely chopped or ground nuts in a dry skillet over medium heat. Stir often so they don't burn. Remove from skillet immediately to stop the cooking process.

Microwave: Spread a single layer of nuts on a microwave-safe plate. Cook on 100 percent power (high) at 1-minute intervals until nuts have a crisp crunch, toasted flavor, and have become fragrant. The amount of time it takes varies according to the type of nut. Nuts will not brown like they would in an oven or skillet.

For oven toasting, spread whole nuts in a single layer on the baking pan so they brown evenly. Keep a close eye on the nuts to prevent burning.

Zucchini Bread

PREP: 25 minutes
BAKE: 55 minutes at 350°F
STAND: overnight
MAKES: 2 loaves (28 slices)

    3 cups all-purpose flour
    1 tablespoon baking powder
 1½ teaspoons ground cinnamon
    1 teaspoon salt
    2 eggs, lightly beaten
 2½ cups coarsely shredded,
      unpeeled zucchini
    2 cups sugar
    1 cup vegetable oil
    2 teaspoons vanilla
    1 cup chopped walnuts or
      pecans (optional)
  ⅔ cup raisins (optional)

1. Preheat oven to 350°F. Grease the bottom and ½ inch up sides of two 8×4×2-inch loaf pans; set aside. In a large bowl stir together flour, baking powder, cinnamon, and salt. Make a well in center of flour mixture; set aside.
2. In a medium bowl combine eggs, shredded zucchini, sugar, oil, and vanilla. Add zucchini mixture all at once to flour mixture. Stir just until moistened (batter should be lumpy). If desired, stir in nuts and raisins.

3. Spoon batter into prepared pans, spreading evenly. Bake about 55 minutes or until a wooden toothpick inserted near centers comes out clean. Cool in pans on a wire rack for 10 minutes. Remove bread from pans. Cool completely on wire rack. Wrap and store overnight before slicing.

To Store: Wrap cooled, uniced loaves in foil or plastic wrap. Store in the refrigerator for up to 1 week. Or place loaves in freezer bags or containers and freeze for up to 3 months. Thaw frozen loaves overnight in the refrigerator.

PER SLICE: *181 cal., 8 g fat (1 g sat. fat), 13 mg chol., 128 mg sodium, 25 g carb., 1 g fiber, 2 g pro.*

Chocolate-Zucchini Bread: Prepare as directed, except stir ¾ cup dark chocolate pieces into the batter with the nuts. After cooling and storing overnight, drizzle loaves with chocolate drizzle. For chocolate drizzle, in a small saucepan heat and stir 3 ounces dark chocolate pieces over low heat until smooth.

PER SLICE: *224 cal., 11 g fat (1 g sat. fat), 14 mg chol., 129 mg sodium, 30 g carb., 1 g fiber, 2 g pro.*

Caramel-Frosted Zucchini Bread: Prepare as directed. After cooling and storing overnight, spread loaves with caramel frosting. For caramel frosting, in a medium mixing bowl combine ¼ cup caramel ice cream topping, 3 tablespoons softened butter, and ¾ teaspoon apple pie spice. Beat with an electric mixer on medium speed until well mixed. Gradually add 1½ cups powdered sugar, beating until combined. If necessary, beat in 1 to 2 teaspoons milk to make desired consistency.

PER SLICE: *225 cal., 10 g fat (2 g sat. fat), 17 mg chol., 150 mg sodium, 34 g carb., 1 g fiber, 2 g pro.*

Honey-Zucchini Bread: Preheat oven to 325°F. Prepare as directed, except reduce sugar to 1½ cups and stir ½ cup honey into egg mixture. Sprinkle batter in each pan with ½ cup granola. Bake for 60 to 70 minutes or until a wooden toothpick inserted near centers comes out clean. If necessary to prevent overbrowning, cover with foil for the last 15 minutes of baking.

PER SLICE: *207 cal., 9 g fat (1 g sat. fat), 13 mg chol., 130 mg sodium, 29 g carb., 1 g fiber, 3 g pro.*

Caramel-Frosted Zucchini Bread

Lemon-Poppy Seed Quick Bread

PREP: 20 minutes
BAKE: 50 minutes at 350°F
STAND: overnight
MAKES: 1 loaf (16 slices)

2 cups all-purpose flour
1 cup sugar
2 teaspoons baking powder
½ teaspoon salt
1 egg, lightly beaten
1 cup milk
¼ cup vegetable oil
1 tablespoon finely shredded lemon peel
2 tablespoons lemon juice
1 tablespoon poppy seeds
2 tablespoons sugar
2 tablespoons lemon juice
1 tablespoon butter

1. Preheat oven to 350°F. Grease the bottom and ½ inch up sides of an 8×4×2-inch loaf pan; set aside. In a large bowl stir together flour, 1 cup sugar, the baking powder, and salt. Make a well in center of the flour mixture; set aside.
2. In a bowl combine egg, milk, oil, lemon peel, 2 tablespoons lemon juice, and the poppy seeds. Add egg mixture all at once to flour mixture. Stir just until moistened (batter should be lumpy). Spoon batter into prepared pan, spreading evenly.
3. Bake for 50 to 55 minutes or until a wooden toothpick inserted near center comes out clean. Cool in pan on a wire rack for 10 minutes.
4. Meanwhile, for lemon glaze, in a small saucepan combine 2 tablespoons sugar, 2 tablespoons lemon juice, and the butter. Heat and stir over medium-low heat until sugar is dissolved. Remove bread from pan. Poke holes in top of warm loaf with a fork; slowly brush with lemon glaze. Cool completely on a wire rack. Wrap and store overnight before slicing.

PER SLICE: *164 cal., 5 g fat (1 g sat. fat), 15 mg chol., 121 mg sodium, 30 g carb., 1 g fiber, 3 g pro.*

To Store: Wrap cooled loaf or mini loaves in foil or plastic wrap. Store in the refrigerator for up to 1 week. Or place in freezer bag or container and freeze for up to 3 months. If frozen, thaw overnight in the refrigerator.

Tangerine-Poppy Seed Quick Bread: Prepare as directed, except substitute finely shredded tangerine or orange peel for the lemon peel and tangerine juice for the lemon juice in bread and glaze. After removing loaf from pan, poke holes in the top of the warm loaf with a fork; slowly brush with glaze.

PER SLICE: *162 cal., 5 g fat (1 g sat. fat), 16 mg chol., 119 mg sodium, 27 g carb., 1 g fiber, 3 g pro.*

Lemon-Cardamom Quick Bread: Prepare as directed, except substitute ½ teaspoon ground cardamom for the poppy seeds. Spread cooled loaf with lemon icing. For lemon icing, in a medium bowl whisk together 1¼ cups powdered sugar, 1 teaspoon finely shredded lemon peel, 4 teaspoons lemon juice, 2 teaspoons light-color corn syrup, and ¼ teaspoon vanilla.

PER SLICE: *187 cal., 4 g fat (1 g sat. fat), 14 mg chol., 114 mg sodium, 35 g carb., 1 g fiber, 3 g pro.*

Make It Mini

Preheat oven to 350°F. Grease bottoms and halfway up sides of three 5¾×3×2-inch loaf pans; set aside. Prepare batter as directed. Spread batter evenly in the prepared loaf pans. Bake about 40 minutes or until a wooden toothpick inserted near the centers comes out clean. Cool in pans on wire rack for 10 minutes. Remove loaves from pans. Poke holes in the tops of the warm loaves with a fork; slowly brush with lemon glaze. Cool completely on wire racks. Makes 3 mini loaves (5 slices per loaf).

Pumpkin Bread

PREP: **25 minutes**
BAKE: **55 minutes at 350°F**
STAND: **overnight**
MAKES: **2 loaves (32 slices)**

3⅓ cups all-purpose flour
2 teaspoons baking soda
2 teaspoons ground cinnamon
1½ teaspoons salt
1 teaspoon ground nutmeg
1½ cups granulated sugar
1½ cups packed brown sugar
1 cup vegetable oil
4 eggs
⅔ cup water
1 15-ounce can pumpkin

1. Preheat oven to 350°F. Grease the bottom and ½ inch up sides of two 9×5×3-inch, three 8×4×2-inch, or four 7½×3½×2-inch loaf pans; set aside. In a large bowl combine flour, baking soda, cinnamon, salt, and nutmeg; set aside.
2. In an extra-large mixing bowl combine granulated sugar, brown sugar, and oil. Beat with an electric mixer on medium speed until well mixed. Add eggs; beat well. Alternately add flour mixture and the water to sugar mixture, beating on low speed after each addition just until combined. Beat in pumpkin.
3. Spoon batter into prepared pans, spreading evenly. Bake for 55 to 60 minutes for the 9×5-inch loaves, 45 to 50 minutes for the 8×4-inch loaves, 40 to 45 minutes for the 7½×3-inch loaves, or until a wooden toothpick inserted near centers comes out clean.
4. Cool in pans on wire racks for 10 minutes. Remove loaves from pans. Cool completely on wire racks. Wrap and store overnight before slicing.

To Store: Wrap cooled, uniced loaves in foil or plastic wrap. Store in the refrigerator for up to 1 week. Or place loaves in freezer bags or containers and freeze for up to 3 months. Thaw frozen loaves overnight in the refrigerator. Before serving, frost or ice as directed.

PER SLICE: *197 cal., 8 g fat (1 g sat. fat), 23 mg chol., 200 mg sodium, 31 g carb., 1 g fiber, 2 g pro.*

Fruitcake-Style Pumpkin Bread: Prepare as directed, except stir one 8-ounce container (1½ cups) chopped mixed candied fruit into the batter. After cooling bread and storing overnight, drizzle with brandy drizzle. For brandy drizzle, in a small bowl stir together 1 cup powdered sugar, 1 tablespoon brandy, and ¼ teaspoon vanilla. Stir in enough additional brandy, 1 teaspoon at a time, to make drizzling consistency.

PER SLICE: *242 cal., 8 g fat (1 g sat. fat), 23 mg chol., 209 mg sodium, 42 g carb., 1 g fiber, 2 g pro.*

Frosted Pumpkin Bread: Prepare loaves as directed. After cooling bread and storing overnight, spread loaves with cocoa-spice frosting. For cocoa-spice frosting, beat 3 tablespoons softened butter with an electric mixer on medium speed for 30 seconds. Beat in 1 cup powdered sugar, 2 tablespoons unsweetened cocoa powder, 1 tablespoon milk, ½ teaspoon ground cinnamon, ½ teaspoon instant espresso coffee powder, and ½ teaspoon vanilla until combined. Beat in 1 cup additional powdered sugar until combined. Beat in additional milk, 1 teaspoon at a time, to make desired consistency.

PER SLICE: *238 cal., 9 g fat (2 g sat. fat), 26 mg chol., 211 mg sodium, 39 g carb., 1 g fiber, 2 g pro.*

Smoky Pumpkin-Cranberry Bread: Prepare as directed, except stir 1 teaspoon ground chipotle chile pepper into flour mixture. Stir 1½ cups chopped fresh or frozen cranberries into the batter.

PER SLICE: *200 cal., 8 g fat (1 g sat. fat), 23 mg chol., 201 mg sodium, 31 g carb., 1 g fiber, 2 g pro.*

Fruitcake-Style Pumpkin Bread

Sweet Cranberry Corn Bread

Corn Bread

PREP: 15 minutes
BAKE: 18 minutes at 425°F
MAKES: 9 servings

- 1   cup yellow, white, or blue cornmeal
- ¾   cup all-purpose flour
- 2   to 3 tablespoons sugar
- 1   tablespoon baking powder
- ½   teaspoon salt
- 1   cup milk or buttermilk
- 2   eggs
- ¼   cup butter, melted
     Honey (optional)

1. Preheat oven to 425°F. Grease a 9×9×2-inch baking pan; set aside. In a medium bowl stir together cornmeal, flour, sugar, baking powder, and salt.

2. In a small bowl whisk together milk, eggs, and melted butter. Add egg mixture all at once to cornmeal mixture. Stir just until moistened (do not overmix). Pour batter into the prepared pan.

3. Bake for 18 to 20 minutes or until golden brown. Cool slightly; serve warm. If desired, serve with honey.

PER SERVING: *183 cal., 7 g fat (4 g sat. fat), 63 mg chol., 313 mg sodium, 29 g carb., 1 g fiber, 5 g pro.*

Corn Muffins: Preheat oven to 425°F. Grease twelve 2½-inch muffin cups; set aside. Prepare batter as directed. Spoon batter into prepared muffin cups, filling each two-thirds full; bake about 15 minutes. Makes 12 muffins.

PER MUFFIN: *130 cal., 6 g fat (3 g sat. fat), 47 mg chol., 224 mg sodium, 17 g carb., 1 g fiber, 3 g pro.*

Corn Sticks: Preheat oven to 425°F. Grease 24 corn stick pans; set aside. Prepare batter as directed. Spoon batter into corn stick pans, filling each half full. Bake for 12 to 15 minutes. Makes 24 corn sticks.

PER STICK: *78 cal., 3 g fat (2 g sat. fat), 28 mg chol., 134 mg sodium, 10 g carb., 1 g fiber, 2 g pro.*

Corn Cakes: Prepare as directed, except add 1½ cups frozen or canned whole kernel corn to the batter. For each cake, spoon about 2 tablespoons batter onto a hot, lightly greased griddle or heavy skillet. Cook over medium heat for 1½ to 2 minutes on each side or until golden brown. Keep cakes warm in a 200°F oven while cooking the remaining cakes. Makes 20 to 24 cakes.

PER CAKE: *92 cal., 3 g total fat (2 g sat. fat), 26 mg chol., 147 mg sodium, 14 g carb., 1 g fiber, 2 g pro.*

Corn Bread Stir-Ins

Customize corn bread for any meal with one of these tasty additions.

Cheesy Tex-Mex: Stir ¼ cup canned diced green chile peppers, ½ cup fresh or frozen whole kernel corn, and ½ cup shredded Monterey Jack cheese with jalapeño peppers into the batter.

Sausage-Parmesan: Cook 6 ounces bulk Italian sausage and ½ cup chopped onion until meat is brown; drain. Add to batter with ¼ cup grated Parmesan cheese.

Sweet Cranberry: Increase sugar to ¼ cup and stir ¾ cup coarsely chopped fresh or frozen cranberries and 1 teaspoon finely shredded orange peel into the batter.

Cheesy Bacon: Stir ¾ cup chopped red sweet pepper, ½ cup shredded cheddar cheese, and 3 slices bacon, crisp-cooked, drained, and crumbled, into batter.

Spicy Herb: Add 4 teaspoons snipped fresh thyme or oregano (or ½ teaspoon dried thyme or oregano, crushed) or ½ teaspoon ground cumin or chili powder to the flour mixture.

Chocolate-Glazed Ginger-Pumpkin Muffins

PREP: **20 minutes**
BAKE: **18 minutes at 400°F**
COOL: **1 hour**
STAND: **30 minutes**
MAKES: **16 muffins**

2 cups all-purpose flour
⅔ cup packed brown sugar
⅓ cup granulated sugar
2 teaspoons baking powder
1 teaspoon ground cinnamon
½ teaspoon ground ginger
¼ teaspoon salt
¾ cup canned pumpkin
½ cup butter, melted
½ cup buttermilk or sour milk
  (see tip, page 16)
2 eggs
1 recipe Chocolate Glaze
1 to 2 tablespoons finely
  chopped crystallized ginger

1. Preheat oven to 400°F. Line sixteen 2½-inch muffin cups with paper bake cups; set aside. In a medium bowl combine flour, brown sugar, granulated sugar, baking powder, cinnamon, ground ginger, and salt. Make a well in the center of the flour mixture; set aside.
2. In a small bowl stir together the pumpkin, melted butter, buttermilk, and eggs. Add egg mixture all at once to flour mixture. Stir just until moistened (batter should be lumpy). Spoon batter evenly into prepared muffin cups.
3. Bake for 18 to 20 minutes or until a wooden toothpick inserted in the centers comes out clean. Remove muffins from muffin cups; cool completely on a wire rack.
4. Dip the tops of the muffins into the Chocolate Glaze, allowing excess glaze to drip off. Place dipped muffins upright on the wire rack. Sprinkle tops of muffins with chopped crystallized ginger. Let stand about 30 minutes or until glaze sets.

Chocolate Glaze: In a medium saucepan heat ½ cup whipping cream, ½ teaspoon vanilla, and, if desired, 1 tablespoon orange-flavor liqueur over medium-high heat just until boiling. Remove from heat. Add 6 ounces chopped bittersweet or semisweet chocolate. Do not stir. Let stand for 5 minutes; stir until smooth.

To Store: Place muffins in a single layer in an airtight container. Cover and store in the refrigerator for up to 3 days.

PER MUFFIN: *240 cal., 12 g fat (8 g sat. fat), 50 mg chol., 165 mg sodium, 31 g carb., 2 g fiber, 4 g pro.*

Chai Breakfast Muffins

PREP: 25 minutes
BAKE: 15 minutes at 350°F
COOL: 45 minutes
MAKES: 24 muffins

1½ cups all-purpose flour
½ cup whole wheat flour
1½ teaspoons baking powder
½ teaspoon baking soda
½ teaspoon ground ginger
¼ teaspoon salt
1¼ cups milk
4 chai tea bags
½ cup butter, softened
1½ cups sugar
½ teaspoon vanilla
2 eggs
¾ cup maple-flavor granola or granola with dried fruit
1 recipe Chai Cream Cheese Icing (optional)

1. Preheat oven to 350°F. Line twenty-four 2½-inch muffin cups with paper bake cups. In a medium bowl stir together all-purpose flour, whole wheat flour, baking powder, baking soda, ginger, and salt. In a small saucepan heat milk just until simmering. Remove from heat. Add tea bags; steep for 5 minutes. Remove tea bags, pressing bags to release tea into saucepan; cool.
2. In a large mixing bowl beat butter with an electric mixer on medium to high speed about 1 minute or until fluffy. Add sugar and vanilla; beat until combined. Add eggs, one at a time, beating well after each addition. Alternately add flour mixture and milk mixture to butter mixture, beating on low speed after each addition just until combined.
3. Spoon batter into prepared muffin cups, filling each about two-thirds full. Use the back of a spoon to smooth out batter in cups. Sprinkle with granola.
4. Bake for 15 to 20 minutes or until a wooden toothpick inserted in centers comes out clean. Cool in muffin cups on wire racks for 5 minutes. Remove muffins from cups. Cool completely on wire racks. If desired, drizzle with Chai Cream Cheese Icing.

Chai-Cream Cheese Icing: In a large mixing bowl combine one 3-ounce package cream cheese, softened; 2 tablespoons butter softened; and 1 teaspoon vanilla. Beat with an electric mixer on medium to high speed until light and fluffy. Gradually beat in 1¼ cups powdered sugar. Whisk in enough cooled brewed chai tea, 1 teaspoon at a time, to reach drizzling consistency.

To Store: Place muffins in a single layer in an airtight container; seal. Store at room temperature for up to 3 days.

To Make Ahead: Place uniced muffins in a single layer in an airtight container; seal. Freeze for up to 1 month. Thaw at room temperature before icing. If desired, drizzle with Chai-Cream Cheese Frosting.

PER MUFFIN: *181 cal., 6 g fat (3 g sat. fat), 35 mg chol., 138 mg sodium, 29 g carb., 1 g fiber, 3 g pro.*

Double Chocolate Muffins

PREP: **15 minutes**
BAKE: **18 minutes at 375°F**
COOL: **10 minutes**
MAKES: **12 muffins**

1¼ cups all-purpose flour
½ cup granulated sugar
⅓ cup packed brown sugar
¼ cup unsweetened cocoa powder
2 teaspoons baking powder
¼ teaspoon baking soda
¼ teaspoon salt
1 cup miniature semisweet chocolate pieces
½ cup vegetable oil
½ cup milk
1 egg

1. Preheat oven to 375°F. Grease twelve 2½-inch muffin cups or line with paper bake cups; set aside. In a medium bowl combine flour, granulated sugar, brown sugar, cocoa powder, baking powder, baking soda, and salt. Stir in chocolate pieces. Make a well in center of flour mixture; set aside.
2. In a small bowl whisk together the oil, milk, and egg. Add oil mixture all at once to the flour mixture. Stir just until moistened.
3. Spoon batter into prepared muffin cups, filling each two-thirds full.
4. Bake for 18 to 20 minutes or until edges are firm (tops will be slightly rounded). Cool in muffin cups on a wire rack for 5 minutes. Remove muffins from muffin cups; serve warm.

To Store: Let muffins cool completely on a wire rack. Place cooled muffins in a resealable plastic bag or an airtight container; seal or cover. Store at room temperature for up to 3 days.

PER MUFFIN: *295 cal., 15 g fat (4 g sat. fat), 19 mg chol., 148 mg sodium, 38 g carb., 2 g fiber, 3 g pro.*

Make It Mini

Preheat oven to 375°F. Line thirty-six 1¾-inch muffin cups with paper bake cups; set aside. Prepare batter as directed. Spoon batter into prepared muffin cups, filling each two-thirds full. Bake for 12 to 15 minutes or until edges are firm (tops will be slightly rounded). Cool and serve as directed. Makes 36 mini muffins.

Sour Cream-Raspberry Muffins

PREP: **25 minutes**
BAKE: **28 minutes at 375°F**
COOL: **5 minutes**
MAKES: **12 muffins**

2 cups all-purpose flour
1 teaspoon baking powder
1 teaspoon baking soda
¾ teaspoon salt
½ cup butter, softened
1 cup granulated sugar
2 eggs
1 teaspoon vanilla
1 8-ounce carton sour cream
1½ cups fresh or frozen raspberries and/or blueberries
1 tablespoon granulated sugar
¼ teaspoon ground cinnamon
Powdered sugar (optional)

1. Preheat oven to 375°F. Grease twelve 2½-inch muffin cups or line with paper bake cups; set aside. In a medium bowl stir together flour, baking powder, baking soda, and salt; set aside.

2. In a large mixing bowl beat butter with an electric mixer on medium to high speed for 30 seconds. Add the 1 cup granulated sugar; beat on medium speed until light and fluffy. Beat in eggs and vanilla just until combined. Alternately add flour mixture and sour cream, beating on low speed just until mixture is moistened.

3. Spoon half of the batter into the prepared muffin cups, filling each about one-third full. Top with half of the berries. Spoon the remaining batter into cups, filling each about two-thirds full. Top with the remaining berries. In a small bowl stir together the 1 tablespoon granulated sugar and the cinnamon; sprinkle evenly over muffin batter.

4. Bake for 28 to 30 minutes or until golden brown and tops spring back when lightly touched. Cool in muffin cups on a wire rack for 5 minutes. Remove from muffin cups. If desired, sprinkle with powdered sugar. Serve warm.

To Store: Cool muffins completely on a wire rack. Store muffins in an airtight container in the refrigerator for up to 3 days. To reheat, wrap muffins in foil. Heat in a 350°F oven for 12 to 15 minutes or until warm.

PER MUFFIN: *216 cal., 10 g fat (6 g sat. fat), 52 mg chol., 298 mg sodium, 29 g carb., 1 g fiber, 3 g pro.*

Cake or Muffin?

Unlike the standard mixing method for muffins and quick breads, these cake-type muffins have a higher sugar and butter content and require the creaming mixing method (see photos, page 24). As a result, the texture is more tender, similar to that of cake.

Banana-Multigrain Streusel Muffins

PREP: 25 minutes
BAKE: 20 minutes at 375°F
COOL: 5 minutes
MAKES: 20 muffins

Nonstick cooking spray
1 cup all-purpose flour
½ cup whole wheat flour
2 tablespoons flaxseed meal
2 teaspoons baking powder
1 teaspoon ground nutmeg
½ teaspoon salt
¼ cup canola oil
¼ cup reduced-fat creamy peanut butter
½ cup packed brown sugar
1 egg
1 cup whole bran cereal
1 cup mashed very ripe bananas (about 3 medium)
¼ cup light sour cream
1 tablespoon vanilla
1 cup buttermilk or sour milk (see tip, page 16)
1 recipe Streusel Crunch Topping

1. Preheat oven to 375°F. Line twenty to twenty-two 2½-inch muffin cups with paper bake cups. Lightly coat bake cups with cooking spray. (Or coat muffin cups with cooking spray.) Set aside. In a medium bowl combine all-purpose flour, whole wheat flour, flaxseed meal, baking powder, nutmeg, and salt. Set aside.

2. In a large mixing bowl combine oil and peanut butter. Beat with an electric mixer on medium speed for 30 seconds. Gradually add brown sugar, beating until combined. Add egg, cereal, bananas, sour cream, and vanilla; beat just until combined. Alternately add flour mixture and buttermilk to banana mixture, beating on low speed after each addition just until combined.

3. Spoon batter into prepared muffin cups, filling each about three-fourths full. Sprinkle Streusel Crunch Topping evenly over batter in muffin cups.

4. Bake about 20 minutes or until light brown and muffin tops spring back when lightly touched. Cool in muffin cups on a wire rack for 5 minutes. Remove from muffin cups. Serve warm.

Streusel Crunch Topping: In a small bowl combine ¼ cup all-purpose flour, ¼ cup rolled oats, ¼ cup packed brown sugar, and ¼ teaspoon ground cinnamon. Add 3 tablespoons canola oil; stir to combine.

To Store: Let muffins cool completely on a wire rack. Store cooled muffins in an airtight container in the refrigerator for up to 3 days. To reheat, wrap muffins in foil. Heat in a 350°F oven for 12 to 15 minutes or until warm.

PER MUFFIN: *172 cal., 7 g fat (1 g sat. fat), 12 mg chol., 143 mg sodium, 24 g carb., 3 g fiber, 4 g pro.*

Ginger-Pear Star Scones

PREP: 30 minutes
BAKE: 8 minutes at 400°F
MAKES: 30 scones

2½ cups all-purpose flour
2   tablespoons packed brown sugar
1   tablespoon baking powder
1   tablespoon finely chopped crystallized ginger
½   teaspoon freshly grated nutmeg (see tip, page 17) or ¼ teaspoon ground nutmeg
¼   teaspoon salt
⅓   cup cold butter, cut up
1   cup finely chopped pear
2   eggs, lightly beaten
⅔   cup whipping cream
    Whipping cream
    Freshly grated nutmeg and/or finely chopped crystallized ginger (optional)
1   recipe Spiced Butter

1. Preheat oven to 400°F. In a large bowl stir together flour, brown sugar, baking powder, 1 tablespoon ginger, ½ teaspoon grated or ¼ teaspoon ground nutmeg, and salt. Using a pastry blender, cut in butter until mixture resembles coarse crumbs. Stir in pear. Make a well in center of flour mixture; set aside.

2. In a medium bowl combine eggs and the ⅔ cup whipping cream. Add egg mixture all at once to flour mixture. Using a fork, stir just until moistened.

3. Turn dough out onto a lightly floured surface. Knead dough by folding and gently pressing it for 10 to 12 strokes or just until dough holds together. Divide dough in half. Lightly roll or pat each half of the dough into a 7-inch circle. Using a 2- to 2½-inch star-shape cutter, cut out scones. Reroll scraps to cut additional scones.

4. Place scones 2 inches apart on an ungreased baking sheet. Brush with additional whipping cream. If desired, sprinkle with additional grated nutmeg and/or ginger.

5. Bake for 8 to 12 minutes or until golden. Serve warm with Spiced Butter.

Spiced Butter: In a small bowl stir together 1 tablespoon sugar, ½ teaspoon finely chopped crystallized ginger, ¼ teaspoon freshly grated nutmeg or ⅛ teaspoon ground nutmeg, and dash ground cinnamon. Stir in ½ cup softened butter until combined. Cover and chill until ready to serve.

To Store: Place scones in an airtight container or resealable plastic bag; cover or seal. Store at room temperature for up to 2 days. If desired, preheat oven to 350°F. Place scones on a baking sheet and heat for 5 to 6 minutes or until warm.

To Make Ahead: Prepare scones as directed. Place cooled scones in a resealable plastic freezer bag. Seal, label, and freeze for up to 2 months. To serve, thaw at room temperature. If desired, preheat oven to 350°F. Place scones on a baking sheet and heat for 5 to 6 minutes or until warm. Serve with Spiced Butter.

PER SCONE: *119 cal., 8 g fat (5 g sat. fat), 35 mg chol., 109 mg sodium, 11 g carb., 0 g fiber, 2 g pro.*

Cranberry-Chocolate Scones

PREP: **20 minutes**
BAKE: **12 minutes at 400°F**
MAKES: **12 scones**

2½ cups all-purpose flour
2 tablespoons sugar
1 tablespoon baking powder
¼ teaspoon salt
⅓ cup cold butter
2 eggs, lightly beaten
¾ cup whipping cream
¼ cup chopped dried cranberries
¼ cup miniature semisweet chocolate pieces
½ teaspoon finely shredded orange peel (see tip, page 102) (optional)
 Whipping cream or milk
1 recipe Orange Drizzle

1. Preheat oven to 400°F. In a large bowl combine flour, sugar, baking powder, and salt. Using a pastry blender, cut in butter until mixture resembles coarse crumbs. Make a well in the center of the flour mixture; set aside.
2. In a medium bowl combine eggs, the ¾ cup cream, the cranberries, chocolate pieces, and, if desired, orange peel. Add egg mixture all at once to flour mixture. Using a fork, stir just until moistened.
3. Turn dough out onto a lightly floured surface. Knead dough by folding and gently pressing it for 10 to 12 strokes or just until dough holds together. Divide dough in half. Pat or lightly roll each portion into a 6-inch circle. Cut each circle into six wedges.
4. Place wedges 2 inches apart on an ungreased baking sheet. Brush wedges with additional cream.
5. Bake for 12 to 14 minutes or until golden. Cool slightly on baking sheet. Drizzle with Orange Drizzle. Serve warm or at room temperature.

Orange Drizzle: In a small bowl combine 1 cup powdered sugar and ¼ teaspoon vanilla. Stir in enough orange juice (1 to 2 tablespoons), 1 teaspoon at a time, to make icing drizzling consistency.

To Store: Place iced scones in a single layer in an airtight container; cover. Store at room temperature up to 2 days.

To Make Ahead: Prepare as directed, except do not drizzle with Orange Drizzle. Place cooled scones in a resealable plastic freezer bag. Seal, label, and freeze for up to 2 months. To serve, thaw at room temperature. If desired, preheat oven to 350°F. Place scones on a baking sheet; heat for 8 to 10 minutes or until warm. Drizzle with Orange Drizzle.

PER SCONE: *291 cal., 14 g fat (8 g sat. fat), 67 mg chol., 203 mg sodium, 38 g carb., 1 g fiber, 4 g pro.*

Make It Mini

Prepare and knead dough as directed, except pat or lightly roll dough into an 8-inch square about ½ inch thick. Cut into 1-inch squares. Place squares 1 inch apart on an ungreased baking sheet. Brush with cream. Bake in the 400°F oven for 8 to 10 minutes or until golden. Cool slightly on baking sheet. Drizzle with Orange Drizzle. Serve warm or at room temperature. Makes 64 mini scones.

Brandy-Soaked Currant, Thyme, and Parmesan Scones

PREP: 25 minutes
CHILL: 30 minutes
BAKE: 20 minutes at 375°F
MAKES: 9 scones

½ cup dried currants
¼ cup brandy or apple juice
1¾ cups all-purpose flour
¾ cup finely shredded Parmigiano-Reggiano cheese (3 ounces)
1 tablespoon baking powder
1 tablespoon sugar
1 tablespoon finely snipped fresh thyme
1 teaspoon freshly ground black pepper
½ teaspoon salt
¼ cup cold butter, cut into small pieces
⅔ cup whipping cream
1 egg
1 tablespoon water

1. In a small saucepan combine currants and brandy. Heat over medium heat just until warm. Remove from heat. Cover and let stand for 15 minutes. Drain.

2. Meanwhile, line a baking sheet with parchment paper; set aside.

3. In a food processor* combine flour, ½ cup of the cheese, the baking powder, sugar, thyme, pepper, and salt; cover and pulse with several on/off turns to combine. Sprinkle butter pieces over flour mixture; cover and pulse with several on/off turns until mixture resembles coarse crumbs. Add drained currants; cover and pulse with several on/off turns to combine. With the motor running, slowly add whipping cream through the feed tube, processing just until combined.

4. Turn dough out onto a lightly floured surface. Knead dough by folding and gently pressing it for 10 to 12 strokes or just until dough holds together. Pat or lightly roll the dough into an 8-inch circle, about ¾ inch thick. In a small bowl whisk together egg and the water; brush over dough circle. Sprinkle with the remaining ¼ cup cheese. Using a pizza cutter or floured sharp knife, cut dough circle into eight wedges. Cover and chill for 30 minutes to overnight.

5. Preheat oven to 375°F. Bake about 20 minutes or until golden. Serve warm.

*Test Kitchen Tip: If you don't have a food processor, combine the flour mixture in a large bowl. Using a pastry blender, cut in butter until mixture resembles coarse crumbs. Make a well in the center of the flour mixture. Add drained currants and whipping cream all at once. Using a fork, stir until mixture is moistened. Continue as directed in Step 4.

To Store: Place scones in an airtight container or resealable plastic bag; cover or seal. Store in the refrigerator for up to 2 days. If desired, preheat oven to 350°F. Place scones on a baking sheet and bake for 5 to 6 minutes or until warm.

PER SCONE: *311 cal., 16 g fat (10 g sat. fat), 75 mg chol., 467 mg sodium, 31 g carb., 1 g fiber, 7 g pro.*

Tomato Pesto Scones with Kalamata Olives

PREP: **35 minutes**
BAKE: **12 minutes at 425°F**
MAKES: **9 scones**

- 1 cup (3 ounces) dried tomatoes (not oil-packed)
- 2 cups all-purpose flour
- 1 0.5-ounce envelope pesto sauce mix
- 2 teaspoons baking powder
- ½ teaspoon baking soda
- ¼ cup cold butter
- ¾ cup milk
- 1 egg yolk
- ½ cup pitted Kalamata olives, coarsely chopped and drained
- 1 tablespoon snipped fresh rosemary
- 1 tablespoon olive oil
  Rosemary sprigs (optional)

1. In a small bowl pour enough boiling water over dried tomatoes to cover. Let stand for 10 minutes; drain well. Remove two of the dried tomatoes; set aside. Chop remaining tomatoes and set aside.

2. Meanwhile, preheat oven to 425°F. Line a large baking sheet with parchment paper; set aside. In a large bowl combine flour, pesto sauce mix, baking powder, and baking soda. Using a pastry blender, cut in butter until mixture resembles coarse crumbs. Make a well in center of the flour mixture; set aside.

3. In a medium bowl combine milk and egg yolk. Add milk mixture all at once to flour mixture. Add the chopped tomatoes, olives, and snipped rosemary. Using a fork, stir just until moistened.

4. Turn dough out onto a lightly floured surface. Knead dough by folding and gently pressing it for 10 to 12 strokes or just until dough holds together. Transfer dough to prepared baking sheet. With floured hands, pat or lightly roll dough into a 9×6-inch rectangle. Using a sharp knife, cut scones into 9 to 15 diamond pieces (do not separate.) Lightly press the 2 reserved tomatoes and, if desired, a few rosemary sprigs into top of dough. Brush with olive oil.

5. Bake for 12 to 14 minutes or until light brown. Gently pull scones apart or cut to separate. Serve warm.

To Store: Place scones in an airtight container or resealable plastic bag; cover or seal. Store at room temperature for up to 2 days. If desired, preheat oven to 350°F. Place scones on a baking sheet and heat for 5 to 6 minutes or until warm.

PER SCONE: *208 cal., 9 g fat (4 g sat. fat), 39 mg chol., 595 mg sodium, 27 g carb., 2 g fiber, 5 g pro.*

A Word About Scones

By definition, scones are light and tender. The dough requires a little TLC during preparation to keep it in top form. Here are a few tips to keep in mind:

- Stir dry ingredients well to evenly distribute the leavening agent.
- When butter is called for, make sure it's cold. Cut fat in only until mixture resembles coarse crumbs.
- Stir in the liquid just until moistened.
- Very gently knead the dough by folding and pressing just to distribute moisture (excessive kneading will develop the gluten in flour and cause toughness).
- If the recipe calls for rolling out the dough, cut as many scones as possible from the first rolling (the second rolling and additional flour will make scones a bit tougher than the first batch).

Flaky Biscuits

PREP: 15 minutes
BAKE: 10 minutes at 450°F
MAKES: 12 biscuits

3 cups all-purpose flour
1 tablespoon baking powder*
1 tablespoon sugar
1 teaspoon salt
¾ teaspoon cream of tartar*
¾ cup cold butter or ½ cup cold butter and ¼ cup shortening
1 cup milk

1. Preheat oven to 450°F. In a large bowl combine flour, baking powder, sugar, salt, and cream of tartar. Using a pastry blender, cut in butter until mixture resembles coarse crumbs. Make a well in the center of the flour mixture. Add milk all at once. Using a fork, stir just until mixture is moistened.
2. Turn dough out onto a lightly floured surface. Knead dough by folding and gently pressing it for four to six strokes or just until dough holds together. Pat or lightly roll dough to ¾-inch thickness. Cut dough with a floured 2½-inch biscuit cutter; reroll scraps as necessary and dip cutter into flour between cuts. Place dough circles 1 inch apart on an ungreased baking sheet.
3. Bake for 10 to 14 minutes or until golden. Remove biscuits from baking sheet; serve warm.

*Test Kitchen Tip: If baking powder or cream of tartar appears lumpy, sift through a fine-mesh sieve before using.

To Store: Place biscuits in an airtight container or resealable plastic bag; cover or seal. Store at room temperature for up to 2 days or freeze up to 3 months. If frozen, remove biscuits from container and wrap in foil; bake in a 300°F oven for 10 to 15 minutes or until warm.

Drop Biscuits: Prepare as directed through Step 1, except increase the milk to 1¼ cups. Using a large spoon, drop dough into 12 mounds onto a greased baking sheet. Bake as directed above. Makes 12 biscuits.

Buttermilk Biscuits: Prepare as directed, except for rolled dough biscuits substitute 1¼ cups buttermilk or sour milk (see tip, page 16) for the 1 cup milk. For drop biscuits substitute 1½ cups buttermilk or sour milk for the 1¼ cups milk.

PER BISCUIT FOR PLAIN, DROP, OR BUTTERMILK: *231 cal., 12 g fat (8 g sat. fat), 32 mg chol., 375 mg sodium, 26 g carb., 1 g fiber, 4 g pro.*

Biscuit Basics

Truly tender biscuits depend on two things: cutting the fat into the flour until it is the right consistency and minimizing the handling of dough once the liquid is added. The former will create pockets of fat for flakiness and the latter will prevent overdevelopment of the gluten in the flour—a surefire tenderness buster.

1. Cut the fat into the flour mixture quickly, leaving coarse, uneven crumbs.

2. Pour the milk into the well in the flour mixture all at once. There is no need to work it in slowly.

3. Gently work the dough with your hands until it is uniform and holds together nicely.

4. Pat the dough into an even thickness on the floured surface.

5. When cutting biscuits, press down quickly and firmly on the cutter. Space the cuts as closely as possible.

Peppery White Cheddar Biscuits

PREP: 25 minutes
BAKE: 13 minutes at 400°F
MAKES: 18 biscuits

- 4 cups all-purpose flour
- 2 tablespoons baking powder
- ½ teaspoon salt
- ½ cup shortening
- ¼ cup butter
- 1½ cups finely crumbled or shredded sharp white cheddar cheese (6 ounces)
- 2 to 3 teaspoons coarsely ground black pepper
- 1½ cups milk
- 1 egg, lightly beaten
- 1 teaspoon water

1. Preheat oven to 400°F. Lightly grease a large baking sheet; set aside. In a medium bowl combine flour, baking powder, and salt. Cut in shortening and butter until mixture resembles coarse crumbs. Add cheese and pepper; mix well. Make a well in center of the flour mixture. Add milk all at once; stir just until moistened.
2. Turn dough out onto a lightly floured surface. Knead dough by folding and gently pressing it for 10 to 12 strokes or just until dough holds together. Divide dough in half. Roll or pat each half into a 6-inch square, about 1 inch thick. Using a sharp knife, cut dough into 2-inch squares. Combine egg and the water; brush tops of biscuits. Place on prepared baking sheet.
3. Bake for 13 to 15 minutes or until golden. Remove biscuits from baking sheet; serve warm.

To Store: Place biscuits in an airtight container or resealable plastic bag; cover or seal. Store in the refrigerator for up to 2 days. To serve, preheat oven to 300°F. Place scones on a baking sheet and bake for 5 to 6 minutes or until warm.

To Make Ahead: Prepare and bake biscuits as directed; cool completely on a wire rack. Place biscuits in a freezer container or bag and freeze up to 3 months. To serve, wrap frozen biscuits in foil and bake in a 300°F oven about 15 minutes or until warm.

PER BISCUIT: *247 cal., 14 g fat (6 g sat. fat), 34 mg chol., 314 mg sodium, 24 g carb., 1 g fiber, 7 g pro.*

Maple Swirl Biscuits

PREP: 35 minutes
BAKE: 18 minutes at 375°F
MAKES: 12 biscuits

- 4 cups all-purpose flour
- 4 teaspoons baking powder
- 1 teaspoon baking soda
- 1 teaspoon salt
- ½ cup cold butter
- 1¼ cups milk
- ¼ cup pure maple syrup
- ½ cup maple sugar or granulated sugar
- 1 tablespoon apple pie spice
- ½ cup butter, softened
- ⅔ cup raisins (optional)
- 2 tablespoons butter, melted
- 1 recipe Maple Glaze

1. Preheat oven to 375°F. Line a 15×10×1-inch baking pan with parchment paper, extending paper over edges of pan; set aside. In a large bowl combine flour, baking powder, baking soda, and salt. Using a pastry blender, cut in the ½ cup cold butter until mixture resembles coarse crumbs. Make a well in the center of flour mixture.
2. Add milk and maple syrup all at once to the flour mixture. Using a fork, stir just until dough forms a ball.
3. On a lightly floured surface, knead dough by folding and gently pressing it for 10 to 12 strokes or just until dough holds together. Place dough between two pieces of parchment paper. Roll or pat dough into a 14×10-inch rectangle.
4. In a small bowl combine maple sugar and apple pie spice. Spread dough with ½ cup softened butter; sprinkle with the sugar-spice mixture. If desired, sprinkle with raisins. Starting from a long side, roll up into a spiral. Pinch seam to seal. Using a sharp knife, cut into 12 slices. Arrange slices, cut sides down, in the prepared pan. Drizzle with the 2 tablespoons melted butter.

5. Bake for 18 to 20 minutes or until golden. Using edges of parchment paper, lift biscuits from pan and place on a wire rack. Cool slightly. Drizzle biscuits with Maple Glaze.

Maple Glaze: In a small bowl combine 1¼ cups powdered sugar and 2 tablespoons pure maple syrup. Stir in enough milk (1 to 2 teaspoons), 1 teaspoon at a time, to make drizzling consistency.

To Store: Place biscuits in a single layer in an airtight container; cover. Store at room temperature for up to 2 days.

To Make Ahead: Bake biscuits as directed; cool completely on a wire rack. Place biscuits in an airtight container or resealable plastic bag; cover or seal. Freeze up to 3 months. To serve, remove biscuits from container and wrap in foil; heat in a 300°F oven for 20 to 25 minutes or until warm. Drizzle with Maple Glaze.

PER BISCUIT: *428 cal., 18 g fat (11 g sat. fat), 48 mg chol., 555 mg sodium, 62 g carb., 1 g fiber, 5 g pro.*

Sage and Pepper Popovers

PREP: 15 minutes
BAKE: 40 minutes at 400°F
MAKES: 6 popovers

- 1 tablespoon shortening or nonstick cooking spray
- 2 eggs, lightly beaten
- 1 cup milk
- 1 tablespoon olive oil
- 1 cup all-purpose flour
- 2 tablespoons grated Parmesan cheese
- 2 teaspoons finely snipped fresh sage or thyme or ½ teaspoon dried sage or thyme, crushed
- ½ teaspoon freshly ground black pepper
- ½ teaspoon salt

1. Preheat oven to 400°F. Using ½ teaspoon shortening for each cup, grease the bottoms and sides of six 6-ounce custard cups or six cups of a popover pan. (Or lightly coat with nonstick cooking spray.) If using custard cups, place the cups in a 15×10×1-inch baking pan; set aside.

2. In a medium bowl beat eggs, milk, and oil with a wire whisk until combined. Add flour; beat until smooth. Stir in Parmesan cheese, sage, pepper, and salt. Fill the prepared cups half full with batter.

3. Bake about 40 minutes or until firm. Immediately after removing from oven, prick each popover with a fork to let steam escape. Turn off oven. For crisper popovers, return to oven for 5 to 10 minutes or until popovers reach desired crispness. Remove popovers from cups; serve warm.

PER POPOVER: *153 cal., 7 g fat (2 g sat. fat), 74 mg chol., 237 mg sodium, 17 g carb., 1 g fiber, 5 g pro.*

High-Rising Popovers

Despite their impressive appearance, popovers are very simple to make, based on five common ingredients—eggs, milk, flour, salt, and oil. When exposed to high heat, the batter magically puffs up in the cups like hot air balloons because of steam that can't escape. This creates popovers with a light and airy interior and a crisp outer crust.

1. Use a pastry brush dipped in shortening to grease the bottoms and sides of each popover cup.

2. Fill the cups about half full with the prepared batter.

3. Immediately after baking, prick each popover with a fork to let steam escape.

Fruit Coffee Cake, recipe page 380

morning favorites

CELEBRATE THE DAWNING OF EACH NEW DAY with homebaked breakfast fare—coffee cakes, cinnamon rolls, fruit-filled turnovers, and more. Get the morning magic started with a play-by-play on our quintessential fruit-filled coffee cake.

Fruit Coffee Cake

Breakfast and brunch spreads demand a coffee cake like this classic version—fluffy, sweet goodness sandwiching a layer of homemade fruit preserves. Add a cup of coffee and breakfast is served!

PREP: 35 minutes
BAKE: 40 minutes at 350°F
MAKES: 9 servings

- 1½ to 2 cups fresh blueberries; fresh red raspberries; sliced, peeled apricots; sliced, peeled peaches; and/or chopped, peeled apples
- ¼ cup water
- ¼ cup sugar
- 2 tablespoons cornstarch
- 1½ cups all-purpose flour
- ¾ cup sugar
- ½ teaspoon baking powder
- ¼ teaspoon baking soda
- ¼ cup butter
- 1 egg, lightly beaten
- ½ cup buttermilk or sour milk (see page 16)
- ½ teaspoon vanilla
- ¼ cup all-purpose flour
- ¼ cup sugar
- 2 tablespoons butter

1. For filling, in a medium saucepan combine fruit and water. Bring to boiling; reduce heat. Cover and simmer (do not simmer raspberries) about 5 minutes or until fruit is tender. Combine ¼ cup sugar and the cornstarch; stir into fruit. Cook and stir over medium heat until thickened and bubbly. Cook and stir for 2 minutes more.
2. Preheat oven to 350°F. In a medium bowl combine the 1½ cups flour, the ¾ cup sugar, the baking powder, and baking soda. Cut in the ¼ cup butter until mixture resembles coarse crumbs (see photos, page 25). Make a well in the center of the flour mixture; set aside.
3. In another bowl combine egg, buttermilk, and vanilla. Add egg mixture all at once to flour mixture. Stir just until moistened (batter should be lumpy). Spread half of the batter into an ungreased 8×8×2-inch baking pan. Spoon and gently spread filling over batter. Drop remaining batter in small mounds onto filling.
4. In a bowl combine ¼ cup flour and ¼ cup sugar. Cut in the 2 tablespoons butter until coarse crumbs form. Sprinkle over batter. Bake for 40 to 45 minutes or until golden. Cool slightly on a wire rack. Serve warm.

Rhubarb-Strawberry Coffee Cake: Prepare as directed, except substitute ¾ cup fresh or frozen cut-up rhubarb and ¾ cup frozen unsweetened whole strawberries for fruit. Continue as directed.

Test Kitchen Tip: For a larger coffee cake, double all ingredients and use a 13×9×2-inch baking pan. Bake for 45 to 50 minutes or until golden. Makes 18 servings.

To Store: Cover cooled coffee cake with heavy foil. Store in the refrigerator for up to 2 days or in the freezer for up to 1 month. To serve, thaw coffee cake if frozen. Reheat coffee cake, covered with foil, in a 300°F oven for 5 to 10 minutes.

PER SERVING: *298 cal., 9 g fat (5 g sat. fat), 44 mg chol., 126 mg sodium, 52 g carb., 1 g fiber, 4 g pro.*

Secrets to Success

Coffee cakes fall somewhere between the categories of bread and cake—sometimes calling for slow-rising yeast, other times calling for quick-rising baking powder. This recipe uses baking powder, so it's quick enough to prepare fresh for a morning meal.

When preparing the fruit filling, thoroughly combine the cornstarch and sugar before adding it to the simmering fruit to prevent lumps of cornstarch from forming. Sprinkle the sugar mixture evenly over the fruit and stir it in quickly.

To keep the cake dough deliciously tender, cut the butter into the flour mixture adequately using a pastry blender (see page 25) or two knives. Toss the liquid into the mixture just until the flour mixture is moistened. Overmixing will develop the gluten in flour and create undesirable toughness.

COOK UNTIL THICKENED Stir the sugar-cornstarch mixture into the cooked fruit. Then cook and stir over medium heat until thickened and bubbly.

SPREAD ON THE FILLING Spoon and gently spread the thickened fruit filling over the batter in the pan.

MOUND REMAINING BATTER Using two spoons, drop the remaining batter in small mounds all over the fruit filling.

SPRINKLE ON TOP Cut butter into a flour-sugar mixture to form coarse crumbs, then sprinkle the crumb mixture on top.

MAKE IT MINE

Make-It-Mine Cinnamon Rolls

Cinnamon rolls are a nostalgic comfort food, but even a classic can be improved. Play around with the dough, filling, and icing ingredients to create a breakfast treat specially designed for your favorite people.

PREP: **45 minutes**
RISE: **1 hour 15 minutes**
BAKE: **25 minutes at 375°F**
MAKES: **12 rolls**

Flour (choose option)
1 package active dry yeast
Liquid (choose option)
½ cup instant mashed potato flakes
⅓ cup butter, cut up
⅓ cup sugar
1 teaspoon salt
2 eggs
Filling (choose option)
¼ cup butter, softened
Icing (choose option)

1. In a large mixing bowl combine 1½ cups of the all-purpose *Flour* and the yeast; set aside. In a medium saucepan heat and stir *Liquid*, potato flakes, the ⅓ cup butter, the sugar, and salt just until warm (120°F to 130°F) and butter almost melts. Add the butter mixture to the flour mixture; add eggs. Beat with an electric mixer on low to medium speed for 30 seconds, scraping the sides of the bowl constantly. Beat on high speed for 3 minutes, scraping the sides of the bowl occasionally. Using a wooden spoon, stir in as much of the remaining *Flour* as you can.

2. Turn dough out onto a lightly floured surface. Knead in enough of the remaining *Flour* to make a moderately soft dough that is smooth and elastic (3 to 5 minutes total). Shape dough into a ball. Place in a lightly greased bowl, turning once to grease surface of dough. Cover and let rise in a warm place until double in size (45 to 60 minutes).

3. Punch dough down. Turn dough out onto a lightly floured surface. Cover and let rest for 10 minutes. Meanwhile, lightly grease a 13×9×2-inch baking pan; set aside. In a bowl stir together *Filling* ingredients; set aside.

4. Roll dough into an 18×12-inch rectangle. Spread ¼ cup butter over dough and sprinkle with *Filling*, leaving 1 inch unfilled along one of the long sides. Roll up rectangle, starting from the filled long side; pinch dough to seal seams. Slice into 12 equal pieces. Arrange pieces, cut sides up, in prepared pan (or choose an *Alternate Shaping*). Cover and let rise in a warm place until nearly double in size (about 30 minutes).

5. Preheat oven to 375°F. Place rolls on middle oven rack. Line a baking sheet with foil; place on bottom rack to catch any drips. Bake for 25 to 30 minutes or until golden. Cool in pan on a wire rack for 10 minutes; remove rolls from pan. In a small bowl combine the *Icing* ingredients. Spread or drizzle rolls with *Icing*.

FLOUR (PICK ONE)

All-purpose flour: 4¼ to 4¾ cups all-purpose flour
Whole wheat flour: 2 cups whole wheat flour (stir in first) and 2¼ to 2¾ cups all-purpose flour
Cocoa powder: ⅓ cup unsweetened cocoa powder (stir in first) and 4 to 4½ cups all-purpose flour

---

LIQUID (PICK ONE)

Milk: 1¾ cups milk
Milk and water: 1 cup milk and ¾ cup water
Half-and-half and orange juice: 1 cup half-and-half, light cream, or milk and ¾ cup orange juice

---

FILLING (PICK ONE)

Brown Sugar and Cinnamon: ½ cup packed brown sugar and 1 tablespoon ground cinnamon
Sugar and Cinnamon: ⅓ cup granulated sugar and 1 tablespoon ground cinnamon

continued on page 384

continued from page 382

Spiced Pecan: ⅓ cup packed brown sugar, ⅓ cup chopped pecans, and 2 teaspoons pumpkin pie spice

Spiced Fruit: ⅓ cup granulated sugar, ⅓ cup chopped dried apples, ¼ cup raisins, 2 teaspoons apple pie spice, and 1 teaspoon finely shredded orange peel

Cranberry and Pistachio: ⅓ cup packed brown sugar, ⅓ cup dried cranberries, and ¼ cup chopped pistachio nuts

Chocolate Chip: ¼ cup packed brown sugar, ¼ cup granulated sugar, and ½ cup miniature semisweet chocolate pieces

SHAPING (PICK ONE)

Cinnamon Roll Ring: Prepare and slice dough as directed, except line a large baking sheet with parchment paper. Arrange dough slices on prepared baking sheet in a circle about 9 inches in diameter, overlapping slices slightly. Let rise and continue as directed. Let rise as directed. Bake in a 350°F oven for 30 to 35 minutes or until golden, covering edges with foil if necessary to prevent overbrowning. Spread or drizzle with Icing.

Cinnamon Twists: Prepare dough and let it rise the first time as directed, except divide dough in half before letting it rest. Line two 15×10×1-inch baking pans with parchment paper; set aside. Roll half of the dough at a time into a 12×8-inch rectangle. Spread with butter; sprinkle *Filling* down half of the rectangle. Fold in half lengthwise; cut into twelve 4×1-inch strips. Twist each strip one or two times and place in one of the prepared baking pans. Repeat with the remaining dough half. Let rise as directed. Bake, one pan at a time, in a 375°F oven for 15 to 20 minutes or until golden. If desired, spread or drizzle twists with *Icing*. Serve warm. Makes 24 twists.

Cinnamon Roll Coffee Cakes: Prepare and roll up dough as directed; slice rolled dough log in half lengthwise. Line two baking sheets with parchment paper. In center of each prepared baking sheet, coil one dough half, cut sides up, to form a snail shape; tuck end under. Let rise as directed. Bake in a 350°F oven for 30 to 35 minutes or until golden, covering edges with foil if necessary to prevent overbrowning. Spread or drizzle coffee cakes with *Icing*.

ICING (PICK ONE)

Powdered Sugar: 1½ cups powdered sugar, ½ teaspoon vanilla, and enough milk to reach desired consistency

Cream Cheese: One 3-ounce package softened cream cheese, 2 tablespoons softened butter, 2½ cups powdered sugar, 1 teaspoon vanilla, and enough milk or orange juice to reach desired consistency

Cocoa: 1¼ cups powdered sugar, 3 tablespoons unsweetened cocoa powder, ½ teaspoon vanilla, and enough milk to reach desired consistency

Cinnamon Roll Ring

Cinnamon Roll Twists

Cinnamon Roll Coffee Cakes

No-Knead Chocolate and Coconut Rolls

PREP: **40 minutes**
RISE: **1½ hours**
BAKE: **15 minutes at 350°F**
COOL: **5 minutes**
MAKES: **9 rolls**

4   cups all-purpose flour
1   package active dry yeast
1   cup milk
⅓   cup sugar
¼   cup butter
½   teaspoon salt
2   eggs
1   13-ounce jar chocolate-
    hazelnut spread
1   cup shredded coconut
    Milk

1. In a large mixing bowl combine 2 cups of the flour and the yeast; set aside. In a small saucepan heat and stir milk, sugar, butter, and salt just until warm (120°F to 130°F) and butter almost melts. Add milk mixture and eggs to flour mixture. Beat with an electric mixer on low to medium speed for 30 seconds, scraping sides of bowl constantly. Beat on medium speed for 3 minutes. Stir in the remaining 2 cups flour. Cover and let rise in a warm place until double in size (45 to 60 minutes).
2. Turn dough out onto a well-floured surface. Cover and let rest for 10 minutes. Lightly grease a large baking sheet; set aside. Roll dough into a 12×9-inch rectangle. Spread ⅔ cup of the chocolate-hazelnut spread over dough, leaving a 1-inch edge along one of the long sides. (Set aside the remaining chocolate-hazelnut spread for the icing.) Sprinkle coconut over chocolate-hazelnut spread. Starting from the long side with the filling spread to the edge, roll up dough into a spiral. Pinch to seal seam. Cut into nine slices. Arrange slices 2 inches apart on prepared baking sheet. Cover and let rise in a warm place until nearly double in size (about 45 minutes).
3. Preheat oven to 350°F. Bake for 15 to 20 minutes or until golden. Cool about 5 minutes; transfer to a wire rack.
4. For icing, in a small bowl stir together the remaining chocolate-hazelnut spread and enough milk to make drizzling consistency. Drizzle icing over rolls. Serve warm.

To Make Ahead: Shape rolls and arrange in pan as directed in Step 2. Cover rolls loosely with plastic wrap. Chill for 2 to 24 hours. Let stand at room temperature for 30 minutes before baking as directed in Step 3.

PER ROLL: *590 cal., 24 g fat (8 g sat. fat), 64 mg chol., 272 mg sodium, 83 g carb., 3 g fiber, 12 g pro.*

Fruit and Almond Cinnamon Rolls with Amaretto Icing

PREP: 45 minutes
CHILL: overnight
RISE: 2¼ hours
BAKE: 30 minutes at 350°F
COOL: 20 minutes
MAKES: 20 rolls

- 1 cup chopped dried apricots
- 1 cup chopped dried sweet cherries
- ¼ cup cherry kirsch or apple juice
- ¼ cup amaretto or apple juice
- ¾ cup warm water (105°F to 115°F)
- 1 package active dry yeast
- ⅔ cup buttermilk
- ¼ cup sugar
- 2 eggs
- 3 tablespoons butter, melted
- 1 teaspoon salt
- 4½ to 5 cups bread flour
- 1 recipe Frangipane Filling
- 1 cup packed brown sugar
- 4 teaspoons ground cinnamon
- 1 recipe Amaretto Icing

1. In a small bowl combine apricots, cherries, kirsch, and Amaretto. Cover bowl tightly and refrigerate overnight.*

2. In a small bowl combine ¼ cup of the warm water and the yeast. Let stand about 10 minutes or until foamy.

3. In a large mixing bowl combine the remaining ½ cup warm water, the buttermilk, sugar, eggs, melted butter, salt, and 2 cups of the flour. Beat with an electric mixer on medium to high speed until smooth. Add yeast mixture; mix well. Using a wooden spoon, stir in enough of the remaining flour, ½ cup at a time, to make a moderately soft dough.

4. Turn dough out onto a lightly floured surface. Knead for 3 to 4 minutes or until smooth and elastic. Place dough in a lightly greased large bowl, turning once. Cover; let rise in a warm place until double in size (1½ hours).

5. Meanwhile, lightly grease a 13×9×2-inch baking pan; set aside. Prepare Frangipane Filling.

6. Turn dough out onto a lightly floured surface. Divide dough in half. Roll one half into a 15×12-inch rectangle. Spread half of the Frangipane Filling over dough, leaving about 1 inch unfilled along the long sides. Spread half of the reserved fruit mixture over Frangipane Filling. Sprinkle with ½ cup brown sugar and 2 teaspoons of the cinnamon. Roll up, starting from a long side; pinch dough to seal seams and ends. Repeat with remaining dough and fillings.

7. Slice each roll into 10 equal pieces. Arrange in the prepared baking pan with 4 rolls across and 5 rolls lengthwise. Cover and let rise in a warm place until nearly double in size (about 45 minutes).

8. Preheat oven to 350°F. Bake rolls for 30 to 35 minutes or until golden. Cool in pan on wire rack for 20 minutes. Spread with Amaretto Icing.

Frangipane Filling: Crumble one 8-ounce can almond paste into a medium mixing bowl. Add ¼ cup softened butter, 3 tablespoons sugar, and ⅛ teaspoon almond extract. Beat with an electric mixer on medium to high speed until smooth. Add 2 eggs, one at a time, beating well after each addition. Beat in 3 tablespoons all-purpose flour and ¼ teaspoon salt.

Amaretto Icing: In a medium mixing bowl beat ½ cup softened butter with an electric mixer on medium speed until smooth. Gradually add 2 cups powdered sugar, beating well. Beat in 2 tablespoons amaretto or other almond liqueur and 2 tablespoons milk (or use ¼ cup milk and ¼ teaspoon almond extract instead of amaretto and milk). Gradually beat in 2 cups additional powdered sugar until smooth.

*Test Kitchen Tip: Or in a small saucepan combine kirsch and amaretto. Carefully heat over medium-low heat just until warm. (If alcohol ignites, cover pan with the lid and remove from heat.) Add apricots and cherries; cover. Remove from heat; let stand for 20 minutes.

To Store: Place rolls in an airtight container. Store at room temperature for up to 2 days.

PER ROLL: *484 cal., 14 g fat (6 g sat. fat), 66 mg chol., 235 mg sodium, 82 g carb., 3 g fiber, 7 g pro.*

Orange-Honey Sweet Rolls

PREP: **45 minutes**
RISE: **1 hour 30 minutes**
BAKE: **25 minutes at 350°F**
COOL: **15 minutes**
MAKES: **15 rolls**

2 packages active dry yeast
1¼ cups warm water (110°F to 115°F)
½ cup nonfat dry milk powder
⅓ cup butter, softened
⅓ cup honey
2 eggs, lightly beaten
2 tablespoons toasted wheat germ
1 teaspoon salt
3 cups white whole wheat flour or all-purpose flour
2 to 2¼ cups bread flour
1 cup golden raisins
¼ cup butter, softened
¼ cup honey
2 teaspoons finely shredded orange peel (see tip, page 102)
1 recipe Orange Icing

1. In a large mixing bowl dissolve the yeast in the warm water; let stand for 5 minutes. Add dry milk powder, the ⅓ cup butter, the ⅓ cup honey, the eggs, wheat germ, and salt. Beat with an electric mixer on low speed for 30 seconds, scraping sides of bowl constantly. Add 2 cups of the white whole wheat flour. Beat on low to medium speed for 30 seconds. Beat on high speed for 3 minutes. Using a wooden spoon, stir in the remaining white whole wheat flour and as much of the bread flour as you can.
2. Turn dough out onto a lightly floured surface. Knead in enough of the remaining bread flour to make a moderately soft dough that is smooth and elastic (about 6 minutes total). Shape dough into a ball. Place dough in a lightly greased bowl, turning once to grease surface of the dough. Cover; let rise in a warm place until double in size (about 1 hour).
3. Punch down dough. Turn out onto a lightly floured surface. Cover and let rest for 10 minutes. Meanwhile, lightly grease a 13×9×2-inch baking pan; set aside.
4. For filling, in a small bowl pour enough cold water over raisins to cover; let stand for 5 minutes. Drain well. In a medium bowl whisk together the ¼ cup butter, the ¼ cup honey, and the orange peel until creamy and well mixed.

5. Roll dough into an 18×15-inch rectangle. Spread the butter-honey mixture to within ½ inch of the edges. Sprinkle with raisins. Starting from a long side, roll up rectangle into a spiral. Pinch seam to seal. Slice spiral into 15 pieces. Arrange pieces, cut sides down, in the prepared baking pan. Cover and let rise in a warm place until nearly double in size (about 30 minutes).
6. Preheat oven to 350°F. Bake about 25 minutes or until lightly browned. Remove from oven. Cool for 1 minute. Carefully invert rolls onto a wire rack. Cool slightly. Invert again onto a serving platter. Drizzle with Orange Icing.

Orange Icing: In a small bowl combine 1 cup powdered sugar and 1 teaspoon finely shredded orange peel (see tip, page 102). Stir in enough orange juice (1 to 2 tablespoons) to make icing drizzling consistency.

To Store: Place leftover rolls in an airtight container. Store at room temperature for up to 2 days. Or freeze uniced rolls for up to 2 months. Thaw at room temperature before drizzling rolls with icing.

PER ROLL: *346 cal., 8 g fat (5 g sat. fat), 48 mg chol., 241 mg sodium, 61 g carb., 4 g fiber, 9 g pro.*

Banana-Coconut Coffee Cake with Macadamia Nut Streusel

PREP: **30 minutes**
BAKE: **35 minutes at 350°F**
COOL: **30 minutes**
MAKES: **18 servings**

3½ cups all-purpose flour
¾ cup flaked coconut
1 tablespoon baking powder
1 teaspoon baking soda
1 teaspoon salt
1 cup butter, softened
¾ cup granulated sugar
¾ cup packed brown sugar
4 eggs
3 ripe bananas, mashed
¼ cup coffee liqueur or strong brewed coffee
¼ cup milk
2 teaspoons vanilla
¼ cup all-purpose flour
¼ cup packed brown sugar
½ teaspoon ground cinnamon
¼ cup cold butter, cut up
½ cup coarsely chopped macadamia nuts
1 recipe Vanilla-Coconut Icing

1. Preheat oven to 350°F. Grease and flour a 13×9×2-inch baking pan; set aside. In a medium bowl stir together the 3½ cups flour, the coconut, baking powder, baking soda, and salt; set aside.
2. In a very large mixing bowl beat the 1 cup butter, ¾ cup granulated sugar, and ¾ cup brown sugar with an electric mixer on medium to high speed until light and fluffy. Scrape sides of bowl; beat for 1 minute. Add eggs, one at a time, beating well after each addition. Beat in bananas, liqueur, milk, and vanilla on low speed just until combined (mixture may appear curdled). Add flour mixture, beating on low speed just until combined. Spoon batter into the prepared pan, spreading evenly.
3. For streusel, in a small bowl stir together the ¼ cup flour, ¼ cup brown sugar, and the cinnamon. Using a pastry blender, cut in the ¼ cup cold butter until mixture resembles coarse crumbs. Stir in macadamia nuts. Sprinkle evenly over top of batter.

4. Bake for 35 to 40 minutes or until a wooden toothpick inserted in the center comes out clean. Cool in pan on a wire rack for 30 minutes. Drizzle coffee cake with Vanilla-Coconut Icing. Serve warm.

Vanilla-Coconut Icing: In a small bowl stir together ¾ cup powdered sugar, 4 teaspoons milk, ½ teaspoon vanilla, and, if desired, a few drops coconut extract until smooth.

To Store: Cover cooled coffee cake with heavy foil or place mini coffee cakes in a single layer in an airtight container. Store in the refrigerator for up to 2 days or in the freezer for up to 1 month.

PER SERVING: *305 cal., 14 g fat (8 g sat. fat), 57 mg chol., 306 mg sodium, 41 g carb., 1 g fiber, 4 g pro.*

Make It Mini

Preheat oven to 350°F. Grease and lightly flour twenty-four 2½-inch muffin cups or line with paper bake cups. Prepare batter as directed. Spoon batter into prepared muffin cups, filling each half to two-thirds full. Prepare streusel as directed; sprinkle over batter in muffin cups. Bake for 18 to 22 minutes or until a wooden toothpick inserted in centers comes out clean. Cool in muffin cups for 5 minutes; remove from pans. Drizzle with Vanilla-Coconut Icing. Serve warm. Makes 24 mini coffee cakes.

Lemon-Foldovers Coffee Cake

PREP: **50 minutes**
RISE: **1½ hour**
BAKE: **25 minutes at 350°F**
COOL: **10 minutes**
MAKES: **12 to 18 servings**

  2 eggs
 ⅓ cup buttermilk
 ½ cup warm water (105°F to 115°F)
  1 package active dry yeast
 ⅓ cup sugar
 ¼ cup butter, melted
1½ teaspoons vanilla
 ½ teaspoon salt
3½ to 4 cups all-purpose flour
 ½ cup sugar
  3 tablespoons finely shredded lemon peel (see tip, page 102)
  1 tablespoon finely shredded orange peel
 ½ cup lemon curd
 ¼ cup butter, melted
  1 recipe Lemon-Cream Cheese Icing

1. Allow eggs and buttermilk to stand at room temperature for 30 minutes. In a large mixing bowl stir together the warm water and yeast. Let stand about 10 minutes or until foamy. Lightly beat the eggs. Add eggs, buttermilk, the ⅓ cup sugar, ¼ cup melted butter, the vanilla, and salt to yeast mixture; mix well.

2. Gradually add 2½ cups of the flour beating with an electric mixer on low speed (dough will be soft and slightly sticky). Beat dough on low speed for 5 minutes. Using a wooden spoon, stir in as much of the remaining flour as you can to make a moderately soft dough (dough will still be slightly sticky). Cover and let rise in a warm place until double in size (about 1 hour).

3. Meanwhile, in a small bowl combine the ½ cup sugar, the lemon peel, and orange peel; mix well, pressing with spoon to release oils from peels. Set aside. Line a 13×9×2-inch baking pan with foil, extending the foil over the edges of the pan. Grease foil; set pan aside.

4. Punch dough down. Turn dough out onto a lightly floured surface. Roll dough into an 18×12-inch rectangle. Using a pizza cutter, cut the dough into eighteen 3×4-inch squares. Spoon a slightly rounded teaspoon of lemon curd into the center of each square. Moisten the edges of the squares with water. Fold squares in half diagonally to make triangles; press edges to seal.

5. Arrange triangles in the prepared pan in two lengthwise rows of nine, sealed corners of the triangles pointing up. Drizzle with ¼ cup melted butter. Sprinkle with lemon peel mixture. Cover and let rise in a warm place until nearly double in size (about 30 minutes).

6. Preheat oven to 350°F. Bake for 25 to 30 minutes or until golden. If necessary, cover with foil the last 10 minutes to prevent overbrowning. Cool in pan on a wire rack for 10 minutes. Use foil to lift coffee cake from pan. Carefully transfer coffee cake to a serving platter. Drizzle with Lemon-Cream Cheese Icing. Serve warm.

Lemon-Cream Cheese Icing: In a medium mixing bowl beat 2 ounces softened cream cheese, 1 tablespoon milk, 1½ teaspoons lemon juice, and ½ teaspoon vanilla with an electric mixer on medium speed until smooth. Beat in 1¼ to 1½ cups powdered sugar to reach drizzling consistency.

To Store: Place any leftover coffee cake in an airtight container; cover. Store in the refrigerator for up to 2 days.

PER SERVING: *385 cal., 11 g fat (7 g sat. fat), 71 mg chol., 196 mg sodium, 66 g carb., 3 g fiber, 6 g pro.*

Raspberry-Apple Kuchen with Warm Cream Sauce

PREP: **30 minutes**
BAKE: **1 hour at 350°F**
MAKES: **16 servings**

  3 cups all-purpose flour
  4 teaspoons baking powder
  1 teaspoon apple pie spice
  ½ teaspoon salt
  ¾ cup butter, softened
1½ cups granulated sugar
  3 eggs
  1 cup half-and-half or
     light cream
  4 large tart cooking apples
1½ cups fresh raspberries
  ⅓ cup granulated sugar
  ¾ teaspoon ground cinnamon
     Powdered sugar (optional)
  1 recipe Warm Cream Sauce

1. Preheat oven to 350°F. Generously grease a 13×9×2-inch baking pan. In a medium bowl stir together flour, baking powder, apple pie spice, and salt. Set aside.
2. In a large mixing bowl beat butter with an electric mixer on medium to high speed for 30 seconds. Add 1½ cups granulated sugar. Beat until light and fluffy, scraping sides of bowl occasionally. Beat in eggs until combined. Alternately add flour mixture and half-and-half to butter mixture, beating on low speed after each addition just until combined. Pour batter into the prepared baking pan, spreading evenly.
3. Peel, core, and thinly slice apples. Beginning at the outside edges of pan, arrange apple slices in a rectangular pattern. Gently press apple slices into batter. Top with raspberries; gently press into batter. In a small bowl stir together ⅓ cup granulated sugar and cinnamon; sprinkle evenly over kuchen.
4. Bake about 1 hour or until a wooden toothpick inserted in the center comes out clean. Cool completely in pan on a wire rack. If desired, sprinkle kuchen with powdered sugar. Drizzle Warm Cream Sauce over kuchen.

Warm Cream Sauce: In a medium saucepan combine 2 cups whipping cream, ½ cup sugar, ½ cup butter, and ½ teaspoon ground nutmeg. Bring to boiling; reduce heat. Simmer, uncovered, for 20 to 25 minutes or until slightly thickened, stirring occasionally. Stir in ½ teaspoon rum extract.

PER SERVING: *502 cal., 29 g fat (17 g sat. fat), 124 mg chol., 298 mg sodium, 59 g carb., 3 g fiber, 5 g pro.*

Adding Alternately

Many batter recipes call for adding dry and wet ingredients alternately to a creamed mixture. The term "alternately" means adding the dry and wet ingredients to the butter-egg mixture in two or three batches, starting with flour, then adding liquid, then flour, and so forth, beating after each addition just until incorporated. This important technique preserves the air bubbles that were whipped in when beating together the butter, sugar, and eggs, creating a light, aerated cake. Take care not to overbeat after each addition or you will cause gluten in the flour to develop (which increases during mixing after flour and liquid come in contact).

Sour Cream-Orange Coffee Cake with Chocolate Streusel

PREP: **20 minutes**
BAKE: **50 minutes at 350°F**
COOL: **15 minutes**
MAKES: **24 servings**

½ cup packed brown sugar
½ cup all-purpose flour
1 tablespoon unsweetened cocoa powder
¼ cup cold butter, cut up
¾ cup miniature semisweet chocolate pieces
½ cup chopped pecans
3¾ cups all-purpose flour
1 tablespoon baking powder
1 teaspoon baking soda
¾ teaspoon salt
2 teaspoons finely shredded orange peel (see tip, page 102)
¾ cup butter, softened
2 cups granulated sugar
2 eggs
1 8-ounce carton sour cream
¾ cup milk
¼ cup orange juice
1½ teaspoons vanilla

1. Preheat oven to 350°F. Grease a 13×9×2-inch baking pan; set aside.
2. For chocolate streusel, in a small bowl stir together brown sugar, the ½ cup flour, and the cocoa powder. Using a pastry blender, cut in the ¼ cup cold butter until mixture resembles coarse crumbs. Stir in chocolate pieces and pecans; set aside.
3. In a medium bowl stir together the 3¾ cups flour, the baking powder, baking soda, and salt. Sprinkle orange peel over top of mixture; using fingers, distribute orange peel evenly through flour mixture. Set aside.
4. In a very large mixing bowl beat the ¾ cup softened butter and the granulated sugar with an electric mixer on medium speed for 2 minutes. Add eggs, one at a time, beating well after each addition. Beat in sour cream, milk, orange juice, and vanilla until combined. Gradually beat in flour mixture on low speed. Beat about 2 minutes more or until smooth.

5. Spread half of the batter in the prepared pan. Sprinkle half of the chocolate streusel evenly over the batter. Using the back of a spoon, press streusel gently into the batter. Spread the remaining batter over streusel. Sprinkle remaining chocolate streusel over batter.
6. Bake for 50 to 55 minutes or until a wooden toothpick inserted near the center comes out clean. Cool in pan on a wire rack for at least 15 minutes. Serve warm or at room temperature.

To Store: Cover and store at room temperature for up to 3 days. Or wrap with heavy foil and freeze for up to 1 month.

PER SERVING: *317 cal., 14 g fat (8 g sat. fat), 44 mg chol., 243 mg sodium, 45 g carb., 1 g fiber, 4 g pro.*

A Tale of Two Leaveners

While the chemistry behind baking soda and baking powder is complicated, here's the gist:

Baking soda, or sodium bicarbonate, requires an acid to help it break down at the right rate and produce the correct amount of carbon dioxide gas to act as a leavener. Acidic ingredients that combine with it include honey, molasses, brown sugar, chocolate, and buttermilk. Without acid, baking soda breaks down too fast, leaving behind an unpleasant soapy taste.

Baking powder is premixed to contain both baking soda and the right amount of acidic ingredient (such as cream of tartar), plus cornstarch to absorb any moisture in the air. When a recipe calls for both of these leaveners, it is so the baking soda will neutralize an added acid, such as the brown sugar in the recipe above. Be sure to thoroughly stir the leaveners into the flour to prevent clumps of either in finished cakes and breads.

Espresso-Bittersweet Yeast Roll Ring

PREP: **45 minutes**
RISE: **1 hour 30 minutes**
BAKE: **25 minutes at 350°F**
MAKES: **1 coffee cake**
(12 slices)

3¼ to 3¾ cups all-purpose flour
  1 package active dry yeast
  ⅔ cup milk
  ⅓ cup butter
  ⅓ cup granulated sugar
  3 teaspoons instant espresso coffee powder or instant coffee powder
  ½ teaspoon salt
  2 eggs
  3 tablespoons butter, softened
  ¼ cup granulated sugar
  1 teaspoon ground cinnamon
  ½ cup chopped almonds, toasted (see tip, page 343)
  ¾ cup bittersweet or semisweet chocolate pieces
  1 cup powdered sugar
  ¼ teaspoon vanilla
  1 to 2 tablespoons brewed espresso or strong coffee, cooled

1. In a large mixing bowl stir together 1½ cups of the flour and the yeast; set aside. In a small saucepan heat and stir milk, the ⅓ cup butter, the ⅓ cup granulated sugar, 2 teaspoons of the instant espresso powder, and the salt just until warm (120°F to 130°F) and butter almost melts. Add milk mixture to flour mixture; add eggs. Beat with an electric mixer on low to medium speed for 30 seconds, scraping sides of bowl constantly. Beat on high speed for 3 minutes more. Using a wooden spoon, stir in as much of the remaining flour as you can.

2. Turn dough out onto a lightly floured surface. Knead in enough of the remaining flour to make a moderately soft dough that is smooth and elastic (5 to 7 minutes total). Shape dough into a ball. Place in a lightly greased bowl, turning once to grease surface of the dough. Cover and let rise in a warm place until double in size (1 to 1½ hours).

3. Punch dough down. Turn dough out onto a lightly floured surface. Cover and let rest for 10 minutes. Roll dough into a 20×12-inch rectangle. Spread with the 3 tablespoons softened butter.

continued on page 400

How to Shape a Yeast Roll Ring

Cutting evenly spaced slits in this yeast roll ring creates an impressive fan during baking.

1. Starting from the long side, loosely and evenly roll dough into a spiral.

2. Using a pastry brush, moisten the ends of dough with water so the dough ring will be easy to seal.

3. Shape dough into a ring on a greased baking sheet. Line up the ends and pinch to seal firmly.

4. Using a sharp knife, make cuts around edge of dough ring, cutting two-thirds of the way to the center.

5. Cut at 1½-inch intervals around the dough ring.

continued from page 399

4. For filling, in a small bowl stir together the ¼ cup granulated sugar, the cinnamon, and the remaining 1 teaspoon instant espresso powder. Add almonds; toss gently to coat. Sprinkle over dough rectangle. Sprinkle evenly with chocolate pieces.

5. Grease a large baking sheet; set aside. Starting with a long side, loosely roll up dough rectangle into a spiral. Moisten edge; pinch firmly to seal. Place spiral, seam side down, on the prepared baking sheet. Bring ends together to form a ring. Moisten ends; pinch together to seal ring. Flatten slightly. Using a sharp knife, make cuts around the edge of the dough ring at 1½-inch intervals, cutting about two-thirds of the way to the center. Cover and let rise in a warm place until nearly double in size (30 to 40 minutes).

6. Preheat oven to 350°F. Bake for 25 to 30 minutes or until bread ring sounds hollow when tapped. (If necessary to prevent overbrowning, cover loosely with foil for the last 5 to 10 minutes of baking.) Transfer to a wire rack. Cool completely.

7. For icing, in a small bowl combine powdered sugar and vanilla. Stir in enough of the brewed espresso to make icing drizzling consistency. Spoon icing over ring.

To Store: Place leftovers in an airtight container and store at room temperature for up to 3 days.

To Make Ahead: Bake and cool as directed. Place cooled, uniced yeast ring in an airtight container or resealable freezer bag; freeze for up to 2 months. Thaw wrapped bread at room temperature about 2 hours. Continue as directed in Step 7.

PER SLICE: *335 cal., 12 g fat (5 g sat. fat), 58 mg chol., 200 mg sodium, 53 g carb., 2 g fiber, 6 g pro.*

In Hot Water

Recipes for yeast bread always call for the liquid to be heated until warm (120°F to 130°F). Follow this recommendation to the T or your finished bread will pay the price. Check the temperature of the water with an instant-read thermometer. If it's too hot, the yeast will die, causing flat bread. (Let the liquid mixture stand until the right temperature is reached or start over.) If the liquid isn't warm enough, the yeast won't activate and your bread won't rise. Yeast may be simple creatures (one-cell plants, to be specific), but they know what they like and won't cooperate without the perfect conditions.

Cinnamon Pecan Bread

PREP: 40 minutes
RISE: 1 hour 30 minutes
BAKE: 20 minutes at 350°F
MAKES: 1 loaf (12 slices)

- 2 to 2½ cups all-purpose or bread flour
- 1 teaspoon active dry yeast
- ½ cup milk
- ¼ cup butter, cut up
- 2 tablespoons sugar
- ½ teaspoon salt
- 1 egg
- 2 tablespoons butter, melted
- 3 tablespoons sugar
- 1½ teaspoons ground cinnamon
- ½ cup chopped pecans
- 1 recipe Powdered Sugar Glaze

1. In a large mixing bowl combine 1 cup of the flour and the yeast. In a small saucepan heat and stir milk, the ¼ cup cut-up butter, the 2 tablespoons sugar, and the salt until warm (120°F to 130°F) and butter almost melts. Add milk mixture to flour mixture. Add egg. Beat with an electric mixer on low speed for 30 seconds, scraping sides of bowl constantly. Beat on high speed for 3 minutes. Using a wooden spoon, stir in as much of the remaining flour as you can.
2. Turn dough out onto a lightly floured surface. Knead in enough of the remaining flour to make a moderately soft dough that is smooth and elastic (3 to 5 minutes total). Shape into a ball. Place dough in a lightly greased bowl, turning once to grease surface of dough. Cover and let rise in a warm place until double in size (1 to 1¼ hours).
3. Punch dough down. Turn dough out onto a well-floured surface. Roll dough into a 12-inch square. Brush the dough with the 2 tablespoons melted butter. Combine the 3 tablespoons sugar and the cinnamon; sprinkle over the butter on dough. Sprinkle with pecans.

Roll up dough, jelly-roll-style. Pinch the seams and the ends to seal. Place roll, seam side down, on a greased baking sheet. Let rise in a warm place until nearly double in size (30 to 45 minutes).
4. Preheat oven to 350°F. Bake for 20 to 25 minutes or until bread sounds hollow when lightly tapped. Transfer bread to wire rack; cool completely. Drizzle Powdered Sugar Glaze over bread.

Powdered Sugar Glaze: In a small bowl stir together ¾ cup powdered sugar and enough milk (2 to 3 teaspoons) to make icing drizzling consistency.

To Store: Place in an airtight container and store at room temperature for up to 2 days. To freeze, wrap uniced, cooled loaf in plastic wrap and place in an airtight container or resealable freezer bag; freeze for up to 2 months. Thaw wrapped loaf at room temperature about 2 hours. Drizzle Powdered Sugar Glaze over bread.

PER SLICE: *221 cal., 10 g fat (4 g sat. fat), 32 mg chol., 160 mg sodium, 30 g carb., 1 g fiber, 4 g pro.*

Brown Sugar-Bacon Monkey Bread

PREP: **35 minutes**
RISE: **45 minutes**
BAKE: **35 minutes at 350°F**
COOL: **10 minutes**
MAKES: **10 servings**

- 4 slices applewood smoked bacon
- 1 cup packed brown sugar
- ⅓ cup Maple-Nut Butter
- ¼ cup whipping cream
- 1 tablespoon vanilla
- ¼ teaspoon five-spice powder or ground allspice
- 1 16-ounce loaf frozen sweet roll dough, thawed
- 1 cup chopped pecans
- 1 cup golden raisins

1. In a large skillet cook bacon over medium heat until crisp. Drain, reserving 2 tablespoons of the drippings in skillet. Drain bacon on paper towels; crumble bacon. Add brown sugar, Maple-Nut Butter, and whipping cream to the skillet; stir until melted. Stir in vanilla and spice.

2. Lightly grease a 10-inch fluted tube pan; set aside. Cut thawed bread dough into 1- to 1½-inch pieces. Arrange one-third of the bread pieces, half of the crumbled bacon, half of the pecans, and half of the raisins in the prepared pan. Drizzle one-third of the cream mixture evenly over the bread pieces in pan. Top with another one-third of the bread pieces and the remaining bacon, pecans, and raisins. Drizzle with another one-third of the cream mixture. Top with the remaining bread pieces and the remaining cream mixture. Cover and let rise in a warm place until nearly double in size (about 45 minutes).

3. Preheat oven to 350°F. Bake for 35 to 40 minutes or until bread springs back when lightly touched. Cool in pan on a wire rack for 10 minutes. Invert onto a serving platter; remove pan. Serve warm.

Maple-Nut Butter: In a food processor combine 1 cup softened butter, ½ cup toasted pecan halves (see tip, page 343), and ¼ cup pure maple syrup. Cover and process until nuts are finely chopped. Store leftover nut butter in refrigerator and serve with pancakes, waffles, or French toast.

PER SERVING: *430 cal., 20 g fat (7 g sat. fat), 48 mg chol., 170 mg sodium, 60 g carb., 3 g fiber, 6 g pro.*

How to Make Monkey Bread

With all those ridges in the fluted tube pan, sometimes sticky recipes don't easily release. The solution: Grease the pan well, making sure you get into all the nooks and crannies. Brushing on shortening with a pastry brush works well (see page 21). To give the glaze time to set and adhere to the bread, let the baked bread cool about 10 minutes before inverting onto the platter.

1. Start by arranging one-third of the bread dough pieces in the greased fluted tube pan.

2. Drizzle one-third of the maple-cream mixture over the bread, bacon, pecan, and raisin layer.

3. Before baking, let the dough rise in a warm place until nearly double in size (about 45 minutes).

Lemon-Almond Cream Bread

PREP: 25 minutes
BAKE: 25 minutes at 375°F
COOL: 10 minutes
MAKES: 1 loaf (10 slices)

½ cup mascarpone cheese
2 tablespoons lemon curd
1 tablespoon all-purpose flour
½ teaspoon almond extract
¼ cup golden raisins
1 16-ounce loaf frozen sweet
   roll dough, thawed
1 egg
1 teaspoon water
1 recipe Lemon Glaze
2 tablespoons sliced almonds,
   toasted

1. Preheat oven to 375°F. Line a very large baking sheet with parchment paper; set aside.
2. For filling, in a small bowl stir together mascarpone cheese, lemon curd, flour, and almond extract. Stir in raisins; set aside.
3. On a lightly floured surface, roll dough into a 13×9-inch rectangle, letting dough relax as necessary while rolling. Transfer dough to the prepared baking sheet. Spoon filling lengthwise down the center of the dough, spreading into a 2½-inch-wide strip. Using kitchen scissors, make cuts at 2-inch intervals along each long side, cutting from the edges almost to the filling. Alternately fold opposite strips of dough at an angle across the filling, lightly pressing ends together in center to seal.
4. In a small bowl whisk together egg and the water; brush loaf with egg mixture. Bake about 25 minutes or until golden.
5. Cool on baking sheet on a wire rack for 10 minutes. Drizzle with Lemon Glaze; sprinkle with almonds. Serve warm or cool completely. Chill within 2 hours.

Lemon Glaze: In a small bowl stir together 1 cup powdered sugar, 1 tablespoon lemon juice, and ½ teaspoon vanilla. Add enough additional lemon juice (1 to 2 teaspoons) to reach drizzling consistency.

To Store: Place bread in an airtight container; cover. Store in the refrigerator for up to 2 days.

PER SLICE: *272 cal., 9 g fat (4 g sat. fat), 48 mg chol., 253 mg sodium, 42 g carb., 2 g fiber, 8 g pro.*

How to Braid Bread

Impressive? Yes. Difficult? No. With a few well-placed cuts and some creative folding, you can turn an ordinary rectangle of rolled bread dough into a showstopping loaf that is worthy of any occasion.

1. Spread filling lengthwise down center of dough, spreading to a 2½-inch-wide strip.

2. On the long sides, make cuts at 2-inch intervals from the edges toward the filling in the center.

3. Alternately fold opposite strips at an angle across the filling. Lightly press the ends together in the center to seal.

4. For a shiny golden crust, brush the loaf with an egg-water mixture before baking.

Strawberry-Chocolate Turnovers

PREP: **30 minutes**
BAKE: **16 minutes at 400°F**
MAKES: **18 turnovers**

1 17.3-ounce package frozen puff pastry sheets (2 sheets), thawed
⅓ cup mascarpone cheese or cream cheese, softened
⅓ cup strawberry jam
4 ounces milk chocolate, chopped
1 egg, lightly beaten
2 tablespoons sliced almonds
  Coarse sugar
2 ounces milk chocolate, melted (optional)

1. Preheat oven to 400°F. Line a large baking sheet with parchment paper; set aside.

2. Unfold puff pastry sheets. On a lightly floured surface, roll each sheet of puff pastry into a 12-inch square. Cut each square into nine 4-inch squares (18 squares total). Spoon 1 teaspoon mascarpone cheese onto center of each pastry square. Top each with 1 teaspoon strawberry jam and 1 tablespoon chopped chocolate. Brush the edges of the squares with egg. Fold the squares in half diagonally to enclose the filling; press edges together with the tines of a fork to seal.

3. Place triangles 2 inches apart on the prepared baking sheet. Prick tops of triangles with a fork. Brush tops with egg; sprinkle with sliced almonds and coarse sugar.

4. Bake for 16 to 20 minutes or until puffed and golden brown. Transfer to a wire rack; cool slightly. If desired, drizzle with melted chocolate.

To Make Ahead: Prepare as directed through Step 2, except do not preheat oven. Place triangles in a single layer in an airtight container; cover. Store in the refrigerator for up to 1 day. Continue as directed in Step 3.

Test Kitchen Tip: The recipe halves easily to make 9 large turnovers or 16 mini turnovers.

PER TURNOVER: *234 cal., 15 g fat (5 g sat. fat), 19 mg chol., 82 mg sodium, 22 g carb., 1 g fiber, 4 g pro.*

Make It Mini

Prepare as directed, except cut each 12-inch pastry square into sixteen 3-inch squares (32 squares total). Spoon ½ teaspoon mascarpone cheese onto center of each pastry square. Top each with ½ teaspoon strawberry jam and 1 teaspoon chopped chocolate. Brush the edges of the squares with egg. Fold the squares in half diagonally to enclose the filling; press edges together with the tines of a fork to seal. Bake for 12 to 15 minutes or until puffed and golden brown. Transfer to a wire rack; cool slightly. If desired, drizzle with melted chocolate. Makes 32 mini turnovers.

Apple-Cheese Danish

PREP: 45 minutes
BAKE: 47 minutes at 375°F
COOL: 45 minutes
MAKES: 12 servings

- 1 17.3-ounce package frozen puff pastry sheets (2 sheets), thawed
- 2 tablespoons butter
- 2½ pounds cooking apples, peeled (if desired), cored, and thinly sliced (about 7 cups)
- 1 cup granulated sugar
- 2 tablespoons all-purpose flour
- 1 teaspoon ground cinnamon
- ⅛ teaspoon ground nutmeg
- 1 8-ounce package cream cheese, softened
- 1 egg
- 1 teaspoon vanilla
  Milk
- 2 tablespoons coarse sugar

1. Preheat oven to 375°F. Lightly grease a 15×10×1-inch baking pan; set aside. On a lightly floured surface, unfold one pastry sheet and roll into a 15×10-inch rectangle. Transfer to the prepared baking pan, pressing dough to edges of pan. Bake about 12 minutes or until golden brown (pastry will puff and shrink from sides of pan). Cool on a wire rack.
2. Meanwhile, in a very large skillet melt butter over medium heat. Add apples; cook in hot butter about 8 minutes or just until crisp-tender, stirring occasionally. In a small bowl combine ½ cup of the granulated sugar, the flour, ½ teaspoon of the cinnamon, and the nutmeg. Sprinkle over apples. Cook and stir over medium-low heat for 2 minutes more; set aside.
3. In a medium mixing bowl combine cream cheese and the remaining ½ cup granulated sugar. Beat with an electric mixer on medium speed until smooth. Beat in egg and vanilla just until combined. Carefully spread cream cheese mixture over baked pastry to within 1 inch of the edges. Spoon apple mixture over cream cheese mixture.
4. On a lightly floured surface, unfold the remaining pastry sheet and roll into a 13×9-inch rectangle (make sure pastry is large enough to completely cover apple mixture). Place on top of apple mixture. Lightly press edges of top pastry to edges of bottom pastry. Lightly brush top pastry with milk. Using a sharp knife, cut a few slits in pastry to allow steam to escape. In a small bowl combine coarse sugar and the remaining ½ teaspoon cinnamon; sprinkle over pastry.
5. Bake for 35 to 40 minutes or until pastry is slightly puffed and golden brown. Cool on wire rack about 45 minutes. Serve warm.

PER SERVING: *438 cal., 25 g fat (9 g sat. fat), 44 mg chol., 184 mg sodium, 51 g carb., 3 g fiber, 5 g pro.*

How to Make an Easy Danish

Because making puff pastry is a time-consuming, laborious activity, there's no question that purchasing frozen prepared puff pastry is the simpler choice. Once thawed, it's easy to work with and creates beautiful flaky crusts and pastries.

1. On a lightly floured surface, roll the puff pastry sheet into a 15×10-inch rectangle.

2. Transfer rolled pastry to the baking pan. Using your fingers, press the dough to the edges of the pan.

3. Spoon cooked apple filling over cream cheese mixture to within 1 inch of the edges.

4. Place the top pastry over the apple filling, being careful not to stretch the pastry.

5. Use a sharp knife to cut slits in the top pastry to allow steam to escape during baking.

Ham and Cheese Slab Pies

PREP: 30 minutes
BAKE: 25 minutes at 400°F
COOL: 10 minutes
MAKES: 12 servings

- 2 3-ounce packages cream cheese, softened
- 2 tablespoons honey mustard
- 1 17.3-ounce package frozen puff pastry sheets (2 sheets), thawed
- 6 ounces thinly sliced Black Forest ham
- ½ of a medium red onion, thinly sliced
- 6 ounces thinly sliced Gruyère, Swiss, or cheddar cheese
- 1 egg
- 1 tablespoon water

1. Preheat oven to 400°F. Line two large baking sheets with parchment paper; set aside. In a small bowl stir together cream cheese and mustard; set aside.
2. Unfold puff pastry sheets. On a lightly floured surface, roll each sheet of puff pastry into a 15×12-inch rectangle. Transfer each pastry sheet to a prepared baking sheet; spread half of each pastry lengthwise with cream cheese mixture, leaving a ½-inch border around edges.
3. Layer ham, onion, and Gruyère cheese over cream cheese, leaving a ½-inch border around edges. In a small bowl whisk together egg and the water. Brush some of the egg mixture on uncovered edges of the pastries. Fold uncovered portion of each pastry rectangle up and over filling. Press edges together with the tines of a fork to seal. Brush tops with egg mixture. Cut decorative slits in top of each pastry for steam to escape.

4. Bake about 25 minutes or until pastries are golden on both the top and bottom. If top browns more quickly than the bottom, cover with foil. Slide pies and parchment paper onto wire racks; cool slightly. To serve, cut crosswise into strips.

To Make Ahead: Prepare as directed through Step 3, except do not preheat oven and do not brush tops of pies with egg mixture. Freeze pies on parchment paper-lined baking pans until firm. Wrap pies tightly with plastic wrap; overwrap with heavy foil. Freeze for up to 2 months. To serve, thaw in the refrigerator for 24 hours. Preheat oven to 400°F. Place on parchment paper-lined baking sheets. Brush with egg mixture; bake and cool as directed.

PER SERVING: *360 cal., 26 g fat (9 g sat. fat), 56 mg chol., 361 mg sodium, 21 g carb., 1 g fiber, 11 g pro.*

Puff Pastry Know-How

Frozen puff pastry is very forgiving in nature, which makes it a pleasure to work with. You do need to plan ahead to give the pastry enough time to thaw. For best results, pull the box from the freezer the night before you plan to use it and let it thaw overnight in the refrigerator.

Spiced Pumpkin Doughnuts

PREP: **35 minutes**
CHILL: **3 hours**
FRY: **2½ minutes per batch**
MAKES: **12 doughnuts + 12 holes**

- 2 tablespoons butter, softened
- ½ cup sugar
- 2 teaspoons baking powder
- ½ teaspoon salt
- ½ teaspoon ground cinnamon
- ¼ teaspoon baking soda
- ¼ teaspoon ground ginger
- ⅛ teaspoon freshly grated nutmeg (see tip, page 17) or a dash of ground nutmeg
- ⅛ teaspoon ground cloves
- ½ cup canned pumpkin
- ⅓ cup buttermilk or sour milk (see tip, page 16)
- 1 egg
- 1 egg yolk
- ½ teaspoon vanilla
- 2 cups all-purpose flour
    Vegetable oil for deep-fat frying
- 1 recipe Spiced Sugar

1. In a large mixing bowl beat butter with an electric mixer on medium to high speed for 30 seconds. Add the ½ cup sugar, the baking powder, salt, cinnamon, baking soda, ginger, nutmeg, and cloves. Beat until combined, scraping sides of bowl occasionally. Beat in pumpkin, buttermilk, egg, egg yolk, and vanilla until combined. Using a wooden spoon, stir in flour until well combined. Cover and chill for 3 hours.

2. On a lightly floured surface, roll dough to a ½-inch thickness. Cut with floured 2½-inch doughnut cutter, dipping cutter into flour between cuts. Reroll as necessary.

3. Fry 2 or 3 doughnuts at a time, in deep hot oil (365°F) about 2½ minutes or until golden, turning once. Using a slotted spoon, remove doughnuts from oil and drain on paper towels. Repeat with remaining doughnuts and doughnut holes. Coat warm doughnuts in Spiced Sugar. Serve warm or at room temperature.

Spiced Sugar: In a small bowl stir together ½ cup sugar, 2 teaspoons ground cinnamon, and 1 teaspoon freshly grated nutmeg (see page 17) or ½ teaspoon ground nutmeg.

To Store: Place leftover doughnuts and holes in an airtight container. Store at room temperature for up to 24 hours.

PER 1 DOUGHNUT AND 1 HOLE: *299 cal., 17 g fat (3 g sat. fat), 37 mg chol., 236 mg sodium, 35 g carb., 1 g fiber, 3 g pro.*

French Market Beignets

PREP: **40 minutes**
CHILL: **4 to 24 hours**
REST: **30 minutes**
FRY: **1 minute per batch**
MAKES: **12 servings**
(36 beignets)

5½ to 6 cups all-purpose flour
 2 packages active dry yeast
 1 cup evaporated milk
 ½ cup granulated sugar
 ½ cup water
 ¼ cup shortening
 1 teaspoon salt
 2 eggs
   Vegetable oil for deep-fat
   frying
   Powdered sugar

1. In a large mixing bowl stir together 3 cups of the flour and the yeast; set aside. In a small saucepan heat and stir evaporated milk, granulated sugar, the water, shortening, and salt just until warm (120°F to 130°F) and shortening nearly melts.
2. Add milk mixture to flour mixture; add eggs. Beat with an electric mixer on low to medium speed for 30 seconds, scraping sides of bowl constantly. Beat on high speed for 3 minutes. Using a wooden spoon, stir in enough of the remaining flour to make a moderately soft dough.
3. Shape dough into a ball. Place in a greased bowl, turning once to grease the surface of dough. Cover and chill for 4 to 24 hours.
4. Turn dough out onto a lightly floured surface. Cover and let rest for 10 minutes. Roll into an 18×12-inch rectangle; cut into thirty-six 3×2-inch rectangles. Cover and let rest for 20 minutes (dough will not double).
5. Preheat oven to 300°F. In a deep saucepan heat 3 inches of oil to 375°F. Fry dough rectangles, a few at a time, in hot oil about 1 minute or until beignets are golden, turning once. Using a slotted spoon, remove beignets from oil and drain on paper towels. Keep warm in oven while frying the remaining beignets. Generously sift powdered sugar over beignets. Serve warm.

PER 3 BEIGNETS: *129 cal., 4 g fat (1 g sat. fat), 14 mg chol., 77 mg sodium, 20 g carb., 1 g fiber, 3 g pro.*

Make It Mini

Prepare beignets as directed, except cut the 18×12-inch dough rectangle into seventy-two 2×1½-inch rectangles. Continue as directed. Makes 72 mini beignets.

Cranberry and Orange Strudel,
recipe page 418

coffee shop

MAKE LIFE SWEETER one pastry at a time with coffee shop treats made at home. Choose from mini-size tarts and cheesecakes, rich éclairs, whoopie pies, flaky baklava, and more. Practice your skills with a no-fuss version of a European favorite—tart cranberry strudel.

Cranberry and Orange Strudel

Flaky, buttery strudel is the hallmark pastry of fine bakeries. Now, with the help of purchased phyllo dough, it's possible to prepare at home. Take it one step at a time to learn how easy it is.

PREP: 40 minutes
CHILL: 2 hours
BAKE: 15 minutes at 425°F
COOL: 15 minutes
MAKES: 12 servings

- 1½ cups cranberries
- 2 cups peeled, cored, and chopped tart apple (about 2 large)
- 1 cup packed brown sugar
- 1 tablespoon water
- 1 teaspoon finely shredded orange peel (see tip, page 102)
- ½ teaspoon ground cinnamon
- 1 3-inch sprig fresh rosemary
- ¼ cup finely chopped pecans
- ½ cup butter, melted
- 16 sheets frozen phyllo dough (14×9-inch rectangles), thawed
- 1 recipe Vanilla Glaze (optional)

1. For filling, in a heavy medium saucepan combine cranberries, apples, brown sugar, water, orange peel, cinnamon, and rosemary. Cook and stir over medium heat about 15 minutes or until liquid is slightly thickened (mixture will get juicy as it cooks). Remove and discard the rosemary; stir in pecans. Cover; chill for 2 hours or until completely cooled.

2. Preheat the oven to 425°F. Line a baking sheet with parchment paper; set aside. Unroll phyllo dough; cover with plastic wrap. (As you work, keep the phyllo covered to prevent it from drying out; remove sheets as you need them.) Place 1 sheet of phyllo on a clean work surface. Lightly brush phyllo sheet with some of the melted butter. Top with another phyllo sheet and brush with butter. Repeat layering, using 8 sheets of phyllo total. Spoon half the filling on top of the stacked sheets, leaving a 1-inch border on the two short sides and one of the long sides and a 2-inch border on the opposite long side. Fold in the short sides 1 inch over the filling. Roll up the phyllo and filling, starting from the long side with the 1-inch border. Seal seam by pressing together with fingers. Brush the tops and sides of the strudel with some melted butter. Place the strudel, seam side down, on the prepared baking sheet. Repeat with remaining phyllo sheets, butter, and filling to make a second strudel.

3. Bake for 15 to 18 minutes or until browned. Carefully transfer strudels to serving plate(s). Cool for 15 minutes. If desired, spoon Vanilla Glaze over strudels. Slice with a serrated knife and serve warm or at room temperature.

Vanilla Glaze: In a small bowl stir together 1 cup powdered sugar, 1 tablespoon milk, and ¼ teaspoon vanilla. If necessary, stir in additional milk, 1 teaspoon at a time, to reach drizzling consistency.

PER SERVING: 258 cal., 11 g fat (6 g sat. fat), 22 mg chol., 213 mg sodium, 38 g carb., 2 g fiber, 2 g pro.

Secrets to Success

The flakiness associated with a strudel comes from layering sheets of paper-thin phyllo dough. When handled properly, phyllo is easy to work with. Here's what you need to know: First, thaw the package of frozen phyllo in the refrigerator overnight as directed on the package. Don't refreeze phyllo once it has been thawed. When ready to use, unroll the phyllo carefully. Immediately cover the stack with plastic wrap and keep it covered the entire time you are working with it, removing only the number of sheets you need at a time. This keeps the sheets from drying out and cracking. As you work, if a sheet breaks, piece it back together, brush it with butter, and stack another sheet on top. Once several sheets are stacked, any torn pieces will be unnoticeable. Brushing with melted butter makes for crisp, flaky layers.

COOK UNTIL THICKENED Combine the filling igredients in a medium saucepan. Cook and stir until mixture appears slightly thickened and bubbly.

STACK AND LAYER For each layer, carefully remove 1 sheet of phyllo from the stack and place over the last sheet. Cover remaining phyllo with plastic wrap.

BRUSH WITH BUTTER With a pastry brush, spread each sheet of phyllo with butter from edge to edge before adding another layer.

TOP WITH FILLING Evenly spread half the cranberry filling over the first stack of phyllo sheets, leaving a 1-inch border on both of the short sides and one of the long sides and a 2-inch border on the opposite long side.

FOLD AND ROLL Fold in the two short sides. Begin rolling the phyllo rectangle from the long side that has a 1-inch border.

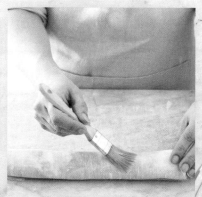

FINISH WITH BUTTER With the seam side down, brush additional melted butter over the strudel once it is rolled. If the butter begins to solidify while working, simply reheat it until melted.

Make-It-Mine Cream Cheese Pastries

Use purchased frozen puff pastry, add flavored cream cheese filling and fresh fruit topping, then serve the most impressive breakfast or brunch.

PREP: **30 minutes**
BAKE: **15 minutes at 400°F**
MAKES: **18 servings**

1 8-ounce package cream cheese, softened
⅓ cup sugar
1 *teaspoon Juice (choose option)*
½ *to 1 teaspoon Flavoring (choose option)*
1½ *cups fresh or frozen thawed Fruit (choose option)*
½ *cup Preserves (choose option)*
1 17.3-ounce package frozen puff pastry sheets (2 sheets), thawed
1 egg
1 tablespoon water

1. Preheat oven to 400°F. Line two large baking sheets with parchment paper; set aside.
2. In a medium mixing bowl beat cream cheese with an electric mixer on medium speed until smooth. Add sugar, *Juice*, and *Flavoring*. Beat until well mixed; set aside. In a small bowl stir together *Fruit* (thawed if frozen) and *Preserves*; set aside.
3. On a lightly floured surface, roll each sheet of the thawed puff pastry into a 10½-inch square. (While rolling out the first sheet of pastry, refrigerate the other sheet so it doesn't get too soft to work with.) Cut each square into nine squares (each 3½×3½ inches). Transfer squares to prepared baking sheets. Using a fork, prick the center of each square, leaving a ½-inch unpricked border around all the edges. In a small bowl beat egg and the water together with a fork. Brush squares with egg mixture. Spread 1 tablespoon of the cream cheese mixture onto the center of each square, leaving a ½-inch border. Top with fruit mixture, spreading evenly over cream cheese mixture.
4. Bake for 15 to 18 minutes or until golden brown. Transfer to wire racks. Cool completely.

JUICE (PICK ONE)
Lemon juice
Lime juice
Orange juice

FLAVORING (PICK ONE)
Vanilla
Almond extract
Coffee flavoring
Lemon flavoring

FRUIT (PICK ONE)
Halved or quartered strawberries
Sliced kumquats
Fresh or frozen blueberries
Chopped or thinly sliced apple
Fresh or frozen pitted tart red or dark sweet cherries
Thinly sliced or chopped pear
Cranberries
Fresh or frozen sliced, peeled peaches
Fresh or frozen raspberries
Fresh or frozen blackberries

PRESERVES (PICK ONE)
Strawberry jam or preserves
Orange marmalade
Blueberry preserves
Apple jelly
Cherry preserves
Blueberry preserves
Peach preserves
Raspberry preserves

Mini Maple Cheesecakes

PREP: 35 minutes
BAKE: 15 minutes at 350°F
COOL: 30 minutes
CHILL: 2 hours
MAKES: 12 mini cheesecakes

    Nonstick cooking spray
2   8-ounce packages cream
    cheese, softened
½   cup packed brown sugar
2   tablespoons milk
1   tablespoon all-purpose flour
2   eggs, lightly beaten
3   tablespoons granulated
    sugar
½   teaspoon freshly grated
    nutmeg (see tip, page
    17), ground cinnamon, or
    pumpkin pie spice
12 sheets frozen phyllo dough
    (14×9-inch rectangles),
    thawed
⅓   cup butter, melted
¼   cup chopped pecans
½   cup pure maple syrup
3   tablespoons milk
4   teaspoons cornstarch
1   tablespoon butter
½   teaspoon vanilla
    Pecan halves, toasted (see
    tip, page 343) (optional)

1. Preheat oven to 350°F. Coat twelve 2½-inch muffin cups with cooking spray; set aside. For filling, in a large mixing bowl beat cream cheese with an electric mixer on medium to high speed until fluffy. Beat in brown sugar, 2 tablespoons milk, and the flour until combined. Beat in eggs on low speed just until combined; set filling aside. In a small bowl combine granulated sugar and nutmeg; set aside.

2. Unroll phyllo dough; cover with plastic wrap. (As you work, keep the phyllo covered to prevent it from drying out; remove sheets as you need them.) Place 1 sheet of phyllo on a work surface; brush with some of the ⅓ cup melted butter and sprinkle with some of the sugar mixture. Top with a second sheet of phyllo. Repeat brushing, filling, and layering four more times (6 sheets total). Brush top with melted butter. Do not sprinkle with sugar mixture.

3. Cut phyllo stack crosswise into thirds, then lengthwise in half to make six squares. Repeat with the remaining phyllo sheets, melted butter, and sugar mixture to make 12 squares total. Gently press squares into the prepared muffin cups, pleating as necessary to fit.

Spoon 1 teaspoon of the chopped pecans into each pastry-lined muffin cup. Divide filling evenly among cups.

4. Bake for 15 to 18 minutes or until pastry is golden and filling is nearly set in the centers. Cool in muffin cups on a wire rack for 30 minutes. Remove from muffin cups. Cover and chill for 2 hours.

5. For topping, in a small saucepan combine maple syrup, the 3 tablespoons milk, and the cornstarch. Cook and stir over medium heat until thickened and bubbly. Cook and stir for 2 minutes more. Remove from heat. Stir in the 1 tablespoon butter and the vanilla; cool. Spoon topping over cheesecakes. If desired, garnish each cheesecake with a pecan half.

To Store: Place topped mini cheesecakes in a single layer in an airtight container; cover. Store in the refrigerator for up to 24 hours.

PER MINI CHEESECAKE: *338 cal., 22 g fat (12 g sat. fat), 89 mg chol., 238 mg sodium, 32 g carb., 0 g fiber, 5 g pro.*

Grand Marnier and Chocolate Tarts

PREP: **25 minutes**
BAKE: **15 minutes at 325°F**
COOL: **30 minutes**
CHILL: **2 hours**
MAKES: **6 tarts**

- 1 cup slivered almonds, toasted (see tip, page 343)
- ½ cup hazelnuts or slivered almonds, toasted (see tip, page 343)
- ¼ cup packed brown sugar
- ¼ cup all-purpose flour
- ¼ cup butter, melted
- ½ cup whipping cream
- ¾ cup semisweet chocolate pieces
- 1 tablespoon Grand Marnier or other orange liqueur*
- ⅓ cup orange marmalade*
- 1 recipe Candied Kumquats (optional)

1. Preheat oven to 325°F. For crust, in a medium bowl combine almonds, hazelnuts, and brown sugar. Transfer to a food processor or blender. Cover and process or blend with on/off pulses until nuts are finely ground; return to bowl. Stir in flour. Stir in melted butter until combined. Press mixture onto the bottoms and into the sides of six 4-inch fluted individual tart pans that have removable bottoms. Bake about 15 minutes or until firm and golden. Cool in pans on a wire rack.

2. In a small saucepan bring whipping cream just to simmering over medium heat. Remove from heat. Whisk in chocolate and Grand Marnier until smooth. Cool about 30 minutes or until chocolate mixture begins to thicken but is still pourable.

3. Spread marmalade over bottom of crust in each tart pan. Carefully pour chocolate mixture over marmalade. Cover and chill about 2 hours or until set. Remove sides of tart pans. If desired, garnish with Candied Kumquats.

Candied Kumquats: Cut 12 kumquats lengthwise into halves, slices, or wedges. In a large skillet or medium saucepan combine ¾ cup sugar and ¾ cup water. Cook and stir over medium-high heat until mixture begins to simmer and is clear. Reduce heat to medium. Add kumquats; simmer for 15 to 20 minutes or until kumquats are softened, turning occasionally. Remove from heat; cool. Drain kumquats on wire rack; if necessary, pat dry with paper towels.

***Test Kitchen Tip:** If desired, use Chambord and raspberry preserves instead of the Grand Marnier and orange marmalade.

PER TART: *643 cal., 38 g fat (15 g sat. fat), 48 mg chol., 95 mg sodium, 76 g carb., 7 g fiber, 8 g pro.*

Make It Mini

Prepare as directed, except lightly grease twenty-four 1¾-inch muffin cups. Press a slightly rounded tablespoon nut mixture into the bottom and up the sides of each of the prepared cups. Bake for 8 to 9 minutes or until crusts are firm and golden. Continue as directed, except gently spoon a slightly rounded ½ teaspoon marmalade into each cooled cup and top with chocolate mixture. (Store any leftover chocolate mixture in a covered container in the refrigerator. Reheat on 50 percent power [medium] in microwave and use as a dessert topping.) Chill tartlets as directed. To serve, run a thin knife around the outside of each tartlet to loosen from the cup. If necessary, use the knife to gently lift tartlets from cups. Garnish as directed. Makes 24 tartlets.

Cranberry Cream Tartlets

PREP: 35 minutes
BAKE: 10 minutes at 325°F
STAND: 15 minutes
CHILL: 4 to 24 hours
MAKES: 8 servings

  2 cups finely crushed gingersnaps (about 30 cookies)
  ¼ cup butter, melted
2⅔ cups water
  1 cup dried cranberries
1⅓ cups sour cream
  ⅔ cup sugar
  ⅓ cup cornstarch
  3 egg yolks, lightly beaten
  ¼ teaspoon salt
  1 teaspoon vanilla
  ½ teaspoon finely shredded orange peel (see tip, page 102)
  1 recipe Vanilla Whipped Cream

1. Preheat oven to 325°F. In a medium bowl stir together crushed gingersnaps and melted butter; press onto bottoms and up sides of eight 4½-inch individual tart pans that have removeable bottoms. Place tart pans on a baking sheet. Bake about 10 minutes or until light brown. Cool completely on a wire rack.
2. In a medium saucepan bring the water to boiling. Remove from heat; stir in dried cranberries. Cover; let stand for 15 minutes.
3. For filling, in another medium saucepan combine sour cream, sugar, cornstarch, egg yolks, and salt. Stir in the water-cranberry mixture. Bring to boiling over medium heat, stirring constantly; reduce heat. Cook and stir for 2 minutes more. Remove from heat. Stir in vanilla and the orange peel. Spoon evenly into prepared tart shells. Cover and chill for 4 to 24 hours.
4. Spoon Vanilla Whipped Cream into a pastry bag fitted with a large star tip. Pipe whipped cream onto the tarts. Remove tarts from pans. Serve immediately.

Vanilla Whipped Cream: In a large mixing bowl combine 2 cups whipping cream and 1 teaspoon vanilla bean paste or 2 teaspoons vanilla extract. Beat with an electric mixer on medium to high speed until soft mounds form. Add ¼ cup powdered sugar; beat on high speed until soft peaks form (tips curl).

Cranberry Cream Tart: Prepare as directed, except press crumb mixture onto bottom and up sides of one 10- or 11-inch tart pan instead of individual pans. Spread filling evenly into prepared crust. Cover and chill as directed.

PER SERVING: *600 cal., 39 g fat (22 g sat. fat), 193 mg chol., 340 mg sodium, 61 g carb., 2 g fiber, 4 g pro.*

Peach Pie Pops

PREP: **50 minutes**
BAKE: **12 minutes at 400°F**
MAKES: **20 servings**

- 1 recipe Pastry for Double-Crust Pie (see page 186) or one 15-ounce package (2 crusts) rolled refrigerated unbaked piecrust
- ¾ cup canned peach pie filling
- 1 tablespoon finely chopped crystallized ginger
- ¼ teaspoon ground cinnamon
  Milk
- 1 tablespoon coarse sugar

1. Preheat oven to 400°F. Prepare Pastry for Double-Crust Pie (if using). On a lightly floured surface, roll half of the dough at a time into a 12-inch circle (or unroll one refrigerated piecrust at a time). Cut dough with a 2½-inch round or star-shape (see right) cookie cutter; reroll scraps as necessary.
2. For peach filling, place pie filling in a medium bowl. Using kitchen scissors, snip fruit into small pieces. Stir in ginger and cinnamon.
3. Spoon 1 slightly rounded teaspoon of the peach filling onto the centers of half of the pastry cutouts. Brush edges with milk. Lay the tip of a lollipop stick on each filled cutout. Top with the remaining pastry cutouts; seal edges with a fork.

4. Place pops 2 inches apart on an ungreased large baking sheet. Brush with additional milk and sprinkle with coarse sugar.
5. Bake for 12 to 15 minutes or until golden brown. Using a spatula, carefully transfer pie pops to wire racks (do not pick up by sticks while hot); cool.

To Store: Layer pie pops between sheets of waxed paper in an airtight container; cover. Store at room temperature for up to 2 days.

PER SERVING: *139 cal., 8 g fat (3 g sat. fat), 6 mg chol., 141 mg sodium, 16 g carb., 1 g fiber, 2 g pro.*

Chocolate Pops: Prepare as directed, except omit the peach pie filing, crystallized ginger, and cinnamon. In a small bowl combine ½ cup powdered sugar, ¼ cup unsweetened cocoa powder, and ¼ cup butter, melted. Spoon 1 level teaspoon of the cocoa mixture onto the centers of half of the pastry cutouts. Continue as directed.

PER SERVING: *160 cal., 10 g fat (4 g sat. fat), 6 mg chol., 158 mg sodium, 16 g carb., 1 g fiber, 2 g pro.*

How to Make Peach Pie Pops

Tender and flaky on the outside with a luscious fruit filling in the center, these handheld pastries are as easy as pie to make. Cut the pastry into a variety of shapes—circles, squares, hearts, or stars. If cutting stars, choose a cutter that has short, fat points so you don't have long points of dough without filling.

1. Spoon a slightly rounded teaspoon of peach mixture onto the centers of pastry cutouts.

2. Brush edges of pastry with milk to help seal pastry edges.

3. Lay the tip of a lollipop stick in the center of each cutout.

4. Place remaining pastry cutouts on top, lining up edges.

5. Using a fork, press down on the edge to seal firmly.

Raspberry Éclairs

PREP: 1 hour 15 minutes
BAKE: 30 minutes at 400°F
MAKES: 12 servings

    1   recipe Raspberry Filling
    1   cup water
    ½   cup butter
    ⅛   teaspoon salt
    1   cup all-purpose flour
    4   eggs
        Fresh raspberries (optional)
    2   ounces white baking
        chocolate with cocoa butter,
        coarsely chopped
    ½   teaspoon shortening

1. Prepare Raspberry Filling. Chill as directed.
2. Preheat oven to 400°F. Line a large baking sheet with parchment paper; set aside. In a medium saucepan combine the water, butter, and salt. Bring to boiling. Immediately add flour all at once; stir vigorously. Cook and stir until mixture forms a ball; remove from heat. Cool for 10 minutes. Add eggs, one at a time, beating with a wooden spoon after each addition until smooth.

3. Spoon dough into a pastry bag fitted with a large plain round tip (about ½-inch opening). Slowly pipe 12 strips of dough 3 inches apart onto the prepared baking sheet, making each strip 4 inches long, 1 inch wide, and ¾ inch high.
4. Bake for 30 to 35 minutes or until golden and firm. Transfer to wire racks; cool completely.
5. To serve, cut éclairs in half lengthwise. Remove some of the soft dough from inside. Pipe or spoon Raspberry Filling into bottom half of each éclair. If desired, add a few raspberries. Replace top halves of éclairs.
6. In a small saucepan heat white chocolate and shortening over low heat just until melted and smooth. Drizzle white chocolate mixture over filled éclairs.

Raspberry Filling: Place 1 cup fresh or thawed frozen raspberries in a blender or food processor. Cover and blend or process until pureed. Strain raspberries through a fine-mesh sieve (you should have about ½ cup); discard seeds. In a medium heavy saucepan stir together ¾ cup sugar and 3 tablespoons cornstarch. Gradually stir in the strained raspberries, 1 cup whipping cream, and 1 cup milk. Cook and stir over medium heat until thickened and bubbly. Cook and stir for 1 minute more. Gradually stir about half of the hot mixture into 5 lightly beaten egg yolks. Return egg yolk mixture to saucepan. Bring to boiling; reduce heat. Cook and stir for 2 minutes. Pour into a medium bowl; stir in 2 tablespoons raspberry liqueur (if desired) and 1 teaspoon vanilla. Tint with red food coloring to desired color. Place bowl of filling in a bowl of ice water; chill for 5 minutes, stirring occasionally. Cover surface with plastic wrap. Chill about 4 hours or until very cold.

PER SERVING: *323 cal., 21 g fat (12 g sat. fat), 188 mg chol., 140 mg sodium, 29 g carb., 1 g fiber, 6 g pro.*

Make It Mini

Prepare as directed, except drop dough by rounded teaspoons 2 inches apart onto a parchment-lined baking sheet. Bake one sheet at a time in a 400°F oven about 25 minutes or until golden and firm. (Keep remaining dough covered while first batch bakes.) Transfer to wire racks; cool completely. Continue as directed in Step 5. Makes about 30 mini puffs.

Ginger Pear Galette

PREP: **25 minutes**
BAKE: **25 minutes at 400°F**
MAKES: **8 servings**

½ of a 17.3-ounce package (1 sheet) frozen puff pastry sheets, thawed
1 egg white, lightly beaten
2 tablespoons all-purpose flour
2 tablespoons granulated sugar
2 tablespoons packed brown sugar
1 tablespoon finely chopped crystallized ginger
1 teaspoon finely shredded lemon peel (see tip, page 102)
2 tablespoons butter
3 large pears, peeled and thinly sliced
Sweetened whipped cream (see tip, page 16) (optional)

1. Preheat oven to 400°F. Line a baking sheet with parchment paper; set aside. On a lightly floured surface, unfold pastry. Roll into a 14×11-inch rectangle; trim to a 12×10-inch rectangle. Place on the prepared baking sheet. Brush edges of pastry with egg white. Cut ½-inch strips from pastry trimmings. Place strips on edges of pastry rectangle, pressing to form raised rim; trim ends. Brush edges again with egg white. If desired, decorate edges with cutouts from pastry trimmings and brush cutouts with egg white. Prick center of pastry rectangle with a fork.

2. For topping, in a small bowl stir together flour, granulated sugar, brown sugar, crystallized ginger, and lemon peel. Cut in butter until pieces are pea size.

3. Sprinkle half of the topping over pastry rectangle. Arrange pear slices on tart, overlapping slightly. Sprinkle remaining topping over pear slices.

4. Bake about 25 minutes or until pastry is golden and pears are tender. If desired, top servings with whipped cream. Serve warm.

PER SERVING: *282 cal., 15 g fat (5 g sat. fat), 8 mg chol., 106 mg sodium, 36 g carb., 3 g fiber, 3 g pro.*

Almond Pastry Fingers

PREP: **30 minutes**
BAKE: **20 minutes at 400°F**
COOL: **4 hours**
MAKES: **4 pastries (48 slices)**

1   **17.3-ounce package frozen puff pastry sheets, thawed (2 sheets)**
1   **12.5-ounce can almond pastry and dessert filling**
1½   **cups white baking pieces**
⅔   **cup slivered almonds, toasted (see tip, page 343) and finely chopped**
     Powdered sugar

1. Preheat oven to 400°F. Line a very large cookie sheet with parchment paper; set aside. Unfold pastry sheets onto a work surface. Cut each sheet lengthwise into two rectangles (four rectangles total). Using a fork, generously prick pastry rectangles all over.
2. Spread the almond filling (about ¼ cup each) over rectangles, spreading to within ¾ inch of the edges. Top evenly with the white baking pieces and almonds. Brush edges of rectangles with water. Fold each rectangle in half lengthwise; gently press edges with fork to seal. Place rectangles 2 inches apart on the prepared cookie sheet.
3. Bake for 20 to 25 minutes or until golden brown. Transfer pastries to a wire rack; cool for at least 4 hours. Generously sprinkle with powdered sugar. Cut each rectangle crosswise into 12 slices.

To Store: Layer pastry slices between sheets of waxed paper in an airtight container; cover. Store at room temperature for up to 3 days or freeze for up to 3 months.

PER SLICE: *119 cal., 7 g fat (2 g sat. fat), 0 mg chol., 57 mg sodium, 13 g carb., 1 g fiber, 1 g pro.*

Filling Puff Pastry

There's so much to love about frozen puff pastry. It's convenience and sophistication wrapped up in one delicious product. And its flaky, buttery goodness is perfect for both savory and sweet recipes. For best results, store puff pastry in the freezer and thaw it overnight in the refrigerator before using.

1. Cut each puff pastry sheet lengthwise into two rectangles.

2. Spread almond filling over rectangles, spreading to within ¾ inch of edges.

3. Fold each rectangle in half lengthwise.

4. Gently press edges with a fork to seal firmly.

Apple Baklava Triangles

PREP: **1 hour**
BAKE: **15 minutes at 375°F**
STAND: **45 minutes**
MAKES: **30 triangles**

¼ cup butter
3½ cups chopped, peeled
  tart apples
¾ cup chopped walnuts
½ cup dried cherries,
  cranberries, or currants
3 tablespoons sugar
½ teaspoon ground cinnamon
1 16-ounce package frozen
  phyllo dough (14×9-inch
  rectangles), thawed
  (40 sheets)
1¼ cups butter, melted
6 ounces Brie cheese, cut into
  thin slices
1 recipe Lemon-Honey Syrup

1. For filling, in a large skillet melt the ¼ cup butter over medium-high heat. Add apples, walnuts, and dried cherries. Cook about 4 minutes or until apples are softened, stirring occasionally; remove from heat. In a bowl stir together sugar and cinnamon; sprinkle over apple mixture and toss gently to combine. Let cool.
2. Preheat oven to 375°F. Line two large baking sheets with parchment paper; set aside. Unroll phyllo dough; cover with plastic wrap. (As you work, keep the phyllo covered to prevent it from drying out; remove sheets as you need them.) Place 1 sheet of phyllo on work surface; brush lightly with some of the 1¼ cups melted butter. Top with second sheet of phyllo. Repeat brushing and layering two more times (4 sheets total). Brush top with melted butter.
3. Cut phyllo stack lengthwise into three strips. Place one cheese slice 2 inches from an end of each strip, cutting cheese to fit if necessary; top with 1 rounded tablespoon filling. To fold into a triangle, bring a corner over filling so short edge lines up with side edge. Continue folding until the end of the strip is reached. Place triangles on one of the prepared baking sheets. Brush tops with melted butter. Repeat with the remaining phyllo, butter, cheese, and filling.
4. Bake for 15 to 18 minutes or until crisp and golden; cool slightly. Transfer all the baked triangles to a 15×10×1-inch baking pan, overlapping slightly if necessary. Drizzle with half of the Lemon-Honey Syrup. Let stand for 15 minutes. Drizzle with the remaining syrup. Let stand for at least 30 minutes before serving.

Lemon-Honey Syrup: In a medium saucepan combine 1 cup sugar, ¾ cup water, 3 tablespoons honey, ½ teaspoon finely shredded lemon peel, 1 tablespoon lemon juice, 2 or 3 sprigs fresh rosemary or thyme (if desired), and 2 inches stick cinnamon. Bring to boiling; reduce heat. Simmer, uncovered, for 20 minutes. Discard rosemary and cinnamon.

PER TRIANGLE: *215 cal., 14 g fat (7 g sat. fat), 30 mg chol., 191 mg sodium, 22 g carb., 1 g fiber, 3 g pro.*

How to Fold Phyllo Triangles

Once brushed with butter, phyllo dough becomes more pliable and is easy to fold and manipulate into an assortment of shapes. These tightly wrapped packets are created by folding phyllo into basic triangle shapes.

1. Start by folding the bottom edge of phyllo up over the filling.

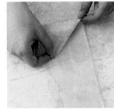

2. Fold phyllo again, taking the pointed end and folding up.

3. Take the corner with the filling and fold over the opposite side.

Saffron-Scented Pistachio-Cranberry Baklava

PREP: 45 minutes
BAKE: 35 minutes at 325°F
MAKES: 24 to 48 pieces

1½ cups pistachio nuts, finely chopped
1½ cups dried cranberries
1⅓ cups sugar
½ teaspoon ground cardamom
¾ cup butter, melted
½ 16-ounce package frozen phyllo dough (14×9-inch rectangles), thawed
¾ cup water
¼ cup honey
1 teaspoon vanilla
½ teaspoon thread saffron, slightly crumbled

1. Preheat oven to 325°F. For filling, in a large bowl stir together pistachio nuts, cranberries, ⅓ cup of the sugar, and the cardamom; set aside.

2. Brush the bottom of a 13×9×2-inch baking pan with some of the melted butter. Unroll phyllo dough; cover with plastic wrap. (As you work, keep the phyllo covered to prevent it from drying out, removing sheets only as you need them.) Layer one-fourth (5 or 6) of the phyllo sheets in the prepared baking pan, brushing each sheet generously with some of the melted butter. Sprinkle with about 1 cup of the filling. Repeat layering phyllo sheets and filling twice more, brushing each sheet with additional butter.

3. Layer the remaining phyllo sheets on top of filling, brushing each sheet with additional butter. Drizzle with any remaining butter. Using a sharp knife, cut baklava into 24 to 48 diamond, rectangle, or square pieces.

4. Bake for 35 to 45 minutes or until golden. Cool slightly in pan on a wire rack.

5. Meanwhile, for syrup, in a medium saucepan stir together the remaining 1 cup sugar, the water, honey, vanilla, and saffron. Bring to boiling; reduce heat. Simmer, uncovered, for 20 minutes. Pour the syrup evenly over slightly cooled baklava in the pan.

To Store: Layer pieces between sheets of waxed paper in an airtight container; cover. Store in the refrigerator for up to 3 days. Or label and freeze for up to 3 months. If frozen, thaw pieces at room temperature for 1 hour before serving.

PER PIECE: *200 cal., 10 g fat (4 g sat. fat), 15 mg chol., 97 mg sodium, 27 g carb., 1 g fiber, 2 g pro.*

Lemon Macarons with Cranberry-Mascarpone Filling

PREP: **40 minutes**
STAND: **30 minutes**
BAKE: **9 minutes at 325°F**
MAKES: **12 sandwich cookies**

1½   cups finely ground almonds
1¼   cups powdered sugar
  3   egg whites
  ½   teaspoon vanilla
  ¼   teaspoon salt
  ¼   cup granulated sugar
  1   teaspoon finely shredded lemon peel (see tip, page 102)
  1   recipe Cranberry-Mascarpone Filling

1. Line three large cookie sheets with parchment paper; set aside. In a bowl stir together almonds and powdered sugar; set aside.

2. In a large mixing bowl combine egg whites, vanilla, and salt. Beat with an electric mixer on medium speed until frothy. Gradually add granulated sugar, about 1 tablespoon at a time, beating on high speed just until soft peaks form (tips curl). Stir in almond mixture and lemon peel.

3. Using a large pastry bag fitted with a ½-inch round tip, pipe egg white mixture into 2-inch flat circles onto prepared cookie sheets, leaving 1 inch between circles. Let stand for 30 minutes before baking.

4. Preheat oven to 325°F. Bake, one sheet at a time, for 9 to 10 minutes or until set. Cool on cookie sheet on a wire rack. Carefully peel cookies off parchment paper.

5. Spread Cranberry-Mascarpone Filling on bottoms of half of the cookies. Top with the remaining cookies, bottom sides down.

Cranberry-Mascarpone Filling: In a medium mixing bowl beat ¼ cup softened mascarpone or cream cheese, 1 tablespoon softened butter, and 1 tablespoon honey with an electric mixer on medium speed until smooth. Gradually add 1 cup powdered sugar, beating well. Stir in 2 tablespoons dried cranberries or cherries, finely snipped, and ½ teaspoon finely shredded lemon peel. Stir in a few drops red food coloring to tint the filling pink. Stir in 2 to 4 teaspoons lemon juice to reach spreading consistency.

To Store: Layer unfilled cookies between sheets of waxed paper in an airtight container; cover. Store at room temperature for up to 3 days or freeze for up to 3 months. To serve, thaw cookies if frozen. Fill cookies as directed in Step 5. (You may store any leftover filled cookies in the refrigerator, but they will soften and be less crisp.)

PER SANDWICH COOKIE: *216 cal., 9 g fat (2 g sat. fat), 9 mg chol., 74 mg sodium, 32 g carb., 2 g fiber, 4 g pro.*

Almond Shortbread Wedges

PREP: **1 hour**
BAKE: **25 minutes at 325°F**
MAKES: **20 cookies**

- ¾ cup butter, softened
- 1 cup powdered sugar
- ¼ teaspoon salt
- 2 teaspoons vanilla
- 1¾ cups all-purpose flour
- 1 recipe Almond-Butter Frosting
- 1¼ cups sliced almonds, toasted (see tip, page 343)

1. Preheat oven to 325°F. In a large mixing bowl beat butter with an electric mixer on medium to high speed for 30 seconds. Add powdered sugar and salt. Beat until combined, scraping sides of bowl occasionally. Beat in vanilla. Beat in as much of the flour as you can with the mixer. Using a wooden spoon, stir in any remaining flour. Divide the dough in half.

2. On an extra-large ungreased cookie sheet, pat each dough portion into a 6-inch circle about ½ inch thick. Leave a 3-inch space between the dough circles. Cut each circle into 10 wedges. Do not separate the wedges.

3. Bake for 25 to 30 minutes or just until the centers are firm and edges are light brown. Recut wedges while warm. Transfer wedges to wire racks; let cool.

4. Frost with Almond-Butter Frosting. Press sliced almonds into frosting on top of wedges.

Almond-Butter Frosting: In a medium mixing bowl beat ¼ cup softened butter with an electric mixer on medium speed for 30 seconds. Gradually beat in 2 cups powdered sugar, ¼ teaspoon vanilla, ¼ teaspoon almond extract, and enough milk (3 to 5 teaspoons) to make frosting spreading consistency.

To Store: Layer cookies in a single layer in an airtight container; cover. Store at room temperature for up to 3 days or freeze for up to 3 months.

PER COOKIE: *227 cal., 12 g fat (6 g sat. fat), 25 mg chol., 112 mg sodium, 28 g carb., 1 g fiber, 3 g pro.*

Mini Raspberry and White Chocolate Whoopie Pies

PREP: 1 hour
BAKE: 7 minutes at 375°F
CHILL: 30 minutes
MAKES: 72 mini whoopie pies

½ cup butter, softened
1 cup sugar
½ teaspoon baking soda
¼ teaspoon salt
1 egg
1 teaspoon vanilla
2 cups all-purpose flour
½ cup buttermilk or sour milk
   (see tip, page 16)
1 recipe White Chocolate and
   Mascarpone Filling
½ cup seedless raspberry
   preserves
   Fresh raspberries (optional)

1. Preheat oven to 375°F. Line a cookie sheet with parchment paper; set aside.

2. In a large mixing bowl beat butter with an electric mixer on medium to high speed for 30 seconds. Add sugar, baking soda, and salt. Beat until combined, scraping sides of bowl occasionally. Beat in egg and vanilla until combined. Alternately add flour and buttermilk to butter mixture, beating on low speed after each addition just until combined.

3. Drop dough by teaspoons 1 inch apart onto prepared cookie sheet. Bake for 7 to 8 minutes or until tops are set. Cool completely on cookie sheet on a wire rack.

4. Spoon White Chocolate and Mascarpone Filling into a large pastry bag fitted with a small star tip. Peel cooled cookies off parchment paper. To assemble, spread about ¼ teaspoon of the raspberry preserves on bottoms of half of the cookies; pipe filling onto preserves. Top with the remaining cookies, bottom sides down. If desired, pipe additional filling onto tops of whoopie pies and top with raspberries. Chill for 30 minutes before serving.

White Chocolate and Mascarpone Filling: In a small heavy saucepan combine 3 ounces chopped white baking chocolate with cocoa butter and ¼ cup whipping cream. Heat and stir over low heat until chocolate nearly melts. Remove from heat; stir until smooth. Cool for 15 minutes. Meanwhile, in a large mixing bowl beat ½ cup softened mascarpone cheese and ¼ cup softened butter with an electric mixer on medium to high speed until smooth. Beat in ½ teaspoon vanilla. Gradually add 4 cups powdered sugar, beating well. Beat in the white chocolate mixture. Chill about 30 minutes to reach piping consistency.

To Store: Place sandwich cookies in a single layer in an airtight container; cover. Store in the refrigerator for up to 3 days or freeze for up to 3 months. If frozen, thaw in the refrigerator for at least 1 hour before serving.

PER MINI WHOOPIE PIE: *91 cal., 3 g fat (2 g sat. fat), 11 mg chol., 39 mg sodium, 15 g carb., 0 g fiber, 1 g pro.*

Rum Babas

PREP: 1 hour
RISE: 1 hour 20 minutes
BAKE: 15 minutes at 350°F
MAKES: 8 or 12 babas

  2 cups all-purpose flour
  1 package active dry yeast
  ⅓ cup milk
  1 tablespoon sugar
  ½ teaspoon salt
  4 eggs
  ½ cup butter
  ¾ cup raisins and/or golden raisins
  1 teaspoon finely shredded orange peel (see tip, page 102)
1½ cups water
  ¾ cup sugar
  ⅓ cup rum or orange juice
  ½ cup apricot preserves
  1 tablespoon water

1. In a large mixing bowl stir together 1½ cups of the flour and the yeast; set aside. In a small saucepan heat and stir milk, the 1 tablespoon sugar, and the salt just until warm (120°F to 130°F).
2. Add milk mixture to flour mixture. Add eggs. Beat with an electric mixer on low to medium speed for 30 seconds, scraping sides of the bowl constantly. Beat on high speed for 3 minutes. Using a wooden spoon, stir in the remaining flour (batter will be very sticky and soft). Cut butter into small pieces; place on top of batter. Cover and let rise in a warm place until double in size (about 1 hour).
3. Grease eight ½-cup popover cups, twelve ½-cup baba molds, or twelve 2½-inch muffin cups; set aside.
4. Stir butter, raisins, and orange peel into batter. Divide batter among prepared cups or molds, filling each one-half to two-thirds full. Cover and let rise in a warm place until batter nearly fills cups or molds (20 to 30 minutes). (Or cover and chill overnight. Let

stand at room temperature for 20 minutes before baking.)
5. Preheat oven to 350°F. Bake for 15 to 20 minutes or until golden. Remove babas from cups or molds and cool on wire racks set over waxed paper.
6. For rum syrup, in a small heavy saucepan stir together 1½ cups water and ¾ cup sugar. Cook and stir over medium heat until sugar is dissolved. Bring to boiling. Boil, without stirring, for 5 minutes; cool slightly. Stir in rum.
7. Prick babas all over with a long-tined fork. Holding the babas upside down, dip two or three times in the rum syrup to moisten. Return babas to wire racks. Spoon any remaining syrup over babas.
8. For glaze, snip any large pieces of fruit in the preserves. In a small saucepan combine preserves and 1 tablespoon water. Cook and stir over low heat until preserves are melted. Brush glaze over babas.

PER BABA: *449 cal., 15 g fat (8 g sat. fat), 124 mg chol., 298 mg sodium, 69 g carb., 2 g fiber, 8 g pro.*

Make It Mini

Prepare as directed, except grease 20 to 24 miniature popover cups or baba cups or forty-eight 1¾-inch muffin cups. Divide batter among cups, filling one-half to two-thirds full. Cover; let rise as directed. Bake about 12 minutes or until golden. Continue as directed. Makes 20 to 24 mini babas or forty-eight 1¾-inch babas.

Sticky Pecan Upside-Down Baby Cakes

PREP: 20 minutes
BAKE: 25 minutes at 350°F
COOL: 5 minutes
MAKES: 12 baby cakes

Nonstick cooking spray
2½ cups all-purpose flour
1 teaspoon baking powder
½ teaspoon baking soda
½ teaspoon salt
⅔ cup packed brown sugar
½ cup butter
⅓ cup honey
1½ cups coarsely chopped pecans
1 teaspoon finely shredded orange peel (see tip, page 102)
3 eggs
2 cups granulated sugar
1 cup vegetable oil
1 8-ounce carton sour cream
2 teaspoons vanilla

1. Preheat oven to 350°F. Lightly coat twelve 3½-inch (jumbo) muffin cups with cooking spray; set aside. In a medium bowl stir together flour, baking powder, baking soda, and salt; set aside.
2. In a medium saucepan combine brown sugar, butter, and honey. Heat and stir over medium heat about 2 minutes or until smooth; remove from heat. Stir in pecans and orange peel; set aside.
3. In a large mixing bowl combine eggs and granulated sugar. Beat with an electric mixer on medium to high speed about 3 minutes or until thick and lemon-color. Add oil, sour cream, and vanilla; beat until combined. Gradually add flour mixture, beating on low speed until smooth.
4. Place 2 tablespoons of the pecan mixture in the bottom of each muffin cup. Spoon a heaping ⅓ cup of the batter into each cup. Place muffin pans on a foil-lined large baking sheet.

5. Bake for 25 to 30 minutes or until a wooden toothpick inserted in the centers of cakes comes out clean. Cool cakes in pans on a wire rack for 5 minutes. Using a sharp knife or thin metal spatula, loosen cakes from sides of muffin cups. Invert onto wire rack. Spoon any pecan mixture remaining in the muffin cups onto cakes. Serve warm or let cool.

To Store: Places cakes in an airtight container; cover. Store at room temperature for up to 2 days.

PER BABY CAKE: *679 cal., 41 g fat (10 g sat. fat), 83 mg chol., 271 mg sodium, 76 g carb., 2 g fiber, 6 g pro.*

Nature's Sweetener

Honey adds the natural, sweet, syruplike qualities to these fragrant little cakes. Produced by bees from flower nectar, honey subtly reflects the color, taste, and aroma of the blossoms from which it was made. Milder varieties made from clover and orange blossoms are good choices for baking because they balance and enhance flavors of other ingredients in baked goods.

Bûche de Noël, recipe page 452

holiday baking

THE HOLIDAYS ARE A TIME to go all out with delightfully decadent goodies of all sorts—homemade pies, cakes, cookies, cakes, and breads. This sweet assortment will help you celebrate in style with flavors crafted just for the season. Get started with a step-by-step guide to creating the classic Bûche de Noël.

Bûche de Noël

Crafted to resemble the long, hard log that was traditionally burned in the hearth during European Christmas celebrations, this dessert is made from sponge cake rolled up around a creamy filling.

PREP: **30 minutes**
BAKE: **12 minutes at 375°F**
CHILL: **30 minutes**
MAKES: **10 servings**

⅓ cup all-purpose flour
⅓ cup cornstarch
¼ cup unsweetened cocoa powder
¼ teaspoon baking soda
¼ teaspoon salt
4 eggs
4 egg yolks
1 teaspoon vanilla
¾ cup granulated sugar
  Powdered sugar
1 recipe Cream Cheese Filling and Frosting
  Sugared cranberries (see tip, page 255) (optional)
  Fresh rosemary sprigs (optional)

1. Preheat oven to 375°F. For cake, grease a 15×10×1-inch baking pan. Line pan with waxed paper. Generously grease waxed paper.
2. Stir flour, cornstarch, cocoa powder, baking soda, and salt through a fine-mesh sieve into a medium bowl. In a large mixing bowl beat eggs, egg yolks, and vanilla with an electric mixer on high speed for 4 to 5 minutes or until thick and lemon color. Gradually beat in granulated sugar, beating on high speed about 2 minutes more or until sugar is almost dissolved. Sprinkle flour mixture, one-third at a time, over egg mixture; using a large rubber spatula, gently fold in flour mixture just until combined. Spread batter evenly in the prepared baking pan. Bake about 12 minutes or until cake springs back when lightly touched.
3. Cool cake in pan on a wire rack for 3 minutes. Loosen the edges of cake with a small knife or thin spatula. Turn cake out onto a clean towel generously sprinkled with powdered sugar. Carefully remove the waxed paper; discard.
4. While cake is still warm, starting from a short side, roll up the cake and towel into a spiral. Cool on a wire rack. Unroll cake; remove towel. With a thin metal spatula, spread the white Cream Cheese Frosting and Filling on the cake to within 1 inch of the edges.
5. Carefully roll up cake (without towel) starting from a short side. Place, seam side down, on serving platter; chill for 30 minutes. With a serrated knife, diagonally cut off a 3-inch slice from one end of the cake. Place the diagonally cut edge of piece against the side of long roll on the serving plate to form a "branch" on the "log."
6. Frost entire cake with the chocolate Cream Cheese Frosting and Filling, carefully "cementing" the limb to the trunk with frosting. If necessary, chill until frosting firms. With the tines of a table fork, create a pattern of "rings" on the cut ends of the roll and "bark" on the rest of the log. Chill until ready to serve. If desired, garnish with Sugared Cranberries and rosemary sprigs.

Cream Cheese Filling and Frosting: In a large mixing bowl beat one 8-ounce package cream cheese, softened; ½ cup butter, softened; and 2 teaspoons vanilla with an electric mixer on medium speed until fluffy. Gradually beat in 4½ cups powdered sugar. Transfer half of the frosting to another bowl. Beat ⅓ cup unsweetened cocoa powder into one portion.

PER SERVING: *540 cal., 22 g fat (11 g sat. fat), 218 mg chol., 260 mg sodium, 81 g carb., 0 g fiber, 7 g pro.*

Secrets to Success

The secret to any filled jelly-roll-type cake is to roll up the cake while it's warm so it will hold that shape later when you fill it without cracking.

Turn the hot baked jelly roll out onto a powdered sugar-sprinkled towel. Lining the pan with parchment or waxed paper helps it come out of the pan easily. Pull the paper off the hot cake. Roll up the cake and towel together. Cool the rolled cake. Carefully unroll the cake to avoid cracking. Fill the cake, then roll it up without the towel.

ROLL THE CAKE While the cake is still hot, roll it up in powdered sugar-dusted towel to shape it. Allow the cake to cool while rolled in the towel.

SPREAD WITH FILLING Unroll the cake. Use a thin metal spatula—an off-set spatula works best—to spread filling evenly over the cake.

REROLL THE CAKE Use the powdered sugar-dusted towel to lift and help roll the cake around the filling.

CUT A BRANCH PIECE Place cake on a serving platter. If desired, cut a piece from the cake log at an angle.

ATTACH BRANCH PIECE Position the cut piece along the side of the cake to resemble a cut branch.

FROST THE LOG Use the thin metal spatula to spread the chocolate-flavor portion of the cream cheese mixture over the cake. If desired, add texture to the ends of the cake with the tines of a fork.

Make-It-Mine Challah

Tweak scrumptiously rich challah to fit any taste or to accompany any meal or dish. Make it sweet, make it savory, make it your own.

PREP: **50 hours**
RISE: **1 hour 30 minutes**
REST: **10 minutes**
BAKE: **25 minutes at 350°F**
MAKES: **3 loaves (48 slices) or 16 mini loaves**

1¾ cups warm water (105°F to 115°F)
   Sweetener (*choose option*)
 2 packages active dry yeast
 4 eggs, lightly beaten
½ **cup Fat** (*choose option*)
 1 tablespoon salt
   Stir-Ins (*choose option*)
7½ to 8 cups bread flour or 7¾ to 8¼ cups all-purpose flour
 1 egg, lightly beaten
 1 tablespoon water

1. In a very large bowl stir together the 1¾ cups warm water, the *Sweetener,* and yeast. Let stand about 10 minutes or until foamy. Using a wooden spoon, stir in the 4 eggs, the *Fat,* and salt. Add *Stir-Ins.* Gradually stir in as much of the flour as you can.
2. Turn dough out onto a lightly floured surface. Knead in enough of the remaining flour to make a moderately soft dough that is smooth and elastic (5 to 7 minutes total). Shape dough into a ball. Place in a lightly greased very large bowl, turning once to grease surface of dough. Cover and let rise in a warm place until double in size (1 to 1½ hours).
3. Punch dough down. Turn dough out onto a lightly floured surface. Divide according to *Shape* chosen. Cover and let rest for 10 minutes. Meanwhile, lightly grease a large baking sheet.
4. *Shape* as desired (see page 457). Arrange on the prepared baking sheet. Cover and let rise in a warm place until nearly double in size (about 30 minutes).
5. Preheat oven to 350°F. In a small bowl combine the 1 egg and the 1 tablespoon water; brush over shaped dough. Bake for 25 to 30 minutes (about 20 minutes for mini loaves) or until loaves sound hollow when lightly tapped. Immediately remove loaves from baking sheet. Cool on wire racks.

SWEETENER (PICK ONE)
½ cup honey
⅔ cup packed brown sugar
¾ cup granulated sugar

FAT (PICK ONE)
Melted butter
Olive oil
Vegetable oil

STIR-INS (PICK ONE)
Garlic and Herb: 4 cloves garlic, minced, and 2 teaspoons dried Italian seasoning, crushed
Mocha: ⅓ cup unsweetened cocoa powder and 2 teaspoons instant espresso coffee powder
Vanilla Bean: scraped seeds from 1 vanilla bean (see page 17)
Feta and Oregano: 1 cup crumbled feta cheese and 1 tablespoon snipped fresh oregano or 1 teaspoon dried oregano, crushed

continued on page 456

continued from page 455

SHAPING

Braids: Divide dough into 3 portions before the 10-minute rest. Divide each portion into thirds to make 9 pieces; roll each piece into a 24-inch rope; braid three ropes together. Repeat with the remaining braids to make 2 more loaves. Makes 3 loaves.

Stacked Braids: Divide dough into six portions before the 10-minute rest. Divide each into thirds to make 18 pieces total. Roll each portion into an 18-inch-long rope. Braid three ropes together; repeat. Brush one braid with water and stack with another braid.

Repeat with the remaining dough portions to make 2 more loaves. Makes 3 loaves.

Side-by-Side Braids: Divide dough into six portions before the 10-minute rest. Divide each into thirds to make 18 pieces total. Roll each portion into an 18-inch-long rope. Braid three ropes together; repeat. Brush one side of each of two braids with water; lay the two braids next to each other so moistened sides are touching. Repeat with the remaining dough portions to make 2 more loaves. Makes 3 loaves.

Spiral Loaves: Divide dough into 3 portions before the 10-minute rest. Divide each portion into thirds to make 9 portions total. Roll each portion into a 24-inch-long rope. Braid 3 ropes together; shape braid into a spiral. Repeat to make 2 more loaves. Makes 3 loaves.

Mini Loaves: Divide dough in half. Roll each half into a 12×7-inch rectangle. Using a pizza cutter or sharp knife, cut twenty-four 7×½-inch strips from each dough half, separating strips a little as you cut. For each mini loaf, braid 3 strips. Place loaves 2 inches

Braiding Dough

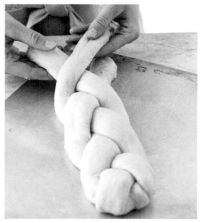

DIVIDE AND ROLL Cut the dough into three pieces. Divide each piece into thirds, for nine pieces of dough total. Roll each piece into a 24-inch-long rope.

START THE BRAID Place 3 pieces of dough on a baking sheet. For easy handling, start from the middle and alternately overlap pieces to create braid.

FINISH THE BRAID Turn the baking sheet around and braid the opposite ends together. Tuck ends under the braid.

Shaping Loaves

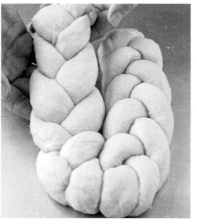

STACKED BRAIDS Create two braids for each loaf. Brush one loaf with water. Top with another loaf. Repeat with remaining loaves to make 3 stacked loaves.

SIDE-BY-SIDE BRAIDS Create two braids for each loaf. Brush one side of each loaf with water. Place loaves side by side with moistened sides touching.

SPIRAL LOAF After dividing and braiding dough, twist each loaf into a spiral on the baking sheet.

Vienna Almond Cutouts

PREP: 20 minutes
CHILL: 2 hours
BAKE: 8 minutes per batch at 350°F
MAKES: 48 cookies

¾ cup slivered almonds, toasted (see tip, page 343)
2¼ cups all-purpose flour
¼ teaspoon salt
1 cup butter, softened
¾ cup sugar
1 egg
1 teaspoon vanilla
½ teaspoon finely shredded lemon peel
¼ teaspoon almond extract (optional)
1 recipe Creamy White Frosting (see page 148)
Paste food coloring
Colored sprinkles, nonpareils, and/or other small decorations

1. In a food processor process toasted almonds with on/off pulses until finely ground. In a medium bowl combine the ground almonds, the flour, and salt. Set aside.

2. In a large mixing bowl beat butter and sugar with an electric mixer on medium to high speed until light and fluffy. Add egg, vanilla, lemon peel, and, if desired, almond extract. Beat until combined, scraping sides of bowl occasionally. Beat in as much of the flour mixture as you can with the mixer. Stir in any remaining flour mixture. Divide dough in half. Cover and chill about 2 hours or until dough is easy to handle.

3. Preheat oven to 350°F. On a lightly floured surface, roll half of the dough at a time to ¼-inch thickness. Using a pizza cutter or a sharp knife, cut dough into 3-inch squares. Place squares 1 inch apart on an ungreased cookie sheet.

4. Bake for 8 to 12 minutes or until edges are light brown and centers are set. Cool on cookie sheet for 1 minute. Transfer to a wire rack; cool completely.

5. Tint Creamy White Frosting with paste food coloring. Decorate cookies with frosting and sprinkles as desired.

PER COOKIE: 106 cal., 9 g fat (4 g sat. fat), 14 mg chol., 48 mg sodium, 18 g carb., 0 fiber, 1 g pro.

How to Decorate Package Cookies

The sweetest gift of all is a tray of cookies dressed up like little Christmas presents. Here's how to create custom gift wrapping designs.

1. Use a pizza cutter or pastry wheel to cut rolled-out dough into squares.

2. Divide frosting and tint as desired. Frost cookies. Decorate with sprinkles.

3. Place extra frosting in pastry bags fitted with flat ribbon or small round tips. Pipe frosting into bows and ribbons.

Sugar Cookies

PREP: **35 minutes**
CHILL: **2 hours**
BAKE: **7 minutes per batch at 375°F**
MAKES: **36 cookies**

⅔ cup butter, softened
¾ cup sugar
1 teaspoon baking powder
¼ teaspoon salt
1 egg
1 tablespoon milk
1 teaspoon vanilla
2 cups all-purpose flour
1 recipe Royal Icing (see page 463)
    Food coloring (optional)
    Colored sugars, candies, and sprinkles (optional)

1. In a large mixing bowl beat butter with an electric mixer on medium to high speed for 30 seconds. Add sugar, baking powder, and salt. Beat until combined, scraping bowl occasionally. Beat in egg, milk, and vanilla. Beat in as much of the flour as you can with the mixer. Stir in any remaining flour. Divide dough in half. Cover; chill dough about 2 hours or until easy to handle.
2. Preheat oven to 375°F. On a lightly floured surface, roll half the dough at a time to ¼-inch thickness. Cut dough with 2½-inch cookie cutters. Place cutouts 1 inch apart on an ungreased cookie sheet.
3. Bake for 7 to 10 minutes or until edges are very light brown. Transfer cookies to a wire rack; cool completely.

4. Add enough water to Royal Icing, 1 teaspoon at a time, just until icing is thin enough to flow over cookies. Tint frosting as desired. Pipe thinned Royal Icing along edges of cookie. Pipe more icing onto center of cookie; using a small thin metal spatula or a knife, spread frosting to outlines. Let dry. If desired, pipe desired colors of additional icing onto dry icing; let dry.

To Store: Layer cookies between sheets of waxed paper in an airtight container; cover. Store at room temperature for up to 2 days or freeze for up to 3 months.

PER COOKIE: *124 cal., 4 g fat (2 g sat. fat), 14 mg chol., 63 mg sodium, 22 g carb., 0 g fiber, 1 g pro.*

Chocolate-Peppermint Cookies: Prepare as directed, except place 2 ounces chopped unsweetened chocolate in a microwave-safe bowl. Microwave on 100 percent power (high) for 30 to 60 seconds or until chocolate melts, stirring once. Cool for 5 minutes. In Step 1, beat chocolate into the butter before adding sugar. Add ½ teaspoon peppermint extract with vanilla. Continue as directed, except bake until edges are firm.

PER COOKIE: *132 cal, 4 g fat (3 g sat. fat), 14 mg chol., 63 mg sodium, 23 g carb., 0 g fiber, 1 g pro.*

How to Flood Cookies with Icing

For a super smooth, edge-to-edge coating of icing, flood cookies with Royal Icing. Here's how to decorate beautifully elegant cookies.

1. To fill a pastry bag with icing, place bag in a large glass. Fold top of bag over the rim of the glass. Fill with icing that has been thinned with water.

2. Snip a very small hole in the end of the bag. Pipe an icing outline on cookie.

3. Pipe additional icing into the center of the cookie

4. Use a thin metal spatula to spread icing to the edges until it meets the icing outline.

5. Allow icing to dry. Pipe additional icing onto cookies. If desired, sprinkle icing with colored sugars or sprinkles while it is wet.

Molasses Cutouts

PREP: **55 minutes**
CHILL: **3 hours**
BAKE: **5 minutes per batch at 375°F**
MAKES: **36 cookies**

- ½ cup shortening
- ⅔ cup granulated sugar
- 2 teaspoons freshly grated nutmeg (see tip, page 17) or 1½ teaspoons ground nutmeg
- 1 teaspoon baking powder
- ¼ teaspoon salt
- ½ cup mild-flavor molasses
- 1 egg
- 1 tablespoon cider vinegar
- 2½ cups all-purpose flour
- 1 recipe Royal Icing Sprinkles, nonpareils, and/or small peppermint candies (optional)

1. In a large mixing bowl beat shortening with an electric mixer on medium to high speed for 30 seconds. Add granulated sugar, nutmeg, baking powder, and salt. Beat until combined, scraping sides of bowl occasionally. Beat in molasses, egg, and vinegar. Beat in as much of the flour as you can with the mixer. Stir in any remaining flour. Divide dough in half. Cover and chill about 3 hours or until easy to handle.

2. Preheat oven to 375°F. Grease a cookie sheet. On a lightly floured surface, roll half of the dough at a time to ⅛-inch thickness. Cut dough with 2½- to 3-inch cookie cutters. Place cutouts 1 inch apart on the prepared cookie sheet.

3. Bake for 5 to 6 minutes or until bottoms are light brown. Cool on cookie sheet for 1 minute. Transfer cookies to a wire rack; cool completely.

4. Divide and tint Royal Icing with food coloring. Place in pastry bags fitted with desired tips; pipe onto cookies to look like vests, dresses, shoes, pants, faces, and more. (If flooding a cookie with icing, add enough water to icing, 1 teaspoon at a time, until icing is thin enough to flow over cookies. Tint frosting as desired. See "How to Flood Cookies with Icing," page 461.) If desired, add sprinkles while icing is wet.

Royal Icing: In a large mixing bowl stir together one 16-ounce package powdered sugar (4 cups), 3 tablespoons meringue powder,* and ½ teaspoon cream of tartar. Add ½ cup warm water and 1 teaspoon vanilla. Beat with an electric mixer on low speed until combined. Beat on high speed for 7 minutes or until stiff. Cover bowl with damp paper towels and plastic wrap. Chill for up to 48 hours.

To Store: Layer cookies between sheets of waxed paper in an airtight container; cover. Store at room temperature for up to 2 days or freeze for up to 3 months.

*Test Kitchen Tip: Look for meringue powder in the cake decorating aisle of hobby and crafts stores.

PER COOKIE: 136 cal., 3 g fat (1 g sat. fat), 5 mg chol., 27 mg sodium, 26 g carb., 0 g fiber, 1 g pro.

How to Decorate Cookie People

Little people made from a gingerbread-style dough are a common sight on holiday cookie trays. Here's how to add a special touch with a customized vest. You can also make dresses, pants, suspenders, and more by flooding with icing as directed on page 461.

1. For a vest, place icing in a pastry bag fitted with a coupler and a small round tip. Pipe an outline of a vest (or other clothing) on a cookie.

2. Remove round tip from coupler. Fit coupler with a small star tip. Pipe tiny stars into the vest outline.

3. If desired, pipe different colors onto cookie for hat, boots, and face. Add candies or sprinkles for accents.

Triple Chocolate Silk Pie

PREP: **30 minutes**
BAKE: **14 minutes at 450°F**
CHILL: **5 to 24 hours**
FREEZE: **35 minutes**
MAKES: **10 servings**

1 recipe Pastry for Single-Crust Pie (see page 195)
4 ounces unsweetened chocolate, coarsely chopped
1 cup sugar
¾ cup butter, softened
1 teaspoon vanilla
¾ cup refrigerated or frozen egg product, thawed
1 recipe White Chocolate Topping
1 recipe Semisweet Chocolate Topping
  Hot fudge-flavor ice cream topping (optional)

1. Preheat oven to 450°F. Prepare Pastry for Single-Crust Pie. On a lightly floured surface, use your hands to slightly flatten pastry. Roll pastry from center to edges into a circle about 12 inches in diameter. Wrap pastry circle around the rolling pin. Unroll into a 9-inch pie plate. Ease pastry into pie plate without stretching it. Trim pastry to ½ inch beyond edge of pie plate. Fold under extra pastry even with the plate edge. Crimp edge as desired.

Generously prick bottom and sides of pastry with a fork. Line pastry with a double thickness of foil. Bake for 8 minutes. Remove foil. Bake for 6 to 8 minutes or until golden. Cool on a wire rack.

2. Meanwhile, in a small saucepan heat and stir unsweetened chocolate over low heat until melted. Remove from heat; cool.

3. In a medium mixing bowl beat sugar and butter with an electric mixer on medium speed about 4 minutes or until light and fluffy. Beat in melted chocolate and vanilla. Gradually add egg, ¼ cup at a time, beating on high speed after each addition and scraping sides of bowl constantly. Spoon chocolate mixture into pastry shell, spreading evenly. Cover and chill for 5 to 24 hours.

4. Spread White Chocolate Topping over top of pie; freeze for 15 minutes. Spread Semisweet Chocolate Topping over white chocolate topping; freeze for 20 minutes. If desired, drizzle each serving with fudge ice cream topping.

White Chocolate Topping: In a small heavy saucepan heat and stir 3 ounces coarsely chopped white baking bar and ¼ cup whipping cream over medium heat until chocolate melts; cool. In a chilled small mixing bowl beat ¾ cup whipping cream with the chilled beaters of an electric mixer on medium speed until soft peaks form (tips curl). Gradually add the white chocolate mixture. Beat just until stiff peaks form (tips stand straight).

Semisweet Chocolate Topping: In a small heavy saucepan heat and stir 3 ounces coarsely chopped semisweet chocolate and ¼ cup whipping cream over medium heat until chocolate melts; cool. In a chilled small mixing bowl beat ¾ cup whipping cream with chilled beaters of an electric mixer on medium speed until soft peaks form (tips curl). Add the chocolate mixture. Beat just until stiff peaks form (tips stand straight).

PER SERVING: *637 cal., 50 g fat (27 g sat. fat), 105 mg chol., 254 mg sodium, 46 g carb., 2 g fiber, 7 g pro.*

Dulce de Leche-Hazelnut-Pumpkin Pie

PREP: 40 minutes
BAKE: 50 minutes at 350°F
MAKES: 8 servings

1 recipe Hazelnut Pastry
1 8-ounce package cream
 cheese, softened
4 tablespoons dulce de leche
1 egg
1¼ cups canned pumpkin
½ cup evaporated milk
2 eggs
⅓ cup sugar
1½ teaspoons pumpkin pie
 spice
1 recipe Dulce de Leche
 Hazelnut Cream

1. On a floured surface, roll Hazelnut Pastry into a 12-inch circle. Ease pastry circle into a 9-inch pie plate without stretching it. Trim pastry to ½ inch beyond edge of pie plate. Fold under extra pastry. Crimp edge as desired.
2. In a small mixing bowl beat cream cheese and 2 tablespoons of the dulce de leche with an electric mixer on medium to high speed for 30 seconds. Add 1 egg; beat on medium speed until smooth. Spread evenly in the pastry-lined plate. Cover and chill for 30 minutes.
3. Preheat oven to 350°F. In a medium bowl whisk together pumpkin, evaporated milk, 2 eggs, ⅓ cup sugar, the remaining 2 tablespoons dulce de leche, and pumpkin pie spice. Carefully pour pumpkin mixture over cream cheese layer.

4. Cover edge of pie loosely with foil. Bake for 25 minutes; remove foil. Bake about 25 minutes more or until filling is set in the center. Cool on a wire rack.
5. Top with Dulce de Leche Hazelnut Cream and, if desired, sprinkle with toasted chopped *hazelnuts (filberts)*.

Hazelnut Pastry: In a bowl stir together 1 cup all-purpose flour, ¼ cup ground hazelnuts (filberts), and ¼ teaspoon salt. Using a pastry blender, cut in ⅓ cup shortening until pieces are pea size. Sprinkle 1 tablespoon ice water over part of the flour mixture; toss gently with a fork. Push moistened pastry to one side of bowl. Repeat moistening flour mixture, using 1 tablespoon ice water at a time, until all of the flour mixture is moistened (¼ to ⅓ cup total). Gather flour mixture into a ball, kneading gently until it holds together.

Dulce de Leche Hazelnut Cream: Place 1 tablespoon dulce de leche in a chilled mixing bowl. If desired, add 2 teaspoons hazelnut liqueur. Beat with an electric mixer on medium speed until smooth. Add 1 cup whipping cream. Beat on medium speed just until stiff peaks begin to form.

PER SERVING: *521 cal., 36 g fat (17 g sat. fat), 155 mg chol., 254 mg sodium, 41 g carb., 2 g fiber, 10 g pro.*

Make It Mini

Prepare as directed, except make 2 recipes of pastry and roll each pastry into a 14-inch circle. Cut the pastry into 3½-inch circles. Ease circles into 2½-inch muffin cups. Prick the bottoms of each a few times with the tines of a fork. Bake crusts in a 450°F oven for 4 minutes. Reduce oven temperature to 350°F. Prepare cream cheese mixture, using 4 ounces cream cheese, 1 tablespoon dulce de leche, 1 egg yolk, and 4 teaspoons sugar. Divide among pastry shells. Prepare pumpkin mixture, using ⅔ cup pumpkin, ½ cup evaporated milk, 1 egg, 3 tablespoons sugar, 1 tablespoon dulce de leche, and ¾ teaspoon pumpkin pie spice. Spread evenly over cream cheese layers. Bake in the 350°F oven for 15 to 20 minutes or until filling is set. Cool for 10 minutes in cups. Loosen edges and remove cups; cool completely. Top as directed. Makes 20 to 24 mini pies.

Peppermint Dream Cake

PREP: 45 minutes
BAKE: 25 minutes at 350°F
COOL: 1 hour
MAKES: 12 servings

    3 eggs
1½ cups all-purpose flour
1½ teaspoons baking powder
 ¼ teaspoon salt
1½ cups sugar
 ¾ cup milk
    3 tablespoons butter
 ½ teaspoon peppermint
      extract
    1 tablespoon liquid red food
      coloring
    1 recipe Fluffy White
      Chocolate Frosting
      Chopped peppermint candy
      canes

1. Allow eggs to stand at room temperature for 30 minutes. Meanwhile, grease bottoms of two 8-inch round baking pans. Line bottoms of pans with waxed paper; grease and lightly flour pans. Set pans aside. In a small bowl stir together flour, baking powder, and salt.
2. Preheat oven to 350°F. In a medium mixing bowl beat eggs with an electric mixer on high speed about 4 minutes or until thick and lemon color. Gradually add sugar, beating on medium speed for 4 to 5 minutes or until light and fluffy. Add flour mixture; beat on low to medium speed just until combined.
3. In a small saucepan heat and stir milk and butter over medium heat until butter melts. Add milk mixture and peppermint extract to batter, beating until combined. Divide batter in half. Pour half of the batter into one of the prepared baking pans. Stir red food coloring into the remaining batter. Pour red batter into the second baking pan.
4. Bake for 25 to 30 minutes or until a wooden toothpick inserted near the centers comes out clean. Cool in pans on wire racks for 10 minutes. Remove cakes from pans. Peel off waxed paper. Cool completely on wire racks.
5. To assemble, cut each cake layer in half horizontally. Place a white cake layer on a serving plate. Spread ¾ cup of the frosting evenly over the cake. Top with a red cake layer; spread evenly with ¾ cup of the frosting. Top with the remaining white cake layer; spread evenly with ¾ cup frosting. Top with the red cake layer. Spread frosting over top and sides of cake.

Sprinkle chopped candy canes over top of cake. Serve immediately or cover and chill for up to 4 hours. Cover and store any leftover cake in the refrigerator.

Fluffy White Chocolate Frosting: In a medium saucepan heat and stir ½ cup whipping cream and 2 tablespoons butter over medium heat until butter melts. Remove from heat. Add 8 ounces chopped good-quality white chocolate (do not stir). Let stand for 5 minutes. Whisk mixture until smooth. Stir in ½ teaspoon peppermint extract. In a chilled large mixing bowl beat 2 cups whipping cream with an electric mixer on medium speed until soft peaks form (tips curl). Fold in white chocolate mixture, half at a time.

To Make Ahead: Bake and cool cake layers as directed through Step 4. Place the cooled cake layers on baking sheets and freeze until firm. Transfer frozen cake layers to separate large freezer bags. Freeze for up to 4 months. Thaw at room temperature before frosting and serving as directed.

PER SERVING: *533 cal., 32 g fat (19 g sat. fat), 139 mg chol., 210 mg sodium, 55 g carb., 0 g fiber, 6 g pro.*

Croquembouche with Maple Cream

PREP: 1 hour
CHILL: 1 hour
BAKE: 20 minutes per batch at 400°F
MAKES: 20 servings

 1 recipe Maple Cream Filling
 ½ cup water
 ½ cup whole milk
 ½ cup butter
 ½ teaspoon salt
 1 cup all-purpose flour
 5 eggs
 1 teaspoon water
 2 cups sugar
 ¼ cup water
 1 tablespoon light-color corn syrup
 ¼ teaspoon lemon juice
    Sea salt flakes (optional)
    Caramel stars (optional)*

1. Prepare Maple Cream Filling. Cover and chill until needed.
2. Meanwhile, preheat oven to 400°F. Line two extra-large baking sheets with parchment paper; set aside.
3. In a large saucepan combine ½ cup water, milk, butter, and salt. Bring to boiling. Immediately add flour all at once; stir vigorously. Cook and stir until mixture forms a ball. Remove from heat. Cool for 10 minutes. Add 4 of the eggs, one at a time, beating well after each addition.
4. Using a pastry bag fitted with a ½-inch round tip, pipe dough into forty-six 1-inch mounds onto prepared baking sheets, leaving 1 inch between mounds. In a small bowl beat the remaining egg and 1 teaspoon water with a fork. Brush puffs with egg mixture.
5. Bake, one sheet at a time, about 20 minutes or until puffs are golden and firm. Cool on baking sheet on a wire rack.
6. Spoon filling into a pastry bag fitted with a ¼-inch round tip. Using a skewer or wooden dowel, gently poke a hole in the bottom of each puff. Insert pastry bag tip into holes and fill puffs with filling.

How to Make Croquembouche

This much-celebrated French dessert is essentially a pyramid of cream-filled pastry puffs stacked and drizzled with caramelized sugar. When you take it one step at a time, this dessert isn't the least bit intimidating.

1. Poke a hole in the bottom of each cream puff. Insert the tip of the pastry bag; squeeze cream filling into centers.

2. On a serving platter, arrange a layer of cream puffs in the center. Repeat with second platter.

3. Drizzle the cream puff circles with caramelized sugar. Add another layer of puffs to each platter.

4. Continue layering puffs and caramelized sugar to build two pyramids. Drizzle tops with caramelized sugar.

continued on page 472

continued from page 471

7. For caramel, in a medium saucepan stir together sugar, the ¼ cup water, the corn syrup, and lemon juice (mixture will be grainy). Bring to boiling over medium heat (do not stir). Increase heat to high. Cook, without stirring, for 6 to 8 minutes or until mixture turns an amber color. Remove from heat; cool slightly.

8. On each of two serving plates, arrange seven puffs in a circle and one puff in the center for the base. With a spoon, lightly drizzle caramel over puffs with quick motions to create thin strands.** Continue adding layers of puffs to make a pyramid, drizzling each layer with additional thin strands of caramel. If caramel becomes too thick, transfer to a microwave-safe bowl and microwave on 100 percent power (high) for 10 to 15 seconds to reach drizzling consistency. If desired, sprinkle layers with sea salt flakes and garnish with caramel stars. Serve immediately or chill for up to 4 hours.

Maple Cream Filling: In a medium saucepan whisk together 1½ cups whipping cream, ½ cup maple syrup, and 3 tablespoons cornstarch. Cook and stir over medium heat until thickened and bubbly (if necessary, whisk to make smooth). Cook and stir for 2 minutes. Remove from heat. Gradually stir about half of the hot mixture into 5 lightly beaten egg yolks. Return yolk mixture to saucepan. Bring to a gentle boil; reduce heat. Cook and stir for 2 minutes more. Remove from heat. Stir in 1 teaspoon vanilla. Pour cream mixture into a medium bowl; cover surface with plastic wrap. Chill for 1 to 2 hours. In a large mixing bowl beat 1 cup softened butter with an electric mixer on medium speed until light and fluffy. Add cream mixture, beating until smooth.

*Test Kitchen Tip: To make caramel stars, line a baking sheet with foil. Drizzle some of the caramel in free-form star shapes onto the prepared baking sheet. Let stand until set. Carefully peel stars off foil.

**Test Kitchen Tip: Keep the drizzles of caramel very light (almost like spun sugar). If the drizzles get too thick, the cream puffs will be difficult to pull from the pyramid once the caramel hardens.

PER SERVING: *346 cal., 23 g fat (14 g sat. fat), 155 mg chol., 91 mg sodium, 32 g carb., 0 g fiber, 4 g pro.*

Chemistry of Caramelizing

Making caramel by boiling a simple sugar and water solution is difficult because of the chemistry involved. If some of the sugar mixture is stirred up onto the sides of the saucepan during cooking, the water will evaporate and cause the sugar particles to crystallize. This sets off a chain reaction in the rest of the caramel mixture that can leave a grainy mess. This caramel recipe uses corn syrup and lemon juice to prevent the problem. The natural sugar in corn syrup acts as an impurity that interferes with crystallization. Adding an acid, such as lemon juice or vinegar, breaks down some of the sugar molecules, which will further inhibit crystallization. Adding corn syrup and lemon juice makes the process practically failproof.

Opera Cake

PREP: 1 hour
BAKE: 8 minutes at 425°F
COOL: 45 minutes
CHILL: 1½ hours
MAKES: 12 servings

   6 egg yolks
   6 egg whites
1⅓ cups slivered almonds
   ⅔ cup powdered sugar
   ⅓ cup milk
   1 teaspoon vanilla
   ½ teaspoon cream of tartar
   ½ cup granulated sugar
   ¼ cup strong brewed coffee
   1 tablespoon coffee liqueur
   1 recipe Coffee Buttercream
   1 recipe Chocolate Ganache
   2 ounces white baking
      chocolate with cocoa
      butter, melted
      Edible glitter and/or luster
      dust (optional)

1. Allow egg yolks and egg whites to stand at room temperature for 30 minutes. Meanwhile, grease three 8×8×2-inch baking pans.* Line bottoms of pans with parchment paper or waxed paper. Grease paper and lightly flour pans; set aside. In a food processor combine almonds and powdered sugar. Cover and process with on/off pulses until nuts are finely ground; set aside.

2. Preheat oven to 425°F. In a medium mixing bowl beat egg yolks with an electric mixer on high speed about 5 minutes or until thick and lemon color. Add milk and vanilla; beat on low speed until combined. Fold in almond mixture; set aside.

3. Thoroughly wash beaters. In a large mixing bowl beat egg whites and cream of tartar on medium speed until soft peaks form (tips curl). Gradually add ¼ cup of the granulated sugar, beating on high speed until stiff peaks form (tips stand straight). Fold half of the beaten egg white mixture into egg yolk mixture; fold egg yolk mixture into remaining beaten egg white mixture. Divide batter among the prepared pans, spreading evenly.

4. Bake for 8 to 10 minutes or until tops are golden. Cool in pans on wire racks for 10 minutes. Remove cakes from pans; remove paper. Cool completely on wire racks (cake layers will be thin).

5. For coffee syrup, in a small saucepan combine the remaining ¼ cup granulated sugar and the coffee. Cook and stir over medium heat until sugar is dissolved and mixture comes to boiling. Reduce heat; simmer, uncovered, for 5 minutes. Stir in liqueur; cool.

6. To assemble cake, place one cake layer on a serving plate. Brush with one-third of the coffee syrup. Spread with half of the Coffee Buttercream. Top with another cake layer; brush with one-third of the syrup. Spread with half of the Chocolate Ganache. Top with the remaining cake layer; brush with remaining syrup. Spread with remaining buttercream. Chill for at least 1 hour or until layers are firm. Spread top with remaining

continued on page 474

continued from page 473

ganache. Using a long sharp knife, trim sides of layers to even.

7. Place melted white chocolate in a small resealable plastic bag. Snip a small hole in one corner of the bag. Drizzle white chocolate over top of cake.** Chill about 30 minutes or until set. If desired, sprinkle with glitter and/or luster dust.

Coffee Buttercream: In a heavy medium saucepan combine ½ cup granulated sugar and 2 tablespoons water; bring to boiling. Remove from heat. Gradually stir about half of the hot mixture into 3 lightly beaten egg yolks. Return egg yolk mixture to saucepan. Cook and stir for 2 minutes. Remove from heat. Stir in 1 tablespoon strong brewed coffee and 1 teaspoon vanilla; cool. In a large mixing bowl beat ¾ cup softened butter with an electric mixer on medium to high speed until light and fluffy. Add cooled egg yolk mixture, beating until combined. If necessary, chill until buttercream reaches spreading consistency.

Chocolate Ganache: In a small saucepan bring ⅓ cup whipping cream just to boiling over medium heat. Remove from heat. Add 4 ounces chopped bittersweet chocolate (do not stir). Let stand for 5 minutes. Stir until smooth. Cool for 15 minutes.

*****Test Kitchen Tip:** If you don't have three 8×8×2-inch baking pans, bake one or two pans at a time, keeping the remaining batter chilled until ready to bake. Cool, grease, line, and flour pans between each batch.

****Test Kitchen Tip:** If you like, decorate the cake with musical notes instead of drizzling with white chocolate. Line a baking sheet with parchment paper or other paper. Draw musical notes and designs on paper with a pencil; cover parchment paper with waxed paper. Pipe melted white chocolate onto waxed paper following the outlines of the notes and designs. Chill about 30 minutes or until set. Carefully lift notes and designs off waxed paper and arrange on top of cake.

PER SERVING: *417 cal., 29 g fat (14 g sat. fat), 180 mg chol., 149 mg sodium, 36 g carb., 2 g fiber, 8 g pro.*

How to Make Musical Notes

Draw designs on parchment paper. Place a sheet of waxed paper over the parchment paper. Pipe melted white chocolate onto waxed paper over the outlines. Chill shapes to harden before removing from the paper.

Baked Alaska with Christmas Rum Pudding Ice Cream

PREP: 30 minutes
FREEZE: 4 hours
BROIL: 2 minutes
MAKES: 10 servings

Vegetable oil
¾ cup dark rum or orange juice
½ cup raisins
½ cup dried cranberries
1½ quarts vanilla ice cream
4 ounces dark chocolate (70 percent cocoa), coarsely chopped
½ teaspoon ground cinnamon
½ teaspoon ground cloves
2 tablespoons dark rum or orange juice
2 tablespoons water
1 tablespoon sugar
1 tablespoon butter, melted
1 10.75-ounce frozen pound cake, thawed
⅓ cup dried egg whites,* such as Just Whites
⅓ cup warm water
⅓ cup sugar

1. Brush a 3-quart metal bowl with oil. Line bowl with plastic wrap, extending the wrap over edges of bowl; set aside.
2. In a small saucepan combine ¾ cup rum, raisins, and dried cranberries. Bring to boiling; reduce heat. Simmer, uncovered, for 5 minutes. Drain and cool.
3. In a large bowl stir ice cream with a wooden spoon just until softened. Stir in raisin mixture, chocolate, cinnamon, and cloves. In a small bowl stir together 2 tablespoons rum, 2 tablespoons water, 1 tablespoon sugar, and melted butter. Cut pound cake into ½-inch slices. Brush cake slices with rum mixture.
4. Pour half of the ice cream mixture into prepared 3-quart bowl, spreading evenly. Layer half of the cake slices on ice cream layer, trimming cake to fit. Top with the remaining ice cream mixture and the remaining cake slices; gently press cake into ice cream. Cover with plastic wrap. Freeze for 4 hours or until firm.

5. Adjust baking rack to the lowest position in oven. Preheat broiler. Line a pizza pan or baking sheet with foil; set aside. For meringue, in a medium mixing bowl combine dried egg whites and ⅓ cup warm water. Beat with an electric mixer on medium to high speed until soft peaks form (tips curl). Gradually add ⅓ cup sugar, beating until stiff peaks form (tips stand straight).
6. Remove plastic wrap from cake. Carefully invert cake and ice cream onto the prepared pan; remove plastic wrap. Quickly spread meringue over cake and ice cream. Using the back of a spoon, add high peaks to the meringue. Broil on the lowest rack for 2 to 4 minutes or just until meringue peaks are golden. Serve immediately.

*Test Kitchen Tip: Look for dried egg whites in the baking section of your supermarket.

PER SERVING: *503 cal., 23 g fat (13 g sat. fat), 86 mg chol., 173 mg sodium, 59 g carb., 3 g fiber, 6 g pro.*

Make It Mini

Cut pound cake into ½-inch-thick lengthwise slices; cut into 2-inch rounds. Brush with rum mixture. Place scoops of ice cream mixture on cake rounds. Cover; freeze for 2 hours or until firm. Prepare meringue as above, except double ingredients. Place 5 rounds at a time on a foil-lined baking sheet. Quickly spread meringue over ice cream and cake. Return to freezer for up to 2 hours. Broil 4 to 5 inches from the heat for 1 to 2 minutes or until brown. Serve immediately. Makes 14 mini desserts.

Caramel Baumkuchen

PREP: 1 hour
STAND: 30 minutes
COOL: 1 hour
MAKES: 12 servings

- 10 egg yolks
- 10 egg whites
- ¾ cup butter
- ¾ cup sugar
- 2 teaspoons finely shredded lemon peel
- 1 teaspoon vanilla
- 1 cup all-purpose flour
- ½ cup cornstarch
- ¼ teaspoon salt
- ¼ cup sugar
- 1 recipe Vanilla Glaze
- 1 recipe Caramel Glaze

1. Allow egg yolks, egg whites, and butter to stand at room temperature for 30 minutes. Meanwhile, grease an 8-inch springform pan; set aside.
2. Preheat broiler. In a medium mixing bowl beat yolks with an electric mixer on high speed about 5 minutes or until thick and lemon color. In an extra-large mixing bowl beat butter on medium to high speed for 30 seconds. Beat in ¾ cup sugar, the lemon peel, and vanilla until combined, scraping bowl occasionally. Add beaten egg yolks, beating until combined. Stir together flour, cornstarch, and salt; stir into egg yolk mixture just until combined.
3. Thoroughly wash beaters. In a large mixing bowl beat egg whites on medium speed until soft peaks form (tips curl). Gradually add ¼ cup sugar, beating on high speed until stiff peaks form (tips stand straight). Fold beaten whites into yolk mixture.
4. Pour ⅓ cup batter into prepared pan, spreading evenly. Broil about 5 inches from heat for 1 to 2 minutes or until light brown. (If necessary, give pan a half-turn for even browning.) Do not overbrown. Pour another ⅓ cup of the batter over first layer, spreading evenly. Broil as directed. Repeat with the remaining batter, making 15 to 17 layers total.

Cool in pan on a wire rack for 10 minutes. Loosen cake from sides of pan. Remove sides of pan; cool cake completely on wire rack.
5. Cut cake into 12 wedges. Place wedges on a wire rack set over waxed paper. Spread Vanilla Glaze over tops of wedges; drizzle with Caramel Glaze. Let stand to set.

Vanilla Glaze: In a medium bowl combine 2 cups powdered sugar, 2 tablespoons milk, and 1 teaspoon vanilla. Stir in enough additional milk, 1 teaspoon at a time, to reach spreading consistency.

Caramel Glaze: In a small saucepan combine 20 unwrapped vanilla caramels and ¼ cup whipping cream. Heat and stir over low heat until caramels are melted. Stir in enough additional whipping cream to reach drizzling consistency.

PER SERVING: *437 cal., 18 g fat (10 g sat. fat), 186 mg chol., 245 mg sodium, 5 g carb., 0 g fiber, 7 g pro.*

How to Make Baumkuchen

To make this European specialty, you will add one layer of batter to the pan and broil it before adding a second layer of batter. This creates well-defined layers within the cake, creating a pastry look.

1. Evenly spread first layer of batter in pan. Broil just until light brown.

2. Spread another layer of batter on baked first layer; broil. Repeat.

Pomegranate Pavlova with Pistachios and Honey

PREP: 35 minutes
BAKE: 1 hour at 250°F
STAND: 1 hour
MAKES: 12 servings

6 egg whites
Dash salt
Dash cream of tartar
1½ cups sugar
1½ teaspoons vanilla
1 teaspoon lemon juice
2½ teaspoons cornstarch
1½ cups pomegranate juice
¼ cup honey
1 tablespoon lemon juice
1½ cups whipping cream
1 tablespoon sugar
1 cup pomegranate seeds
¼ cup pistachio nuts, coarsely chopped

1. Allow egg whites to stand at room temperature for 30 minutes. Meanwhile, line a baking sheet with parchment paper or foil. Draw a 9-inch circle on the paper or foil. Invert paper or foil so the circle is on the reverse side.

2. Position baking rack in center of oven. Preheat oven to 250°F. For meringue, in a large mixing bowl beat egg whites, salt, and cream of tartar with an electric mixer on medium speed until soft peaks form (tips curl). Add 1½ cups sugar, 1 tablespoon at a time, beating on high speed until stiff peaks form (tips stand straight). Beat in ½ teaspoon of the vanilla and 1 teaspoon lemon juice. Sift cornstarch over egg white mixture; fold in gently.

3. Spread meringue over circle on paper or foil, building up edges slightly to form a shell. Bake for 1 hour (do not open door). Turn off oven; let meringue stand in oven with door closed for 1 hour.

4. Meanwhile, for pomegranate syrup, in a small saucepan combine pomegranate juice, honey, and 1 tablespoon lemon juice. Bring to boiling over medium heat; reduce heat. Boil gently, uncovered, for 30 to 40 minutes or until mixture is reduced to ½ cup. Transfer syrup to a small bowl; cool.

5. In a chilled large mixing bowl beat whipping cream, 1 tablespoon sugar, and the remaining 1 teaspoon vanilla with chilled beaters of the mixer on medium speed until stiff peaks form (tips stand straight).

6. Carefully lift meringue off paper or foil and transfer to a serving plate. Spread with the whipped cream. Sprinkle with pomegranate seeds; drizzle with the pomegranate syrup. Top with pistachio nuts.

PER SERVING: *280 cal., 12 g fat (7 g sat. fat), 41 mg chol., 54 mg sodium, 41 g carb., 0 g fiber, 3 g pro.*

Make It Mini

Prepare as above, except halve the meringue recipe. Line 2 large baking sheets with parchment paper. Draw six 3-inch circles on each paper. Invert paper so the circles are on the reverse side. Spread the meringue over the circles, building up the edges slightly to form a shell. Bake in the 250°F oven for 45 minutes (do not open door). Turn off oven; let meringues stand in oven with door closed for 1 hour. Halve the amount of pomegranate syrup, sweetened whipped cream, pomegranate seeds, and pistachios. Top meringues as above. Makes 12 mini pavlovas.

Butterscotch Marble Cake,
recipe page 484

everyday baking

THERE'S ALWAYS TIME TO BAKE a homemade dessert when you start with a cake or cookie mix. Use one as the starting point for superb desserts, bars, and cookies that tout from-scratch flavor in a fraction of the time.

Butterscotch Marble Cake

With decadent swirls of chocolate and butterscotch-flavor batter, your family and friends will never guess this homespun dessert started with a white cake mix. And there's no reason to tell them!

PREP: 20 minutes
BAKE: 55 minutes at 350°F
COOL: 2 hours
MAKES: 12 servings

- 1 package 2-layer-size white cake mix
- 1 4-serving-size package butterscotch instant pudding and pie filling mix
- 1 cup water
- 4 eggs
- ¼ cup vegetable oil
- ½ cup chocolate-flavor syrup
- 2 ounces sweet baking chocolate, chopped
- 2 tablespoons butter
- ¾ cup powdered sugar
- 1 tablespoon hot water

1. Preheat oven to 350°F. Grease and flour a 10-inch fluted tube pan; set aside.

2. In a large mixing bowl combine cake mix, pudding mix, the 1 cup water, the eggs, and oil. Beat with an electric mixer on low speed just until combined. Beat on medium speed for 2 minutes, scraping sides of bowl occasionally.

3. Transfer 1½ cups of the batter to a medium bowl; stir in chocolate syrup. Pour light-color batter into the prepared pan. Top with the chocolate batter. Using a table knife or spoon, gently cut through batters to swirl them together.

4. Bake for 55 to 60 minutes or until a wooden toothpick inserted near the center comes out clean. Cool in pan on a wire rack for 15 minutes. Remove cake from pan; cool completely on wire rack.

5. For icing, in a small saucepan combine sweet baking chocolate and the butter. Heat and stir over low heat until melted and smooth. Remove from heat. Stir in powdered sugar and the 1 tablespoon hot water. If necessary, stir in additional hot water, 1 teaspoon at a time, until icing reaches drizzling consistency. Drizzle the icing over the cake.

To Store: Place cake in an airtight container. Store at room temperature for up to 3 days or freeze for up to 2 months.

PER SERVING: *377 cal., 14 g fat (4 g sat. fat), 76 mg chol., 467 mg sodium, 60 g carb., 1 g fiber, 5 g pro.*

Secrets to Success

Cake mixes take a lot of the work out of making a cake. The dry mixes contain all of the flour, leavening, and flavorings needed to make a cake. You just add water, oil, and eggs. Once baked, the result is a fine-textured cake that is supremely moist and delicious. You can create homemade flavor in desserts made from cake mixes by adding different ingredients. In the Butterscotch Marble Cake recipe, half of the batter is flavored with chocolate syrup, then swirled into the butterscotch-flavor batter for a lovely marbled effect. Tweaking boxed baking mixes requires a few extra steps before or after you put the cake in the oven, but the overall recipes are still much simpler to create than a 100 percent from-scratch recipe. These shortcuts make great desserts on busy weeknights.

GREASE THE PAN Use a pastry brush to brush a thin layer of shortening over the inside of a fluted tube pan. Be sure to coat the insides of the grooves.

LIGHTLY FLOUR THE PAN Sprinkle a little flour into the pan; tap so flour covers all greased surfaces. Tap out any extra flour.

PREPARE CHOCOLATE BATTER Transfer 1½ cups of the cake batter to a bowl. Pour the chocolate-flavor syrup over top.

COMBINE WELL Using a spatula, combine the chocolate-flavor syrup and the light-color batter.

PLACE BATTERS IN PAN Pour light-color batter into prepared pan. Spoon chocolate batter in mounds over top.

MARBLE THE BATTERS Gently swirl a knife or spoon through both batters to create a marbled effect. Bake as directed.

Make-It-Mine Whoopie Pies

Whip up a different creation every time you make these whoopie pies with your choice of cake mix, fillings, toppers, and more.

PREP: **30 minutes**
BAKE: **10 minutes at 350°F**
CHILL: **1 hour**
MAKES: **12 sandwich cookies**

  1 *package 2-layer-size Cake Mix* (choose option)
⅓ cup butter, melted
  2 eggs
¼ *cup Liquid* (choose option)
    Toppers (choose option)
  1 3-ounce package cream cheese, softened
½ *of a 16-ounce can Frosting* (¾ *cup*) (choose option)

1. Preheat oven to 350°F. Line two large cookie sheets with parchment paper; set aside. In a large bowl stir together *Cake Mix*, melted butter, eggs, and *Liquid* with a wooden spoon until smooth and thick.
2. For each cookie, drop dough from rounded measuring tablespoons 2 inches apart onto prepared cookie sheets. Immediately sprinkle dough mounds with *Toppers*.
3. Bake for 10 to 12 minutes or until cookies are light brown and edges are set. Transfer cookies to a wire rack; let cool.

4. For filling, in a medium mixing bowl beat cream cheese with an electric mixer on medium speed just until smooth. Beat in *Frosting* just until combined.
5. Spread a slightly rounded tablespoon of filling on the bottoms of half of the cookies, spreading filling to edges. Top with remaining cookies, bottom sides down, lightly pressing cookies together. If desired, roll edge of filling in additional *Toppers*. Cover and chill for at least 1 hour before serving.

CAKE MIX (PICK ONE)
Chocolate
White
Yellow
Red velvet
Spice

LIQUID (PICK ONE)
Water
Milk
Orange juice
Strong brewed coffee

TOPPERS (PICK ONE)
Multicolored, red, or white sprinkles or jimmies
Finely chopped pecans or walnuts
Sliced almonds
Finely snipped dried apricots
Finely chopped crystallized ginger
Miniature semisweet chocolate pieces
Chocolate-covered coffee beans

FROSTING (PICK ONE)
Chocolate
White
Vanilla

To Store: Layer unfilled cookies between sheets of waxed paper in an airtight container; cover. Store at room temperature for up to 3 days or freeze for up to 3 months. To serve, thaw cookies if frozen. Assemble as directed in Steps 3 and 4. For filled cookies, wrap individually in plastic wrap. Store for up to 2 days in the refrigerator or freeze for up to 3 months.

Gooey Chocolate-Caramel Cake

PREP: **15 minutes**
PREP: **according to package directions at 350°F**
STAND: **30 minutes**
MAKES: **15 servings**

1 package 2-layer-size German chocolate cake mix
1 14-ounce can sweetened condensed milk
1 12-ounce jar caramel-flavor ice cream topping
1 8-ounce container frozen whipped dessert topping, thawed
3 1.4-ounce bars chocolate-covered English toffee, chopped

1. Preheat oven to 350°F. Grease and lightly flour a 13×9×2-inch baking pan; set aside.
2. Prepare cake mix according to package directions. Pour into prepared pan. Bake according to package directions. Cool cake in pan on a wire rack.
3. Using the handle of a wooden spoon, poke holes about 1 inch apart over top of cake. Slowly pour sweetened condensed milk over cake, then slowly pour caramel topping over cake. Let stand for 30 minutes.
4. To serve, spread dessert topping evenly over cake. Sprinkle with chopped toffee.

To Store: Cover leftover cake with foil or place mini cakes in an airtight container. Store in the refrigerator for up to 24 hours.

PER SERVING: *440 cal., 14 g fat (8 g sat. fat), 12 mg chol., 348 mg sodium, 663 g carb., 0 g fiber, 4 g pro.*

Make It Mini

Prepare as directed, except grease and lightly flour twenty-four 2½-inch muffin cups. Spoon batter into prepared cups, filling each about one-half to two-thirds full. Bake in the 350°F oven for 18 to 20 minutes or until tops spring back when lightly touched. Cool for 5 minutes in cups; remove and cool completely on wire racks. Return cooled cupcakes to muffin cups. Using a long wooden skewer, poke holes in cakes. Pour sweetened condensed milk over cakes; then pour caramel topping over cakes. Let stand for 30 minutes. Transfer cupcakes to a serving plate. Spoon or pipe whipped topping onto cakes; sprinkle with chopped toffee. Makes 24 mini cakes.

Dulce de Leche Cake

PREP: **1 hour**
BAKE: **40 minutes at 350°F**
COOL: **1 hour**
CHILL: **overnight**
MAKES: **12 servings**

- 1 package 2-layer-size white cake mix
- ¾ cup butter, softened
- 5 eggs
- ½ cup water
- 2 tablespoons finely shredded orange peel (see tip, page 102)
- 1 recipe Dulce de Leche Cream
- 1 recipe Sweetened Whipped Cream Frosting (see page 148)
- 1 recipe Caramelized Sugar Drizzle (optional)

1. Preheat oven to 350°F. Grease and flour a 10-inch springform pan;* set aside.

2. In a very large mixing bowl beat cake mix, butter, eggs, and the water with an electric mixer on low speed until combined. Beat on medium speed for 2 minutes more (batter will be thick). Stir in orange peel. Spread batter in the prepared pan.

3. Bake about 40 minutes or until a wooden skewer inserted near the center comes out clean. Cool in pan on a wire rack for 10 minutes (cake may sink slightly during cooling). Loosen cake from side of pan; remove sides. Using a wide metal spatula, lift cake from pan bottom and transfer to a wire rack. Cool cake completely on wire rack.

4. Using a long serrated knife, cut the cake in half horizontally to make two layers. Place one layer, cut side up, on a serving plate. Slide pieces of waxed paper underneath the cake layer on all sides to catch drips. Spread ½ to ¾ cup of the Dulce de Leche Cream on top of layer. Top with the second cake layer, cut side up. Press down lightly. Spread ½ to ¾ cup of the Dulce de Leche Cream over cake. Cover and chill overnight. If necessary, cover and chill any remaining Dulce de Leche Cream.

5. Spread Whipped Cream Frosting over top and sides of cake. Remove waxed paper from under the cake. If desired, just before serving, drizzle cake with Caramelized Sugar Drizzle. Serve with any remaining Dulce de Leche Cream.

Dulce De Leche Cream: In a large saucepan combine half of a 14-ounce can sweetened condensed milk and one 13.4- to 15-ounce can dulce de leche.** Cook over medium heat just until boiling, stirring frequently. Remove from heat. Transfer to a bowl. Cover; cool for 5 minutes.

Caramelized Sugar Drizzle: In a large heavy skillet cook ⅓ cup sugar over medium-high heat until sugar starts to melt, shaking skillet occasionally. Do not stir. When sugar starts to melt, reduce heat to low and cook about 5 minutes or until all of the sugar is melted, stirring as needed with a wooden spoon. Remove from heat. Immediately drizzle caramelized sugar over frosted cake.

***Test Kitchen Tip:** If your springform pan does not have a tight fit, line the outside of the pan with foil. If you don't have a 10-inch springform pan, divide batter between two greased and floured 9-inch round baking pans. Bake according to timings on cake mix package.

****Test Kitchen Tip:** Look for dulce de leche in the ethnic section of your supermarket or at Mexican specialty markets.

To Store: Loosely cover any leftover cake and store in the refrigerator for up to 2 days.

PER SERVING: *582 cal., 33 g fat (19 g sat. fat), 174 mg chol., 475 mg sodium, 64 g carb., 0 g fiber, 9 g pro.*

Upside-Down Apricot-Caramel Cake

PREP: 30 minutes
BAKE: 35 minutes at 350°F
COOL: 25 minutes
MAKES: 14 servings

Nonstick cooking spray
2 15- to 17-ounce cans unpeeled apricot halves in light syrup, undrained
¾ cup packed brown sugar
¼ cup butter
¾ teaspoon ground cinnamon
1 package 2-layer-size spice cake mix
½ cup quick-cooking rolled oats
¾ cup caramel-flavor ice cream topping
Sweetened whipped cream (see tip, page 16) (optional)

1. Preheat oven to 350°F. Lightly coat a 13×9×2-inch baking pan with cooking spray. Set aside. Drain apricot halves, reserving juice in a 2-cup glass measuring cup. In a small saucepan combine brown sugar, butter, cinnamon, and 2 tablespoons of the reserved juice. Cook and stir over low heat until sugar is dissolved. Spread brown sugar mixture evenly over bottom of prepared baking pan. Arrange apricot halves, cut sides down, on the brown sugar mixture; set aside.

2. Prepare cake mix according to package directions, except stir oats into dry cake mix and substitute reserved apricot syrup for the water listed in package directions. Discard any remaining syrup. Pour batter evenly over apricot halves in pan, being careful not to disturb apricots.

3. Bake for 35 to 40 minutes or until a wooden toothpick inserted near the center comes out clean. Cool in pan on a wire rack for 10 minutes. Carefully invert onto a large serving platter. Cool for 15 minutes.

4. To serve, cut warm cake into squares. Drizzle with ice cream topping. If desired, top with sweetened whipped cream.

PER SERVING: *315 cal., 6 g fat (3 g sat. fat), 9 mg chol., 321 mg sodium, 63 g carb., 1 g fiber, 3 g pro.*

Make It Mini

Prepare as directed, except lightly coat fourteen 10-ounce custard cups or ramekins with nonstick cooking spray. Spread brown sugar mixture over bottoms of cups. Place apricot halves, cut sides down, in cups. Divide batter between the cups, filling one-half to two-thirds full. Bake for 15 to 18 minutes or until a wooden toothpick inserted in centers comes out clean. Cool in the custard cups for 5 minutes. Loosen cakes from cups with a sharp knife. Invert onto a platter. Cool for 10 minutes. Serve as directed. If you do not have enough custard cups or ramekins, bake in batches and refrigerate batter while first batch bakes.

Praline Crunch Cake

PREP: **30 minutes**
BAKE: **30 minutes at 350°F**
COOL: **2 hours**
MAKES: **16 servings**

2 tablespoons molasses
Water
1 tablespoon instant coffee crystals
1 package 2-layer-size yellow cake mix
3 eggs
⅓ cup vegetable oil
⅓ cup all-purpose flour
1 tablespoon packed brown sugar
½ teaspoon ground cinnamon
3 tablespoons butter
⅓ cup coarsely chopped pecans
1 recipe Coffee Frosting

1. Preheat oven to 350°F. Grease a 13×9×2-inch baking pan; set aside.
2. Place molasses in a 2-cup glass measuring cup. Add enough water to equal 1⅓ cups total liquid; stir to combine. Transfer liquid to a large mixing bowl. Stir in coffee crystals until dissolved. Add dry cake mix, eggs, and oil. Beat with an electric mixer on low speed until combined. Beat on medium speed for 2 minutes. Pour batter into the prepared baking pan, spreading evenly.
3. Bake about 30 minutes or until a toothpick inserted in the center comes out clean. Cool cake completely in pan on a wire rack.
4. Meanwhile, for praline topping, in a small bowl stir together flour, brown sugar, and cinnamon. Using a pastry blender, cut in butter until crumbly. Stir in pecans. Knead with fingers until mixture begins to cling together (mixture should form small moist clumps). Spread clumps evenly in an ungreased 15×10×1-inch baking pan. Bake about 10 minutes or until light brown. Spread topping on a piece of foil; cool.

5. Spread cooled cake with Coffee Frosting; sprinkle with topping.

Coffee Frosting: In a medium mixing bowl beat ¼ cup softened butter with an electric mixer on low speed for 30 seconds. Beat in 1 cup powdered sugar. In a small bowl stir 1 teaspoon instant coffee crystals into ¼ cup half-and-half, light cream, or milk until dissolved. Add coffee mixture and 1 teaspoon vanilla to butter mixture; beat until combined (mixture may appear curdled). Gradually beat in 2½ cups additional powdered sugar until smooth. If necessary beat in additional half-and-half, light cream, or milk, 1 teaspoon at a time, to make frosting spreading consistency.

PER SERVING: *369 cal., 15 g fat (6 g sat. fat), 54 mg chol., 263 mg sodium, 58 g carb., 0 g fiber, 2 g pro.*

Almond Brickle Ring Cake

PREP: 15 minutes
BAKE: 45 minutes at 350°F
COOL: 2 hours
MAKES: 12 servings

- 1 package 2-layer-size French vanilla cake mix
- 1 4-serving-size package vanilla instant pudding and pie filling mix
- 4 eggs
- 1 cup water
- ½ cup butter, softened
- 1 teaspoon almond extract
- ¾ cup toffee pieces
- 1 cup powdered sugar
- 1 tablespoon milk
- ¼ teaspoon almond extract
  Milk (optional)
  Purchased almond brittle, coarsely crushed, or toffee pieces

1. Preheat oven to 350°F. Grease and flour a 10-inch fluted tube pan; set aside.

2. In a large mixing bowl combine cake mix, pudding mix, eggs, the water, butter, and the 1 teaspoon almond extract. Beat with an electric mixer on medium speed for 2 minutes. Fold in the ¾ cup toffee pieces. Pour batter into the prepared pan, spreading evenly.

3. Bake for 45 to 50 minutes or until a wooden toothpick inserted near the center comes out clean. Cool in pan on a wire rack for 15 minutes. Remove cake from pan; cool completely on wire rack.

4. For glaze, in a small bowl combine powdered sugar, milk, and the ¼ teaspoon almond extract. If necessary, stir in enough additional milk, 1 teaspoon at a time, to reach drizzling consistency. Drizzle glaze over cake. Immediately sprinkle crushed almond brittle over glaze on cake.

To Store: Place cake, mini cakes, or cupcakes in an airtight container. Store at room temperature for up to 3 days or freeze for up to 2 months.

PER SERVING: *427 cal., 18 g fat (10 g sat. fat), 96 mg chol., 573 mg sodium, 61 g carb., 0 g fiber, 4 g pro.*

Make It Mini

Prepare as directed except grease and flour 12 fluted 1-cup tube pans or twenty-four 2½-inch muffin cups (or line muffin cups with paper bake cups). Divide batter among pans or cups, filling each about half full. Bake for 15 to 18 minutes for tube pans (12 to 15 minutes for muffin cups) or until a wooden toothpick inserted in centers comes out clean. Cool in pans on wire racks for 5 minutes. Remove cakes from pans; cool completely on wire racks. Continue as directed in Step 4. Makes 12 mini cakes or 24 cupcakes.

Pumpkin Cheesecake Bars with Chocolate Topping

PREP: 35 minutes
BAKE: 40 minutes at 350°F
CHILL: 2 to 24 hours
MAKES: 48 bars

- 1   17.5-ounce package oatmeal cookie mix
- ½   cup butter
- 2   8-ounce packages cream cheese, softened
- 1¾ cups sugar
- 3   eggs
- 1   15-ounce can pumpkin
- 1   teaspoon vanilla
- ½   teaspoon pumpkin pie spice
- ¼   teaspoon salt
- 1   cup semisweet chocolate pieces (6 ounces)
- ¼   cup butter
- 48 pecan halves

1. Preheat oven to 350°F. Line a 15×10×1-inch baking pan with foil, extending the foil about 1 inch over edges of pan. Lightly grease foil; set pan aside. For crust, place cookie mix in a large bowl. Using a pastry blender, cut in the ½ cup butter until mixture resembles coarse crumbs. Press mixture evenly onto the bottom of the prepared baking pan. Bake about 10 minutes or until set.

2. In a large mixing bowl beat cream cheese and sugar with an electric mixer on medium speed until combined. Add eggs, one at a time, beating on low speed after each addition just until combined. Stir in pumpkin, vanilla, pumpkin pie spice, and salt. Pour pumpkin mixture over hot crust, spreading evenly.

3. Bake for 30 to 35 minutes more or until filling is slightly puffed around edges and just set in center. Cool in pan on a wire rack.

4. In a small microwave-safe bowl combine chocolate and the ¼ cup butter. Microwave on 100 percent power (high) for 30 to 60 seconds or until softened; stir until smooth. Spread chocolate mixture over uncut bars. Top with pecan halves. Cover and chill for 2 to 24 hours. Using edges of the foil, lift uncut bars out of pan. Cut into bars.

To Store: Place bars in a single layer in an airtight container; cover. Store in the refrigerator for up to 3 days.

PER BAR: *173 cal., 11 g fat (5 g sat. fat), 31 mg chol., 117 mg sodium, 18 g carb., 1 g fiber, 2 g pro.*

Viennese Almond Bars

PREP: **25 minutes**
BAKE: **40 minutes at 350°F**
MAKES: **30 bars**

1 17.5-ounce package sugar cookie mix
¼ cup cold butter
4 ounces cold cream cheese
½ cup sliced almonds, toasted (see tip, page 343) and finely chopped
1 8-ounce can almond paste
¼ cup sugar
1 egg
2 to 3 tablespoons milk
⅔ cup seedless raspberry preserves
¼ cup sliced almonds, toasted (see tip, page 343)

1. Preheat oven to 350°F. Line a 13×9×2-inch baking pan with foil, extending foil about 1 inch over edges of pan. Lightly grease foil. Set pan aside.

2. Place cookie mix in a large bowl. Using a pastry blender, cut in butter and cream cheese until mixture resembles coarse crumbs. Stir in the finely chopped almonds. Measure 1 cup of crumb mixture and set aside for topping. Press the remaining crumb mixture onto the bottom of the prepared pan. Bake about 15 minutes or until set.

3. In a large mixing bowl combine almond paste, sugar, and egg. Beat with an electric mixer on medium speed until combined. Beat in milk, 1 tablespoon at a time, until mixture is spreadable. Spoon almond paste mixture in small mounds on crust; gently spread to within ¼ inch of edge. In a small bowl stir the preserves to soften; spread preserves evenly over the almond paste mixture. Sprinkle with the reserved crumb mixture. Top with the ¼ cup sliced almonds.

4. Bake for 25 to 30 minutes or until the topping is light golden brown. Cool in pan on a wire rack. Using the edges of the foil, lift the uncut bars out of the pan. Cut into diamond- or square-shape bars.

To Store: Place bars between sheets of waxed paper in an airtight container; cover. Store at room temperature for up to 3 days or freeze for up to 3 months.

PER BAR: *174 cal., 8 g fat (2 g sat. fat), 15 mg chol., 70 mg sodium, 24 g carb., 1 g fiber, 2 g pro.*

Cranberry-Almond Cookie Wedges

PREP: 20 minutes
BAKE: 18 minutes at 350°F
MAKES: 32 cookies

- 1 17.5-ounce package sugar cookie mix
- ¼ teaspoon almond extract
- ½ cup butter
- 1 cup dried cranberries
- 1 tablespoon milk
- ¾ cup sliced almonds
  Coarse or granulated sugar

1. Preheat oven to 350°F. Line two 9×1½-inch round cake pans with foil, extending foil over edges of pans. Set pans aside.
2. Place sugar cookie mix in a large bowl. Sprinkle almond extract over cookie mix. Using a pastry blender, cut in butter until mixture resembles coarse crumbs. Stir in dried cranberries. (Dough will be crumbly.)
3. Divide mixture between the two prepared pans; press firmly onto bottoms of pans. Brush tops lightly with milk. Top with almonds. Sprinkle with sugar.

4. Bake for 18 to 20 minutes or until the centers are set and tops are light brown. Cool in pans on wire racks. Using the edges of the foil, lift cookie rounds out of the pans. Cut each round into 16 wedges.

To Store: Place cookies between sheets of waxed paper in an airtight container; cover. Store at room temperature for up to 2 days or freeze for up to 3 months.

PER COOKIE: *119 cal., 5 g fat (2 g sat. fat), 8 mg chol., 62 mg sodium, 17 g carb., 0 g fiber, 1 g pro.*

How to Prepare the Dough

This shortbread-style cookie starts with a cookie mix, but omits the egg. With just butter to bind the ingredients, the result is a deliciously tender, crumbly cookie flecked with cranberries and topped with almonds.

1. Cut in the butter with a pastry blender until the mixture looks like coarse crumbs.

2. Press the crumbly mixture firmly onto the bottom of foil-lined pan.

Gooey Mixed-Nut Bars

PREP: 25 minutes
BAKE: 45 minutes at 350°F
MAKES: 32 bars

Nonstick cooking spray
1 package 2-layer-size yellow cake mix
½ cup butter
4 eggs, lightly beaten
1 cup packed brown sugar
½ cup light-color corn syrup
⅓ cup butter, melted
1 teaspoon vanilla
½ teaspoon ground cinnamon
2 cups mixed nuts, coarsely chopped

1. Preheat oven to 350°F. Line a 13×9×2-inch baking pan with foil, extending the foil about 1 inch over edges of pan. Lightly coat foil with cooking spray; set pan aside.
2. For crust, place cake mix in a large bowl. Using a pastry blender, cut in the ½ cup butter until mixture resembles coarse crumbs. Press mixture evenly onto the bottom of the prepared baking pan. Bake for 15 to 20 minutes or until light brown and set.
3. Meanwhile, in a medium bowl combine eggs, brown sugar, corn syrup, the ⅓ cup melted butter, vanilla, and cinnamon. Stir in mixed nuts. Pour nut mixture over hot crust.

4. Bake about 30 minutes more or until bubbly around the edges. Cool in pan on a wire rack. Using the edges of the foil, lift uncut bars out of pan. Cut into bars.

To Store: Layer bars between sheets of waxed paper in an airtight container; cover. Store in the refrigerator for up to 1 week or freeze for up to 3 months.

PER BAR: *207 cal., 11 g fat (4 g sat. fat), 39 mg chol., 155 mg sodium, 26 g carb., 1 g fiber, 3 g pro.*

Carrot Cake Bars

PREP: **30 minutes**
BAKE: **20 minutes at 350°F**
MAKES: **32 bars**

1 package 2-layer-size yellow or white cake mix
2 eggs
½ cup vegetable oil
¼ cup milk
2 teaspoons grated fresh ginger or ½ teaspoon ground ginger
1 teaspoon vanilla
1 cup finely shredded carrots (2 medium) (see "How to Finely Shredded Carrots," below)
½ cup golden raisins
1 recipe Extra-Creamy Cream Cheese Frosting or one 16-ounce can cream cheese frosting
¼ cup finely chopped walnuts or pecans, toasted (see tip, page 343)

1. Preheat oven to 350°F. Lightly grease and flour a 15×10×1-inch baking pan; set aside.

2. In a large mixing bowl combine cake mix, eggs, oil, milk, ginger, and vanilla. Beat with an electric mixer on medium speed until combined. Stir in carrots and raisins. Pour batter into the prepared pan, spreading evenly.

3. Bake for 20 to 22 minutes or until top springs back when lightly touched. Cool in pan on a wire rack. Frost with Extra-Creamy Cream Cheese Frosting. Sprinkle with nuts. Cut into bars.

Extra-Creamy Cream Cheese Frosting: In a large mixing bowl combine half of an 8-ounce package cream cheese, softened; ¼ cup butter, softened; and ½ teaspoon vanilla. Beat with an electric mixer on medium speed until light and fluffy. Gradually beat in 2½ to 3 cups powdered sugar to make frosting spreading consistency.

To Store: Place bars in a single layer in an airtight container; cover. Store in the refrigerator for up to 3 days.

PER BAR: *184 cal., 9 g fat (2 g sat. fat), 21 mg chol., 138 mg sodium, 25 g carb., 0 g fiber, 2 g pro.*

How to Finely Shred Carrots

The secret to moist and fluffy carrot cake and bars is to make sure the carrots are finely grated. Shred carrots by hand with a grater instead of buying bags of preshredded carrots. Those pieces are too thick and heavy and will sink to the bottom of the cake. Note: 1 medium carrot equals about ½ cup finely shredded carrot.

Finely shredded carrots make all the difference. Use the fine grates on a box or hand grater.

Cherry Crumb Bars

PREP: **20 minutes**
BAKE: **45 minutes at 350°F**
MAKES: **16 bars**

      Nonstick cooking spray
 1   17.5-ounce package oatmeal
      cookie mix
 ½   cup butter
 1   egg, lightly beaten
 1½ teaspoons vanilla
 ½   teaspoon almond extract
 1   16-ounce package frozen
      unsweetened pitted tart
      red cherries, thawed and
      drained
 ¼   cup granulated sugar
 ½   cup powdered sugar
 1   to 2 teaspoons milk

1. Preheat oven to 350°F. Line a 9×9×2-inch baking pan with foil, extending the foil about 1 inch over edges of pan. Lightly coat foil with cooking spray; set pan aside.
2. Place cookie mix in a large bowl. Using a pastry blender, cut in butter until mixture resembles coarse crumbs. Measure 1 cup of crumb mixture and set aside for topping. Stir egg, 1 teaspoon of the vanilla, and the almond extract into the remaining crumb mixture until combined. Press egg mixture evenly onto the bottom of the prepared baking pan.
3. In a medium bowl stir together cherries and granulated sugar; spoon evenly over cookie layer in pan. Sprinkle with the reserved 1 cup crumb mixture.
4. Bake about 45 minutes or until topping is golden. Cool in pan on a wire rack.

5. For icing, in a small bowl stir together powdered sugar and the remaining ½ teaspoon vanilla. Stir in 1 to 2 teaspoons milk to make icing drizzling consistency. Drizzle icing over bars (see tip, page 510). Let stand until icing is set. Using the edges of the foil, lift uncut bars out of pan. Cut into bars.

To Store: Place bars in a single layer in an airtight container; cover. Store in the refrigerator for up to 3 days or freeze for up to 3 months.

PER BAR: *240 cal., 12 g fat (5 g sat. fat), 27 mg chol., 202 mg sodium, 31 g carb., 0 g fiber, 3 g pro.*

Chocolate Chip and Peanut Butter Cookies

PREP: **35 minutes**
BAKE: **8 minutes per batch**
at **375°F**
MAKES: **30 cookies**

⅔ cup crunchy peanut butter
½ cup butter, softened
½ cup granulated sugar
½ cup packed brown sugar
1 egg
2 cups packaged biscuit mix
1½ cups milk-chocolate-and-peanut-butter pieces or semisweet chocolate pieces
1 teaspoon shortening

1. Preheat oven to 375°F. In a large mixing bowl combine peanut butter, butter, granulated sugar, and brown sugar. Beat with an electric mixer on medium speed until creamy. Add egg, beating until combined. Add biscuit mix, beating on low speed just until combined. Stir in 1 cup of the chocolate pieces.

2. Drop dough by rounded measuring tablespoons about 2 inches apart onto an ungreased cookie sheet.

3. Bake for 8 to 10 minutes or until bottoms begin to brown. Cool cookies on cookie sheet for 1 minute. Transfer cookies to a wire rack; let cool.

4. In a small saucepan combine the remaining ½ cup chocolate pieces and the shortening; heat and stir over low heat until melted and smooth. Cool slightly. Drizzle cooled cookies with the melted chocolate mixture.

To Store: Place cookies in a single layer in an airtight container; cover. Store in the refrigerator up to 3 days or freeze for up to 3 months.

PER COOKIE: *190 cal., 11 g fat (5 g sat. fat), 15 mg chol., 181 mg sodium, 20 g carb., 1 g fiber, 2 g pro.*

Easy Cleanup of Chocolate Drizzle

When drizzling cookies or bars with melted chocolate or drippy icings, first place the items to be drizzled on waxed paper or parchment paper. (Or place them on wire cooling racks set over waxed paper.) Drizzle the chocolate over the cookies, letting excess drip off onto the waxed paper. Let cookies stand until chocolate is set. When you remove the cookies to a serving platter, simply throw out the waxed paper and all the mess with it.

index

general high-altitude issues

At altitudes higher than 3,000 feet above sea level, water boils at lower temperatures, causing moisture to evaporate more quickly than at sea level. This can cause foods to dry out during cooking and baking. Because of the lower boiling point, foods that are steamed or boiled take longer to cook. Also lower air pressure may cause baked goods that use yeast, baking powder, baking soda, egg whites, or steam to rise excessively, then fall.

suggestions for baking

These estimates are based on an altitude of 3,000 feet above sea level; at higher altitudes you may need to alter these measures proportionately. Make just one change at a time and see how each affects the results.

cakes

- Increase the baking temperature by 15°F to 25°F to help set the batter.
- For cakes leavened by air, such as angel food, beat the egg whites only to soft peaks; otherwise the batter may expand too much.

For cakes made with shortening, you may want to try any one of the following:

- Decrease the baking powder by ⅛ teaspoon per 1 teaspoon called for;
- Decrease the sugar by up to 1 tablespoon for each 1 cup called for;
- Increase the liquid by 1 to 2 tablespoons for each 1 cup called for.

For cakes that contain 1 cup or more of fat or chocolate:

- Reduce the shortening by 1 to 2 tablespoons per 1 cup and add an egg to prevent the cake from falling.

cookies, breads and pies

- Cookies generally yield good results at high altitudes, but if not, try slightly increasing baking temperature; slightly decreasing baking powder or soda, fat, and/or sugar; and/or slightly increasing liquids and flour.
- Muffins, biscuits, and muffinlike quick breads generally need little adjustment, but if they develop a bitter or alkaline flavor, decrease baking soda or powder slightly. Because cakelike quick breads are more delicate, you may need to follow adjustment guidelines for cakes.
- Yeast breads will rise more quickly at high altitudes. Allow unshaped dough to rise only until double in size, then punch it down. Repeat this rising step once more before shaping dough. Flour tends to be drier at high altitudes and sometimes absorbs more liquid. If your yeast dough seems dry, add more liquid and reduce the amount of flour next time.
- Piecrusts usually don't need adjustment, though slightly more liquid may be needed.

metric

product differences

Most of the ingredients called for in the recipes in this book are available in most countries. However, some are known by different names. Here are some common American ingredients and their possible counterparts:

- Sugar (white) is granulated, fine granulated, or castor sugar.
- Powdered sugar is icing sugar.
- All-purpose flour is enriched, bleached or unbleached white household flour. When self-rising flour is used in place of all-purpose flour in a recipe that calls for leavening, omit the leavening agent (baking soda or baking powder) and salt.
- Light-color corn syrup is golden syrup.
- Cornstarch is cornflour.
- Baking soda is bicarbonate of soda.
- Vanilla or vanilla extract is vanilla essence.
- Green, red, or yellow sweet peppers are capsicums or bell peppers.
- Golden raisins are sultanas.

volume and weight

The United States traditionally uses cup measures for liquid and solid ingredients. The chart below shows the approximate imperial and metric equivalents. If you are accustomed to weighing solid ingredients, the following approximate equivalents will be helpful.

- 1 cup butter, castor sugar, or rice = 8 ounces = ½ pound = 250 grams
- 1 cup flour = 4 ounces = ¼ pound = 125 grams
- 1 cup icing sugar = 5 ounces = 150 grams
- Canadian and U.S. volume for a cup measure is 8 fluid ounces (237 ml), but the standard metric equivalent is 250 ml.
- 1 British imperial cup is 10 fluid ounces.
- In Australia, 1 tablespoon equals 20 ml, and there are 4 teaspoons in the Australian tablespoon.
- Spoon measures are used for smaller amounts of ingredients. Although the size of the tablespoon varies slightly in different countries, for practical purposes and for recipes in this book, a straight substitution is all that's necessary. Measurements made using cups or spoons always should be level unless stated otherwise.

common weight range replacements

Imperial / U.S.	Metric
½ ounce	15 g
1 ounce	25 g or 30 g
4 ounces (¼ pound)	115 g or 125 g
8 ounces (½ pound)	225 g or 250 g
16 ounces (1 pound)	450 g or 500 g
1¼ pounds	625 g
1½ pounds	750 g
2 pounds or 2¼ pounds	1,000 g or 1 Kg

oven temperature equivalents

Fahrenheit Setting	Celsius Setting	Gas Setting
300°F	150°C	Gas Mark 2 (very low)
325°F	160°C	Gas Mark 3 (low)
350°F	180°C	Gas Mark 4 (moderate)
375°F	190°C	Gas Mark 5 (moderate)
400°F	200°C	Gas Mark 6 (hot)
425°F	220°C	Gas Mark 7 (hot)
450°F	230°C	Gas Mark 8 (very hot)
475°F	240°C	Gas Mark 9 (very hot)
500°F	260°C	Gas Mark 10 (extremely hot)
Broil	Broil	Grill

*Electric and gas ovens may be calibrated using celsius. However, for an electric oven, increase celsius setting 10 to 20 degrees when cooking above 160°C. For convection or forced air ovens (gas or electric), lower the temperature setting 25°F/10°C when cooking at all heat levels.

baking pan sizes

Imperial / U.S.	Metric
9×1½-inch round cake pan	22- or 23×4-cm (1.5 L)
9×1½-inch pie plate	22- or 23×4-cm (1 L)
8×8×2-inch square cake pan	20×5-cm (2 L)
9×9×2-inch square cake pan	22- or 23×4.5-cm (2.5 L)
11×7×1½-inch baking pan	28×17×4-cm (2 L)
2-quart rectangular baking pan	30×19×4.5-cm (3 L)
13×9×2-inch baking pan	34×22×4.5-cm (3.5 L)
15×10×1-inch jelly roll pan	40×25×2-cm
9×5×3-inch loaf pan	23×13×8-cm (2 L)
2-quart casserole	2 L

u.s. / standard metric equivalents

⅛ teaspoon = 0.5 ml	
¼ teaspoon = 1 ml	
½ teaspoon = 2 ml	
1 teaspoon = 5 ml	
1 tablespoon = 15 ml	
2 tablespoons = 25 ml	
¼ cup = 2 fluid ounces = 50 ml	
⅓ cup = 3 fluid ounces = 75 ml	
½ cup = 4 fluid ounces = 125 ml	
⅔ cup = 5 fluid ounces = 150 ml	
¾ cup = 6 fluid ounces = 175 ml	
1 cup = 8 fluid ounces = 250 ml	
2 cups = 1 pint = 500 ml	
1 quart = 1 litre	